EMERGING
GLOBAL
CITIES

EMERGING GLOBAL CITIES

Origin, Structure, and Significance

ALEJANDRO PORTES
AND ARIEL C. ARMONY

Columbia University Press
New York

Columbia University Press

Publishers Since 1893

New York   Chichester, West Sussex

cup.columbia.edu

Library of Congress Cataloging-in-Publication Data

Names: Portes, Alejandro, 1944– author. | Armony, Ariel C., author.

Title: Emerging global cities : origin, structure, and significance / Alejandro Portes
and Ariel C. Armony.

Description: New York : Columbia University Press, 2022. | Includes bibliographical
references and index.

Identifiers: LCCN 2022012585 | ISBN 9780231205160 (hardback) |
ISBN 9780231205177 (trade paperback) | ISBN 9780231555876 (ebook)

Subjects: LCSH: Megacities. | Urbanization. | City planning.

Classification: LCC HT166 .P6383 2022 | DDC 307.1/216—dc23/eng/20220315

LC record available at https://lccn.loc.gov/2022012585

Cover design: Elliott S. Cairns

Cover image: Xavier Cortada, *Emerging Global Cities*, 2021

CONTENTS

ACKNOWLEDGMENTS

A study of the scope that we set for ourselves—identifying, analyzing, and comparing cities in the contemporary global system—could not have come to fruition without a series of fortunate events and coincidences, and without the cooperation and faithful support of a number of people. Aside from our collaborating authors, listed in the title page and in individual chapters, Portes benefited from his affiliation with New York University–Abu Dhabi, where he taught fall courses over five years. There he met Rana Tomaira—a scholar of Middle Eastern and urban affairs—who, in addition to authoring the chapter on Dubai, she also furnished sage counsel and gave valuable inputs to our analysis of global cities. Also at NYU-Abu Dhabi, David Cook-Martin, then chair of the Social Studies Department, provided decisive support for the project and organized a symposium on our previous book—*The Global Edge: Miami in the Twenty-First Century*—in which several urban scholars, including Professor Tomaira, participated.

Armony's position as Vice Provost for global affairs at the University of Pittsburgh made possible a number of trips to different parts of the world, including Singapore and Dubai, as well as to other cities that were subsequently striving for a comparable position of global prominence. In 2015, Portes paid an extensive visit to Singapore at the invitation of Professor Min Zhou, then head of Sociology at Nanyang Technological University. This visit provided firsthand knowledge about the economic and social characteristics of the city and their surprising similarities with those that he had observed in Miami and Dubai.

The enriching discussion generated by the presentation of our book on Miami at the University of Pittsburgh in March 2019 played an important part in shaping our ideas for this project. The insights from many colleagues at Pittsburgh and informants in places such as Hong Kong were vital for gathering information and finetuning our understanding of the different cases included in this book. Armony's ongoing collaboration with colleagues at the University of São Paulo's Programa de Pós-Graduação Integração da América Latina (PROLAM/USP)—in particular, Professor Lucilene Cury—and his interactions with colleagues at Newcastle University in the United Kingdom, and with businesspeople and government officials in Lagos, were important in shaping our perspectives and helped us produce a nuanced analysis that was sensitive to the often-conflicting perspectives on "global cities."

As the study gradually took form, it received crucial support from several colleagues who followed the project from the start. In particular, we must acknowledge with gratitude the input of Professors Min Zhou and Philip Kasinitz. Zhou was not only the gracious host of Portes during his visit, but she also continued to provide advice based on her extensive knowledge of Singapore. She carefully reviewed the chapter dedicated to that city and evaluated the initial prospectus for the book, offering valuable insights and recommendations.

On his part, Philip Kasinitz played the star role at a symposium on our previous book on Miami, organized by the University of Miami Institute for Advanced Study of the Americas (UMIA) in April 2019. During his intervention, Kasinitz advanced several important observations and a key insight that helped guide our then-incipient work on this project in a new direction. He went on to suggest Columbia University Press as a suitable publisher for the book and subsequently contributed a strongly positive and also detailed critical evaluation of the initial prospectus.

During the past decade, Portes has been affiliated with the University of Miami, with dual appointments at its Law School and Department of Sociology. This affiliation provided an invaluable vantage point for observing the evolution of the city and the complex features of its economy and social structure. The president of the University of Miami, Julio Frenk, and Felicia Knaul, director of UMIA and Frenk's spouse, provided a cordial and supportive environment for our work, with UMIA organizing several symposia to highlight several past publications, including the *Global Edge*. Portes acknowledges with gratitude this stance on the part of university leaders, including the university provost, Jeffrey Duerk, and the dean of the College of Arts and Sciences, Leonidas Bachas.

From 2010 to 2014, Armony held the Martha Weeks Professorship of Latin American Studies at the University of Miami, where he directed the Center for

Latin American Studies and led the foundation of UMIA. These years afforded him the opportunity to observe firsthand the core attributes of Miami as an emerging global city and to engage with residents and local organizations. At the University of Pittsburgh, where he has directed the University Center for International Studies (UCIS) in addition to acting as vice provost, he benefited from many workshops, conferences, and symposia on cities organized by the area and thematic centers under UCIS, as well as from diverse collaborations with partners around the world. These collaborations helped him explore issues of economic development, race relations, migration, social justice, and climate change in comparative perspective, as cities are built and rebuilt.

At the University of Miami Law School, our colleague David Abraham was an assiduous and careful interlocutor, taking part in the symposia organized by UMIA and using his vast knowledge of Miami to contribute several astute observations and correctives to our analysis on the city. Subsequently, the newly appointed chair of the Sociology Department, Alexis Piquero, engaged both with our prior book and with the present study. A world-renowned criminologist, Piquero has drawn on his expertise to provide several key insights and points of comparison on civil life and crime patterns in the three cities that are at the center of our study.

Also at the University of Miami, the work of Portes's assistant, Maria F. Briz, deserves special mention. Maria contributed in multiple ways to this project from the start. Her contribution extended well beyond transcribing successive versions of each chapter and alerting the authors to new developments in Miami and new research material in other cities. It also included an indefatigable and always positive attitude. More than anyone else, she furnished the necessary technical infrastructure to make this book possible.

At the University of Pittsburgh, the continuous support of Chancellor Patrick Gallagher and Provost Ann Cudd—who moderated a lively discussion about the ways Miami and Pittsburgh were being shaped by the forces of globalization in early 2019—has been vital from the very beginning. It has been challenging to balance the administrative responsibilities that come with a senior leadership role and the extraordinary challenges posed by the global pandemic with a complex intellectual project such as this one. Armony's colleagues at UCIS, particularly the Senior Leadership Team, stepped up many times to get things done and showed a great deal of patience when simultaneous demands rose to high levels. At Newcastle University, where Armony spent two months as a visiting professor in fall 2021, he greatly benefited from the wonderful hospitality and stimulating intellectual environment provided by the leadership of the university and colleagues in the faculty of Humanities and Social Sciences, particularly the School of Geography, Politics and Sociology.

Armony's executive assistant, Janet Kosko, was an extraordinary companion in this long journey, which would have been impossible without her support, excellent disposition, and unparalleled professionalism. For Armony, one of the most gratifying aspects of this project has been the opportunity to work with two incredibly talented young scholars, Rosa Hassan De Ferrari and Anthony Ocepek. They worked tirelessly on many essential tasks, conducted superb research, offered invaluable insights and perspectives, and put contagious enthusiasm into every step of the project. This book would not have been possible without them.

Lastly, we owe a debt of gratitude to our editor at Columbia University Press, Lowell Frye. From the start, he demonstrated a positive and supportive attitude toward our work, guiding us through the complex process of obtaining approval from the various internal boards for the book prospectus that culminated with the award of a publication contract. The several months invested in this process coincided with those in which we worked to move this comparative project forward by completing successive chapters in record time.

Portes gratefully recognizes his spouse, Patricia Fernandez-Kelly, for her steady support at each stage of this project as he traversed the world and maneuvered through the inevitable ups and downs of a complex project. As with everything he does, Armony has had the unconditional, loving support and encouragement of Mirna Kolbowski, Ian Armony, and Alan Armony. This is the trio that gives meaning to every single moment. He would not have been able to embark on this project, stick with it, and drive it to completion without their determination to be there no matter what, their great sense of humor, and their regular—and indispensable—dose of sanity.

The comparative vision that this study represents and the range of topics that it covers could not have been assembled without the support of everyone already mentioned. Whatever merit the final product has, it is largely due to their contributions. Whatever limitations and mistakes it contains are our responsibility.

EMERGING
GLOBAL
CITIES

INTRODUCTION

The idea for this book was inspired by two events. First, in the summer of 2018, we published our first coauthored book on the evolution of the city of Miami, *The Global Edge: Miami in the Twenty-First Century.*[1] In the fall of that year, Portes traveled to the United Arab Emirates (UAE) to teach a course at the New York University campus in Abu Dhabi (NYU-AD). During this time in the UAE, he repeatedly traveled to Dubai, just one hour away from the NYU-AD campus. As he contemplated Dubai's skyline, the idea occurred to him of how similar it was to that of Miami. Further conversations with NYU urban scholars, including Professor Rana Tomaira, who would become a key collaborator on this project, made clear that the resemblance was more than superficial. The condominium towers and huge shopping malls in both cities were there for a reason—for selling luxury units to wealthy foreigners, taking their money in the malls and hotels, and luring them to invest the rest in the local international banking center.

In March 2019, we jointly presented our recently published book at the University of Pittsburgh. In conversations during that visit, the idea for this project began to fall into place. As we looked at the similarities between Miami and Dubai, we started to pay attention to a third city, Singapore. A few years earlier, we had both visited Singapore on separate occasions and had been impressed by its extraordinary economic and educational achievements, as well as by its cityscape. "Just like Miami," an academic acquaintance at a local university remarked to one of us about the city. At that time, we had not begun to work on our book on the transformation of Miami, and the remark passed over unnoticed. But now the similarities between the three cities became increasingly apparent, both in their outward appearance and in their distinct roles in the global economy. Upon reflection and further research, we concluded that they were rather unique, since we could not identify other metropolitan areas that had similar profiles or played the same strategic economic and cultural roles in their respective regions.

The second event that inspired this book took place during a visit by Armony to the Universidade de São Paulo, Brazil, in August 2019. He was there to participate in a symposium on "World Cities" that featured the host city and Miami as key case studies. The presentations by the Brazilian colleagues conveyed an interest in São Paulo's global dimensions and its similarities to and differences from Miami. They emphasized aspects of the city that signaled its globalizing position, but it was clear that, despite São Paulo's status as a megacity and cultural center, the undisputed hub for Latin America and the Caribbean was Miami. As Armony, now vice provost for global affairs at the University of Pittsburgh, traveled to different parts of the world, the conversations in other cities resembled those in São Paulo, regardless of the language or environment. Almost everywhere, those in government, academia, and business were concerned with their city's global appeal for investment, wealth, and lifestyle. Rankings that looked at metrics—from business and investment performance to livability, air connectivity, and diversity—were often quoted in city halls, university auditoriums, and corporate offices. Narratives of success played a fundamental role in shaping this global conversation.[2]

Competition for recognition and capital inflows in the world economy is fierce. Many cities aspire to become the "next Dubai" or the "next Singapore," or to displace Miami as the "capital of the Americas." An essential element of this race is the branding of cities as safe and desirable places for investment and consumption. Just as cars and airlines seek to gain favorable attention, cities also brand themselves, inventing catchy labels to advertise their most appealing features and attempting to conceal less charming aspects such as deep socioeconomic inequalities. These efforts include deliberate attempts to attract investments (in capital and in physical and intangible infrastructure) and members of what Richard Florida has termed the "creative class" (highly trained people in tech, banking and finances, law, healthcare, arts, etc.).[3] They also include branding the city in various forms as a center for arts fairs, hi-tech expositions, concerts, and major sports and cultural events. It would be but a slight exaggeration to say that leaders of every city attempting to increase their visibility and position in the world economy engage in these various types of branding efforts.

For several reasons, such efforts—no matter how motivated or expensive—tend to fail, at least in terms of catapulting a city into a permanent position of prominence. Multinational corporations and wealthy investors are skittish and do not easily position their regional headquarters or trust their billions to just any one place. Similarly, members of the creative class are highly selective about where they plan to live, work, and invest. For that reason, history records numerous examples from the last century into the present of what we term "global hopefuls"—cities that, at one point or another, were poised to attain positions of global or regional importance but eventually failed to do so.

As we looked into the global competition among cities to achieve some level of distinction and visibility beyond their region, we paid attention to cities outside the Dubai-Miami-Singapore trio. We focused on a selected group of global hopefuls, realizing that the specific histories of these urban places could bring much to the study, particularly if we were to identify their key differences from those cities that have raced ahead to central positions.

The number of those hoping to project themselves beyond their immediate region was not limited to a handful of cases. Barcelona, Mumbai, Shanghai, Sydney, and Toronto were among the urban centers with valid global aspirations. In the end, we settled on three cases. The first is New Orleans, which despite being the third-largest urban economy in the United States in the mid-nineteenth century and a city fully expected to become the natural entrepôt of hemispheric trade in the twentieth century, never reached its potential. Its story offers a fascinating counterpart to the emergence of Miami as a hub for the region. The other two are megacities, the largest and most economically important urban centers of sizable countries but with aspirations to transcend their national position by placing themselves on the global stage. São Paulo is a megacity with ambitions beyond its regional standing in Brazil and South America, and Lagos is the largest and most economically important city in Nigeria, which brands itself as the "new African Dubai." We devote individual chapters to each of these cities.

Sustaining a city's global position depends on a variety of factors. The futures of cities are uncertain. Histories of urban expansion and decline can evolve over centuries or morph over one human lifetime. Climate change, pandemics, and geopolitical conflict can alter the fate of cities.[4] This is why we decided to incorporate the case of Hong Kong—a city that, by many standards, had already achieved prominence in the global economy and a central status in its region of the world,[5] but that has seen that status threatened due to political reasons.

The experience of Hong Kong, until recently far ahead of Singapore and Dubai in financial and commercial prominence and now experiencing the tightening control of Beijing, is a key counterfactual that puts to the test the preconditions for global emergence and significance advanced by our theory.

GLOBAL CITIES AND URBAN STUDIES

Like other urban scholars, we were impressed by Saskia Sassen's immensely influential study of New York, London, and Tokyo, which she identified as the three key global cities.[6] She did this, not on the basis of their size or national significance, but because of their function in the capitalist world economy. They are urban entities suspended, as it were, above their respective national spaces and playing a command-and-control role for financial and economic activities extended worldwide. Sassen's prime insight was that, while communications and transportation innovations made possible the decentralization of industrial production and commercial distribution on a global basis, the coordination of their multiple functions could not be decentralized. On the contrary, the more productive and commercial activities spread in space, the more they required a tightly controlled central presence among key decision-makers who interacted in close physical contact with one another. These actors are located in the nerve centers of the world economy; these are the global cities.

In the best sociological tradition, Sassen's study was not limited to identifying the economic role of these cities, but went on to study them from within, including their culture, ethnic composition, and class structure. She identified a central social fact, namely, the bifurcation of the urban population between a minority working and profiting from international trade, finance, and other globalized activities and a majority whose occupations were purely local in scope, modestly remunerated, and commonly insecure.[7]

The increasing inequalities in economic returns and opportunities between elites and the rest of the urban population made the undoubted achievement of these cities in becoming "global" less than universally celebrated. Life in them became challenging and precarious for a working population compelled to live from paycheck to paycheck in a service economy largely geared toward the tastes and luxury consumption of a privileged minority. Following Sassen and others, a focus on "durable inequality" became paramount in urban studies.[8]

After Sassen, urban studies focused roughly on three main areas of concern. First, there developed a school geared to rank-ordering cities in the world according to the importance of the economic activities concentrated in these urban spaces and the number and relative proportion of the creative class living or working in them.[9] Second, a mostly ethnographic literature focused on the conditions of life in cities of the advanced world and the plight of specific racial and ethnic minorities living in them, particularly African Americans.[10] Third, a continuing literature on cities of the formerly called "Third World", pioneered by Janet Abu-Lughod, Jorge Hardoy, Richard Morse, and others.[11] These studies focused on the quasi-perennial subordination of these cities to the needs and dictates of the centers of the capitalist economy, the difficulties in escaping this situation, and the vast inequalities between peripheral elites in protected and secluded areas and the mass of the urban population living in shantytowns and other irregular settlements.[12]

All three of these schools tend to neglect a phenomenon that is apparently of tangential importance but that points to a significant departure from received knowledge. This is the emergence of urban places that, rising from positions of inferiority and insignificance in the world economy, have reached the status of important players in the fields of international commerce, real estate, finance, and the arts. The significant fact is that these cities emerged seemingly from nowhere and without any deliberate sponsorship from global elites. They rose from below and, as we will see, through a variety of quite distinct historical sequences.

When we refer to "emerging global cities," we take the word "global" critically, acknowledging that it is a highly contested term. Critics have noted that the concept of global city carries the risk of elevating "single or small groups of urban examples to be paradigmatic; that is, to offer apparent lessons for all other urban areas."[13] They have also argued that the attempt to define a city as global carries "the risk of focusing too much on single, isolated spaces, on specific senses of time and on particular representations within cities."[14] Using "sector-specific" and "place-specific" indicators to define the global status of cities, they said, misses the opportunity to understand "the urban as the co-presence of multiple spaces, multiple times and multiple webs of relations, tying local sites, subjects and fragments into globalizing networks of economic, social and cultural change."[15] Hierarchical conceptions of cities are viewed not only as reductionist but also as notions that reproduce North American and Eurocentric worldviews of urban life.

Our analysis recognizes these tensions. We are interested in understanding how cities such as Dubai, Miami, and Singapore evolved into their present condition, without necessarily presenting them as models to be followed by other cities. By adopting a mode of analysis that is historical, we delve deep into the varied social encounters that take place in urban spaces and the local and regional impact of state governance and administrative systems.[16] This analysis allows for a more nuanced understanding of globality in the context of the capitalist world system.

STUDYING THE EMERGING GLOBAL CITY

Reflecting on the trio of cities that we came across, several things became increasingly obvious. First, each of them played a similar role, in their respective region of the world, to those previously described by Sassen on a global scale. Second, the rise of Dubai, Miami, and Singapore to positions of economic, financial, and cultural prominence did not happen by chance, but was the consequence of decisive and sustained efforts by key actors that took advantage of propitious geopolitical conditions. Only in this manner were they able to best their regional rivals vying for the same position of prominence. Third, while these were the *only* cities that we could identify with a comparable profile worldwide, many others were attempting to surpass them or achieve the same level of prominence but without similar success, at least up to the present.

There are four basic questions to be answered: First, why did these cities emerge, assuming some of the entrepôt functions that were supposedly reserved for established global cities? Second, what were the historical conditions that facilitated their emergence, and who were the key actors behind them? Third, what is the ethnic and class structure of these new centers? Fourth, to what extent have they followed the pattern of older global cities, bifurcating their population into an elite profiting from international activities and a working mass in insecure jobs and employment in the informal economy?

As in Sassen's study, answers to the third and fourth questions can provide a response to the first two, which often lead to celebratory accounts of the vision and prowess of the leaders who guided their respective urban centers to a position of global prominence. The cities that fit into this profile are not industrial centers, or even places of high-tech innovation. Nor are they necessarily the largest urban economies in their respective countries. The basic characteristic that defines them is their position as coordinating centers for a multistranded complex of economic activities. They are places where international banks and global corporations feel sufficiently confident to establish their regional head-quarters, and where the wealthy in their respective regions come to make real estate investments and otherwise "park" their capital to protect it from the inse-curities of their own countries.

Despite their very different origins and history, Dubai, Miami, and Sin-gapore are remarkably similar in their present economic profile and social structure. All three boast enormous ports and airports serving as centers for international trade and points for the transshipment of commodities to other nations and cities in their respective regions. All three feature major banking and financial centers operating as coordinating centers for multiple forms of investment, mergers, and acquisitions on an international scale. All three have developed a vast real estate sector, building and marketing office and residential space for investors worldwide, but especially in their respective regions. The impressive skylines characteristic of these cities is a direct prod-uct and reflection of their respective real estate industries and the "growth machine" that runs them.[17]

Finally, all three have become important tourist destinations and regional centers for commercial art. For this purpose, they have taken advantage of their locations fronting warm and attractive seashores—Miami by the Atlantic, right north of the Tropic of Cancer, Dubai by the Persian Gulf, and Singapore by the southern Indian Ocean. Tourism was always Miami's raison d'être, having been cre-ated as a resort for northerners escaping frigid temperatures in winter. Building on this role, the city has developed music festivals, sport events, and arts fairs that have turned it into a year-round touristic attraction. Most prominent of these is the December Art Basel fair, imported from Switzerland, which brings to the city reportedly more millionaires and billionaires in private planes than those who attend the Superbowl every year.[18]

Building tourist centers in Dubai and Singapore has been more difficult. A desert location with temperatures around 40°C for most of the year make Dubai a forbidding place to visit. With determination and capital, city leaders turned the situation around, building artificial islands in the Gulf, creating the largest commercial mall in the world, and topping it with the highest needle-like sky-scraper—the Burj Khalifa.[19] Placed on a distant island, almost lost in the Indian Ocean, Singapore also has had little chance to attract tourists to itself. Again, decisive action by the leaders of the city-state reversed the situation. They created nature parks, malls, museums, and accessible beaches and promoted these attractions while courting companies and investors to do business in the island. One could come to Singapore to invest one's money in a new luxury condominium or a profitable stock transaction and, at the same time, have a nice beach vacation with one's family. The islet of Santosa across downtown became the centerpiece of Singapore's tourist scene.[20]

The arrival of these new urban actors needs to be seen in the context of the steady growth of an economy that is rich in "intangibles," that is, "investment in ideas, in knowledge, in aesthetic content, in software, in brands, in networks and relationships."[21] This latest episode in the evolution of the world economy is a function of a number of changes in the capitalist system, including an increased role of services in the economy, continuous market liberalization, and innovation in information technology and management systems. There is a reinforcing relationship between globalization and the requirement to build more complex institutions, networks, and organizations on the one hand, and the necessity to augment intangible investments in institutional capabilities, complex systems, and business processes on the other.[22]

Cities, particularly those fraught with the arduous challenge of postindustrial reinvention, have sought to replicate the templates of "intangible-intensive" metropolises such as New York and London with limited success.[23] Our trio of cities has taken advantage of a niche in the intangible economy. As noted, these cities are not power centers of science and innovation, but they have successfully profited from their strategic location and bolstered it by combining physical and intangible assets.[24] They took advantage of the steady growth of international trade and secured a predominant position as transportation and financial hubs in the regional and global arenas by leveraging top-notch physical infrastructure, business-driven information technology investment, organizational know-how, and international agreements. More importantly, as we will discuss throughout the study, they consistently invested in the institutional infrastructure of the rules, norms, and regulations that provide predictability and certainty for international investors.[25]

THE STUDY

The series of events that led to the rise and consolidation of Dubai, Miami, and Singapore as regional centers in the world economy are mostly different, indicating that there is no set "recipe" for urban places aspiring to the same position. At the end, however, all three managed to take advantage of their unique geographic locations and to couple them with institutional innovations that gained the confidence of capital—both corporate and private. The following chapters tell this story, coupling it with an analysis of the population of these cities and the ways they adjusted to the opportunities and challenges of an internationalized economy and an increasingly cosmopolitan culture and social life. These cities embody many of the complexities that characterize urban environments in the twenty-first century, from migration and victimization to materialism and conspicuous consumption.

The book is organized as follows. The first chapter presents a general historical introduction to the relationship between capitalist development and the city from early medieval times onward. The successive stages of this evolving relationship culminate with the rise of global cities in the twentieth century and of emerging ones in the twenty-first. This introductory chapter is followed by three corresponding to the trio of successful emerging cities that we have identified: Dubai, Miami, and Singapore. Each of them is authored or coauthored by one of our collaborators: Rana Tomaira, Brandon P. Martinez, and Larry Liu.

The book then shifts gears to focus on the contemporary urban scene and the practices and efforts of different city elites to distinguish themselves in what has become an intense global competition. We discuss the evolution of these practices and provide examples of them in order to introduce a detailed study of another trio of cities—New Orleans, São Paulo, and Lagos—that, at one point or another, closely approached the coveted status of strategic world entrepôts but that have not done so, at least up to the present. The cases of these selected cities that fell behind or that, for other reasons, have not succeeded in their aspirations to global prominence serve as a necessary counterpoint to those that have and bring into light the strategic factors accounting for the difference. Each of these individual histories is coauthored by one or more of our collaborators: Larry Liu, Rosa Hassan De Ferrari, and Anthony Ocepek.

The exceptional case of Hong Kong closes our analysis of emerging cities. The concluding chapter brings together major findings of the study, with a focus on their key implications for urban theory and the lessons that they carry for the future, including the threats—physical and political—to be confronted by the so-far winners in global competition. The conclusion also situates these groups of cities in the context of current discussions about climate migration and other phenomena that will continue to shape the planet.

While struggles for hegemony mark the long-term history of capitalism and urbanization, it has become evident that issues of politics and culture largely determine its present course. The stability and predictability of political regimes are a precondition for the economic development of cities and their role and significance in the contemporary world. Similarly, the rise of a global culture and the manipulation of symbols have acquired central importance to the pursuit of prominence, competing with actual industrial production. Many major corporations in the advanced world do not own factories of any kind, nor do they produce anything but symbols. This symbolic culture—from the intangible products spawned by Wall Street to the selective branding of peoples and places—characterizes the world where we live and where cities, global or not, vie for space and distinction.

PART I

CHAPTER 1

THE ROLE OF CITIES IN THE CAPITALIST ECONOMY

An Overview

In surveying the classic and contemporary social science literature on the city, one is struck by two things: first, the profound fascination that the city has had for scholars throughout history; and second, the very partial ways in which the phenomenon of urbanization has been described and understood. Confronted with the complexity and size of the modern city, students of urbanization have followed one of two paths. Either they have lapsed into hyperbole and impressionistic descriptions of the "urban way of life," or they have described the conditions and problems of particular groups in the city.

Characteristic of the first strand are Louis Wirth's classic essay on the culture of urbanism, George Simmel's social-psychological theories of the metropolis and mental life, and the analysis of "urbane" social forms by Scott Greer.[1] Characteristic of the second are William F. Whyte, *Street Corner Society*; Gerald Suttles, *The Social Order of the Slum*; Mitchell Duneier, *Slim's Table*; and countless studies of homelessness, the Black ghetto, Hispanics, Asians, and other ethnic groups in the city.[2]

A third perspective on urbanization is provided by demography and ecology. Here, attention is focused on what may be called the "skeleton" of urban forms: how many people live in a city and how they are distributed in space. Counting how many people there are, how many migrate in or out, and how they are distributed by age, gender, or race is a necessary first step for analyzing urban forms, but by no means does it constitute a complete description of the nature of the city or the character of urban phenomena. Demographic data often need to be explained. The compilation of this information should prompt the analyst to ask important questions, such as why people move in one direction or another, why they gather in particular locations, what accounts for their distribution in more or less desirable urban spaces, and so forth. The required theoretical framework to develop answers to these questions is not provided by demography itself but must be sought elsewhere.

An understanding of the emergence and development of the city as a unique and self-contained social form rests on two general assumptions:

I.   The emergence of urban agglomerations and the particular form that they take are dependent on the mode of production and distribution of the products that are dominant in specific historical periods.

II. The city, as known today, is a unique formation modeled by the requirements of the capitalist mode of production, first on a local and then on a global basis.

MEDIEVAL CITIES

The story of modern capitalism does not begin in the sixteenth century, as asserted by Immanuel Wallerstein, but in the ninth.[3] That obscure era, with Europe reeling from the military victories of Islam and the loss of the Mediterranean, is when the seeds of what was to come were planted. To be sure, cities shriveled by the loss of trade. As Pirenne stresses, the ninth century was the century of "no markets," but the old Roman urban system endured because the Catholic Church preserved its administrative system based on urban dioceses ruled by bishops.[4]

These were pitiful enclosures: no more than a few hundred meters long and wide protected by a wall and a moat. Inside, one would find the cathedral, the residences of the bishop and his clerical and military retinue; some open space for the weekly market; more churches; and the granaries where the tribute in kind of the servile peasants from the outskirts was warehoused. In comparison with the brilliant cities of antiquity, these were sad places indeed, and the shriveling of urbanism in that century of no markets reflected faithfully the change from a commercial mode of production to a subsistence one.[5]

But the bishops and, in the following century, the Catholic Church as a whole succeeded in persuading the landed nobility to undertake the reconquest and recapture of the Holy Lands. The succession of crusades that followed occupied those lands but did not manage to retain them; yet they did reopen the

Mediterranean to Christian fleets and thereby revived the east-west commercial flow of which Europe had been deprived for two centuries. From the Belgian historian Henri Pirenne and the British historian Maurice Dobb, we learn what happened next.[6] Mediterranean trade revived the cities and, once again, shifted the European center of gravity south, culminating in the emergence of the great Italian commercial city-states of Venice, Florence, Pisa, and Genoa.[7] To be sure, Venice was never fully locked out from Mediterranean trade because its close ties with Constantinople and the willingness of its seamen to trade with anyone, Muslims included, spared it the fate of Marseilles and other coastal cities in the centuries of Islamic domination. But, as Islamic domination receded, other Italian cities joined the trade—Genoa and Pisa being paramount. It was in Genoa, according to the Italian economist Giovanni Arrighi, where the first "systemic" cycle of capitalist accumulation emerged in the sixteenth century.[8]

While the great Italian city-states endlessly fought one another for control of the Mediterranean and its trade routes, farther north equally fundamental developments were taking place. Spurred by the currents of trade from the Mediterranean and then from the recently pacified North Sea, towns regained their stature as commercial centers and nurtured new market-oriented social classes, such as artisans and merchants. These were soon to unite in guilds and challenge the power of the rural-based nobility. That "marvelously indented" coast of northern Europe promoted the rise of new port towns in Flanders and the Low Countries—Antwerp, Bruges, Ghent, and others.[9] In their struggles to escape the exactions of nobility and clergy, the townsmen counted with their growing numbers and their control of money.

Indeed, this confrontation is what Marx had in mind when he identified the most basic source of historical change in the struggle between existing social relationships of production and a rising new mode of production.[10] Medieval artisans and merchants represented the latter, and, in one city after another in central and northern Europe, they succeeded in extracting "charters" from a declining and economically pressed nobility. As Max Weber emphasized, charters—akin to the bill of rights of the time—conferred on the towns the right of self-government and on their inhabitants protection from servile duties and other feudal exactions. "City air made men free," and, in Weber's account, it made "citizens" out of urban residents, creating a new territorially based form of community. No longer did people belong to their families or clans; now they were part of an urban community largely delimited by the space within city walls.[11]

This was, by no means, full-fledged capitalism, and a number of historical events had to occur in the succeeding centuries to bring that about, but the chartered autonomous cities of the twelfth and thirteenth centuries were the birthplace of capitalist development. The static world of the dark Middle Ages gave way to a new market-driven dynamism; the religious superstitions and fears of an early era were replaced by rational calculation.[12] The rebellion of the towns and their increasing ascendance culminated in the Lutheran and then Calvinist reforms. When the Augustinian monk Martin Luther nailed his ninety-five theses to that chapel door at Wittenberg, he had no idea of the momentous transformation that his gesture was to unleash. For it was the towns and their inhabitants who converted en masse to the new religious doctrine, grounded in rational opposition to the Catholic superstitions and fears of the past.[13] The Protestant Reformation and the Catholic Counter-Reformation reflected and corresponded well, at the ideological level, to the transformations undergone at the base of the economic infrastructure. Production for the market and rational calculation of profit replaced subsistence production and the medieval exploitation of a servile peasantry by nobility and clergy alike.

INDUSTRIAL CITIES

Merchants were not the dominant class in the early northern European cities. That role belonged to craftsmen and artisans grouped in increasingly powerful guilds. Compared to them, merchants of the tenth and eleventh centuries were rather pitiful add-ons to the guild-dominated towns. The economic activity carried on in these towns could be properly called "petty commodity" production, where master craftsmen worked side-by-side with a few journeymen; where the quality and price of a good were strictly regulated; and where, with some exceptions, urban goods were sold in local markets. As whenever direct producers hold power, these medieval towns were fairly egalitarian and democratic, resisting exactions by kings and feudal lords and keeping church privileges in check.[14]

Guild democracy was short-lived, however, because an alliance of the wealthier merchants, nobles, and royal houses succeeded, in less than half a century, in restoring class privileges. The remarkable transformation of the pathetic tradesmen of the eleventh century into the merchant plutocracy of the fourteenth century could not have been achieved without bypassing guild restrictions and regulations and focusing on long-distance trade: "In the first place, so much commerce in those times, especially foreign commerce, consisted either of exploiting some political advantage or scarcely veiled plunder. Secondly, the class of merchants, as soon as it assumed any corporate form was quick to acquire the powers of monopoly, which fenced its ranks from competition and served to turn the terms of exchange to its own advantage in its dealings with producer and consumer."[15]

Monopoly, that golden tool of merchant capital, was then the key to the transformation of the class structure of medieval cities from guild democracy to places ruled by a merchant plutocracy in alliance with the territorial rulers of France, England, Italy, and elsewhere. In the process, the enriched traders did not hesitate to surrender the hard-earned urban freedoms enshrined in city charters in exchange for the military protection provided by kings.[16] In time, merchants also sought to gain the status of the nobility and its privileges by purchasing their way into the lingering feudal aristocracy.

With guild power mortally wounded, European cities of the fourteenth and fifteenth centuries featured a growing inequality between the nobility, clergy, and enriched merchant bourgeoisie, which grew even wealthier by lending to the royal houses and farming their taxes, and the growing mass of the dispossessed. These were not industrial cities yet, nor were the trading activities of the merchants competitive commercial capitalism, as they relied on monopoly and hereditary privileges protected by the crown: "In general for those who had both capital and privileged position in the major gilds, investments in the export trade to the Levant or across the Alps into France and the Rhineland, or farming the Papal revenues and granting mortgage loans on the estates of princes was more lucrative than the exploiting of dependent craftsmen and the development of industry."[17]

Nevertheless, underneath all these privileges, there arose an enterprising class of direct producers made up of former guild craftsmen, enterprising squires in the countryside, and the lower strata of the merchant class. They recruited workers among the ever-growing mass of the poor, in both the cities and the countryside. Large "manufactories," some employing hundreds, rose in French cities like Sedan, Rheims, and Lyons, as well as in London and English cities of the Midlands.[18] They produced consumer goods both for the local market and for export, while continually chafing under the restrictions to commerce enforced by the monopolists and the mercantilist monarchies. Not surprisingly, Calvinism and later forms of Puritanism made deep inroads among the majority of the population subjected to this oppression.[19]

In due time, mass discontent was going to explode in popular revolutions that united the mass of the dispossessed in city and countryside against the privileges of the crown, the nobility, and the enriched merchant class. In both England and France, these revolutions cost the monarch his head, along with those of many of the privileged class. While separated by 150 years, both revolutions were led by the rising entrepreneurial and industrial bourgeoisie. Cromwell himself was a gentleman farmer, and many of his lieutenants were recruited among artisans and shopkeepers. The same was the case in France a century later, where both Girondins and Jacobins were led by liberal lawyers, professionals, and entrepreneurs.[20]

In both cases, the shock troops of the revolution were provided by the dispossessed floating mass, in city and countryside—the *levelers* in England and the so-called *sans-culottes* in France. Once victorious, their hopes for equality and radical distribution of wealth were promptly negated by the property-owning bourgeoisie: "Thus we have displayed with remarkable clearness the contradictory feature that we find in every bourgeois revolution: while this revolution requires the impetus of the most radical element to carry through its emancipating mission to the end, the movement is destined to shed large sections as soon as these radical elements appear, precisely because the latter represent the small man or the dispossessed whose very claims call in question the rights of large-scale property."[21]

The abolishing of royal and noble commercial privileges gave way to a new era of free trade that directly benefited the rising industrial class. Even the restoration of the two monarchies did not succeed in setting back the clock of history. In England, the return of Charles II after Cromwell's death did nothing to alter the radical measures taken during the Commonwealth, and when Charles's successor, James II, attempted to reinstate royal privileges, he was promptly sent on his European travels again, being replaced by William of Orange and a Parliament-controlled constitutional monarchy: "While it is true that the bourgeois revolution in seventeen-century England went only a relatively small distance in its economic and social policy, it had achieved enough to accelerate enormously the growth of industrial capital in the next half-century."[22]

The French republic went much farther, and while the first restored Capetian king, Louis XVIII, followed the cautious example of Charles II two centuries earlier, his successors attempted again to restore royal privileges and were duly deposed.[23] In both England and France, the long-term winning class was the urban industrial bourgeoisie, which reorganized foreign trade to its benefit and proceeded to transform the masses of the dispossessed into the new industrial proletariat. The subordinate classes, who had fought so hard to abolish royal and noble privileges, now found themselves in an arguably worse situation, being rapidly turned into the "beasts of burden" of industrial capital.[24] That transformation, consolidated in the nineteenth century, gave rise to new social and political realities—bourgeois democracy and the industrial city. They set the scene for an enormous expansion of European economies and, in the coming century, the increasingly violent confrontation between the beneficiaries of this expansion and the exploited urban proletariat. Marx dedicates much of the first volume of *Capital* to the refined cruelties inflicted on the working classes by their employers, and in the rest of this work he explains the instability of this exploitation under the capitalist mode of production.[25]

As always, the city played a central role as locus, instrument, and reflection of the new mode of production. Just as the rising merchant capital of earlier centuries found its center in the enriched cities of the Hanse and northern Italy, now its successor—industrial capital—was to pivot and change the urban scene of central and northern Europe and then move to the cities of the American Northeast and Midwest, transformed by massive European migration in the wake of the country's own industrial revolution.[26] As in France, England, and Germany, the "robber barons" who led American capitalism displayed profound indifference to the plight of the working man, with the difference that the masses that they exploited came mostly from abroad as southern and eastern European immigrants.[27]

By and large, industrial cities were grimy places. They grew in size by internal or foreign migration, but the noise, dirt, and pollution of their industrial plants, the deep poverty of working-class living quarters, and the vast disparities between these districts and those inhabited by the bourgeois classes made them unfriendly and threatening places. Even the well-to-do could not escape the consequences of industrial capitalism. The Cuyahoga River in Cleveland caught fire because of the vast amount of pollutants discharged in it; the sky over Pittsburgh was permanently gray from the smoke belched out by its steel mills; mutilations and premature deaths were counted by the millions among the unfortunates compelled to work in the mines and the mills. The era of industrial capitalism was also the moment when British hegemony over the rest of the world consolidated and London arose as the first global city.[28]

The British pound simultaneously became the world currency, issued by the Bank of England and controlled by financiers in the City. While the industrial bourgeoisie controlled the real productive economy, English financiers underwrote imperialist ventures. The world was fully occupied by the European powers, with colonial economies reorganized to serve the centers as sources of raw materials and markets for manufactured products.[29]

Within industrial cities in Europe and North America, the ceaseless struggle between labor and capital gave rise to a seemingly unending series of strikes and mass rallies, often repressed violently. The solution to working-class unrest proposed by Henry Ford early in the twentieth century—high wages for the workforce so that it could become, in turn, a purchaser of manufactured goods—was applied only to a limited number of industries. Strikes continued, including the Great Steel Strike of 1919. The triumph of the Bolshevik Party in Russia gave new impetus to socialist and communist movements in North America and Europe. The stock market collapse of 1929 and the ensuing Great Depression were the final straw. To many observers of the time, it seemed that capitalism was at its end and, along with it, the industrial cities that it had spawned.[30]

It did not happen that way. Massive New Deal interventions into the American economy, the rise of Keynesianism as the new economic orthodoxy, and World War II intervened. The war's victor—the United States—rose as the unquestionable hegemonic power in the world, with New York gradually replacing London at the center of gravity of the global economy. The networks of world finance converged in Manhattan, and, on cue, the dollar replaced the pound as the global currency.[31]

Taking advantage of that hegemony, American industrial corporations approached their unions to draft a new historical pact that, in effect, put Henry Ford's idea into general practice: industrial workers were granted higher wages and negotiated for annual increases, job security, and other benefits in exchange for labor peace. Internal markets permitted sustained upward mobility from within the firm for corporate employees. After the pact was reached in the late 1940s, major industrial strikes practically disappeared.[32]

The ensuing three decades of *Pax Americana* had visible effects in both American and European cities. Industry continued to concentrate in them with the by-now familiar effects on grime and pollution, but, along with them, new stable subdivisions of middle-class housing emerged. These were populated by an industrial working class made secure by the pact reached earlier between capital and labor. Referred to as the "primary" labor market, these well-paid and secure jobs made possible a more egalitarian income distribution within cities, while also contributing to sustained national growth. The 1950s were easily the most egalitarian period in America since its industrial revolution. By 1952, the share of income going to the top 10 percent of American taxpayers had declined from 45 percent in the 1930s to 32 percent and that going to the top 1 percent had dropped from 20 to 10 percent relative to 1928 figures. As Sassen notes, "A large share of manufacturing workers were in the middle-earnings jobs during the post-war period of high growth in the United States and the United Kingdom."[33]

THE POSTINDUSTRIAL CITY

This happy state of affairs was brought to an abrupt end by the heightened international competition in durable manufactured goods coming primarily from the defeated Axis powers in World War II. Germany and, especially, Japan took the world by storm with well-made cars, machine tools, and other manufactured goods, cheaper and better than those made by American industrial corporations. Challenged from their comfortable prior hegemony, these corporations did not respond by seeking to improve their own quality and efficiency, but by resorting to the "spatial fix" of moving production to cheaper locations in the Third World. In the process, American corporate managers did not vacillate in ditching the "historical pact" with their own workers, who suddenly found themselves at the mercy of the world economy.[34]

This is what Bluestone and Harrison referred to as the "Great U-Turn."[35] In a few years, the industrial belt in the American Northeast and Midwest had become the "Rust Belt," with dozens of shriveled towns housing a suddenly redundant blue-collar population. European industry followed suit, especially in Great Britain, where the industrial Midlands became similarly ravaged.[36] As always, cities became loci, vehicles, and reflections of the rapid changes in the mode of production. Redundant industrial cities saw their populations decline and their real estate markets collapse. To survive, these postindustrial places sought to reinvent themselves as service centers or as tourist destinations. Universities and hospitals took the place of industry as the major urban employers. However, unlike manufacturing, which had supported a middle-income lifestyle for its workers, service employment became split into a minority of well-paid professionals and managers and a mass of low-paid manual workers, with little else left in the middle. The labor market ceased to resemble a pyramid, with most of the working population in the middle-income levels, to become more like an "hourglass" with occupations and incomes bifurcated between a skilled and well-remunerated minority and the rest of the population.[37]

Urban space in postindustrial cities reflected faithfully these changes. Grime and industrial pollution disappeared, giving way to defunct factories and empty warehouses, plus street after street of abandoned or rapidly decaying housing—the former abode of the industrial working class.[38] Such cities did not disappear, but their social structure and physical appearance became very different. In cities like Detroit, Flint, and Cleveland, the built environment evaporated, giving way to empty land; population diversity declined; and homelessness, informal street vending, and other reflections of spreading poverty became common. Taking advantage of the suddenly affordable urban centers, young professionals returned to some of these cities, turning lofts and abandoned apartments downtown into newly renovated living places.[39]

This process of gentrification infused new life into some downtowns and other selected residential areas, but it did not include the former industrial working class, many of whose members were displaced to make way for the new gentrifiers. Postindustrial cities in America became more racially polarized because a significant part of the displaced industrial working class was composed of African Americans who had migrated north in search of employment in earlier decades. The gentrified urban centers in these cities remained solidly white, while large tracts of the surrounding decayed housing were populated by Blacks.[40]

The banks, finance houses, universities, and hospitals that employed skilled professionals in the new "ed and med" urban economy protected themselves by landscaping their surroundings in attractive ways that blocked the sea of urban decay beyond. Employment for the unskilled and semiskilled working class focused increasingly on providing services for the classes above—cleaning houses, repairing newly gentrified property, caring for the wealthy elderly and infirm, and performing the myriad manual jobs required by service institutions. These became the only available forms of employment; the rest of the former industrial working class survived through invented employment in an expanding informal economy, street drug vending, and petty crime, as well as through paltry subsidies from a shrinking welfare system.[41]

The physical appearance of the postindustrial city differed sharply from that of its predecessor. Instead of continuous and walkable inhabited space, there emerged a series of "islands" inhabited by governmental, educational, medical, and other service institutions and their professional employees plus posh commercial malls, all surrounded by a no-man's land of boarded-up working-class housing, empty land, and places where the illegal trades made it too dangerous to walk alone.

PERIPHERAL CITIES

It is a familiar fact that urban civilization did not start in the West, as the first known cities in history were founded elsewhere—in Egypt, Mesopotamia, China, and India. Rulers and warlords assembled people together in selected physical destinations and for their own purposes. While these cities of antiquity could reach considerable size and fulfill a number of functions, their inhabitants derived no particular status from living there because their social identities and solidarity were based on their family and kinship group, not on the places where they lived.[42]

It is only in the eleventh and twelfth centuries in medieval Europe where we see the emergence of an "urban community" whose inhabitants leave behind kinship loyalties and religious superstition to bind themselves together in defense of urban freedoms and the pursuit of rational economic enterprise: "Here the burgher joined the citizenry and swore his civic oath as an individual. This personal membership in the local association of the city, not his kinship or tribal affiliation, was the basis of his legal rights as a citizen."[43]

As we have seen before, it was these autonomous, commercially oriented territorial entities that provided the cradle for capitalism and that were, in Weber's terms, the locations for the rise of its "spirit." Three centuries later, capitalist economic practices and orientations had evolved into an imperialist system that eventually subdued the entire world. Whatever their functions and their loyalties had been before, non-Western cities in the new European colonies were systematically conquered, eliminated, or reconstructed to serve the economic goals of the colonizing powers.[44] Without exception, these powers treated peripheral cities not as autonomous or productive entities but as subordinate places of administration from where surpluses—in the form of raw materials, foodstuffs, precious metals, and other goods—were channeled to the European metropolis.

When newly colonized territories did not contain suitable urban agglomerations, the Europeans created them. The Spanish, in particular, were adept at founding cities in the Americas. Such cities did not emerge organically to serve the economic and administrative needs of a settled population but were imposed by fiat as instruments for political and military control. Under the Ordinances for Discovery and Population promulgated by King Philip II in 1573, cities were founded everywhere in the conquered territories in accordance with a prescribed uniform design.[45] This colonizing strategy created an urban system in the Americas that has lasted to our day. As shown in table 1.1, most of the twenty largest cities in Latin America already existed by the end of the sixteenth century. The Portuguese crown followed a similar strategy in Brazil but with a focus on coastal settlements that left the interior of the vast colony untouched. São Paulo, Rio de Janeiro, and Recife were also founded in the sixteenth century, but the large interior city of Belo Horizonte did not emerge until the nineteenth century.[46]

The second massive wave of European colonization coincided with the last phase of the French-British struggle for world hegemony and the final emergence of Britain as the prime industrial power in the nineteenth century. Neither the French nor the British were adept at founding cities, adapting instead precolonial urban formations for their purposes. That was the strategy followed by the East India Company as it played regional chieftains against one another and eventually replaced the Mughal Empire as the dominant political and military force in the subcontinent.[47] The same happened in the Middle East, where British and French forces put themselves in place of the retreating Ottoman Empire and occupied former Turkish administrative and political centers.[48]

Neither the towns founded by Spain and Portugal in the earlier phase of European conquest nor those occupied by France and England in the nineteenth century ever evolved into autonomous political entities in the model of medieval European towns, nor did they develop into industrial centers after the pattern of British, French, and then North American cities in the nineteenth and early twentieth centuries. Peripheral cities remained instead administrative and commercial places involved primarily in trade with the global capitalist centers. In India, the British East India Company busied itself with deindustrializing the country so that it could serve as a source of raw materials for English and

TABLE 1.1 Population and founding year of the twenty largest cities in Latin America and the United States

City and country (2017)	Estimated metro population (1,000s)[a]	Year founded[b]	U.S. metro area (2010)	Estimated metro population (1,000s)[c]	Year founded[b]
São Paulo, Brazil	21,243	1554	New York	18,920	1626
Mexico City, Mexico	20,400	1521	Los Angeles	12,849	1781
Buenos Aires, Argentina	12,740	1536	Chicago	9,474	1833
Rio de Janeiro, Brazil	12,281	1565	Dallas	6,403	1846
Lima, Peru	10,852	1535	Houston	5,977	1836
Bogota, Colombia	9,800	1538	Philadelphia	5,971	1681
Santiago, Chile	6,582	1541	Washington, D.C.	5,610	1790
Belo Horizonte, Brazil	5,156	1897	Miami	5,582	1896
Guayaquil, Ecuador	5,000	1537	Atlanta	5,288	1847
Quito, Ecuador	4,700	1534	Boston	4,561	1630
Monterrey, Mexico	4,560	1579	San Francisco	4,345	1850
Guatemala City, Guatemala	4,500	1776	Detroit	4,292	1701
Guadalajara, Mexico	4,424	1521	Riverside	4,246	1893
Porto Alegre, Brazil	4,405	1742	Phoenix	4,211	1871
Fortaleza, Brazil	4,019	1654	Seattle	3,449	1853
Recife, Brazil	3,996	ca. 1550	Minneapolis	3,286	1867
Salvador, Brazil	3,920	1889	San Diego	3,106	1850
Medellin, Colombia	3,731	1675	St. Louis	2,815	1764
Cordoba, Argentina	3,645	1573	Tampa	2,789	1834
Cali, Colombia	3,400	1563	Baltimore	2,714	1729

[a] "Largest Cities in the World and Their Mayors," City Mayors Foundation, http://citymayors.com/statistics/largest-cities-mayors-1.html.

[b] *Encyclopedia Britannica*; Alejandro Portes and John Walton, *Urban Latin America: The Political Condition from Above and Below* (Austin: University of Texas Press, 1976).

[c] U.S. Census Bureau, 2010 Decennial Census.

Scottish factories and as a market for their manufactured products.[49] Local elites in the nominally independent new countries of former Spanish America were content with adhering to the British regime of free-trade imperialism, exporting raw materials and foodstuffs to the industrial centers and importing railways and manufactured goods from them. Cities, especially those that were ports, became nodes for this unequal exchange, which relegated Latin American economies to a permanently subordinate role.[50]

The American republic did not follow the European imperialist adventures, but rather devoted its energies to colonizing itself or, more properly, colonizing its own continent from east to west through a series of successful wars and fortunate acquisitions.[51] Unlike in Spanish America, cities were not imposed by fiat to subdue a hostile hinterland, but rather emerged gradually following the contours of trade. In the model of the early settlers of New England, occupying the land came first and towns arose subsequently to serve the commercial and administrative needs of a settled rural population. This is the reason that, as shown in table 1.1, North American cities were not created all at once but emerged over several centuries as the country advanced in its process of self-colonization.

Beyond early examples of industrialization such as São Paulo, by the mid-twentieth century many peripheral cities in the Global South had begun to industrialize, but industrialization seldom lifted them beyond their traditional subordinate status. The policy of import substitution industrialization (ISI) was strongly advocated by, among others, the U.N. Economic Commission for Latin America under the leadership of Argentine economist Raúl Prebisch.[52] ISI registered some notable successes, particularly in Asian nations like Japan and, subsequently, South Korea and Taiwan. In most countries, however, ISI policies were compromised by a series of macroeconomic contradictions. Multinational corporations were allowed to jump the tariff barriers set up by ISI and become "national" in their respective adopted countries (e.g., Ford "Argentina," Westinghouse "do Brazil," etc.). Once there, they outcompeted authentic national firms, thereby subverting the very purpose of ISI.[53]

In terms of urbanization, the principal result of ISI policies was to bring about a quantum leap in the concentration of the population in one or two cities per country. The condition of urban "primacy" whereby the major city, as in Argentina or Mexico, or a duopoly, as in Brazil, exceeds the combined population of the next three or six cities became exacerbated by the location of ISI industries in the largest urban centers, thereby triggering large-scale labor migration toward them.[54] During the ISI years, in the mid-twentieth century, the relentless growth of urban primacy was seen as unstoppable.

However, the contradictions and recurrent trade imbalances that eventually did away with ISI brought in their wake a reassertion of the dominant capitalist centers in defense of free trade, market opening, and the end of autonomous industrial policy in peripheral nations. The result was the emergence of the Washington Consensus, which opened the economies of countries in Africa, Asia, and Latin America to global trade under conditions not too different from those that predominated under nineteenth-century British free-trade imperialism.[55] Starting with the Mexican debt crisis of the 1980s, country after country in the world peripheries, especially Latin America and Africa, lifted barriers to foreign investments and trade, dismantling in the process the domestic industrial plant so painfully built during the ISI period.

Not coincidentally, the new free-market orthodoxy emerged at a time when industrial corporations in North America were ditching the "historical pact" with their own workers and casting about for new exploitable labor sources with which to confront the global competition in manufactured goods started by Japan. Countries like Mexico, Colombia, Pakistan, Vietnam, Malaysia, and Egypt did not suddenly become deindustrialized, but their process of industrialization took a radically new turn as low-cost production platforms for multinational corporations, primarily American.[56] The rise of these new export platforms mirrored faithfully the decline of the old industrial cities in the world centers, as well as that of the fledgling peripheral industries built during the ISI period. Mexican, Malaysian, Vietnamese, and especially Chinese workers were now hired by the thousands to produce the same components and final goods previously manufactured in the industrial plants of the capital core but at a fraction of the cost in labor.

The new policy became known as export-oriented industrialization (EOI). From the standpoint of "Third World" urbanization, one of its most important consequences was to put an end to the relentless rise of urban primacy. As old industries built under import substitution policies disappeared, the migratory "pull" exercised by primate cities weakened, to be substituted by rechanneled migration to the new export platforms in secondary cities and regions. A telling, but not the sole, example is Mexico, where the growth of the capital city slowed significantly, to be substituted by the rapid rise in population of export-oriented *maquiladora* cities, such as Tijuana and Juárez, situated in the border with the United States.[57]

Whether under ISI or EOI auspices, the most significant feature of peripheral cities is that they never managed to leave behind their condition of subordination to the global capitalist centers. Even the largest, such as Mexico City, São Paulo, Jakarta, or Lagos, never managed to become global centers for capital accumulation and decision making themselves. Their primary role, as in colonial times, was to serve as administrative and market nodes for their respective national economies and to play an entrepôt role between those economies and the capitalist world centers.[58]

The systemic role of such cities is not unimportant because they coordinate vast trade and financial flows for large regions inhabited by millions of people. Yet the decisions that ultimately make or break their economic fates are made elsewhere. The role of peripheral urban centers in the global economy is ultimately to organize the production and export of raw materials and foodstuffs, as in colonial times, and, in addition, to facilitate the emergence of industrial export platforms under the auspices of foreign multinational corporations. As during the period of British free-trade imperialism, these cities remain subordinate.

THE GLOBAL CITY

In fact, most formerly industrial cities in Europe and North America regressed to the role that cities had in preindustrial times as administrative centers and local marketplaces. Some cities located by the sea and in other attractive places pursued a new future as tourist destinations. For the most part, however, the sad landscape of industrial abandonment and economic paralysis was the norm. Notable exceptions were the few cities that managed to concentrate administrative and financial services for an economy extending well beyond their own physical locations. By one of those peculiar turns in the history of capitalism, the global economy came to require increasing physical concentration of its command -and-control functions at the same time that industrial production and commercial logistics decentralized worldwide.[59]

Saskia Sassen was the first to highlight this pattern in the contemporary world economy. She noted that, despite the expansion of long-distance communication facilities, major decisions on investments and trade affecting millions the world over were made by a few major players and their staff in close contact with one another. That is why the headquarters of major banks, multinational corporations, legal and auditing firms, and large consulting firms cluster close to one another in a few designated places. These are the global cities. They permit face-to-face contact, nearly instantaneous decisions, and fluid interaction among key economic players, as the occasion demands.[60]

Sassen identified New York, London, and Tokyo as such cities and then described their main characteristics. They all left their industrial past behind, as the manufacturing function decentralized on a global scale. What they produce instead are financial instruments—bonds, derivatives, stock options, and the like; instantaneous sales and purchases of such instruments in specialized exchanges; and corporate decisions affecting long-term investments and disinvestments on a mass scale. The class structure of such places has become increasingly polarized between capital owners, highly paid executives, and skilled professionals and the rest of the population. To work in an office in Wall Street or London, one needs very specialized training, commitment, and luck.

Most of the people in these cities work in a myriad of services—education, health, leisure, recreation—many of them catering to the needs and tastes of the dominant classes. Most of these service jobs in restaurants, laundries, transportation, and delivery services of all kinds are staffed by a semiformal and informal proletariat composed largely of immigrants. Unlike members of the old industrial working class, members of the new one in global cities are often part of a "gig" economy, paid irregularly and without job security. Workers rapidly shift from job to job, depending on a demand that is ultimately generated by the higher-income classes and the institutions that employ them.[61]

The postindustrial global city is neither peaceful nor solidary. Instead, it is fragmented between a core of highly capitalized firms, their managers, and staff and the millions making a living in the fractured economy below. In between are salaried professionals and technicians employed by a number of indispensable services in education, health, and local commerce. While challenging and unpromising to those with limited skills, employment prospects in global cities are still quite superior to those in formerly industrial ones that have not found a niche in the new globalized economy. The economic outlook in such cities is grim, which is why their youths often abandon them and why they manage to attract few immigrants. The rise of the global city, epitomized

by New York and London, would appear to bring to a conclusion the evolution of capitalism born in the cradle of medieval European towns and of
the capitalist world system launched in the sixteenth century by imperialist
European nations.

However, the latest episode in the continuing evolution of the world capitalist economy has been the arrival of new actors that seek to imitate, in their
respective regional spheres, the achievements and experience of established
global cities. This development has been prompted by the very evolution of the
capitalist system, which requires still more centers for coordination of financial
transactions and international trade. Naturally, every city, especially those struggling with postindustrial decline, has sought to imitate the models of New York,
London, and Tokyo; few, however, have succeeded.[62]

To succeed in this endeavor requires a unique combination of factors: a privileged geographical location, an iron will among local elites to move ahead in
global competition, and an institutional apparatus free of graft and capable of
carrying out the necessary policy innovations. This is a difficult combination.
Those few cities that have achieved this feat may be labeled "emerging global
cities." The present book focuses on their experiences, as well as those of other
urban places that have come close to that achievement but that, for a variety of
reasons, have fallen short.

URBAN STUDIES IN THE AGE OF GLOBALIZATION

Following Sassen's lead, the vast social science literature on contemporary
urbanization has focused on what makes cities competitive, attracting capital
and investments to themselves and becoming the abode of what Richard Florida
calls "the creative classes."[63] In urban geography, in particular, the result has been
the emergence of various rankings of cities based on a number of economic and
political criteria, but ultimately reflecting how close or distant they are to the
ideal type of global city.[64] A journal like *Global Networks* can be consulted for a
number of examples.

Parallel to the attempt to convert the concept of global cities into a set of
empirical measures, there has emerged a critical literature that accuses Sassen
and her successors of focusing on the core and celebrating the superiority of
the advanced world to the neglect of urban trends and problems in poorer

lands. Jennifer Robinson's critique of the global city literature exemplifies this stance:

> Part of the adverse worldly impact of their urban theories is . . . a consequence of the geographical division of urban studies between urban theory, broadly focused on the West, and development studies focused on places that were once called "third-world" cities. . . . One of the consequences of these overlapping dualisms is that understandings of city-ness have come to rest of the experiences of a relatively small group of mostly western cities, and cities outside the West are assessed in terms of this pre-given standard of . . . urban economic dynamism.[65]

Neil Brenner, arguably the leading figure in this critical literature of "planetary urbanization," pitches his argument at a high level of abstraction to reassess theories of global city formation and related theories.[66] Taking his clue from Henri Lefebvre's exploration of the capitalist laws of motion and their urban manifestations, Brenner concludes that "the relentless implosion-explosion of social-spatial relations through capitalist industrialization . . . must today be placed at the analytical epicenter of critical urban theory."[67]

This is highly abstract material, with few concrete references or examples of how the process of urbanization actually unfolds in specific countries or regions. Nevertheless, Brenner's work provides powerful support for Robinson's contention that the literature on global or world cities has evolved with increasing indifference to what is taking place in poorer regions of the world economy.

These alternative and competing strands of the literature on contemporary urbanization provide a necessary framework for our own study of emerging global cities. On the one hand, it is undeniable that theorizing and research on global cities is decidedly core-centric, focused primarily on the "winners" of the competitive struggle for hegemony, while leaving behind the evolution of cities in less fortunate peripheral regions. On the other hand, the research literature on "Third World" urbanization has emphasized this other side of the coin, namely, the evolving forces in the capitalist world economy that have kept these cities in a subordinate place, assigned a subsidiary role in the circles of capitalist accumulation.[68]

Yet this polarization neglects the admittedly exceptional experiences of cities and countries in the periphery that have managed to overcome the heavy burden of underdevelopment and the associated expectations about their "proper" role in the world economy in order to climb up to positions of greater wealth and power. At the national level, the historical experiences of Japan and, subsequently, of South Korea and Taiwan have been the subject of a vast literature focused on the political and economic forces that allowed them to enter the ranks of the First World.[69] Neglected in this literature is the history of specific cities that have managed to do likewise.

Their study is important not only because these experiences may show to others the path forward, but also because they provide a bridge to the competing literatures on world cities—always situated in the advanced countries—and subordinate ones in the rest of the world. In contrast to the past literature on peripheral urbanization, the study of these exceptional new global cities demonstrates that there are "degrees of freedom" in the world economy, even though the path forward is difficult.

The emerging global cities that are the subject of this book are located, geographically and financially, at the "edge" of the world economy. They have in common that they have left behind their industrial past or never had one. Nor are they centers of high-technology innovation such as the cities in Silicon Valley or the cities of Austin or Boston. Instead, the pillars of their economies tend to imitate the four sectors of the established global centers: banking and financial institutions, transportation and commerce on a world scale, construction and real estate speculation for expatriate buyers, and tourism. The class structure of such places is also increasingly polarized between capital owners, managers, investors, and skilled professionals in a multiplicity of services and a semiproletariat hired for low wages and on a temporary basis. The national and ethnic origins of these subordinate classes vary significantly among these cities.[70]

Unlike the class structure of emerging global cities, which tends to be quite similar, what they have to offer by way of attraction to prospective visitors and tourists varies greatly. In some places, it is sun and sand; in others, a highly advanced medical system; in others, a specialized arts scene. While entertainment and leisure attractions are common to all, none has relied so far on gambling as a key component of a tourist offer.

Like the major global cities originally identified by Sassen, emerging ones are also a threesome. We identify Dubai, Miami, and Singapore as the urban places that most closely approach this characterization. Hong Kong may be a fourth that, in several ways, is ahead of the others in financial and commercial centrality.

Of late, however, Hong Kong has confronted a near-fatal situation from the combined threat of political takeover by the Chinese communist regime and mass protests against that prospect by the resident population. While the initial momentum of its past achievements in all four sectors previously described continues to make Hong Kong a power to be reckoned with, its prospects for maintaining and consolidating its global status in the long term are dim.

The three other emerging global cities have in common that they were all peripheral and, as such, destined to a subordinate role similar to so many other cities outside the capitalist core. The political leader credited with the rise of Singapore, Lee Kuan Yew, titled his account of these events *From Third World to First: The Singapore Story*.[71] Like Dubai, Singapore emerged from the status of a secondary colony in the former British Empire. Miami was a peripheral winter resort in the American urban system. The complex sequence of factors that led these cities to leap ahead of others and acquire parallel economic structures and class profiles will be the subject of the coming chapters. The dramatic case of Hong Kong will also deserve detailed attention. Finally, we also examine selected instances of other cities that have aspired to the same global role and possess some, but not all, the requisite characteristics. What these are and why it is so difficult to combine them in order to break the stranglehold of subordination and underdevelopment in the capitalist world economy will be a central focus of our conclusion.

CHAPTER 2

DUBAI

From Marginal Gulf Town to Regional Hub

RANA TOMAIRA

A t the onset of 2020, just as Dubai was preparing to host Expo2020, which was scheduled to open in October, things were still looking good for Dubai. There were high hopes that the Expo would boost Dubai's economy, which never fully recovered from the 2008 crisis. The six-month event, to be hosted for the first time in the Arab region, generated a lot of hype. As is the case with all high-visibility events that Dubai hosts, an expensive marketing strategy advertised this anticipated landmark event. The target was to attract 25 million visitors, with 70 percent coming from overseas. The Expo was meant to generate economic growth partly through spending on the event and its infrastructure and architecture. More importantly, it was hoped that the event would bring in more indirect investments. The total investment amount was estimated at AED 122.6 billion (approximately US$33.2 billion).[1]

A few months into 2020, as the coronavirus pandemic unfolded, the global economy came to a standstill. Not only was Expo2020 postponed, but the ensuing shutdown was also a major blow to Dubai's economy. Capital Economics, a leading economic research company based in London, saw Dubai as the most vulnerable economy in the Arab region because its economy had the highest percentage (32 percent) of sectors negatively affected by social distancing, namely, wholesale and retail trades, hotels and restaurants, arts and recreation, and food sectors. Furthermore, Capital Economics was already skeptical about the Expo's ability to boost the economy given the high amount of debt of Dubai's government and of the government-related entities (GREs), the latter equaling 80 percent of GDP, or $88.9 billion.[2] This new reality had many observers speculating on what the future of this emerging global city would look like. It seemed that a bailout scenario by Abu Dhabi, reminiscent of 2009, was very likely, except that this time the economic impact was larger.

On the other hand, some government officials had faith that Dubai would be able to weather the storm. As the only global city in the region, Dubai has the experience and flexibility that neighboring economies do not have. This leads observers to count on the ability of decision-makers to "respond quickly to challenges," as stated by the director-general of Dubai's economic department.[3] Perhaps the shrinkage in the economy today would allow the city to rescale and restructure it in a way that could be beneficial in the future. However, throughout its history Dubai has enjoyed autonomy in pursuing economic policy. Is this autonomy compromised in the current circumstances?

Much has been written about the thriving globalized sectors of Dubai. This emerging global city has managed to leapfrog and position itself as a major hub and service center for the movement of people, goods, and capital. The great economic success of Dubai, which took off in the 1990s, positioned the city as the poster child of diversification away from the oil rentier model dominant among Gulf states. The success of Dubai has led other Gulf states to adopt the "Dubai model" as their main strategy for economic diversification away from oil.[4] Given the current economic crisis and the growing regional competition from Gulf cities emulating Dubai's economic strategies, Dubai finds itself at a crossroads. Either it succeeds in its rebound and ventures into new market niches that will sustain its economic advantage, or it will lose a significant portion of its market share.

THE MAIN ARGUMENT

Much of the literature on Gulf cities, and on Dubai in particular, follows an "exceptionalism" frame of analysis. The city's current model of integration with the global economy is often seen as a historical break from a traditional past. This view has also been celebrated by the royal families, who see themselves as being both the leaders of modernity and the guardians of heritage. This approach neglects two facts: (1) the history of fluid trade and migration, and (2) the central political role of British imperialism in concentrating power in the hands of ruling families.[5] In the past decade and a half, a growing number of scholars have been challenging this view and showing that there is continuity between Dubai's past and its present. Works by Hanieh, Kanna, Keshavarzian, Marchal, Ramos, and others have rejected the exceptionalism argument and have developed a framework that studies the Gulf and its development as part of a global process that has produced its current form of integration with the global economy.[6] This chapter builds on that framework.

Furthermore, the analysis presented here focuses on regional issues, which are often excluded from the discourse on Dubai as a global city. In his seminal work, *Money, Markets, and Monarchies*, Hanieh shows that national, regional, and global scales are not separate levels. Relations between these scales are "understood to be jointly formed and co-constituted."[7] His work contributes to the missing regional focus by looking at the rise of the global Gulf in relation to the fall of traditional regional powers. This chapter builds on this work but situates Dubai within its region, highlighting the fundamental role of geopolitics, political stability, and the fall of traditional Arab centers of gravity in explaining how Dubai rose to become the only city in the Arab region to achieve global economic prominence.

The sections that follow begin with an overview of the major events that shaped Dubai's economic trajectory. A large body of literature has focused on the city's history and the features of its global economy; to avoid repeating these discussions, this chapter emphasizes three points: (1) how the city managed to carve out its global niche; (2) how it secured economic power through autonomy and dependence; and (3) how it manages to seize opportunities and act quickly before others do the same.

At the onset, it is important to point out four essential characteristics that underlie this particular case. These are by no means specific to Dubai and may very well exist in other emerging global cities. However, they have been central to the developmental path of Dubai.

The first characteristics is the hereditary power structure and the highly centralized decision-making process. Absolute power rests with the ruler, supported by a small number of close aides, who presides over and directly runs the state and who is the central driver of the economy.

Second, the state and ruling family are not distinguishable. When we say "state," we mean the "ruling family," the al-Maktoums. State ownership is synonymous with family ownership. While Dubai is often hailed as a model of the free market, it is very much a *dirigiste* economy where the state is the guiding and dominant economic force. It leads the way by opening up new opportunities for investment and capital accumulation and is directly involved in the economy through its GREs.

Third, the private sector and the ruling class are intertwined to the extent that, at the level of individuals, they are often one and the same. This is the result of state formation and class formation occurring hand in hand. Adam Hanieh articulates this point well, stating that "members of the ruling family who hold high-ranking state positions should simultaneously be considered part of the 'private' capitalist class and, in a related fashion, where prominent non-royal private capitalists simultaneously serve in the state apparatus."[8] Hanieh explains that this is not a new observation in the Arab world. It has always been a topic of debate because it deviates from the conventional economic literature that separates the "state sector" from the "private sector." "Understanding the state as an institutional relation of class thus implies that many of the individual personnel related to the institutions of the state can simultaneously be considered part of the capitalist class. This is a pronounced feature of the way that capitalism has developed in the GCC and, in many cases, the 'capitalist class' should be understood as inclusive of state personnel and individuals from the ruling family."[9]

More important is that the development of the "capitalist class" was not insulated from the global capitalist system. On the contrary, class formation in Dubai and the Gulf in general was integrated early on, long before the discovery of oil, into the world market. To use Hanieh's words, "The global economy is part of the actual essence of the Gulf itself—the development of the global 'appears' through the development of the Gulf."[10]

Fourth, a point often overlooked is the centrality of geopolitics. Since its early days as a port, Dubai's rulers have enjoyed a symbiotic relationship with colonial powers and had no reason to challenge colonial interests in the Gulf. Trucial States respected maritime peace agreements imposed by Britain to facilitate British trade in return for stability and protection.[11] After the decline of British influence and presence in the region, the Gulf states shifted their alliance to the new global power, the United States. This alliance with the West ensured political stability for the Gulf states and enabled cities like Dubai to make and execute long-term plans. The case of Dubai and other emerging global cities reveals that political, economic, and physical security are paramount for economic growth and long-term strategic planning. In Kiren Chaudhry's seminal piece on social instability and economic deprivation in the Arab region, she contends that the lack of political stability, which is prevalent in the Arab world, creates a volatile environment that can be more detrimental for people's lives than stable poverty.[12] Sources of instability in this region are built into its resource structure, regional politics, and international interventions. Instability and insecurity undermine the formation of the stable preferences necessary for political action. They also work against cross-regional collaboration.

BETWEEN AUTONOMY AND DEPENDENCE

Unlike in other parts of the Arab region, colonial powers, beginning with the Venetians, the Portuguese, the Dutch, and then the British, were never interested in the management of societies in the Gulf region. Nor were they interested in the Gulf as a market or destination for their trade.[13] They were mainly interested in its role as a trade route, a safe passageway for European trading ships. This fact gave some room for ruler autonomy on the domestic level, which served Dubai well, despite the weakness of its ruling al-Maktoum family vis-à-vis its counterparts in Sharjah, Ra's al-Khaimah, and Abu Dhabi.

Signs of autonomy in Dubai were apparent as early as 1820. Davidson explains that when the British political resident, Britain's most senior representative to the Gulf, visited the lower Gulf for the first time, he noted that Dubai seemed to enjoy some autonomy.[14] Eventually, this autonomy was further cemented as the al-Maktoum family benefited from the rivalry between the Qawasim of Ra's al-Khaimah and Sharjah and the al-Nahyan family of Abu Dhabi.

The Qawasim, whose influence spread from Ra's al-Khaimah in the north to Sharjah, passing through Um al-Quwain and Ajman, were the troublemakers in the eyes of Britain. They had a substantial fleet of 500 ships and sought to impose a fee on British ships for navigating Gulf waters.[15] They also allied themselves with the growing religious Wahabi or al-Muwah'iddun movement from the hinterland, which was hostile to anti-Muslim entities and rejected British guardianship.[16] Fearing a threat to their trade and their allies, the British took military action against the Qawasim. The defeat was swift, and the Qawasim agreed to a peace treaty. Jim Krane writes: "Historians differ on their views of the British assaults. Traditionally, the narrative follows the British line that the attacks were a justified response to Arab piracy. Recent research disagrees. Using documents from the East India Company's archives, historians—including Sharjah ruler Sheikh Sultan al-Qassimi—say the British decision to destroy Qawasim shipping was made to snuff the competition. The incessant alarms over Arab piracy were more smoke than fact, used to justify sending the Royal Navy on its punitive mission."[17]

The military attack and destruction of the Qawasim fleet in 1819 were a defining moment that ushered in the era when colonial powers maintained a continuous military presence in the Gulf.[18] This presence began with Britain and was then taken over by the United States. Colonial military ships required fueling and maintenance, and Dubai's port developed into the major docking point for these ships. This relationship sealed Dubai's fate—and that of the United Arab Emirates (UAE)—as symbiotically intertwined with imperialism and militarism. The weakening of the Qawasim, al-Maktoum's closest tribal challenge, meant that the latter had room to maneuver and carve out an autonomous political space for Dubai. They did this through seizing economic opportunities while making sure to keep a friendly relationship with the British.

After their defeat, the Qawasim diverted their attention away from the British toward Abu Dhabi and the troubling provocations from the Nahyan family. Therefore, it was in the Qawasim's interest that Dubai remained autonomous and free from Abu Dhabi's influence. They were willing to protect this independence, which functioned as a buffer between them and Abu Dhabi. The ruler of Dubai capitalized on this rivalry to fortify his town. The al-Maktoum family governed by negotiating and building alliances to protect themselves against the more powerful clans to their north and south. They kept a neutral stance and avoided getting caught up in the tribal wars between the Qawasim and Nahyan families.[19]

Dubai's early relationship with Britain brought another layer of protection that was seminal in cementing the regional role that Dubai would play in antipiracy truces and agreements. Britain was quick to realize that its interest lay in supporting Dubai's autonomy. As Davidson states, the simple act of signing peace treaties or truces, which were meant to last into the future, legitimized these rulers and gave them an advantage over other local elites in the eyes of Britain, therefore securing their protection by the colonial power.[20] These treaties were first signed in 1820 and were routinely extended until December 1, 1971, when a union between six sheikhdoms formed the United Arab Emirates.

On their part, the sheikhs of the Trucial States were satisfied with the arrangements that placed Britain as their political guardian and controller of foreign policy. They benefited politically (through protection) and economically (through subsidies) from their dependency on Britain. For Britain, the subsidies meant that the rulers would continue to honor the peace treaties. For the rulers, this relationship allowed them to be less financially dependent on merchant elites through taxation.[21]

As for the power structure, the British political resident, the highest diplomatic official of the British Empire, had more power and higher status than the sheikhs. The rulers were willing to accept this incomplete sovereignty in return for Britain's support of their seats of rule. Protecting the Trucial State system was a priority for Britain. It could not tolerate any maritime disruptions of its British East India Company, which monopolized trade in the Indian Ocean region. Adam Hanieh explains:

> Britain's major concern was the exclusion of other colonial and regional powers from the Gulf region, and the continued profitable engagement with pearling and other trade. These interests in the Gulf were subordinate to a broader colonial framework centered upon enduring control over India. . . . As a result of this economic subordination to British-controlled trade, the ruling *shuyoukh* (pl. Sheikh) along the Gulf's coast were largely dependent on British support for their survival. The British were fully cognizant of this fact, and pursued a clearly articulated policy of divide-and-rule within the region—breaking the territory into many small sheikhdoms that would be reliant on an external power for their survival—and embodied in a treaty between the ruler and the British.[22]

It was important for Britain to guard its monopoly on the Gulf sheikhdoms and prevent any foreign entity from setting its economic foot in the region. Britain's aim was never the development of the region. When a conflict of interest arose, the wishes of the colonial power trumped everything else. On many occasions, Britain was the obstacle in the face of development efforts in Dubai, as it blocked outside interests in the nascent town as well as foreign entrepreneurs who were willing to introduce new technologies to the pearling industry.[23] In fact, this ban extended beyond pearling equipment and included other technologies. Interestingly, the ban included British-made radios to keep the people away from political messages that could harm Britain's interests. Furthermore, Britain took direct action to prevent the proliferation of pan-Arab and anticolonial sentiments in Dubai and other Gulf towns brought there by Arab expatriates. On some occasions, the British interfered directly, such as by removing unruly Arab educators from schools and replacing them with obedient counterparts.[24]

REGIONAL TRADE AND THE RISE OF DUBAI AS A MAJOR PORT

Trade began to flourish under the rule of Sheikh Maktoum bin Butti (1833–1852), the first independent ruler of Dubai. Dubai began to establish its position as a major port in the second half of the nineteenth century. Sheikh Maktoum bin Hasher al-Maktoum, who ruled between 1894 and 1906, took the decision to remove trade barriers and fees.[25] By the end of the century, Dubai was further integrated into Britain's trade routes and was declared the principal port for British merchants in the Gulf region.[26]

It took a few "bad decisions" elsewhere and good decisions at home to cement Dubai's position as the major port in the Gulf. Two of these decisions stand out. The first occurred around 1904 when the government in Tehran decided to impose taxes on the port of Bandar Lingeh, as well as other restrictive laws that targeted the Arab population in the southern coastal regions. This development led the majority of prominent merchants to relocate their businesses and families to the more welcoming port of Dubai. These merchants were immediately welcomed by the rulers in Dubai and were offered protection and land near the creek for them to settle.[27]

These Persian merchants were a tremendous benefit to the city because they brought with them trade expertise and access to new markets in Asia and Africa, establishing the path for Dubai's growth as a port city in the early twentieth century. Britain then added Dubai as a port of call for its India Steam Navigation Company, which reinforced the decline of Bandar Lingeh as the main trading center in the Gulf.[28] In the 1920s, the government in Persia imposed policies to increase taxes, secularize and modernize the populations in the southern coastal cities, and prevent schools from teaching in Arabic. These policies sent a second wave of merchants relocating their businesses to Dubai. A third wave arrived as a result of political unrest in Iran and the decision by Britain to impose an embargo in Iranian ports during World War II.[29]

The first blow to Dubai's economy came about in the late 1920s with Japan's commercialization of cultured pearls. The global recession of 1929 also had a negative impact on the demand for Dubai's pearls. Until then, the pearl trade had been the main source of income for the merchant class, which shared power and revenue with the ruling family.[30] With the drastic decline of the pearl industry, the main source of economic livelihood for Dubai's inhabitants, a new source of income had to be found. Beginning in the 1930s, Dubai began to sell twenty-five-year oil exploration concessions to British companies and charge air landing fees to British aircraft. Growing traffic in and out of Dubai as a result of aviation and oil concessions increased the demand for infrastructure.[31]

The second policy that strengthened Dubai's trade position occurred in the 1950s when India banned gold trade and limited the textile market.[32] This created an opportunity for Dubai, especially after the fall of the pearl industry, to position itself as a reexport trading port. Most of this trade revolved around gold. By the mid-twentieth century, merchants had shifted to gold trade and Dubai had replaced Kuwait as the main exporter of gold to India. This happened with the help of the British Bank of the Middle East in Dubai, which offered free dollars for gold trade.[33] Dubai quickly became the trading link between the Indian subcontinent and Europe as its merchants took advantage of this new role. Among those merchants was the businessman Saif Ahmad Al-Ghurair, founder of the Al-Ghurair Group, today one of the largest Emirati conglomerates.[34]

In terms of economic strategy, Dubai's rulers were keen on establishing a business-friendly environment open to investors and seizing opportunities to expand the space for capital accumulation. Keshavarzian writes: "The relative weakness of the royal family in terms of revenue is particularly important given that its grip on state power was rendered tenuous (even symbolic) by Dubai's status as a 'protected state' of Britain until 1971. The weakness vis-à-vis local and international forces during the state-building era encouraged the royal family to adopt a pro-market outlook and policies in the second half of the twentieth century."[35]

The establishment of the Land Law of 1960 by Sheikh Rashid was the milestone for the establishment of a land market under state control in Dubai. With the help of British consultants and urban planners, the law was modeled after the Sudanese land law. At that time Sudan was under British rule, so Sudanese consultants were hired to draft the law. The law allowed Dubai nationals to claim ownership of land after proving that they had lived on the property for a set period of time. All other unclaimed land belonged to the ruler, including reclaimed land.[36] The law had a fundamental effect on the ruler's consolidation of power. Ramos explains: "The law was also an essential step to define land capitalization for wealth accumulation and should be understood as directly linked to the first master plan as part of the larger strategy to both invest in Dubai as a territory through large infrastructure projects and take advantage of the resulting land value increase from these projects. The law also helped to guarantee the loans needed for these projects by capitalizing land for wealth accumulation."[37]

As a result of the ruler owning the vast majority of land in the emirate, the pace of land development accelerated and drove the demand for infrastructure. The wealth generated from the increase in land values went directly to the ruler, allowing him more political autonomy. Another milestone was the discovery of oil in 1966 and its export beginning in 1969. Despite its small amount, it supplied Dubai's ruler with revenue to finance investments in the large infrastructure projects necessary for driving economic growth. This financial autonomy further entrenched the ruler's political autonomy vis-à-vis the local population, on the one hand, and the ruling families of the other emirates, on the other.

After the establishment of the federal UAE in 1971, and knowing that their emirate could not rival the massive oil wealth of Abu Dhabi, the rulers in Dubai continued their strategy of diversifying the economy away from oil. With foreign policy and security taken care of at the federal level, Dubai had ample space to pursue an outward-oriented economic strategy. This strategy gave Dubai an economic trajectory different from that of Abu Dhabi. While Abu Dhabi resembled the classic model of an oil-rich rentier economy, Dubai gained the reputation of a diversified economy pegged to the global market.

> Dubai's position as a regional port began to grow when Port Rashid opened in 1972 near the city's center. That same year, Sheikh Rashid bin Said al-Maktoum decided that it should be followed by a second larger and deeper port; Jebel Ali Port, which opened in 1979 was one of the largest ports in the world. Much like Singapore, Dubai set itself on a path of *"build it and they will come"* by investing in large infrastructure projects and counting on attracting future demand. This has been a major characteristic of decision-making in Dubai up until today. In the case of the ports, it proved to be a wise decision by the leadership despite discouragement by advisors back then.[38]

This is similar to what happened in Singapore, as described in chapter 4, where the leader, Lee Kuan Yew, decided to go against "outside advisers" and build the new international airport at Changi air base, miles away from the city center.

Initially, Jebel Ali was intended to serve as a docking port for U.S. and NATO aircraft carriers, but this role was delayed, and eventually Jebel Ali outstripped Port Rashid to become the busiest port in the Middle East and the largest port for container traffic in the Gulf.[39] In 1999 Dubai Ports International (DPI) was founded, and in 2005 it merged with the Dubai Ports Authority to form Dubai Ports World (DP World), one of the largest cargo logistics companies in the world.

Dubai's success has been emulated by other cities in the UAE. Abu Dhabi's port of Khalifa and Sharjah's port also developed into major containership ports. Even so, other regional competitors are on the rise, namely, the ports of Jeddah and Dammam in Saudi Arabia and of Salalah in Oman. In the 1970s Dubai's share of UAE shipping stood at 95 percent. Today it's at 75 percent, but with a significant increase in volume. Dubai's foreign trade ratio to GDP compares to that of Singapore and Hong Kong (figure 2.1).[40]

In summary, and contrary to the prevalent perception that it is a newcomer to the network of globalized and cosmopolitan regions, the Gulf has had a long history of being a medium of trade flows connecting Asia, Europe, and Africa. The history of the rise of Dubai as a major regional port is a testament to the fact that Dubai was already integrated into global capitalism before the discovery of oil in the emirates. This fact deviates from the commonly held view that the

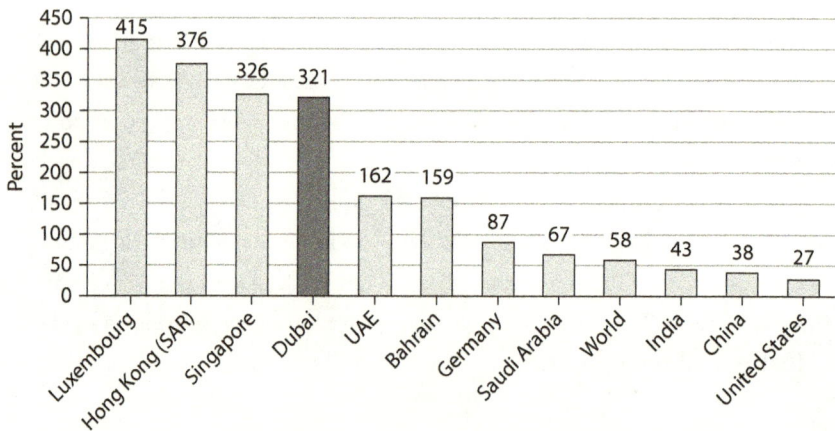

2.1 Dubai's foreign trade ratio to GDP, 2017–2018.

Source: Dubai Economic Report 2019

discovery of oil was the turning point that intertwined its economy with the global economy.[41] In the words of Keshavarzian: "The Gulf has been a vehicle, and not a barrier, for socioeconomic intercourse and imperial expansion. Since World War II and the creation of the Middle East nation-state system, economic activities have not lost their social dimensions, but have been augmented by a whole host of new technologies, economic institutions, and markets, most prominently the petroleum economy. Thus, the Persian Gulf region has a long history of what may be construed as 'globalization' and 'cosmopolitanism.'"[42]

THE POPULATION OF DUBAI

Historically, movements of people, especially merchants, between Gulf towns were very common. Tribal migration from inlands of the Arabian Peninsula to coastal cities like Dubai dates back to the 1700s and was prompted by the promise of a better life due to trade.[43] The beginnings of Dubai as an autonomously ruled entity dates to 1833, when 800 members of the al-Bu Falasah section of the Bani Yas ruling family in Abu Dhabi left to settle in Dubai.[44] The al-Maktoums were the most prominent of the al-Bu Falasah family.

Dubai's merchant community in its prestate years had always been cosmopolitan, characterized by fluidity and freedom of movement and trade.[45] Keshavarzian describes Gulf merchants as follows: "Although these merchants invested in land and property, their capital and social acumen were highly mobile and responsive to shifts in duties and customs regimes. Therefore, these ports competed to attract long-distance trade, with customs offices enticing this mercantile capital by reducing their rates or even establishing 'free ports.' In turn, merchants who already had region-wide footholds moved, or threatened to do so, in response to changing customs duties and rivalries."[46]

Direct British rule in India (the British Raj) in 1858 opened the door for Indian merchants to settle in Dubai after 1865. These merchants, referred to as *Banians*, took on banking services, textile and retail trades, and shopkeeping activities. With time they became the second-largest economic class after tribal Arab merchants who focused on pearling, fishing, and trading.[47] A second wave of Indian migrants came in the 1930s. These were the *Baluchis*, who worked as porters.[48]

The decision in 1904 to eliminate taxes in Dubai's port, discussed earlier, brought about the first wave of migrant merchants from the ports in Persia, especially from Bandar Lingeh. In the beginning, these merchants established a base for their trading businesses in Dubai on a temporary basis, but as the tax system in Persia became permanent, they accepted the offer made by Dubai's ruler and brought their families to settle there. They settled the area known as Bastakiyya, named after the Bastak district in Persia.[49] The Persians constituted the third group of Dubai's merchants.

Persian migrants were the second group, after the Indians, to shape Dubai's social and economic structure after the 1833 arrival of the al-Bu Falasah. The effect of the immigration of Iranian merchants on Dubai's economic activity was evident in the significant increase in the frequency of cargo ships and passenger vessels: from five visits per year to two per month.[50] Apart from a few hostile incidents, Persian merchants were assimilated into Dubai's society and were welcomed by the rulers. Davidson estimates that about one-half of Dubai's "indigenous" population today is of Persian origin.[51] In addition to migrants from Persia and South Asia, other migrant groups from Bahrain and Iraq settled in the city. These merchant communities developed a vibrant trade economy in Dubai before the discovery and extraction of oil.

IMMIGRATION FROM ABU DHABI AND SHARJAH

Dubai did not only attract migrants from other countries, but was also perceived by merchants from other Trucial States as a city more favorable for doing business and more welcoming of strangers. By the 1920s, a merchant community had flourished in Abu Dhabi as a result of the pearl trade. However, these merchants could not realize their business ambitions because the rulers of Abu Dhabi at the time were not open to strategies for economic development. Eventually, these merchants made their way to Dubai and settled there. Abu Dhabi's aversion to investment and economic development worsened under the leadership of Shakhbut bin Sultan al-Nahyan to the extent that it lagged far behind Dubai and Sharjah in terms of services such as education, health, and banking. Sheikh Shakhbut was eventually deposed in 1966 and replaced by his brother Zayed, who had been ruler of the nearby city of Al-Ayn.[52]

Similarly, mounting economic problems in Sharjah as a result of a series of bad decisions drove away the town's merchants toward the neighbor to the south. The first wave settled in Dubai in the mid-1930s. Subsequent groups of merchants followed suit, as they sought more opportunities to expand their businesses. This trend continued well into the 1950s and 1960s as more merchants gravitated toward the more economically progressive lands ruled by the al-Maktoums.[53]

Up until the 1930s and the fall of the pearling industry, Dubai's merchant class enjoyed political power because the ruling family was economically dependent on it. Their power was evident in October 1938 when 400 merchants from various families, including the ruler's, tried to impose political and economic reforms on Sheikh Said. This attempt was not successful, and Sheikh Said was able to retain absolute power with the help of the British and some Bedouin tribes.[54] As mentioned earlier, Britain's air landing fees and oil concessions ensured that the rulers were economically and politically more powerful than the merchants. The discovery of oil in 1966 further cemented this reality.

According to rentier theory, rent flows directly into the hands of the state or, in this case, the rulers, which gives them great autonomy to steer the economy in the direction they want.[55] As a result, rulers become the ultimate decision-makers. They can reorganize society by co-opting existing classes, creating new classes, and dismantling others. This was very much the case in Dubai.

A TRANSIENT POPULATION

The development of a society hugely dependent on migrant labor is not unique to Dubai. This is a feature seen in all six Gulf countries as a result of the oil boom and the subsequent increase in demand for professional expertise as well as for semiskilled labor. At present, the size of the migrant workforce in the UAE, and in Dubai specifically, is extraordinarily high, around 90 percent of the population today.

To facilitate the influx of the labor force necessary for the economy, the UAE made it easy for workers to come and reside for work purposes for as long as needed, but without becoming citizens. This was a conscious decision that ensured certain rights and generous welfare benefits only to citizens while, at the same time, allowing workers to enter and restricting their full social integration in line with economic and political needs. The discovery of oil, and later the export of oil, were turning points in terms of the pace and scale of migration. The early "expat" waves came to work in the oil industry.[56] It would seem natural that the vast majority of this labor would come from non-Gulf Arab countries, given similarities in culture, religion, and language. However, this was true only for Saudi Arabia and Kuwait, which were not under Britain's control.[57] In contrast, British control in Dubai and the other Trucial States discouraged the importation of labor from other Arab countries because the British feared the proliferation of nationalist movements and hostility toward Britain. As a result, most skilled labor came from the United Kingdom, and most semiskilled labor from British colonies in the Indian subcontinent. Unskilled workers were locals who had lost their livelihoods after the end of the pearl trade.[58]

The subsequent oil booms of 1973 and 1979 saw a surge in labor migration to the UAE and other Gulf states. By then, all of these states were independent, and oil wealth led to rapid construction and infrastructure development in various sectors. Consequently, the country opened its doors to large numbers of migrant workers as well as professionals. Migrants from South and Southeast Asia became attractive because they were less expensive, were willing to come without their families, and did not carry the potential risk of Arab migrants, who often came with ideas of pan-Arabism, communism, and socialism. Additionally, being non-Arabs meant that they would not want to assimilate, which ensured that they would remain foreign.[59] As the economy grew, so did Dubai's population, from 183,187 in 1975, to 370,788 in 1985, 690,420 in 1995, 1,321,453 in 2005, 2,446,675 in 2015, and 3,411,200 in 2020 (figure 2.2). Today, foreigners constitute around 92 percent of the population of Dubai. The huge demand for construction workers meant that the vast majority of migrants were single male

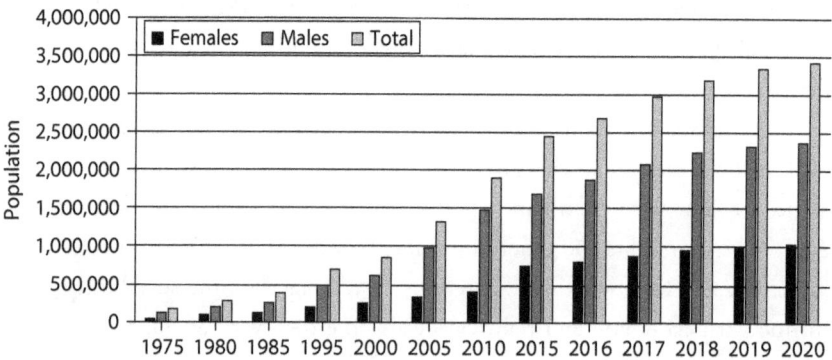

2.2 Dubai's population by gender, 1975–2020.

Source: Dubai Statistics Center

workers. This is why Dubai's population pyramid is hugely skewed toward males, especially those twenty-five to forty-four years old.

Another important reason that Dubai was able to easily recruit its workforce from Asia and later from Africa from the 1980s onward was that stringent regulations for visas and work permits in Europe led people to look for alternative markets.[60] Dubai was a welcoming destination because of its relatively easy tourist and business visa process, usually taken care of through airlines or travel agencies.

Because migrants remain foreigners and cannot become citizens, the labor market is divided between citizens or locals and migrants. This division extends to wages, benefits, and sectors of employment. Government jobs go mainly to citizens, who also favor them, while the private sector in Dubai is dominated by foreigners, who constitute 98 percent of the total. The migrant community is also divided by nationality and level of skill.

Migrants are classified as permanently transient, regardless of the time spent living and working in the UAE. Gulf cities have benefited from the brain drain from other Arab countries due to wars, unrest, and economic hardship. Oil wealth and political stability have managed to lure thousands of professionals from other Arab countries. Very few cities compete with Dubai when it comes to cosmopolitanism, as around 90 percent of the city's population are foreigners who come from about 200 countries. In 2018, citizens accounted for 7.9 percent of Dubai's population of 3.19 million.[61] The rest were foreigners, with South Asia representing the lion's share. The very high percentage of foreign labor has both advantages and disadvantages. The advantages are mainly due to the extreme flexibility of this labor force.

Unemployment rates are always low in a place like Dubai. Redundant labor simply leaves the city when it is no longer needed. While reliance on imported labor leads to a highly transient labor force, the government benefits because it can recruit skills from around the world in a short time, as opposed to spending years growing these skills locally. As economic needs change, the workforce can change accordingly. In times of economic downturn, excess labor is sent back home. When demand rises again, foreign workers are brought in. The long process of educating and reeducating the labor force, faced by other countries, is bypassed in the case of Dubai, which means that changes in vision regarding the economy can be implemented relatively quickly.[62] At the same time, the government does not have to bear the consequences of rising unemployment during economic downturns. However, while this flexibility is an advantage at the level of the state, especially in the service sector, it is not an advantage for entrepreneurs and companies in the innovation business. The high cost of hiring and terminating employees is a huge burden on companies. In addition, considering Dubai's stated goal of fostering a knowledge-based economy, a temporary workforce with a high rate of turnover becomes a disadvantage.

DUBAI AS A REGIONAL CENTER OF GRAVITY

On the regional front, Dubai has been the recipient of skilled labor and professionals from other Arab countries. As in the other emerging global cities, incoming migrants are both low- and semiskilled, but the attraction of high-skilled workers continues to increase to fuel the city's service sectors, including fintech industries. The lack of job opportunities and stability in these workers' home countries is the main driver of this brain drain. The regional rise of Gulf cities was accelerated by the fall of traditional regional powers and cities in the Arab world. As a result, the patterns and geographies of accumulation shifted within the region, causing the focal points to shift as well. More importantly, investor-friendly policies and a reliable legal infrastructure for business enabled Dubai to become the go-to city for the regional headquarter offices of multinationals. This could not have happened without a legal and regulatory infrastructure that attracted businesses and foreign investors. With time, Dubai became the model to be emulated, as its impact on the more traditional Arab cities could be felt and seen. Dubai's influence on these cities was driven by local governments and foreign investments, especially from the Gulf.[63]

The central role that Gulf cities play today in the Arab region is manifested at many levels: economic, political, and cultural. A combination of push factors at home and pull factors in a city like Dubai leads many professionals and young families to seek employment opportunities there. According to the annual ASDA'A BCW Arab Youth Survey, the UAE ranked top for eight consecutive years, ahead of Canada and the United States, as the country where Arab youths would like to live. In 2019, 44 percent of Arab youths chose the UAE, up from 20 percent in 2015 and 35 percent in 2018.[64] With high unemployment rates among Arab youth, especially in the Levant and North Africa, the main attractions to the UAE are the job opportunities and the attractive salaries, in addition to safety and security.

In *Money, Markets, and Monarchies*, Hanieh puts forth a compelling argument that highlights the often-missing regional dimension of Gulf capital. His analysis links global, regional, and Gulf factors through a detailed examination of the powerful reach of Gulf finance in the Arab region. Dubai became a hub for the movement of people, goods, and capital in a region dominated by political volatility and turmoil. Along with other Gulf cities, it was able to fill the regional gap left by the political and economic deterioration of traditional leaders like Cairo, Baghdad, Beirut, and Damascus. The 1978 signing of the Camp David peace treaty with Israel isolated Egypt, the heavyweight of the Arab world. Lebanon's civil war played a profound role in the demise of Beirut, the cosmopolitan Arab city and a regional cultural center. The series of devastating wars in Iraq since the 1980s and the ongoing war in Syria have left these countries in unstable conditions for years to come. The resulting vacuum was quickly filled by Dubai and other Gulf cities as they gradually became the leading political, urban, and economic centers in the Arab region.[65]

The regional reach of Dubai has expanded beyond the economic realm and more recently into the art and culture scene. The growth of this soft power further entrenches the prominence of Dubai in the minds of many Arabs experiencing the various manifestations of a failed state at home. Numerous initiatives ranging from literary prizes, cultural festivals, and art exhibitions have mushroomed in the last decade and a half. The International Prize of Arab Fiction, associated with the Booker Prize Foundation in London, was founded in Dubai in 2008. Today, it is one of the most prominent literary prizes in the Arab world. Like almost everything else done in Dubai and the UAE in general, it is a form of branding, an offshoot of a mother institution usually based in Europe.

Similarly, the Dubai International Film Festival (DIFF), founded in 2004, is considered the leading film festival in the region. Dubai also hosts jazz festivals, marathons, tennis championships, golf tournaments, food festivals, Dubai's design week, the Dubai World Cup horse-racing event founded in 1996, and the Arab Hope Maker prize for philanthropy initiated in 2017. In addition to residents, these events draw participants and audiences from all over the world.

Since the beginning of this century, Dubai has ushered in the era of commercial arts and culture in the UAE. Like the São Paulo Art Biennial, Miami's Art Basel, and New Orleans's Jazz and Heritage Festival, Dubai's art and cultural events are illustrative of efforts by aspiring and emerging global cities to use art and culture to promote their global brand. The international expatriate population played an important role in driving this development. In 2006, Christie's opened in Dubai and hosted its first auction in the Middle East. In 2009, the UAE became the first Gulf country to have a permanent pavilion at the Venice Biennale.[66] The Alserkal Avenue attests to the rise of the art scene in Dubai. This is a 50,000-square-foot area of galleries, restaurants, a theater, and an outdoor cinema that continuously host concerts and art exhibits. Additionally, investments in large-scale art venues in Abu Dhabi and in the local art in Sharjah have boosted the UAE's reputation globally as a center for art showcasing and a market for art products. At a time when countries in the region face deteriorating economic conditions, a city like Dubai becomes a land of opportunity for many artists and professionals.

GROWTH OF DUBAI'S ECONOMY

The strategy that pushed Dubai's economy forward was partly due to the understanding by Dubai's rulers, specifically Rashid and later his son Mohammed, that they needed to stay ahead of their wealthier neighbors: Saudi Arabia, Kuwait, and especially Abu Dhabi. This meant that Dubai would have to act quickly to seize economic opportunities.[67] It would have to build projects ahead of demand. This "build it and they will come" strategy still holds true today.

Keshavarzian explains that after the oil boom of the 1970s, international capital saw in the Gulf region, especially in Dubai's ports and free-trade zones, an opportunity for economic expansion at a time when Western economies were collapsing.[68] The free-trade zones were ideal sites for foreign investment because they allowed complete repatriation of profits. While Abu Dhabi established its position as the sheikhdom with the strongest military and political power, Dubai secured its position as the main commercial hub. This early division of responsibility freed Dubai from the burden of foreign policy and allowed its leaders to focus on the development of the emirate as a regional trading center.

With oil production peaking in Dubai in 1991 and then falling afterwards, the rulers set out to diversify its economy away from oil. As a result, the city is often hailed as an example of an economy that managed to diversify away from the hydrocarbon rentier model prevalent among its neighbors. The current ruler of Dubai, Sheikh Mohammed bin Rashid al-Maktoum, has been a central force, even before assuming power in 2006, in putting the city on an accelerated path to becoming a global center for finance, tourism, and investment.[69] This business model took off in the mid-1990s and was a necessary step in safeguarding the emirate's autonomy within the UAE federal system, especially in relation to Abu Dhabi.[70] This period of economic growth coincided with accelerated globalization worldwide. The timing allowed Dubai to leapfrog into becoming a global service center without having to go through an industrial phase, as was the case in other parts of the world, including Singapore. As a result, the sectors that saw the fastest growth were those most connected to and dependent on the global economy, namely, ports and free-trade zones, shipping and reexport, aviation, tourism, real estate, and global finance. The connection between real estate and financial markets is a crucial aspect of economic diversification in Dubai. Buckley and Hanieh refer to this phenomenon as "diversification by urbanization," which constitutes a significant portion of wealth generation in the emirate.[71] The process of rapid urbanization and the proliferation of megaprojects has had a direct impact on the development of financial markets and ultimately on capitalist class formation.

However, from the onset, the growth of Dubai as a port city was concerned with distribution, not production.[72] When Gulf Cooperation Council (GCC) countries decided to abolish double taxation of reexported goods, Dubai flourished as a regional hub for reexports.[73] In the last decade, reexporting constituted the largest share of export activity (figure 2.3). Most reexports go to the GCC countries, other Arab countries, and Asian countries.

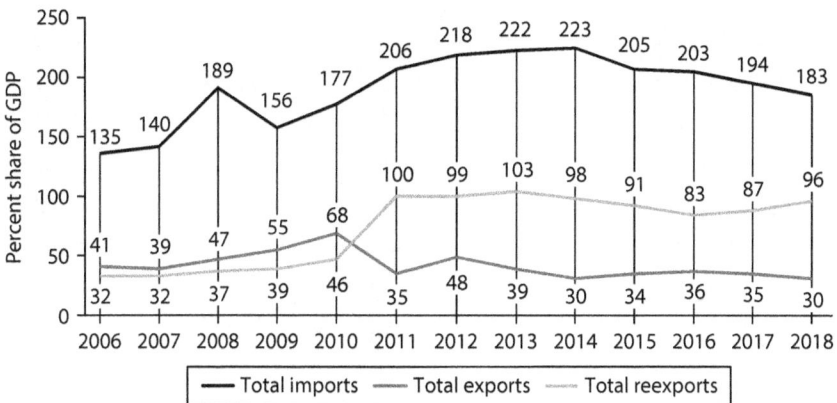

2.3 Dubai's merchandise exports, imports, and re-exports as percentage share of GDP, 2006–2018.

Source: Dubai Economic Report 2019

Dubai's economy is often associated with neoliberal ideas and the free market. Mobility has a lot to do with this perception. The large volumes of capital, people, and goods in the small emirate feed the idea that it is a haven for the free market. Moreover, Dubai's successful economic rise is frequently invoked to highlight the failure of statist policies and rentier economies elsewhere in the region. Missing from this picture of a neoliberal haven is Dubai's heavily centralized planning and decision-making structure, which is the main driver of the economy. A closer look at Dubai's economy reveals that common classifications and frames of analysis cannot be applied here. With 85 to 90 percent of the population being foreign, movement of people and labor is highly regulated and controlled by the state, with increasing intervention as one goes down the labor chain.

The government structure comprises for-profit state-owned corporations referred to as GREs. These companies are pillars of Dubai's economic model. They lead the way for investment into new sectors, and because of their governmental status, they quickly create an environment of trust and security that encourages private companies to join in. Krane writes:

> Dubai's portfolio of businesses is huge. Dubai World is one such group, with its profitable port operator DP World and glamor developer Nakheel, responsible for the Palm islands. Emirates airline and Dubai Aluminum are 100 percent state-owned, as are investment funds Istithmar and Dubai International Capital, a slew of property developers, banks, and several others. Each is run along conventional corporate lines, financing investments with debt or earnings. . . . The companies aren't subject to civil service hiring rules. They get special access to the ruler and bypass the bureaucracy. Sheikh Mohammed asked them all to develop internationally, and several are dominated by foreign investments, especially DP World, property developer Sama Dubai, and increasingly Emaar, partly state-owned and building neighborhoods in more than a dozen countries. Sheikh Mohammed's own Dubai Holding Group, with its Jumeirah hotel brand, operates the same way.[74]

Krane argues that these state-owned corporations challenge conventional wisdom on the direct involvement of the state in the economy.[75] Apart from developmental states like Japan and the Asian Tigers, the state-owned enterprise model has largely been associated with public-sector failure and incompetence in most countries. The case of Dubai dispels the common wisdom that a state's direct role in the economy is bound to fail. More important is the fact that these state-owned enterprises are expected to generate revenue. They behave as independent companies, each with its own profit-and-loss account. They form an essential base for generating revenue for the state. "State-owned enterprises, however, are believed to generate 'hefty earnings,' with sources estimating income at 8 to 12 percent of the GDP. These entities encompass such firms as Emirates Airlines, Dubai Airport, Dubai Aluminum Company, Etisalat (the national phone company), Dubai Dry Dock, and the multitude of entities included in Dubai World and Dubai Holding. Their exact contribution to the economy is not known outside the innermost circles."[76]

The central role of the state in Dubai's economy does not necessarily mean that the economy is completely formal, nor does it mean that the state is insulated from the larger sociopolitical context. Being a major hub for the movement of capital, goods, and people highlights two things. First, the informal economy—including money laundering—is an integral part of Dubai's economy. Second, the city's economy actually depends on the political instability in surrounding countries.[77] As described in chapter 3, this pattern is similar to what happened in Miami, which became a destination for middle and upper classes in Latin America and the Caribbean seeking to protect their assets from political instability in their own countries.

FREE-TRADE ZONES AND THE ESTABLISHMENT OF A LAND MARKET

The foundations for free-trade zones were established by the emirate in the 1970s as a mechanism to assert sovereignty and ensure a flow of rent to the elites.[78] In fact, the establishment of Jebel Ali, the first free-trade zone in Dubai, and the proliferation of this model later on were at the heart of nation building; as Keshavarzian writes, "the Gulf's free trade zones intersect with new patterns of state sovereignty, regional security, and capital accumulation."[79]

Moreover, the timing of the process of state building was important for the economic and political trajectory of the state. Keshavarzian explains that "state-building, defined as developing a final and absolute political authority over a territory and population, was taking place at the same moment as the rise of modern global capitalism."[80] Hanieh affirms this statement and goes on to say that global capitalism since World War II should not be viewed as an external effect on Gulf economies. To the contrary, to repeat a quote given earlier in this chapter, "the global economy is part of the actual essence of the Gulf itself—the development of the global 'appears' through the development of the Gulf."[81]

Land ownership is at the center of how the rulers of Dubai managed to increase their power vis-à-vis the merchants. As mentioned earlier, a master plan prepared by British consultants in 1960 laid down the process by which the ruler could privately own land that is not used in order to put it to better use. Today, the state owns the overwhelming majority of land in Dubai. Privately owned land is distributed between four families, with Al Futtaim owning 62 percent and private development constituting only 1 percent of the urban area.[82]

Based on this reality, the rulers of Dubai used land and land development to accumulate capital. Building large infrastructure projects increased the land value and became a major source of income for the state. This also applied to reclaimed land around Dubai Creek. The high cost of dredging and reclaiming land incurred by the ruler would be offset by the sale or lease of the land later on. Additionally, the law allowed rulers to use the land as a guarantee to obtain the bank loans needed for various infrastructure projects.[83]

The strategy was outward oriented: to attract investors from abroad to establish businesses in Dubai. However, a major deterrent for potential investors was the 1984 Commercial Companies Law issued by the federal government in Abu Dhabi and made applicable to all seven emirates. The law required that a local sponsor or *kafeel* had to own at least 51 percent of any registered company in the UAE. This put a severe constraint on foreign investors. The ruler of Dubai, Sheikh Rashid bin Sa'id al-Maktoum, wanted to avoid confrontation with Abu Dhabi and therefore resorted to the free-zones strategy. The free-trade zones are geographically designated areas where certain economic, financial, and legal regulations do not apply. Most importantly, these zones allow 100 percent foreign ownership. The free zones were the means by which Dubai was able to bypass the ownership regulations dictated by the federal law.[84]

Established in 1985, Jebel Ali was the pioneer free-trade project located next to the Jebel Ali port. Keshavarzian explains that choosing to locate Jebel Ali far from Dubai's city center and close to the border with Abu Dhabi was a political move to strengthen the power of al-Maktoum vis-à-vis the al-Nahyans, the rulers of Abu Dhabi. The Jebel Ali port was one of the bargaining tools; it ensured

Dubai's commitment to the union in return for Abu Dhabi allowing Dubai to build the port.[85]

The timing of the establishment of the Jebel Ali free-trade zone could not have been better because both the Iran-Iraq War and the Lebanese civil war were raging. Merchants found it attractive to locate their businesses in the new free zone, which saw rapid growth in the number and variety of companies registered.[86] Although Jebel Ali was not the first global free-trade zone, its huge success takes credit for spreading the concept around the world. When it was first inaugurated in 1985, the first in the region, it included 19 companies. By the end of the 1990s, the number of companies was over 2,000. Today it has more than 7,000 companies with 135,000 workers.[87] At present, Dubai has more than twenty free zones, not all of which are geographically confined and involve trade in physical products.

The aim behind the proliferation of nonindustrial free-trade zones was to continue to circumvent the federal law, which does not allow more than 49 percent foreign ownership of a business. Free zones like Media City and Internet City and others allow 100 percent foreign ownership in certain industries. They are especially attractive to the services and technology industries. Their establishment led to a significant rise in the number of technological start-ups in Dubai.

FUTURE OPPORTUNITIES AND CHALLENGES

Generally speaking, diversifying an economy away from oil is a good strategy. However, according to Davidson, the downside of Dubai's diversified economy is that it has made Dubai more dependent on foreign economies.[88] In other words, the more connected the city is to the global economy, the weaker it is in the face of a global economic crisis. However, what actually matters is what kinds of sectors a global city relies on. In Dubai's case, these are mostly service sectors that depend on sustained outside demand. Tourism, free zones, air travel, real estate, and many services related to these sectors are highly dependent on external factors and are therefore more exposed to economic shocks.[89] This dependency explains why Dubai was the hardest hit in the 2008–2009 economic crisis when compared to other cities in the region.

In 2016, Dubai's ruler, Sheikh Mohammed, launched Dubai Industrial Strategy 2030. The vision aims, among other goals, to "increase the total output and value-addition of the manufacturing sector," "enhance the depth of knowledge and innovation," and "promote environmentally friendly and energy-efficient manufacturing."[90] It is clear from this strategy that Dubai is trying to do what it always has done: stay ahead of potential competitors by tapping into new market niches for wealth generation. With other Gulf countries trying to compete with Dubai, especially Saudi Arabia, and with the high cost of living in Dubai compared to other cities in the region, Dubai needs to reinvent its economic base. Being the incumbent global city in the region, it has, to its advantage, the infrastructure and the ability to make some decisions easily because it has been there first as a major commercial and financial center, driven by a forward-looking and outward-oriented leadership in terms of business and investment.

However, to succeed as an economy based on knowledge, innovation, and manufacturing requires significant changes in institutional infrastructure and policies. While this is not the focus of this chapter, it is important to note that the ability to attract and retain talent and innovation is crucial for global cities seeking to be at the forefront of the production of knowledge and innovation. According to Hvidt, "The higher the number of expat knowledge workers relative to national knowledge workers, the higher the risk to the national economies if all or a portion of the workers for some reason were inclined to leave the country."[91] This concern, as well as the harsh negative effects of the Covid-19 pandemic on the economy, has prompted Dubai to recently roll out new laws aimed at mitigating the high risk of a predominantly transient workforce. Some of these new laws are at the federal level.

These new laws can be summarized as follows. In October 2020 Dubai initiated a scheme to attract professional expatriates to settle in Dubai while working remotely anywhere in the world. The city would offer these expatriates the necessary infrastructure to bring their families and make Dubai their home for as long as needed.[92] A month earlier, Dubai announced a visa program that would allow people above fifty-five years of age to retire in the city. It used to be that an expatriate who retired had to leave Dubai and could not have his or her visa extended. More important is the UAE federal law announced in November 2020 that aims to retain highly educated and qualified foreign workers by extending a ten-year visa (as opposed to the current annual or two-year visa) to all doctors, PhD holders, and highly skilled workers in specific engineering and technology fields.[93]

It is too early to say if Dubai will be able to embark on a major diversification from its existing economic base. Dubai never fully recovered from the 2008–2009 economic crisis. Back then it was saved from defaulting by Abu Dhabi through loans and bonds, which Dubai issued to the central bank of the UAE. The coronavirus crisis and the lockdown measures have made the situation much worse. The city's economy has been hard hit, especially in tourism and aviation. It is unclear if a new bailout from Abu Dhabi is under way. If it is, this could alter the relationship between the two emirates, possibly reducing the space for economic autonomy that Dubai has so far enjoyed.

The 2008 financial crisis and the Covid-19 pandemic have shown that an emerging global city like Dubai is especially vulnerable to external shocks because it depends on global flows of people, capital, and goods. An economic base that is outward oriented and intertwined with the global economy is a double-edged sword. In good times, it attracts consumers and investors from around the world. In bad times, it suffers from people and capital flight. Additionally, while Dubai has benefited from its political stability in a volatile region, this advantage could change given the unpredictability of geopolitical dynamics in that region. Furthermore, competition from other Gulf states, namely, Saudi Arabia, has gained momentum in recent years. No longer will many companies and expatriates put up with the high cost of living and doing business in Dubai because of the lack of alternatives. The rapid and sweeping policy changes in the largest economy and most populated Gulf country pose major challenges to the economic edge that Dubai has enjoyed for the past three decades. Beginning in 2021, Saudi Arabia took several steps that could be seen as a direct challenge to Dubai. In an attempt to lure corporate offices away from Dubai, the Saudi government began offering incentives for companies to move their headquarters to Saudi Arabia.[94] In February, it announced that by 2024 it will stop doing business with companies whose headquarters are not located in Saudi Arabia.[95] Similarly, the kingdom is moving on the port front and is attracting foreign investment, especially from China, to expand its ports. Another dramatic move that targeted Dubai's status as a regional trade hub was to exclude goods produced in the UAE free zones from preferential tariffs.[96]

Historically, Dubai has dealt with challenges by leading the way into new market niches. However, as neighboring economies are competing with it in what it does best, Dubai needs to be more creative. Today, to stay ahead of the rest, it is implementing new policies that aim to expand its economic base and retain the expatriate population. As explained earlier in this chapter, Dubai's population composition makes it much more nimble in shifting economic priorities and implementing new policies compared to its competitors. In addition, regional economic dynamics may be able to accommodate growing competition so that it produces complementary competitive advantages instead of cannibalism. To put it more clearly, growing competition may push Dubai to new areas of economic advantage through a process of creative destruction instead of economic demise. For now, it is too soon to tell in which direction these changes will unfold.

The Dubai Metro, the world's longest fully automated metro network (75 kilometers), November 2012.
(Courtesy of A. Ross)

Boats on Dubai Creek in Deira, with an aerial view of old Dubai.
(Courtesy of A. Ross)

The Burj Al Arab Hotel.

(Courtesy of A. Ross)

Aerial view of the sunrise over Dubai's skyscrapers.
(Courtesy of A. Ross)

The Dubai Fountain Show at the Burj Khalifa.
(Courtesy of A. Ross)

The illuminated Jumeirah Lakes Towers Metro Station, with the Dubai Marina and Dubai Internet City skyline at night.
(Courtesy of A. Ross)

Dubai at night, seen from Deira.
(Courtesy of A. Ross)

The Burj Khalifa, the tallest building in the world.
(Courtesy of A. Ross)

CHAPTER 3

MIAMI

From Winter Resort to Hemispheric Capital

WITH THE COLLABORATION OF BRANDON P. MARTINEZ

The average condominium price in the One Thousand Museum tower in downtown Miami, affectionately dubbed "The Scorpion," was $6,940,000 in 2020 with a per-square-foot average of $1,288. Penthouse dwellings in the same building went for more than $20 million. The "Scorpion" is the first exoskeletal tower in the city, an innovation brought by its Iranian architect Zaha Hadid from similar buildings in Dubai. While cranes continue erecting new towers, the skyline of downtown Miami is fairly complete. It is also quite impressive. From the waters of Biscayne Bay, one gazes at an uninterrupted chain of skyscrapers, the third-tallest collection in the nation, housing financial and law firms, massive hotels, entertainment complexes, and thousands of individual residences in the sky. The total of such residences in 2018 was 44,372.[1]

From downtown looking out to sea in 2020, one would see one pleasure cruiser after another—the massive multistoried boats operated by Carnival, Royal Caribbean, and Norwegian lines out of the largest cruise port in the world. For a city that was given up for lost in the 1980s, some proclaiming it "paradise lost" and a Central American "banana republic," it has been quite a transformation. No one contemplating the Orange Bowl, occupied by thousands of destitute Cuban refugees arriving from the port of Mariel in 1980, or the large tracts of burned-out buildings after the latest Black riot in the same year, would have given much for the place. Housing in Miami in those days went for a pittance.[2]

The president of the University of Miami, Julio Frenk, likes to say that "geography is destiny" and that Miami's privileged geographical position prefigured its brilliant future. But that argument is limited. The city had the same geographical position for much of the last century without becoming much more than a winter resort for northern elites.[3] Miami shared with other cities, such as Havana, the capital of Cuba, and New Orleans, at the mouth of the Mississippi River and at the center of the Gulf of Mexico, an enviable position at the midpoint between the Americas, but that potential had to be somehow activated.[4]

To the extent that Miami has become an emerging global city, its evolution cannot be traced to the industrial era or to a preindustrial role as a market settlement because the place did not exist for most of the nineteenth century and never had an industrial past. It leapfrogged over those stages of urban history characteristic of established global cities such as New York and London. Instead, it was assigned a role as a recreational extension of established cities in the American Northeast and Midwest, a "billion-dollar sandbox," built as a part-year playground for the rich and powerful.[5] That destiny, shared with other winter resorts along the Florida coast, enabled the city to escape the ravages of the industrial era and to build from scratch. But, from the standpoint of its founders, it had one economic driver—the sun—and one function—fun and retirement for those who could afford it.[6]

True enough, from time to time, Spanish-speaking escapees from political troubles in their own lands arrived in South Florida, but they were regarded as little more than a nuisance. Those who triumphed politically returned home, and those who did not found employment in Miami's hotels and tourist attractions. Over time, a transplanted white elite emerged to rule over the built-up sandbox, and they did so with a typical southern-style certainty of white Anglo-Saxon superiority and the relegation of others—Blacks, Jews, and Spanish speakers—to subordinate positions in the social and economic hierarchies.[7]

This was the Miami that the initial waves of Cubans escaping the communist revolution in their island encountered. From their point of view, local city politics mattered little because their concern was to establish an alliance with the U.S. federal government to overthrow the Castro regime in Cuba. They were also initially regarded with compassion and even sympathy by local elites, who expected them to return home soon. It did not happen that way. The defeat of the exiles' invading force at the Bay of Pigs in 1961 also meant the sudden transformation of Cubans into a stable component of Miami's population. The confrontations that followed brought the city to the very edge of political and economic chaos.[8] No one at that time could have anticipated that, barely a quarter of a century later, Miami would boast the second-largest banking and financial services concentration in the East, only exceeded by New York.[9]

THE EARLY DAYS

The struggle between the old Anglo power structure of Miami—coalescing around the "Non-group"—and the rising Cuban business and political establishment developed gradually for two decades. The old leaders of the city regarded their task as preserving Miami as a pristine winter resort for use by people like themselves. Those coming from the Caribbean for political or economic reasons were seen as an intrusion or, at best, a new source of manual labor. For the Cuban exile population, the defeat of its brigade at the Bay of Pigs and the subsequent resolution of the missile crisis of 1962, in which the United States committed itself not to invade Cuba in exchange for removal of the Soviet missiles from the island, meant the end of all hope for return.[10]

Reluctantly at first, they turned their energies and know-how to rebuilding their lives in South Florida, but they suddenly discovered that their former allies in the struggle against communism had turned into rivals. For the Anglo establishment of Miami, the newly settled Cuban population was just another ethnic minority to be controlled and managed. As a Black leader of the time put it: "In those days, I said to Cubans in a speech that there was going to be a day when white folks are going to try to treat you like niggers. They're going to put you again in your place as they do with all minority groups. But unlike Black Americans, Cubans had no history of being kept in their place and, as a result, they responded differently. We Black folks were saying to white folks, 'Let us in.' Cubans were saying to white folks, 'Let us in so that we can take over.'"[11]

Having assessed the situation, Cuban leaders created the "Mesa Redonda" as an alternative decision center to the Anglo Non-group. Their efforts moved in two directions simultaneously: to naturalize and register to vote as soon as possible and to build up their firms. The confrontation between the two power blocs came to a head during the exodus of Mariel in 1980. Following the occupation of the Peruvian embassy by thousands of Cubans wishing to leave their country, the Castro government opened the port of Mariel and invited all Cuban refugees with relatives in the island to come and retrieve them. A massive flotilla organized itself in South Florida to do precisely that.[12]

Then, in another brilliant political maneuver, Fidel Castro decided to get rid of common criminals and other "undesirables" in Cuba by forcing them into the exiles' boats along with their relatives. The following chaotic exodus hit Miami like a bomb. Feeling cornered, the Anglo establishment mounted a campaign through its mouthpiece, the *Miami Herald*, asking the federal government to stop the exodus and resettle the new arrivals away from South Florida. Most of the hostility in the *Herald*'s articles was directed not at the Castro regime, but at the "strident exile community" that was sponsoring the flotilla. On June 26, 1980, a *Herald* editorial strongly criticized President Jimmy Carter for failing to end the exodus: "The President consciously let the threat of mob reaction intimidate him into ignoring the law and allowing his own policies to be trampled."[13]

On July 24 and 25, 1980, a series of *Herald* articles focused on the crime wave attributed to Mariel refugees. Miami Beach reported a crime increase of 34 percent since the refugees' arrival. On September 18, a front-page article denounced a crime wave in Little Havana, the perpetrators being Mariel refugees: 775 more robberies than in 1979; 284 percent more auto thefts; 110 percent more assaults.[14]

In seeking to advance its policy goals, the *Miami Herald* identified the Cuban exile community as its major opponent and acted aggressively against it. In the course of articulating its goals, the newspaper displayed both great energy and notable ineffectiveness. Predictably, the end result of this offensive was to produce a powerful reaction in the Cuban exile community. Previously concerned with getting rid of the Castro regime in the island or getting their relatives out of it, exile leaders reacted to the unexpected attack from their supposed allies in the struggle against communism by organizing themselves for domestic politics. As a Cuban-American Dade County official of the time put it: "The Anglo power structure is scared to death about the Cuban rise in this community. It has tried cooptation through an 'Interethnic Relations Committee' of the Miami Chamber of Commerce which was really a sham . . . there was then the antibilingual referendum which was a slap in our face. People began to feel 'more Cuban than anyone.' The plan today is to try to elect a Cuban mayor of the city and perhaps one or two state legislators."[15]

In the end, the contest between the two power elites did not end in compromise but in the complete rout of the older leadership. Monolingual Anglos left Miami in droves while their institutions fell, one after another, in the former exiles' hand. Knight-Ridder, the parent company of the *Miami Herald*, also left Miami; its former editor, David Lawrence, resigned and was replaced by a new leader of Cuban origin, Alberto Ibargüen.[16] By the mid-1990s, the mayoralties of Miami-Dade County, the city of Miami, Coral Gables, and other major municipalities in the area were in the hands of Cubans or Cuban Americans. There were three elected Cuban-American congressmen, and most state legislators from Dade County were also of Cuban origin.[17]

This was the outcome that many native Anglos had feared, as they anticipated that the area would become a "banana republic," similar to failed states in the Caribbean and Central America.[18] It did not happen that way because of a unique combination of factors. First, the U.S. federal government kept a close watch on the area, removing from office and arresting corrupt officials. Second, the exiled business class quickly saw that the geographical location of Miami created unique opportunities. Rather than looking north, they looked south, repeatedly visiting the capitals of Caribbean and South American countries. Once there, they proceeded to inform wealthy investors and bankers of the advantages of doing business in Miami rather than in distant New York. Investors in Miami received the same protections afforded by American property laws, and they could also conduct business in an attractive climate and in their own language.[19]

Cuban American bankers established "correspondent" relations with a number of Central and South American banks while lobbying the Florida State legislature for a law allowing foreign banks to establish branches or regional offices in the state. They were also instrumental in creating the Florida International Bankers Association (FIBA). FIBA and most of its affiliates settled in Miami, creating a large banking and financial services concentration in the Brickell district of the city.[20]

The vision that informed these bankers' activities and that eventually permeated the entire local business community was one of Miami as a center of global finance and trade—the economic capital of the Americas. That vision, replacing that of a provincial tourist resort, eventually gained traction from the activities not only of Miami-based entrepreneurs and bankers but also of economic actors in other countries. First, western European and Middle Eastern banks and businesses came to see Miami as the "natural" place to base their Latin American operations, further adding to the cosmopolitan character of the place. Second, middle and upper classes in Latin America and the Caribbean came to regard Miami as the logical place to protect their assets from unstable political conditions in their own countries. Owning property in Miami became de rigueur for the Latin American rich and even for the continent's middle classes. They could come to Miami on business and, while at it, slip in a vacation by the beach and shop in Miami Beach's famed Lincoln Road.[21]

In the wake of these developments, construction and real estate became a major pillar of the local economy. The impressive skylines of luxury apartment towers by Biscayne Bay and the Atlantic Ocean were created by a local "growth machine" that targeted foreigners, primarily well-heeled Latin Americans, but later western Europeans and Russians, as clients. They bought these apartments for the same reason already described—wealth protection—as well as for investments. Many such units were acquired by companies rather than by individuals and were often left vacant.[22] As instruments for wealth protection and growth, they have also been utilized for years by corrupt politicians and drug smugglers seeking to launder their assets.

Drug trafficking and money laundering still exists in South Florida, but they now are a pale reflection of what they once were. The money laundering trade in the 1970s and 1980s actually had another positive consequence for the local economy. Beyond the major impulse it created for the construction and real estate sectors, it placed Miami front and center in the perceptual field of wealthy individuals and corporations throughout Latin America and the Caribbean. Thereafter, doing business in the United States required, at least as a first step, coming to Miami. The heavy presence of major Latin American banks, such as Espirito Santo or Banco Popular in the Brickell district, reflects this reality.[23]

Hence, the political takeover of the city by the former exiles from Cuba, instead of marginalizing it as many predicted in the early days, turned it in the direction of becoming a cosmopolitan entrepôt. This was due largely to the vision of an exiled business class whose initiatives are now institutionalized in a major financial district and a flourishing real estate industry. Spanish rose to parity with English in the business world, while Miami's own place in the world economy rose to that of a key regional center.

OTHER MAKERS OF A GLOBAL CITY: COMMERCE, TOURISM, AND ART

In the wake of the events just described, Miami was no longer valued because of its winter temperatures but was redefined and reactivated to become a hemispheric center of trade. Port Miami and the Miami International Airport (MIA) became, next to real estate and banking, prime motors of the local economy. In 2018, Port Miami received 2,205 ships and transited 9,162 million tons of merchandise, figures that made it the largest port in the U.S. East Coast south of New York. By 2015, Port Miami was offering super post-Panamax gantry cranes capable of handling cargo ships up to twenty-two containers wide. Deep dredging of its oceangoing channel lane made Port Miami the only logistical hub south of Virginia capable of handling fully laden post-Panamax vessels. In addition, it became the largest cruise capital in the world. In 2012, more than 4 million passengers traveled to Miami to embark on their dream cruise. By 2018, the number had reached 6 million.[24]

A multilane tunnel and rapid freight rail link the port to the airport. Airfreight at MIA reached 2.25 million tons in 2017, putting it at the top of U.S. airports, ahead of Los Angeles (LAX) and New York (JFK). In terms of international tonnage, MIA ranks ninth in the world and is the only U.S. airport among the top ten. Naturally, MIA's trade partners are overwhelmingly Latin American, with Brazil and Colombia accounting for 30 percent of the total. Only two non–Latin American nations, China and Switzerland, rank among the top ten. In terms of perishable goods, such as flowers and agricultural products, MIA accounts for 71 percent of total U.S. imports, followed at a distance by JFK in New York. A total of 35.6 million passengers traveled through MIA in 2010; by 2018, the figure had grown to 45 million, turning it, next to Atlanta, into the largest passenger airport in the Southeast.[25]

Tourism has always been Miami's raison d'être. As T. D. Allman once remarked, it is the metropolis founded on the desire to escape freezing temperatures in the North.[26] With the passage of time, however, the seasonal tourist industry has become an all-year affair. Festivals and parades of all kinds dot the calendar, and tourist-driven spots like South Beach and Wynwood have become, to use Hemingway's expression about Paris, a perennial "moveable feast."[27] A powerful, and unexpected, contribution to this trend has been commercial art. Next to New York and Los Angeles, Miami has become a major hub in the art world. With eleven art fairs per year, the city surpasses other major centers, including London and Amsterdam. Only New York and Paris have more.[28]

This development can be traced to the arrival of the Art Basel Winter Fair in Miami. Just as Julia Tuttle, an early Miami settler, persuaded magnate Henry Flagler to extend his railroad to South Florida by sending him a bouquet of orange blossoms in the middle of winter, Mary Rubell went to Basel and persuaded its art leaders to bring their fair to Miami in December.[29] Sun and warm weather were certainly part of the attraction, but so was the emergence of a vigorous center for Latin American art, anchored on the city's hegemony in the region. In Miami-Dade County, there are now over 40,000 full-time jobs in the art sector, with a payroll of over $1.3 billion and over $150 million in taxes paid to the local and state governments.[30]

Major sculptures and paintings dot the city, with entire neighborhoods now defined by the kind of art that they exhibit and promote. The large paintings covering the walls of the formerly derelict Wynwood district are the major, but not the only, example. The nearby impoverished Allapattah district has just opened its own art museum, and there are also museums, galleries, and art festivals in Coconut Grove, Coral Gables, Little Haiti, and Miami Beach (north and south). The county government has strongly supported this development by endowing its Arts Council with an annual budget of over $17 million, one of the largest in the country on a per capita basis.[31]

Public art and art sold in galleries are no longer exclusively Latin American. The Perez Art Miami Museum (PAMM) now features exhibits from the world over, as does the Lowe Art Museum at the University of Miami and the Frost Museum at Florida International University. Miami has become a magnet for painters and sculptors from North America and Europe, with many actually paying for space to have their art featured on the walls of Wynwood.[32] This development has added powerfully to the sense of cosmopolitanism in Miami. The city has left behind its role as a seasonal tourist resort and is no longer just a financial and commercial hub. As one of the senior partners in a major law firm in downtown Miami noted recently: "I am not sure that we are an emerging global city; I think that we have already arrived."[33]

THE ETHNIC MOSAIC

The population of metropolitan Miami is ethnically diverse.[34] By 2014, Hispanics already constituted the absolute majority, 66 percent; Blacks represented 16.7 percent and non-Hispanic whites 14.7 percent, having declined from 61.1 percent in 1960. By 2020, the Hispanic population had reached 70 percent of the total.[35] If non-Hispanic whites represent the "mainstream" of the American population, then that mainstream has disappeared in Miami. In other words, the index of dissimilarity, calculated for other American cities on the basis of how many minorities must move to "majority" (i.e., white) areas to eliminate spatial segregation, makes no sense in Miami because there are only a few, and diminishing, non-Hispanic white places to move to. Table 3.1 presents the evolution of the area's population in the last half century. The recent political history of the place is well reflected in these figures.

TABLE 3.1 Miami-Dade County, population by decade and ethnicity, 1970–2020

Year	Number of people (1,000s)			
	Total	Hispanic	Black	Non-Hispanic white/other
1970	1,268	299	190	782
1975	1,462	467	237	765
1980	1,626	551	284	773
1985	1,771	768	367	656
1990	1,967	968	409	618
1995	2,084	1,555	446	519
2000	2,253	1,292	457	534
2005	2,402	1,455	497	483
2010	2,551	1,621	526	442
2015	2,703	1,794	554	395
2020	2,858	1,972	583	342
	Percentages			
1970	100.0	27.6	15.0	65.7
1975	100.0	31.9	16.2	52.3
1980	100.0	35.7	17.5	47.5
1985	100.0	43.4	20.7	37.0
1990	100.0	49.2	20.8	31.4
1995	100.0	55.4	21.4	24.9
2000	100.0	57.3	20.3	23.7
2005	100.0	60.6	20.7	20.1
2010	100.0	63.5	20.6	17.3
2015	100.0	66.4	20.5	14.6
2020	100.0	69.0	20.4	12.2

Source: Miami-Dade County, Department of Planning and Zoning, *General Statistical Data*, 2020, www.miamidade.gov/finance/library/genstat04.pdf.

The mainstream population in Miami-Dade is now resolutely of Latin American and Caribbean descent, and this population and the Black population firmly adhere to their own distinct and separate patches of urban territory. This fact makes the area a majority-minority city, except that the two groups are quite distinct, maintaining their own separate social and geographical identities. Remarkably, the foreign-born now exceed half the population (51.6 percent) of Miami-Dade County, making it the only metropolitan area in the United States to have a majority immigrant population. About 90 percent of the foreign-born come from Latin America and the Caribbean, Cuba being the largest source.

This exceptional demographic profile contrasts with the apparent "normalcy" of everyday life in the city, where English is still the unchallenged official and business language; where American economic, political, and judicial institutions are dominant; and where the standards of personal achievement and success are the same as elsewhere in the nation. One hears a lot of Spanish (and some Haitian Creole and Portuguese) in Miami, but the people who speak it accept that they live in an English-ruled world and that, to succeed in it, there is no alternative to full-fledged English learning and acculturation.

The absolute demographic dominance of Hispanics and the rapid decline of the Anglo white population also mean that an increasing number of property capitalists and of those leading and managing banks in Miami's financial district are now Latino/a. This fact fits with the rise of the Cuban enclave economy in the 1960s and 1970s and the subsequent success of Cuban entrepreneurs and their offspring. While Anglo and, increasingly, European capitalists and executives are also found at the top of the commercial and financial world, the Latin American presence in these circles is indisputable. That presence is also deeply felt in the art world in terms of both artists and entrepreneurs. Politically, economically, and culturally, Miami now moves to a resolute cosmopolitan Latin beat.

The national and ethnic origins of the present population of Miami are too diverse to cover in their entirety, but apart from the most prominent players—Cubans, American Jews, and the remaining Anglos—other nationalities and ethnicities play a significant role, demographically and socially. Of these, none is more important than the native Black population, which has been in and with the city since its beginnings. To this group must be added other sizable immigrant groups that have also established a durable and visible presence. Miami's

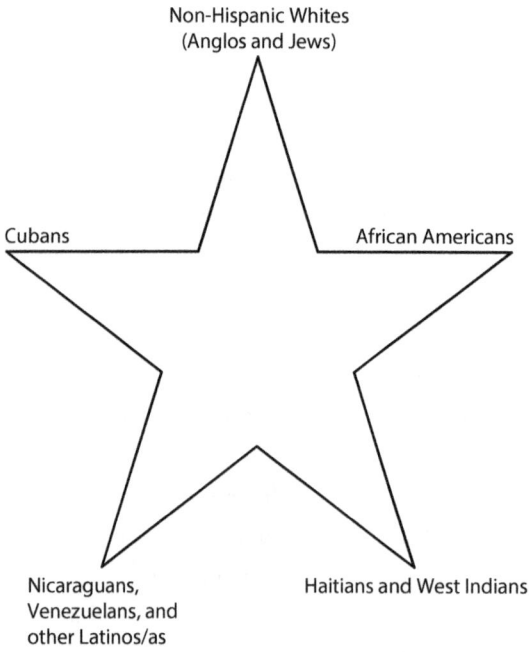

Non-Hispanic Whites
(Anglos and Jews)

Cubans

African Americans

Nicaraguans,
Venezuelans, and
other Latinos/as

Haitians and West Indians

3.1 Miami's ethnic mosaic.

Source: Alejandro Portes and Ariel Armony, *The Global Edge: Miami in the Twenty-First Century* (Oakland: University of California Press, 2018), 150.

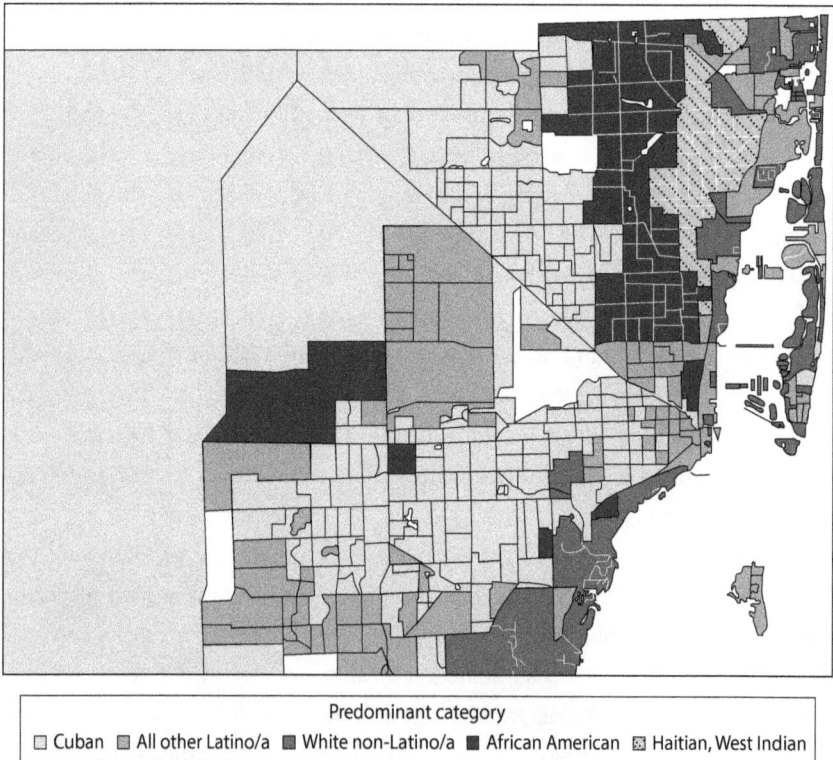

Predominant category

☐ Cuban ▨ All other Latino/a ■ White non-Latino/a ■ African American ▨ Haitian, West Indian

3.2 Geographical distribution of the principal ethnic groups in the Miami-Dade metropolitan area.

ethnic mosaic can be portrayed as a five-pointed star where Cubans and American Anglos and Jews occupy the best-known angles, but where the other three weigh significantly in the present mix. Figure 3.1 presents this star, and figure 3.2 locates the main ethnic groups in the metropolitan area.

AFRICAN AMERICANS

The story of how railroad and hotel magnate Henry Flagler marched his "Bahamian artillery" to the election that made Miami a city in 1896 is well known, as is the story of the subsequent relegation of these Bahamians and other Black people to Overtown and then Liberty City in the days of segregation.[36] More significant for our purposes is what has taken place during the last twenty-five years. African Americans have maintained a stable demographic presence in the metropolitan area, representing 19 percent of the county's population, but this sizable presence has not translated into comparable political and economic power. By most accounts, African Americans are still at the bottom of the ethnic hierarchy politically and economically, having been surpassed by more recent immigrant groups, including those of the same racial origins. Median household incomes are significantly below the county average of $55,998, while Blacks are overrepresented in the population receiving food stamps (25.5 percent countywide) or Supplemental Security Income (7 percent).[37]

The African American population concentrates in certain areas of Miami and in the municipalities of Florida City, Opa Locka, and Miami Gardens. In Miami, Overtown—close to the central district—has been a traditional Black residential area. It is now heavily decayed and threatened with extinction by the advancement of the Arts and Entertainment District and the construction of the Miami World Center and the Miami Central Complex. Only the Lyric Theater remains as a reminder of the story of the district.[38] Colored Town, as it was known, attracted the likes of Ella Fitzgerald, Muhammad Ali, and even sociologist W. E. B. Du Bois throughout the early and mid-1900s. However, much of the Black population from Overtown was displaced by the construction of Interstate 95 in the 1960s and followed the highway north, through Allapattah, Liberty City, Opa Locka, and Miami Gardens.[39]

Liberty City is most known for Liberty Square, the first public housing project for Black families; built in the 1930s, it was featured in the Barry Jenkins

Academy Award–winning film *Moonlight*. A massive redevelopment of Liberty Square is now under way with contributions from the county, the federal government, and the Related Group, a private development firm responsible for much of the skyline of condominium towers downtown.[40]

Just north of Liberty City is the municipality of Opa Locka. Together with Florida City in the far south of the county, Opa Locka features the lowest median household incomes in the county ($17,908), with 40 percent of the population currently living below the poverty line.[41] The city is home to a large collection of Moorish Revival architecture, much of which is nationally registered for preservation, built by the city founder Glenn Curtis. While the city has received much attention for corruption scandals, recent actions by architects and artists (both local and national) have brought a new spotlight to the northern suburb. Most recently, a sculpture by artist Hank Willis Thomas was installed at Town Center Apartments in the city, showing that public art can be found far from the confines of the gentrifying Wynwood district.[42]

Just north of Opa Locka and reaching the Broward County line lies Miami Gardens. This is where many middle-class African American families escaping Overtown and Liberty City have settled. They have been joined there by large numbers of West Indian and Haitian immigrants. Miami Gardens's population is three-fourth Black and, at 112,200 inhabitants, is the largest predominantly Black city in Florida.[43] Miami Gardens is also ruled by Blacks. Although street crime is high, local government under Mayor Oliver Gilbert III did a good job attracting businesses and middle-class residents to the area.

Miami Gardens does not feature areas of concentrated wealth, as in Coral Gables or Brickell Avenue, but it does not have the desolate streets of Liberty City or Opa Locka either. Its median household income is close to the county average ($42,398), and over half of the businesses in the city are owned by Blacks. The area's main claim to fame lies in its sponsorship of the Orange Bowl, a nationwide televised event presided over with panache by the current mayor and his assistants.[44] The rest of the year, the city is anchored by the principal institutions that call it home—two universities and the Dolphin football stadium.

Institutional discrimination in Miami is reflected in the fact that city leaders, even leaders of immigrant groups of color, generally view African Americans as a "problem" to be solved or neutralized rather than as a human resource. For these leaders, the general quiescence and increasing apolitical character of the Black American community are actually assets rather than issues to be overcome. The almost complete absence of Black Americans from Miami's power elite extends even to the leadership of progressive Miami Gardens. The city could as well be over the county line for all the downtown movers and shakers care. As one of our informants puts it: "Take the Orange Bowl. It is advertised nationally as 'The game from Miami,' not from the Gardens. Nobody knows where Miami Gardens is. That is why the mayor is a 'flamboyant figure.' He has to be in order to make his presence felt."[45]

Back in the 1980s, repeated riots in Liberty City—such as the so-called Miami Riot in 1980, triggered by the acquittal of a group of white police officers charged in the beating death of a Black citizen—and frequent confrontations between Cubans and African Americans over a number of issues were features of Miami life and culture. The city was "on edge" at the time, not only because of the political struggle between Anglo and Cuban elites, but also because of the mobilization of Black Americans to confront the threat of double subordination—being shunted aside not only by a traditional southern elite, but also by a newly arrived foreign minority.

Twenty-five years later, Black areas of town were mostly politically inert, though race relations continued to be tense. An African American attorney clarified what had taken place: "The major change in Miami in the last quarter of a century is that it has become a Spanish-dominated city. Hispanicity is now its core and has become institutionalized. For other groups in this city, it is not just resignation or despair; it is the acceptance of how things are now."[46]

The response of the Black middle class was to move to the extreme north of the county, turning Miami Gardens into its political center. Wealthier Blacks became dispersed throughout the metropolitan area, exercising their new right to live wherever they wished. Though small in number, Black elite families can be found in the most exclusive neighborhoods—such as Aventura, Miami Beach, and even Fisher Island. At the opposite end, the Black working poor and, in increasing numbers, the nonworking poor have been left to their own devices, confined to the traditional slum areas of Overtown, Liberty City, and Opa Locka.[47]

National mobilizations to protest police violence against Blacks in 2020 also took place in Miami, but the tone of the protests in that city was different. Protestors were not only African American but young people of all ethnicities incensed by the images of police aggressiveness and brutality against unarmed citizens. For the most part, these scenes featured white police officers beating or shooting African Americans. None of these events happened in Miami, and none is likely to happen in the future. City and county police are primarily Latino/a and are led by Cuban-American officers. In Miami Gardens, the police force is predominantly African American. Thus the sharp racial confrontations present in other American cities do not happen in Miami. There are scarcely any native whites left, and the Black population features a substantial number of immigrants from Haiti, Jamaica, and the West Indies. The mindset of these immigrants is quite different, being focused, as we shall see next, on economic ascent and political integration.

In earlier decades, however, from the 1950s to the 1980s, Miami did experience a number of massive Black protests and riots.[48] As in other southern cities, they involved confrontations between young African Americans and a largely white police force. Today the transformation of Miami in the direction of multiethnicity and a strong Latin presence is also reflected in the character of its police force. It is not imprinted with the Jim Crow southern legacy, and, for the most part, it polices people of the same ethnic background.[49]

HAITIANS

The archbishop of Miami, Thomas Wenski, made his name as a young priest by championing the cause of a downtrodden and largely forgotten group. Haitians, "the refugees nobody wants," as Alex Stepick referred to them, had been arriving in Miami since the 1970s. Those caught at sea by the U.S. Coast Guard were promptly returned, but others found their way in. In 1980, a large influx of Haitians managed to enter by hitching their fortunes to the Mariel exodus from Cuba. Advocates for the Haitians pointed out the patent injustice that, while refugees from Cuba were promptly admitted into the United States, those from Haiti were summarily turned back. In the end, the federal government relented, but it refused to grant refugee status to either group. Instead, a new label was invented for both of them: "entrants, status pending."[50]

Destitute and heavily discriminated against because of their color, Haitians settled in one of the poorest areas of Miami, adjacent to Liberty City. The place was originally called Lemon City, but with the appearance of brightly colored Caribbean small shops and restaurants, it was rebaptized Little Haiti. Still, no one went there, and even African Americans kept their distance from the new arrivals. Then Father Wenski made his appearance. He got the Miami Archdiocese to let him occupy an abandoned nuns' convent nearby and turn it into a community center. With Haitian labor, he repaired the church and garden and rebuilt the convent. Notre Dame d'Haiti was born, becoming the spiritual home of the downtrodden refugees. Before community leaders could emerge to take up their cause, Father Wenski was the voice that spoke for the Haitians. Sunday Mass at Notre Dame d'Haiti was something to behold—men and women dressed in their finest and the ritual prayers recited and sung with rhythmic claps and a Caribbean beat.[51]

Gradually, the community improved, as Haitians borrowed a page from what Cubans had done on the other side of town and started operating a number of small businesses. Little Haiti patterned itself deliberately after Little Havana, although it fell quite short of its model. The causes were directly traceable to the two groups' contrasting modes of incorporation. Early Cuban refugee waves were uniformly white; they brought a great deal of education and businesses expertise and were warmly received by the U.S. government and public as allies in the global struggle against communism. The U.S. Congress enacted the Cuban Adjustment Act in the 1970s, granting legal access and refugee status to all Cuban escapees from communism. The Small Business Administration and other federal agencies put in place a panoply of programs to support Cuban enterprises in Miami and the revalidation of professional titles from the island.[52]

None of this happened with the Haitians, whose reception by the government and American society at large was quite negative. Haitian efforts at business development were thwarted by lack of capital and pervasive discrimination. A colorful Haitian Caribbean Marketplace was built in the heart of the community, hoping to attract tourists from downtown. No one came. White tourists made no distinction between Little Haiti and nearby Liberty City, both seen as equally threatening Black areas. In a few years, the Caribbean Marketplace had to close its doors.[53]

Relations between the two major Miami Black communities were, at best, tense. African Americans did not regard the arrival of Haitian refugees as a benefit to themselves. Speakers of a foreign tongue and carriers of a vibrant but different culture, they were regarded at best as strangers and, at worst, as competitors for housing, jobs, and social services. Instances of solidarity and common mobilization by both Black communities did happen, but they were, by and large, exceptional. On their part, Haitians manifested a distinct reluctance to assimilate to African American culture and identity. Carriers of a rich national tradition themselves, they did not see any gain in casting their lot with the most downtrodden group in the local ethnic mosaic. Tensions between American Blacks and Black Haitians were well reflected in repeated clashes at Edison Senior High, the school that youths from both communities shared.[54]

Changes during the last two decades, however, have been rather dramatic. Haitian entrepreneurs and civic leaders eventually succeeded in creating their own enclave. While it still could not match the Cubans' enclave, it acquired its own political and economic identity. Notre Dame d'Haiti is still there, and the Caribbean Marketplace has reopened its doors, but the core of the community has moved north, to the city of North Miami. Resettlement of the former refugees there has totally transformed local politics and civic life. North Miami's mayor in 2021 was Philippe Bien-Aimé, born in Haiti. Two of the four council members were also Haitian. A drive around the city preceding the last municipal election pointed to a large number of posters of candidates for mayor and city commissioner; they were invariably Haitian. The local high school, North Miami Senior High, has become "the" Haitian educational center, featuring classes in French and Haitian Creole. At $40,661, median household incomes in North Miami are close to the county's figures, and the increasing political visibility of this Haitian community has propelled one of its own, Jean Monestine, to a seat as county commissioner and to a prominent position on the county board.[55]

Resettlement of Haitian families into North Miami and out of Little Haiti has been due, in part, to the sudden popularity of the latter. The Wynwood area, now experiencing explosive growth fueled by its art scene, is directly south of Little Haiti. Since land and buildings have been snapped up in Wynwood, artists, gallery owners, and developers have started looking north. The formerly forlorn Lemon City is now in the local growth machine's crosshairs as the next frontier for expensive condominium towers and malls. Ironically, this new development has triggered a defensive reaction among Haitian community activists to maintain their old community. It may have been poor and isolated, but it was theirs. In the words of Marlene Bastien, community leader and a candidate for the Miami-Dade Commission: "Through their efforts and determination, Haitians were able to lift this area to the level of a cosmopolitan neighborhood that is now desirable to others . . . the Caribbean Marketplace has re-opened, but there are developers already interested in buying it. In the nineteen eighties, there were lots of protests and mobilizations in defense of Haitian refugees in this area. That historical memory is worth preserving."[56]

When a community shifts from struggling for survival to defending its historical memory of success, things have surely improved. Haitians are still not part of the power elite in the Miami metropolis, nor are they part of its growth machine, but they have established a solid and visible presence as members of its ethnic mosaic. This relative success stands in contrast with what has happened to the African American population, which, with the partial exception of Miami Gardens, is still confined to the bottom of the city's social and economic hierarchies.

NICARAGUANS

Latin American dreams of power often end up in Miami dust. Two Cuban presidents are buried in the Woodlawn Cemetery fronted by Calle Ocho (Southwest Eighth Street). They were joined there by the latest Nicaraguan dictator, Anastasio Somoza. He only had two years to enjoy his plush Miami Beach mansion before he passed. His overthrow by the Sandinista Revolution in 1979 was the prelude for a near-repeat performance of the Cuban drama two decades earlier. Like the Cuban upper classes had done following the arrival of communism to power, the Nicaraguan elites promptly moved their property and themselves to Miami. The middle classes followed in the early to mid-1980s, creating a visible presence in the westernmost suburb of Sweetwater. Small Nicaraguan businesses started to proliferate in that city, imitating, in all particulars, what had happened earlier in Little Havana.[57]

The local middle school was duly renamed Ruben Dario Middle High, and busts of the great Nicaraguan poet proliferated in the emerging Nicaraguan enclave. The population was there to fuel this development, as hundreds of thousands of Nicaraguan refugees moved to Miami during the late 1980s. As with the Cubans before, all sorts of ethnic organizations proliferated. The decade saw the emergence of the Miami-Managua Lions Club, the Nicaraguan-American Bankers Association, the Association of Nicaraguan Architects and Engineers of Florida, the Nicaraguan Medical Association, *La Estrella de Nicaragua* newspaper, and many others. Los Ranchos restaurant, a direct import from Managua, became an instant hit, spawning five branches throughout the metropolitan area.[58] All signs were there for a repeat performance of what Cubans had done and the rise of a second powerful Latin group in Miami.

It did not happen, and the causes of that outcome are instructive. They had to do less with the education and motivation of the new exiles than with the circumstances surrounding their arrival. As already discussed, in the wake of Castro's revolution, Cubans had been received with open arms by the federal government and American society at large. Circumstances two decades later were quite different. Embarked in an all-out effort to prevent another communist regime in its backyard, the Reagan administration did not see the arrival and settlement of Nicaraguan refugees in the United States as helpful. Instead, it sought to keep discontent with the Sandinista dictatorship bottled up in Nicaragua and encouraged escapees to join the Contra military effort in Honduras rather than settling in Miami.[59]

While leaders of the Contra movement were given refugee status in the United States and their Miami headquarters were supported by the CIA, the attempt by rank-and-file Nicaraguans to join the exodus was decisively resisted. Thousands of would-be asylees were deported by the Immigration and Naturalization Service (INS), and those granted asylum were not provided with any resettlement assistance. In the late 1980s, the INS even mounted a major operation at the Texas border aimed at summarily adjudicating asylum requests by arriving Nicaraguans and immediately sending back those rejected.[60]

This negative reception played havoc with the refugees' effort to consolidate their community in Miami. Except for the earlier elite waves and those directly involved in the Contra war, Nicaraguans arriving in the late 1980s were treated no better than undocumented immigrants, denied asylum and confined to economic penury. Their minds occupied with obtaining a work permit, escaping the INS if denied, and surviving in the informal economy, the new refugees were in no condition to build a viable economic enclave. Unlike the Cubans, they lacked the legal security and external assistance that had proven so decisive in the latter's success.

The single card in the Nicaraguans' favor was their reception by the local Cuban community. By the late 1980s, Cubans had consolidated their own enterprises and occupied prominent positions in the local political structure. They saw the Nicaraguans as brothers-in-arms, suffering under another communist dictatorship supported by the Castro government and seeking, like themselves, refuge and assistance to rebuild their lives. Thus, as the federal government tried to stop the exodus and make life difficult for those arriving in South Florida, the local government in Miami took exactly the opposite stance.[61]

Witnessing the "inhuman" conditions suffered by Nicaraguan refugees in a private homeless shelter, the Cuban city manager of Miami at the time, Cesar Odio, ordered it closed and made arrangements to move the refugees to Bobby Maduro Stadium, a facility built by wealthy Cubans in the 1950s and the spring training site of a major league baseball team, the Baltimore Orioles. Odio assured the refugees that they would receive the same consideration given to Cuban Mariel entrants. His action mobilized squads of city rescue workers—welders fenced off the entrance to the baseball field, carpenters built partitions, and cots were placed along the stands in neat rows. The auxiliary Cuban Catholic bishop of Miami, Agustín Román, paid a visit; doctors from the Pasteur Clinic—run and staffed by Cuban-American physicians—set up an examination room under a stairway.[62]

Two days after Odio's original declaration, the Cuban-American manager of Miami-Dade County, Joaquín Aviño, unveiled a plan to build a temporary trailer camp to house new arrivals. A week later, Odio flew to Washington, D.C., to persuade INS commissioner, Alan Nelson, to reverse the policy of denying work permits to newly arrived Nicaraguans. Despite the pleas of the Florida senators at the time to "regain control of our borders," Nelson granted Odio's request. Upon returning to Miami, Odio went directly to the stadium, where he was cheered and had bestowed upon him the title of "Father of the Nicaraguan refugees."[63]

Arriving in Miami and seeing how their spring training camp had been transformed, the Orioles promptly made arrangements to move to Sarasota. Never mind—what happened in Bobby Maduro Stadium was symbolic of what took place in the community at large. To a man, Cubans lined up behind the new refugees, committing their considerable economic and political resources to the effort to protect and resettle them. That effort culminated in the passage by the U.S. Congress of the Nicaraguan Adjustment and Central American Relief Act (NACARA) in 1997, which granted the new refugees legal resident status and the right to work in the United States. NACARA was initiated and steered through Congress primarily by the Cuban-American delegation from Miami. Cuban-American congressman Lincoln Diaz-Balart wrote the bill.[64]

Cuban support played a decisive role in facilitating resettlement of the large population of Nicaraguan refugees in Miami, but it was insufficient to bring it to a position of political prominence or consolidate a strong economic presence. In addition to federal reluctance to commit resources to the new refugees, a second key development conspired against consolidation of a Nicaraguan enclave. The victory of the Contra rebellion in the late 1980s and the return of democracy to Nicaragua in 1990 promptly created a return flow of political leaders, entrepreneurs, and professionals. The incoming Nicaraguan administration under newly elected president Violeta Chamorro lobbied heavily for the return of the former exiles and appointed many of them to prominent positions in government.[65]

This development short-circuited the consolidation of a strong Nicaraguan community in Miami. Existing ethnic organizations shriveled or disappeared. A dense traffic of people and goods arose between Miami and Managua, with multiple flights per day. With Nicaraguan democracy restored, the U.S. government strongly encouraged the former refugees to go back, while the Cuban community saw no reason to continue supporting them. Thereafter, Nicaraguans still living in South Florida were no different from other economic migrants; only their protected status under the enduring NACARA legislation gave them an edge.

Unlike with the Cubans, the Nicaraguan exodus lacked finality, being interrupted by changing political circumstances at home. Ironically, the triumph of the Contra war spelled out the end of a viable Nicaraguan enclave in Miami. Even the return of the Sandinistas to power via electoral politics a few years later did not reignite the exodus. By then, the die was cast. The Nicaraguan and Nicaraguan-American population of Miami is still quite sizable, numbering about 150,000 in 2020. Politically and economically, however, it is nearly invisible. Nicaraguans have repaid the solid assistance received from Cuban leaders by supporting their initiatives and power. Cuban candidates have consistently counted on the Nicaraguan vote.[66] In recent years, many former Nicaraguan refugees have left their fledgling community in Sweetwater to settle in East Little Havana. While Ruben Dario High is still there and the Divine Providence Church in Flagler and 102nd Avenue is still regarded as the "cathedral of Nicaraguans," much of this population has opted to leave the far west of the metropolitan area and reoccupy places of former Cuban concentration.[67] Unlike Cubans and even Haitians, who have imprinted Miami with many symbols of their presence and culture, there are few such icons in areas where Nicaraguans concentrate. A little memorial to fallen members of the defunct Nicaraguan National Guard at Yambo restaurant in Little Havana and scattered busts of Rubén Darío here and there are all that exist at present.

OTHER GROUPS

Miami's ethnic mosaic comprises many other groups that, if not as sizable or as settled as those discussed previously, are nevertheless increasingly important. Miami's Latino/a population is now more than half non-Cuban. Aside from Nicaraguans, the fastest-rising nationality is Venezuelans escaping the disastrous Maduro regime in their country. Concentrated in the city of El Doral, Venezuelans have come to resemble the first stages of the Cuban and Nicaraguan flows, with former elites and an increasing number of professionals migrating to Miami.[68]

El Doral is an affluent municipality with a median household income of $77,418 in 2020, well above the county average. The concentration of Venezuelans there reflects both the elite character of this population and their earnest hope that their country does not follow, in the end, the example of Cuba. Venezuelans in Miami are not yet considered political refugees "proper." Many travel frequently back to their country to visit family, attend to their businesses there, and bring needed resources. Close proximity of Doral to the MIA is thus a valuable feature of their new place of settlement.[69]

As in the case of Nicaraguans, the Venezuelan movement into Miami still lacks finality. Yet, while in the Nicaraguan case the exodus was interrupted by the one-time defeat of the Sandinistas at the polls, in the case of Venezuelans, it is defined by political uncertainty, economic crisis, and instability back home. Eligible voters in El Doral were able to elect a Venezuelan mayor of the city, but he was subsequently defeated by a Cuban-American candidate. Despite considerable economic resources, this lack of finality in their settlement pattern has so far prevented the consolidation of a strong Venezuelan political presence in Miami.

Other sizable South American migrant groups include Argentines, Brazilians, Colombians, and Ecuadoreans. They are formed primarily by upper- and middle-class businesspeople and professionals. As in the case of Venezuelans, many are former members of the elite escaping bouts of political instability or threatened by populist takeovers. Once in Miami, South American immigrants have dispersed throughout the metropolitan area, failing to create a visible presence anywhere. There is no identifiable "Little Bogota" or "Little Rio" that would reflect the presence of these groups. For most of their members, settlement in Miami is also regarded as tentative. They retain houses in their respective countries, divide their time between these countries and South Florida, and often remain more concerned with politics back home than in their adopted city.

As in the case of Venezuelans, lack of permanent settlement decisively weakens their political presence, despite sizable numbers. While South American immigrants often complain about the Cubans' firm hold on political and economic power, the underlying reason is that earlier Cuban exiles and their children represent the only national group that made a collective decision to adopt Miami as "their" city. As discussed previously, the exodus from Cuba is inextricably linked to the rise of Miami in the global economy. Miami's place in the Americas has been strengthened by the arrival and economic resources of other Latin American groups displaced from their respective countries by political instability. None, however, has repeated the Cuban exile experience.

Jamaicans and other West Indians represent another sizable immigrant community in South Florida, but, unlike Haitians, these Black groups have not created a distinct economic or political presence either in Miami-Dade County or in Broward County (Fort Lauderdale) to the north. Migration from Jamaica and other West Indian nations is mostly nonpolitical, triggered by various economic motives. Although ethnographic reports point to the desire of many West Indians to differentiate themselves from Black Americans, they end up settling in middle-class suburban Black areas such as Miami Gardens. As a longtime observer of this community notes, its basic motto is "don't make waves." According to this informant: "There are over 350,000 Jamaicans and other West Indians in Dade and Broward counties, but you will not know it. There is not a single West Indian mayor or any other senior elected official in either county. They are content with letting others rule in their place. However, they also try to keep their distance from American blacks."[70]

North of Miami Beach is the wealthy municipality of Sunny Isles. Recently, it has experienced a growing concentration of Russians and Ukrainians, accompanied by the emergence of Russian restaurants and ethnic shops. For the most part, this emerging presence is due to the purchase of luxury apartments by wealthy Russian entrepreneurs. Climate and the desire to take their money out of their unpredictable country have fueled this new inflow in a pattern that resembles the behavior of South American elites. Unlike the latter, however, Russians have concentrated in a single spot, and the presence of so many well-heeled Russian families in Sunny Isles has attracted a secondary inflow of other eastern European migrants seeking to provide these families with a range of culturally defined services. Hence, the white and blonde people that one sees frequenting bars and shops in the northern beaches of Miami are not the Anglos of yesteryear, but mostly eastern Europeans. Signs in the Cyrillic alphabet fronting a number of restaurants and other businesses complete the transformation.

MIAMI IN COMPARATIVE PERSPECTIVE

> In the late 1950s, Miami experienced three "tipping" points: the advent of air conditioning, the invention of jet propulsion, and the arrival of Cubans. The three had nothing to do with each other, but their convergence made the city what it is today.
>
> Alberto Ibargüen, president, Knight Foundation

According to Ibargüen,[71] air conditioning allowed Miami to become an all-year city rather than a winter village; jet propulsion brought it within two or three hours from New York City, Boston, Bogota, and Mexico City; and Cubans turned the city inside out, reorienting it to the rest of the hemisphere and then the world. Remnants of the "winter village" still exist. Arguably, some of the quaintest are the mechanical bridges that dot major transportation avenues across Biscayne Bay and the Miami River.

These bridges open on demand or at regular intervals to allow boat traffic through the bay and river. Built for an era when cars and buses were few and yachts and sailboats even scarcer, they have now become choke points in the city's present transportation crisis. Of these bridges, none is more visible than the one across the Miami River linking Biscayne Boulevard and Brickell Avenue. Built at the confluence of the river and bay and adorned by an impressive statue of a Tequesta warrior, the original tribe inhabiting the place, the bridge has become a regular scene of confrontation between marine and street life. It is the most direct link between booming downtown and the financial Brickell district, yet its frequent openings for an intense river traffic snarl automobiles and buses at peak times of the day.

Cross that bridge when you can and you will find yourself in a jungle of high-rises inhabited by banks from all over the world and, farther afield, luxury condominium towers, ritzy restaurants and night clubs, and an enchanting bayfront promenade. The owners of the apartments, the patrons of the restaurants, and the joggers by the bay are invariably white—native Anglo, European, or Cuban—the top echelon of Miami's income distribution. The servers in the restaurants and night clubs come, however, in a wide variety of colors.

Return to downtown and the river again, this time going west on Flagler Street, and, in just four blocks, you are in a different world. The word *fritanga*—meaning Nicaraguan restaurant—is everywhere, as are all kinds of businesses advertising in Spanish. The people in the streets are uniformly poor Latin Americans—Nicaraguans, Hondurans, and other Central American migrants.[72]

The spatial character of urban phenomena cannot be better illustrated than in these contrasting images located just a few hundred meters from one another. They are, however, only a single illustration of the complex ethnic mosaic of this city. As in established global cities like New York and emerging ones like Dubai, wealth and privilege are but a short distance away from struggling migrant populations. The two coexist in a symbiotic relationship where migrants and minorities fulfill the manifold labor needs of firms and individuals at the top of the economic hourglass. So far, these economic and spatial inequalities have not led to violent political confrontation, partly because the old working class—composed primarily of African Americans—has been marginalized and also because the new laboring classes are formed by immigrants, who are more interested in individual economic survival and progress than in local politics. The ethnic heterogeneity of Miami's present population discourages frontal confrontations, so common in the city's past when it was a southern-style, white-ruled town.

Miami differs in that respect from other nearby coastal cities that, at some point, also competed for the role of hemispheric commercial and financial center. New Orleans, the subject of chapter 6, is a case in point. The former capital of the Louisiana territory remains firmly ensconced in the post–Civil War Black-white racial division and continuous conflict. No major Latin American or other immigrant group arrived to dilute that confrontation, so the city stayed southern and as such declined politically and economically. As elsewhere in urban history, Miami became the locus, vehicle, and reflection of the transformations brought about by the arrival of so many foreign groups—from Cuba first and then from the rest of the Western Hemisphere. Without them, the city by Biscayne Bay would not have acquired the economic relevance and cultural prominence described in this chapter.

There are some notable similarities between the emerging global cities that are the central subjects of this book—Dubai, Miami, and Singapore. As seen in table 3.2, Miami International Airport, Singapore Changi Airport, and Dubai

TABLE 3.2 Indicators of airport traffic in Miami, Singapore, and Dubai, 2008–2019

	2008	2009	2010	2011	2012	2013	2014	2015	2016	2017	2018	2019
Miami International Airport												
Total flights	317,519	351,417	376,208	323,635	391,195	399,140	402,663	412,915	414,234	413,287	416,032	416,773
Total passengers	34,063,531	33,886,025	35,698,025	32,793,034	30,467,444	40,562,948	40,562,948	44,350,247	44,584,603	44,071,313	45,044,312	45,924,466
Total cargo (tons)	1,992,029	1,717,091	2,024,032	1,738,861	2,127,772	2,144,445	2,144,445	2,210,776	2,220,733	2,284,184	2,348,024	2,307,025
Singapore Changi Airport												
Total aircraft arrivals and departures	231,926	240,360	263,593	301,711	324,722	343,765	341,386	346,334	360,490	373,201	386,042	382,342
Total passengers	37,694,824	37,203,978	42,038,777	46,543,845	51,181,804	53,726,087	54,093,070	55,448,964	58,698,039	62,219,573	65,627,356	68,282,840
Total cargo (tons)		1,752,121	1,700,892	1,826,381	1,867,748	1,840,955	1,850,000	1,870,000	2,000,000	2,140,000	2,140,000	
Dubai International Airport												
Total flights landed	270,376	280,476	307,283	326,341	344,656	373,534	357,842	407,315	420,870	413,940	414,252	
Total passengers	37,441,440	40,901,752	47,180,628	50,973,514	57,684,466	66,496,469	70,475,471	78,014,828	83,669,850	88,242,099	89,149,388	86,396.757
Total cargo (tons)	1,731,808	1,829,257	2,070,040	1,995,353	2,146,833	2,450,533	2,077,445	2,357,567	2,418,256	2,510,557	2,486,830	

Note: Total flights include scheduled, nonscheduled, and military flights.

Sources: Airport authorities' annual reports.

International Airport have followed a similar pattern of growth during the last decade in all the relevant indicators: total flights, total passengers, and total cargo tonnage. Dubai International has advanced most rapidly in numbers of passengers, but otherwise figures for all three are of a comparable order of magnitude. The same story is graphically portrayed in figure 3.3a–c.

(a)

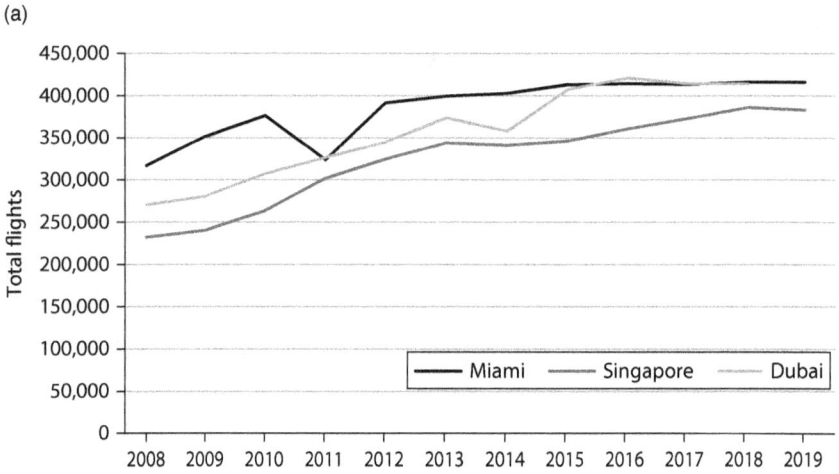

(b)

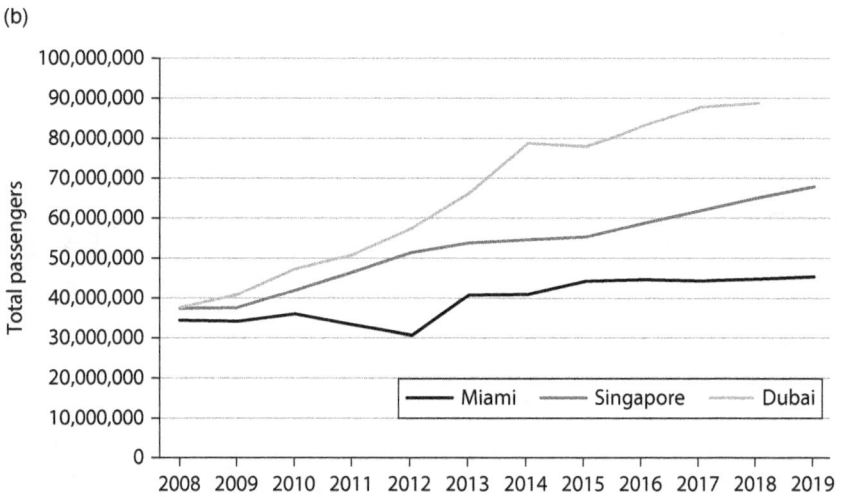

3.3 International airports compared: Miami International, Singapore Changi, and Dubai International.

(c)

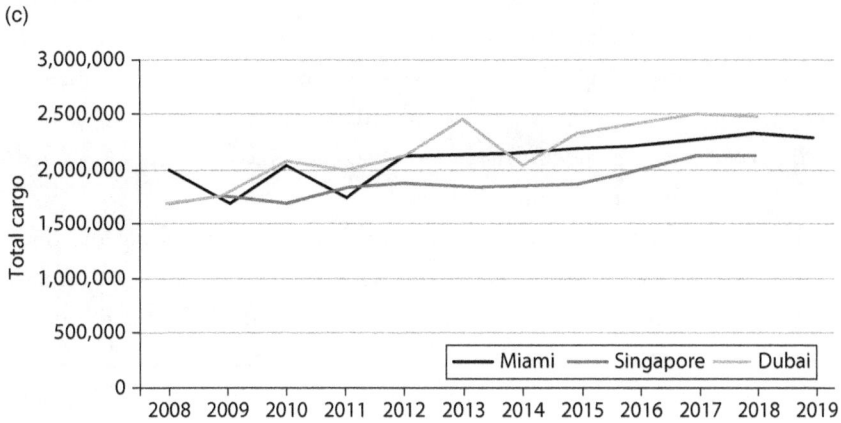

3.3 (continued)

Table 3.3 presents some final statistics for the three cities. The Miami metropolitan area is the largest and Singapore, built on a tiny island, the smallest. Yet
Singapore's domestic product is far larger, more than doubling those of the other
two cities. Because, at almost 6 million, Singapore's population is also the largest, its GDP per capita and per capita income come close to comparable figures

TABLE 3.3 Summary statistics for Miami-Dade County,
Dubai, and Singapore

	Size of metro area (sq km)	Population of metro area	GDP (USD)	GDP per capita (USD)	Median household income (USD)	Per capita income (USD)
Miami-Dade	6,296.7	2,761,581	164,632	59,615.15	55,998 (2018)	26,838
Dubai	4,112.9	3,192,275	114,539	35,880.17	61,914 (2014)	
Singapore	725.7	5,638,676	356,829	63,282.40	81,120 (2019)	24,339,

Sources: Miami-Dade County, *Analysis of Current Economic Trends*, 2018; Dubai Statistics Center,
2018; Department of Statistics, Singapore, 2018.

for Miami. Per capita figures, however, are averages that are sensitive to extreme values. A class of very wealthy bankers and real estate entrepreneurs in Miami tends to pull these averages upward. However, when median statistics, which are not sensitive to extreme values, are considered, the overall economic superiority of Singapore becomes evident. The median household income in the city-state is much larger than that of Miami.

These differences must be taken into account when comparing the three areas to one another as well as to others. Nevertheless, their strategic similarity as nodal points for vast regions justifies their being singled out and brought together for analysis. In their own different ways, all three managed to climb up the ranks of the capitalist world economy, from insignificant peripheries to areas with a central role in its contemporary operation and future development. While recognizing this undeniable achievement, the dangers and limitations facing their future—from rising inequality to the parallel rising of the oceans—must also be taken into account. These issues are discussed in detail in the conclusion to this book.

Downtown Miami.
(Courtesy of Zeinab K. Chatila)

The American Airlines Arena, Miami. Visible behind it is the Freedom Tower, a museum to Cuban exiles, which was built as a replica of the Giralda Tower of Seville and originally the headquarters of the *Miami News*.
(Courtesy of Zeinab K. Chatila)

The Pérez Art Museum Miami (PAMM). In the background is the One Thousand Museum Tower Building was completed in 2019. Designed by the Iranian architect Zaha Hadid, it is the first exoskeleton building in Florida.
(Courtesy of Zeinab K. Chatila)

The Miami Beach shoreline. Biscayne Bay can be seen in the background.
(Courtesy of Zeinab K. Chatila)

The Miami Marlins baseball stadium. The bond required to build it nearly bankrupted the city and led to the recall referendum of the then Miami mayor, Carlos Alvarez.
(Courtesy of Zeinab K. Chatila)

The Ermita de la Caridad del Cobre Church. Built with the contributions of Cuban exiles, it sits on Biscayne Bay facing toward Cuba.
(Courtesy of Zeinab K. Chatila)

The Eternal Flame, located at S.W. 8th Street, Little Havana. It was built in honor of the fallen at the Bay of Pigs. The caption reads: "To the Martyrs of the Assault Brigade 2506. April 17, 1961."

(Courtesy of Zeinab K. Chatila)

Domino Park in Little Havana, Miami.
(Courtesy of Zeinab K. Chatila)

CHAPTER 4

SINGAPORE

From Fishing Village to World-Class Metropolis

WITH THE COLLABORATION OF LARRY LIU

T he story of the rise of Singapore to its present world-class status among other Asian Tiger states (Taiwan, Hong Kong, South Korea) has been told many times and in many different ways by journalists, social scientists, and development experts. Most accounts sound common themes, such as the decisive character of the republic's early leadership, its incorruptibility, and its commitment to capitalism as the only way out of underdevelopment. Other features of the "Singapore model" have garnered less attention. One of them is the refusal of the city-state's leaders to follow "expert" advice by international agencies and consultants who were focused more on short-term expedient solutions than on long-term development outcomes.

An example is the decision to relocate the international airport to Changi, a former British Royal Air Force base located about nine kilometers from the city's center. In the early 1970s, a series of international consultants recommended the addition of a second runway to the existing Paya Lebar airport, close to the central business district, as the least costly and fastest way to alleviate air traffic congestion. The proposal was initially accepted by the Singaporean cabinet, but then Prime Minister Lee Kuan Yew intervened: "I was not satisfied and wanted the option of moving to Changi to be re-considered. I have flown over Boston's Logan Airport and been impressed that the noise footprint of planes landing and taking off was over water. A second runway at Paya Lebar would take aircraft right over the heart of Singapore city."[1] In June 1975, the Singaporean government approved moving the international airport from Paya Lebar to Changi. In Lee's words, it was "the best $1.5 billion investment we ever made."[2]

A second example was the policy of the Singapore Civil Aviation Authority to deliberately build over capacity, again contradicting immediate cost-benefit calculations and foreign advice. Within three years of Changi's inauguration and when capacity at Terminal I was still ample, the government approved construction of a new terminal. Even as the Civil Aviation Authority was celebrating the inauguration of Terminal II, it announced plans to build a third.[3]

The intent of that policy was to signal to airlines flying to South and Southeast Asia that Singapore was their natural hub because of its superior facilities and capacity and that it was better than the competition from other major airports nearby such as Bangkok and Kuala Lumpur. Through such forward-looking and well-planned government policies, the Singaporean economy grew steadily, reaching a GDP of US$339 billion in 2020 and a GDP per capita of US$59,797, which is higher than the GDP of many European countries.[4] If capitalism was the engine that promoted Singapore's forward march in the global economy, it was *dirigiste* capitalism guided by a committed political leadership.

THE EARLY YEARS

Ancient Singapore

The Kingdom of Singapura was founded in 1299 by Sang Nila Utama, the Srivijayan prince from Palembang (South Sumatra, Indonesia). Singapura is Sanskrit for "Lion City," after Sang was fascinated by the beauty of a lion he encountered on the island.[5] During the fourteenth century, Singapore was known as Temasek and was a trading port under the influence of Java, the Siamese kingdoms (Thailand), and India.[6] The last raja of Singapura was toppled in 1398 after a naval invasion by the Majapahits, who controlled the island thereafter.[7] In 1613, Portuguese raiders burned down the settlement, and it remained in obscurity for nearly two centuries.[8] The Dutch then conquered the Malacca peninsula in 1641, displacing the Portuguese.[9]

British Colony, 1819–1942, 1945–1959

The British, in turn, displaced the Dutch in 1819, when the British commander Stamford Raffles seized Singapore and made the island a port.[10] The sultanate that included Singapore was internally divided between Sultan Tengku Abdul Rahman and his older brother Tengku Long, who was living in exile. The British East India Company smuggled Tengku Long into Singapore and declared him the rightful sultan, in exchange for the right to create a trading post in the port. The British introduced a free-trade policy without taxing trade, and the island immediately attracted migrant groups such as Malays, Chinese, Arabs, and Indians.[11]

In the early years, the largest immigrant group was the Malays, but by the 1830s the Nanyang Chinese, who had earlier settled throughout Southeast Asia, had become dominant.[12] Later Chinese migrants came from the southern provinces of China (Guangdong, Fujian), the flow picking up with the end of the Qing dynasty's ban on emigration.[13] The migration pattern was heavily skewed toward males, who either left their family in China or went to Singapore without a family. Women were discouraged from migrating. To handle the vagaries of migration, men joined secret societies tied to their ancestral hometown or dialect group (Hokkien, Teochiu, Cantonese, and Hakka). The secret societies organized unskilled labor and controlled economic niches like shipping, transportation of cotton, gambling, and prostitution. Some merchant middlemen became quite wealthy, but most migrants were poor laborers who were forced to work for low wages while paying off the cost of their voyage. The Chinese specialized in different activities: the Hokkien became active in trade, shipping, banking, and industry; the Teochiu worked in agricultural and rubber production; the Cantonese were artisans; and the Hakka or Hainanese worked as servants, sailors, and unskilled laborers.[14] The Fujianese developed a thriving import trade in Fujianese tea, which was avidly consumed among Chinese immigrants in Malaya.[15]

Malay migrants were fishermen, boatmen, woodcutters, or carpenters. Indians tended to be soldiers posted by the British East India Company. Some were convicts, making Singapore a detention center for Indian prisoners. Rather than punishing the convicts, Raffles adopted the policy of rehabilitating them as brickmakers, carpenters, ropemakers, printers, weavers, tailors, and construction workers.[16] A unique community were the *peranakan* Chinese, who were Chinese men intermarrying with Malay women and their descendants and who displayed a mixture of Chinese, Malay, and Western cultures.[17]

Over the course of two centuries, Singapore experienced a substantial increase in its population (see table 4.1), which rapidly changed from being Malay-dominant to Chinese-dominant (see tables 4.1 and 4.2). The main drivers of immigration were the high demand for labor in public works, the free-trade environment, and

TABLE 4.1 Population of Singapore, 1819–2021

Year	Population
1819	~ 5,000
1824	10,683
1840	35,389
1860	81,734
1881	137,722
1901	226,842
1921	418,358
1950	938,144
1970	2,074,507
1990	3,047,132
2010	5,076,732
2021	5,453,566

Source: Department of Statistics, Singapore, https://www.singstat.gov.sg/modules/infographics/population. For 1819–1921, see Saw Swee-Hock, "Population Trends in Singapore, 1819–1967," *Journal of Southeast Asian History* 10, no.1 (1969): 36–49. For 1950–2021, see Department of Statistics, Singapore.

TABLE 4.2 Percent distribution of Singapore population by race, 1824–2017

Year	Chinese, %	Malays, %	Indians, %	Others, %
1824	31.0	60.2	7.1	1.7
1836	45.9	41.9	9.9	2.6
1849	52.9	32.2	11.9	3.0
1871	56.8	27.1	11.9	4.0
1891	67.1	19.7	8.8	4.3
1911	72.4	13.8	9.2	4.7
1931	75.1	11.7	9.1	4.2
1947	77.8	12.1	7.4	2.8
1967	74.4	14.5	8.1	3.0
1997	77.0	13.9	7.7	1.3
2017	74.3	13.4	9.0	3.2

Source: For 1824–1967, see Saw Swee-Hock, "Population Trends in Singapore, 1819–1967," *Journal of Southeast Asian History* 10, no.1 (1969). For 1997–2017, see Data.gov.sg: https://data.gov.sg/dataset/resident-population-by-ethnicity-gender-and-age-group?view_id=ce206ba3-ea36-46fe-9e9a-6351a9c6805f&resource_id=f9dbfc75-a2dc-42af-9f50-425e4107ae84.

the legal stability provided by British colonial rule.[18] Early political domination by the business community, which had a high demand for unskilled labor, meant that there were virtually no immigration restrictions under British rule.[19] The migration level continued to be very high in the early part of the twentieth century before consolidating at a lower figure until the beginning of the twenty-first century. At this point, the proportion and number of the foreign-born population picked up again (see table 4.3). As of June 2021, the resident population of Singapore (citizens and permanent residents) was 3.98 million, while the nonresident population was 1.46 million (26 percent of total).[20]

Raffles noted the geographic significance of Singapore in a letter to a friend, in which he considered Singapore to be "by far the most important station in the East; and, as far as naval superiority and commercial interests are concerned, of much higher value than whole continents of territory."[21] Raffles was an enlightened ruler and created government regulations that made property sales transparent, ensured free-trade status, and followed English common law (except in Malay matters of religion, marriage, and inheritance, which were regulated by Muslim law). He believed in preventive forms of crime regulation rather than punishment and introduced monetary payment for nonviolent offenses. He shut

TABLE 4.3 Singapore foreign-born population, 1921–2015

Year	Foreign-born population	Percentage of total
1921	301,913	72.2
1931	358,291	64.2
1947	411,716	43.9
1957	515,751	35.7
1970	530,883	25.6
1980	527,153	21.8
1990	727,262	24.1
2000	1,351,691	34.5
2010	2,164,794	42.6
2015	2,543,638	45.3

Source: For 1921–1980, see Swee-Hock, Saw. 2012. *The Population of Singapore*, 3rd Edition. Singapore: Institute of Southeast Asian Studies, pp. 62, 64. For 1990–2015, see Macrotrends.net: https://www.macrotrends.net/countries/SGP/singapore/immigration-statistics.

down gambling dens and taxed the sale of liquor and opium. He abolished slavery in 1823, although debt bondage remained a common form of financing migration to Singapore. Raffles left Singapore for Britain in 1823. In 1824, the Anglo-Dutch Treaty confirmed British claims over Singapore and Malacca, while Indonesia reverted to Dutch control. With the Dutch out of the way, Britain in turn forced Malay rulers to cede Singapore to the full control of the British East India Company.[22] In 1826, Singapore joined the Straits Settlement under the jurisdiction of the British Raj.[23]

Until the end of the 1860s, Chinese and Malay piracy threatened the Singapore trade route, but it was stamped out through improvements in British ship technology and an agreement with Ibrahim, prime minister of Johore, and the Qing Empire to crack down on piracy. By midcentury, only a few kilometers close to the port were developed, while the interior was dense jungle and mangrove swamps. Singapore's attempts to introduce plantation agriculture failed. The exceptions were the thriving pepper plantations[24] and, since the 1890s, following the rise of automobiles, rubber plantations.[25]

Successful entrepôt trade and plantation production created affluent Chinese businessmen who were Anglicized and culturally identified with the British Empire. They were eager to associate with British royals and sent their children to British universities. They financially supported Britain's efforts during World War I and celebrated the British military victory. Simultaneously, Singapore Chinese businessmen also retained ties to their ancestral homeland and, thanks to their British citizenship, were confident in going back and forth between China and the island colony. The Qing rulers and later the Nationalists under Sun Yat-sen cultivated cultural connections with the Singapore Chinese via clubs, debating societies, Chinese-language schools, and newspapers. Thus there developed a division between the British-oriented Chinese and the China-oriented Chinese. This division was to have significant political consequences later.

Singapore sat out World War I and profited during the Roaring Twenties from tin and rubber sales, but the Great Depression in the 1930s hit it hard. The government limited immigration with the Immigration Restriction Ordinance of 1930 and the Aliens Ordinance of 1933. The latter set quotas on immigrants and landing fees for aliens. The interwar period also resulted in overseas Chinese political activism, as both the Nationalist Kuomintang (KMT) and the Chinese Communist Party (CCP) set up local branches. Chinese Singaporean businesspeople funded the anti-Japanese resistance of China and organized a boycott of Japanese goods. In the end, however, Japan invaded and then seized Singapore in 1942, treating the Chinese population most harshly. On arrival, the Japanese massacred between 25,000 and 50,000 Singaporean Chinese and subjected the rest to beatings and executions. Those with wealth were forced to contribute funding for the Japanese war effort.[26]

With the Japanese surrender in August 1945, the British regained control over the island. Their first major act was the fateful decision to split Singapore from Malaya, which had hitherto been the regional capital for British rule. When talk of a Malaysian Federation emerged in the early 1960s, it became a contentious and fraught process, especially for the Kuala Lumpur Malay elite, who saw their power threatened by the inclusion of Chinese-dominated Singapore.[27]

In 1953, the colonial government implemented constitutional reform, which introduced legislative elections set for 1955. This election resulted in the formation of two major political parties, the Singapore Labour Front (LF) led by the Sephardic-Jewish lawyer David Marshall and the People's Action Party (PAP) led by the young Cambridge-educated lawyer, Lee Kuan Yew. PAP was divided between Lee's moderate wing and the radical leftist trade union wing under Lim Chin Siong. Lee was the undisputed party leader because he served as defense lawyer for the influential trade unions. LF and PAP were both anti-imperialist parties, promising their voters a push toward independence from the British Empire.[28]

LF won the first election, and David Marshall became Singapore's first chief minister. Marshall was the first proponent of multilingualism and mutual respect between communities.[29] He faced two powerful opponents. The radical trade unions struck against the ruling government even when there was no wage-bargaining issue. Marshall also faced opposition from the British governor, Sir Robert Black, who interfered in ministerial appointments. Due to lack of compromise, Marshall resigned and was succeeded by LF's other leader, Lim Yew Hock. Lim successfully negotiated statehood for Singapore, passed a citizenship law to provide nationality to all individuals born in Singapore and Malaya, another law to complete Malayanization of the civil service, and an education law to declare the four main languages—English, Chinese (Mandarin), Malay, and Tamil—valid for instruction.[30] In 1957, Lim ordered the imprisonment of the radical communist wing of the PAP, which allowed the moderates under Lee Kuan Yew to consolidate their power.[31]

Self-Government Administration, 1959–1963

The second legislative election in 1959 was handily won by Lee's PAP, which has continued to rule Singapore to the present without interruption. Lee became the nation's founding prime minister. PAP was well organized and had a platform of honest efficient government, social and economic reform to promote development, and union with the Federation of Malaya. The last-mentioned became a sticking point within PAP. Lee favored unification with Malaya because he felt that Singapore needed to integrate into a bigger market to remain viable. In a September 1962 referendum, 70 percent of Singaporeans voted for unification with Malaya to form the nation of Malaysia, which formally emerged in September 1963. The Malay leader, Tunku Abdul Rahman, was originally opposed to the merger with Singapore because it would detract from his explicitly Malay nationalist agenda. However, he was even more afraid of a communist takeover of Singapore if the Lee government failed. Tunku wanted Singapore to become the New York of Malaya, not a "second Cuba."[32] Consequently, he demanded the arrest of Singaporean communist leaders, with which Lee happily complied as it reduced internal opposition against his rule.[33]

Lee Kuan Yew delivered on his developmentalist agenda by creating investor tax incentives to build export-oriented manufacturing products and protective tariffs against imports. The government set up an industrial estate in the Jurong area and attracted foreign labor-intensive textile firms. To pacify the masses, Lee's government created the Housing and Development Board (HDB), which was tasked with clearing slums and constructing public housing. The government also substantially hiked education spending to improve literacy.[34]

Malaysian Federation, 1963–1965

The merger revealed the fundamental fault lines between the Malayan and Singaporean regimes. The Federation was brought up in the Singapore parliamentary election, which gave Lee's PAP another landslide, but it faced substantial opposition from Indonesia, which considered itself the rightful hegemon in the region. Political harmony in the duopoly was further strained by a Malaysian propaganda campaign directed at Singapore Malays to demand more government subsidies. Lee believed in meritocracy, the promotion of the best and brightest.[35] This position implicitly favored the educated and business-minded Chinese over the Malays.[36]

Lee advocated for a "Malaysian Malaysia" (instead of a Malay Malaysia), where all citizens were equal irrespective of race.[37] In contrast, Tunku and the Malaysian UMNO (United Malays National Organization) held the view that the Bumiputra ("sons of the soil," i.e., Malays) had a right to control the political institutions and collect rentlike benefits (scholarships, civil service quotas, trade licenses, land) in exchange for not interfering with the Chinese doing business on Malaysian soil.[38]

The political conflict was expressed in the April 1964 Malaysian general elections when PAP won one seat in Malaysia, which UMNO regarded as a political threat. In July 1965, Singapore's finance minister, Goh Keng Swee, negotiated with UMNO for Singaporean independence.[39] Tunku finally expelled Singapore from the Federation (the vote occurred with Singapore abstaining), in August 1965. The expulsion led to the founding of the independent Republic of Singapore. Many knowledgeable observers, including Lee Kuan Yew himself, had serious doubts about the country's economic survival.

REPUBLIC OF SINGAPORE AND LEE KUAN YEW, 1965-1990

When asked a few years later whether Singapore's leadership had "a model in mind," Lee Kuan Yew replied, "No, we borrowed in an eclectic fashion elements of what Hong Kong was doing, what Switzerland was doing, what Israel was doing, and we improvised. I also went to Malta, to see how they ran the dry docks."[40]

Countries and cities seeking to establish themselves in the world economy ceaselessly study one another and copy from one another, but the results are not uniform. An important reason is what economists call "path dependence" or the inertial force of existing institutions and culture, so that what happens today will largely determine what will take place tomorrow.[41] If, for example, a country is endowed with a favorable geographic position, if it has an educated and disciplined workforce, and if its laws are administered impartially and fairly, it will be in a much better position to launch an economic takeoff than if the opposite is the case.

In the case of Singapore, path dependence was a decidedly mixed process. Its favorable geographic position was balanced by its tiny size, just 580 square kilometers, and the existence of a dynamic, business-oriented middle class confronted a militant, Communist-led union movement and a strong nationalist bent among some members of the business class. This segment supported stronger ties with China and was highly critical of the pro-English attitude of Lee and PAP. In the words of one of the radical pro-China leaders, Tan Lark Sye, "If we do not take steps to preserve our culture now—in 40 or 50 years, we shall no longer call ourselves Chinese."[42]

All of this is to say that the popularized view of Singapore as a success story riding on Chinese business acumen and British legal tradition is only partially accurate. The outcome was not a foregone conclusion, and the direction that history took depended on three key factors. First, Lee Kuan Yew and his faction of the PAP were resolutely opposed to becoming "a communist outpost of Peking."[43] The second factor was the strong support of the British government, the still-powerful colonial power in the region. The third was the anticommunist stance of Malaysia under Tunku Abdul Rahman and his organization (UMNO), who supported Lee's decision to eliminate the communist wing of his own party.[44]

Lee's main concern upon independence was to ensure the "survival" of his nation and people.[45] This was made complicated by Singapore's dependence on Malaysian raw materials, most importantly, fresh water.[46] On the flip side, he no longer had to accommodate Malay nationalist priorities. He could thus pursue his political vision, which included (1) a multicultural framework on cultural relations, (2) authoritarianism in politics, and (3) developmentalism in economic policy. Lee believed that the high incomes generated by economic growth could sustain Singapore's national defense, which was necessary to fend off Indonesian and Malaysian attempts at hegemony.[47] The three main pillars of the Singaporean system have been laid out by Chua Beng Huat, who argued that PAP received electoral power by combining social democracy (public housing, trade union representation in parliament) with state capitalism (sovereign wealth fund, government-linked companies, state promotion of multinational corporations) and multicultural policies (bilingual policy, racial quotas in housing and employment) but to the exclusion of democracy and liberalism.[48] These priorities deserve further elaboration.

Multiculturalism

With respect to cultural policy, Lee advanced English first in both education and administration in order to attract foreign (especially U.S. and Western) investment. This policy would also signal to the three major ethnic groups (Chinese,

Malay, and Indian) that no ethnicity was above any other.[49] People would learn English and their respective mother tongue (Mandarin, Malay, Tamil) in school. In 1965, the government established a Constitutional Commission on Minority Rights, which was tasked with promoting ethnic and cultural diversity. It also promoted integrated schools and public housing. The latter was made possible by the fact that the newly created housing stock (mainly high-rises) was owned by the state and organized with strict racial quotas, thus overcoming the previous segregation in ethnic slums.[50] Ethnically mixed apartment blocks prevented the rise of self-enclosed and separatist communities, which are prevalent in cities such as Miami, where enclaves of different ethnic groups have a distinct socio-spatial dimension that has led to racial and ethnic tensions. At the same time, the government celebrated ethnic diversity and ethnic cultural festivals, with the caveat that, although "we come from different places, we are all Singaporeans now."[51] Most importantly, the race riots of the early 1950s had to be prevented from happening again.[52]

The housing estates were self-contained satellite towns with their own schools, supermarkets, malls, community hospitals, clinics, food courts, sports and recreational facilities, and train and bus stops connecting them to other parts of town. PAP used the housing estates politically by promising to upgrade the buildings in exchange for votes.[53] Most importantly, housing was sold to the occupants, turning them into homeowners. Widely diffused homeownership (93 percent in 2003) gave citizens a stake in society and made them more content without ballooning state social spending.[54]

The all-important message about the need for interethnic harmony is inculcated repeatedly in elementary and secondary school students. In social studies courses, students are exposed in detail to the experiences of ethnically fractured countries at war with themselves because of their internal divisions. Northern Ireland and Sri Lanka are studied from this perspective, and their experiences are contrasted with the successful management of ethnic divisions in Singapore.[55] While the Chinese are the absolute majority of the population, as well as economically and politically dominant, this deft management of interethnic relations has prevented potentially fatal confrontations, particularly with Malays, whose home country is next door.[56] It helped that the winning Chinese party was not pro-China, but pro-Britain, and that it militantly opposed a possible takeover by Chinese communists.

Authoritarian Politics

The small elite at the top of the PAP agreed from the start on two principles: first, that Western-style capitalism was the only way to move the economy forward and, second, that Western-style democracy was *not* the right political model for the country because it would risk electoral takeover by the communist extreme left, followed by the virtual annexation of the small island to China. Instead, PAP opted for a form of "guided" democracy in which freedom of expression was allowed, if kept within prescribed bounds, and elections were regularly staged, to be invariably won by the ruling party.[57] The PAP leadership offered the Singaporean citizens a reasonable deal: political compliance in exchange for tangible economic benefits, including employment and housing, plus the promise of a still better future.

The elections after independence registered continued PAP electoral victories without notable opposition. The government pressured voters to support PAP or risk being excluded from public housing programs. Opposition politicians were silenced by arbitrary detention via the Internal Security Act.[58] The government has also used defamation lawsuits to bankrupt opposing political party candidates or disqualify them from running for office. Authorities have also gerrymandered electoral districts by converting single-member districts into group representation constituencies (GRC), which force political parties to nominate six candidates and win the entire GRC in order to win seats.[59]

Authoritarianism is not confined to party politics but also permeates the press, which became directly controlled by the state in the early 1970s.[60] Liberal theorists like Fareed Zakaria have criticized Singapore for advancing a form of political authoritarianism that cannot be reconciled with liberal capitalism.[61] Lee's reply was that the most capable, least corrupt rulers who raised people's standard of living deserved to be in power,[62] and that unstable, democratic government was worse than what Singapore had.[63] Furthermore, his theory was that Singapore was a small country that had only a few talents. These could not be split evenly across many political parties but had to be absorbed into the party-state.[64] With respect to the harsh treatment of the political opposition, Lee retorted that communists, whom he fought against in the 1960s, were much worse.[65]

Economic Developmentalism

Independence made Singapore's economy more vulnerable because of emerging tariff barriers with Malaysia. However, Singapore was helped by the normalization of relations with Indonesia, which had been very hostile during the brief Federation era.[66] The Lee government pivoted the economy toward the wealthy countries (first the United States and Japan; later South Korea, China, and the Gulf[67]). It wooed foreign capital but realized the difficulty posed by restive labor relations and strikes. After fresh elections in 1968, in which PAP took all the seats in parliament, the government passed new labor laws that permitted longer working hours, reduced holidays, and gave employers more autonomy for hiring, firing, and promotion. Strikes could only be held after a secret ballot majority vote of union members.

The National Trades Union Congress (NTUC), the national labor union, agreed to the law in exchange for the government's promise to limit worker exploitation; to allow individual workers to appeal unjust treatment; and to create a Central Provident Fund (CPF), a mandatory saving scheme to guarantee worker pensions, unemployment compensation, sick leave, a medical savings account, and even down payment for housing purchases. The labor laws established a tripartite (employer, labor, government) industrial relations structure that enhanced productivity, attracted foreign investments, and virtually eliminated labor strikes.[68] These laws also created a firm link between NTUC and PAP, as many unionists became PAP politicians.[69]

While Singapore has no minimum wage law, the tripartite National Wage Council (NWC) produces a nonbinding wage agreement that is widely implemented.[70] Controlling labor unrest was fundamental to the initial stages of economic development, which was based on attracting foreign capital to produce cheap manufactured goods for export.

With labor relations secure, and with tax incentives and full repatriation of profits and capital to foreign investors in place, the next part of the industrial strategy was to set up the Jurong Town Corporation to transform the southern coast of Singapore into an industrial estate.[71] Other smaller estates were formed in Kallang Park, Tanjong Rhu, Redhill, Tiong Bahru, and Tanglin Halt.[72] By the late 1970s, 271 factories employed 32,000 workers, mainly producing for export.[73] The government promised foreign investors prudent macroeconomic policies, including a state budget surplus and a stable Singapore dollar.[74] Few developing

countries would have been willing to tolerate Singapore's level of foreign investment and the power of foreign corporations in their economies. Singapore did
it because of the urgency of the economic situation following independence
and the strength of its government apparatus.[75] In 1974, the government created
Temasek Holdings, Singapore's sovereign wealth fund, to manage the country's
financial reserves. A second sovereign fund, GIC Private Limited, was founded in
1981 to manage foreign financial holdings. The significance of these wealth funds
is that, instead of channeling state resources toward improving living standards,
they were used to increase the economic power and autonomy of the state. "In
effect, Singapore exchanged an outflow of national savings for an inflow of private foreign capital."[76]

Singapore created at the same time a big oil industry, which included exploration rigs, oil refining, and oil storage centers. When the British announced a
military pullout in the early 1970s, the government successfully converted the
military facilities into a civilian, commercial shipyard for shipbuilding and
repair. By 1975, Singapore was the world's third-busiest port behind Rotterdam
and New York.[77]

The country's push to upgrade the content of exports from low-skilled,
labor-intensive production to high-skilled, high-technology production occurred
in the late 1970s.[78] For instance, the British pharmaceutical company Beecham
Pharmaceuticals set up a technologically advanced semisynthetic penicillin plant
in Singapore.[79] The next step in the development process was to attract foreign
multinationals to set up their regional headquarters for South Asia in Singapore.
Political stability combined with a rock-solid protection of private property
ensured that this policy succeeded.

The final step in this developmental saga was the creation of a formidable
banking and financial center. To attract corporate and individual deposits
throughout the region and provide facilities for increasingly complex financial
transactions, Singapore took advantage of its privileged strategic geographical
position midway between the financial centers of New York and London. Of
late, it has benefited from the political difficulties of the main regional financial center, Hong Kong, which is seriously wounded by the end of its political
autonomy from China. Banks and finance corporations have taken note and have
started to move their office facilities out of Hong Kong and into Singapore.[80] The
Global Investor Program fast-tracks permanent residency for rich individuals
from Asia who invest at least S$2.5 million in local businesses or have a family

office with at least S$200 million in assets; this program has become more popular thanks to the turmoil in Hong Kong and the raging pandemic in the rest of Southeast Asia.[81]

Every stage in the economic rise of Singapore has been accompanied by close collaboration with foreign capital—from foreign direct investment in factories producing low-tech goods for export to the fast rise of banking and financial services as the core of the city-state economy. Given the multiples critiques of how less developed countries have "opened up" to foreign capital,[82] the question is how Singapore accomplished this feat.

The answer boils down to two facts: first, an outstanding, competent, and honest civil service and, second, an unshakable dirigiste approach on the part of the government elite. The best and brightest of Singapore's young were sent abroad for training, and upon return they were employed in the civil service, paid at levels comparable to those in private industry, and given regular promotions and rewards. Combined with severe punishments given to those found guilty of corruption, this policy ensured a capable and efficient bureaucracy with which to implement government directives.[83]

The second factor involved a refusal by the Singaporean elite to leave the task of development solely in the hands of private capital. Instead, as already documented, Lee and his team closely monitored and directed the process from above. Instead of allowing salaries to Singaporean workers to be spent solely on consumption, the government implemented a forced savings scheme through the Central Provident Fund that provided a noninflationary way of financing works of infrastructure—ports, airports, roads, telecommunications, and mass transit: "Through helping to assure MNCs required rate of profitability, domestic savings also drew in the MNCs entrepreneurship, technology, and access to world markets."[84]

The combination of an incorruptible bureaucracy and a proactive stance toward private capital has been identified in prior studies as the key to the rise of a developmental state and to successful national development.[85] Singapore's history fully illustrates this point.

Singapore's economic development is reflected in GDP figures, which were only US$516 per capita in 1965, the year of independence (US$3,800 for the United States), but increased to US$62,700 in 2018, a much higher figure than comparable ones for its Southeast Asian neighbors. The trend is graphically illustrated in figure 4.1.

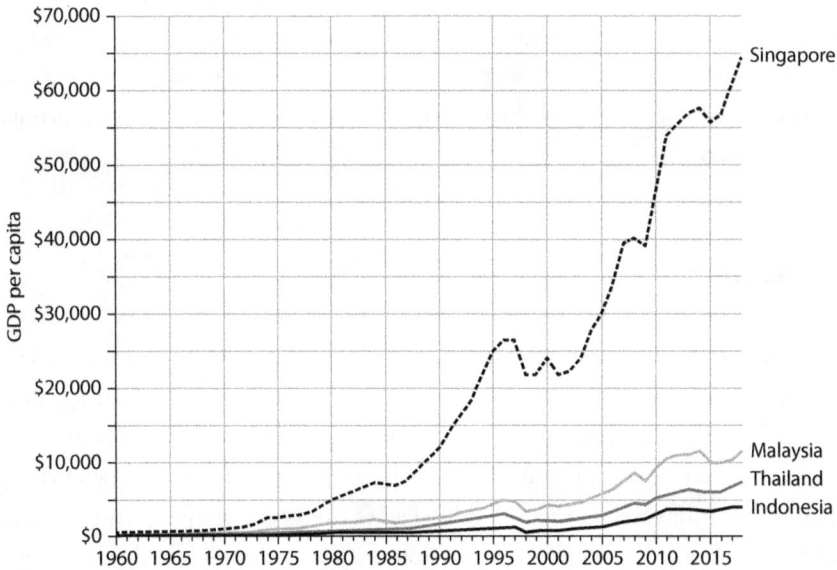

4.1 GDP per capita of Singapore (in 2016$USD).

Source: World Bank

The outstanding economic record of Singapore has also heavily depended on foreign migration. The continuing high GDP growth rates depend on both low- and high-skilled migrant workers. This has produced some nativist resentment against immigrants, whose children begin to compete for school spots,[86] and it has also created overcrowding in public transit, on beaches, and in parks.[87] The ultra-low fertility rate of domestic women (1.1 in 2020) makes Singapore's economy extremely dependent on foreign workers.[88]

As of 2019, 24.5 percent of the population (1.4 million) were foreign-born workers. About a million arrived on work permits for low- or semiskilled workers that year. They are drawn from India, Bangladesh, China, Myanmar, and the Philippines. Low-skilled workers are not allowed to switch employers and are deported if fired. High-skilled workers arrive via the Employment Pass scheme, which is fairly flexible.[89] They tend to come from the United States, Britain, France, Australia, Japan, and South Korea. Since the 1990s, high-skilled workers have also come from China and India, which explains the rise in the Indian population share from 7 to 9 percent. Since 2011, anti-immigrant resentment has resulted in a tightening of migration policy. Singaporeans, who struggle to find work, believe that foreigners are competing for their jobs.[90] However, Lee Kuan Yew always emphasized that immigration is essential to Singapore and can only function with the American concept of multiculturalism, welcoming people from all countries.[91]

CONCLUSION

The rise of Singapore from a fishing village to a world-class city can be attributed primarily to a charismatic and pragmatic leadership that took advantage of a limited set of assets from the start. A strategic geographical location and a tradition of efficient administration under the British Empire were some of these pluses. But against them, the leadership had to overcome nearly insurmountable obstacles—from the lack of natural resources, even water, to trade union agitation and a powerful political opposition bent on an alternative project—to convert the island into an outpost of the rising Chinese empire.

Max Weber's point about the transformative power of charisma finds no better illustration than the experience of this city-state.[92] Indeed, Singapore was not transformed; it was built from scratch through an integrated series of audacious policy decisions. These turned the island from a cheap labor source of manufacturing for export into a commercial, financial, and transportation hub for the entire region.

Each step in the process presented its own challenges that had to be met. Air traffic congestion forced the relocation of the airport from Paya Lebar to distant Changi. Lack of water and the attempt by Malaysia to increase water costs by a usurious rate (from $0.008 per cubic meter to $0.045) led the government to invest in a massive water desalinization and water reclamation project.[93]

Lastly, the city literally ran out of land as its economy and population steadily increased. Singapore responded to this constraint by making more land through massive importation of foreign sand and later by resorting to the Dutch impoldering method.[94] As a result, Singapore's landmass increased from 580 square kilometers to 720. The reclamation of land from the sea as a feature of the built environment is also seen in other emerging global cities—Dubai, for example—as well as in global hopefuls such as Lagos. Like other successful new global cities, Singapore has gradually transformed its economy to be grounded on the four pillars of maritime and air commerce; financial and banking services; construction and real estate; and tourism and leisure.[95]

Growing and supporting the tourist sector has been particularly difficult given the location of the island, far away from the major tourist-generating regions of western Europe and North America. To stimulate tourism, as in Dubai and Miami, the city has built distinct architecture and amenities, such as Gardens by the Bay, to bolster its international appeal. The government has even gone against its ethos of asceticism and discipline to allow the building of a gambling casino in the islet of Santosa to compete with the surging gambling industry of Macao.[96] The casino is open mainly to foreigners and, to discourage locals from visiting it, the government charges Singaporeans a very steep entry fee.[97]

Singapore's economy is now solidly established as a new global economy. As shown in table 4.4, the number of airport passengers arriving in the city-state far surpasses the number arriving in Miami, and the number of tourists

TABLE 4.4 Indicators of economic activity in Miami, Singapore, and Dubai

	Miami	Singapore	Dubai
Container traffic (TEU[a]), 2020[b]	1.066	36.6	13.5
Airport passengers, 2019[c]	45,924,466	68,300,000	86,396,757
International visitors, millions, 2018[d]	5.8	14.67	15.93
Construction spending, billions (USD)[e]	$18.7 (2019)	$22.1 (2021)	$3.2 (2018)
Median household income[f]	$55,998 (2017)	$81,120 (2019)	$61,914 (2014)

[a] Twenty-foot equivalent unit.

[b] Miami: Florida Ports Council, https://flaports.org/ports/portmiami/. Singapore and Dubai: "Top 50 Ports in the World in 2015," World Shipping Council, https://www.worldshipping.org/top-50-ports.

[c] Port Authority of New York and New Jersey, *2019 Airport Traffic Report*: https://www.panynj.gov/content/dam/airports/statistics/statistics-general-info/annual-atr/ATR2019.pdf.

[d] Miami: https://www.travelweekly.com/North-America-Travel/Insights/International-visitors-fuel-record-tourism-numbers-for-Orlando-Miami. Other cities: Mastercard: https://newsroom.mastercard.com/wp-content/uploads/2019/09/GDCI-Global-Report-FINAL-1.pdf.

[e] Miami: https://ccorpinsights.com/wp-content/uploads/2020/10/CCORP20Q3_MarketOverview-v1-MIA.pdf; Dubai: Meed: https://www.meed.com/dubai-construction-must-get-lean-in-2020/.

[f] Miami: Miami-Dade County, *Analysis of Current Economic Trends, Miami* (2018): http://archive.miamigov.com/Finance/CAFR/City%20Of%20Miami%20Comprehensive%20Annual%20Financial%20Report%20For%20the%20Fiscal%20Year%20Ended%20September%2030,%202018%20(Ev)%20SECURED.pdf. Singapore: Department of Singapore Statistics: https://tablebuilder.singstat.gov.sg/table/TS/M810361. Dubai: Dubai Statistics Center: https://www.dsc.gov.ae/Report/T%2001.pdf.

is almost triple the number coming to Miami, despite Miami's fame as a prime tourist destination. In maritime container traffic, Singapore is in a category by itself, doubling that of Dubai and being thirty times the corresponding figure for Miami. When median incomes, which eliminate the effect of positive outliers, are compared, Singapore easily outranks other emerging global cities, exceeding the figure for Dubai by almost $20,000 and that for Miami by $25,000.

Going forward, arguably the principal challenge facing Singapore is the death of its founder and the consequent fragmentation of the political leadership. Lee Kuan Yew died in March 2015, and immediately conflicts emerged among his children, especially between the new prime minister, Lee Hsien Loong (LHL), and his brother Hsien Yang (LHY). The latter went so far as to leave the PAP and join a new opposition party, the Progress Singapore Party (PSP). Rumors are that LHL is grooming his own son, Li Hongyi, the director of a government technology firm, to succeed him as prime minister, although Hongyi denies interest in a political career.[98] These signs of conflict at the top are entirely predictable. Another central concept in Weber's political sociology—the routinization of charisma—is helpful in understanding present developments.[99] With the disappearance of the original charismatic figure, its successors are likely to revert to more self-seeking pursuits, including competition to inherit the mantle of the leader. In the process, the symbols and ideals inherited from the charismatic figure are likely to become routinized into rituals and ceremonies aimed at keeping the loyalty of the faithful while leaders pursue their own goals.[100]

So far, the PAP has managed to retain its iron hold on political power, and the famed incorruptibility and efficiency of the Singaporean bureaucracy have not been visibly tarnished. But signs of dissension have started to emerge. The founder of the PSP, Tan Cheng Bock, a former minister in the government, argued that the new political party was necessary because of the rising erosion of good governance, transparency, and accountability under the PAP regime.[101] While PSP failed to enter parliament, the main opposition, the Workers' Party, gained ten seats in the 2020 elections, more than in its entire history, and its leader, Pritam Singh, was appointed the first official leader of the opposition in Singapore history. However, the Workers' Party only fielded twenty-one candidates for ninety-three constituency seats. Hence, their objective is to check PAP from the opposition bench, not to displace PAP in power. Whether Singapore can continue its path forward as a global city with a formally Western-style democratic regime or fall back into the traditional, corrupt autocracy so common in its surrounding region depends on how the current struggles of succession and transmission of power play out. Routinization of charisma does not always lead to catastrophic outcomes, but the process is riddled with multiple obstacles.

Singapore's recent democratization trend raises the question of whether it is on a fundamentally different trajectory than Hong Kong, which is becoming more tightly controlled by mainland China and hence less democratic. The possibilities for democratization are much greater for Singapore because the first generation of leaders has left the political stage, similar to Taiwan's process of democratization initiated by Chiang Ching-kuo after the death of Chiang Kai-shek, and also because Singapore has been a sovereign country and, unlike Hong Kong, is not subject to external pressures to remain authoritarian. Importantly, from the perspective of global cities, Singapore might be able to attract foreign labor and capital much more easily than Hong Kong by combining rule of law with a modicum of liberal democratic norms.

Singapore, the seat of many multinational corporations doing business in southeast Asia.

The Marina Bay Sands, a casino resort. Its opening in 2010 marked Singapore's turn toward tourism.

The Supertree Grove Trees from the Lily Pond at Gardens by the Bay, which opened in 2012 and had over 50 million visitors by 2018.

ION Orchard Shopping Mall at Orchard Road. Orchard Road is a major tourist attraction and holds upscale department stores, restaurants, and coffeehouses.

Clarke Quay was named after Sir Andrew Clarke, Singapore's second governor (1873–1875). It contains many restaurants and nightclubs. River taxis and cruises ferry around tourists.

PART II

CHAPTER 5

GLOBAL HOPEFULS

An Overview

T he preceding chapters discussed the evolution of cities and their interaction with the rise of the capitalist world system, introduced and justified the concepts of "global cities" and "emerging global cities," and presented three studies of cities that, in our view, are emerging global cities. We must now focus attention on another group of cities that, for one reason or another, have not managed to reach global status. These include New Orleans, a city that in the past was regarded as a rising "star" in the competition for hegemony and power. New Orleans was the third-largest American city in size and economic significance in the mid-nineteenth century and a logical candidate for the role of "capital of the Americas," a role that was eventually assumed by Miami. The other two cities are actually larger than those studied so far, being economic and political centers of large countries but with aspirations to place themselves on the global scene. These are São Paulo, the largest and most economically important city in Brazil, and Lagos, which plays a similar role in Africa's largest country, Nigeria.

Before launching into a detailed analysis of this tercet, we wish to call attention to a near-universal phenomenon that serves to frame and focus these disparate experiences. This is the rising competition among urban places for some kind of extranational distinction and visibility. This phenomenon also justifies our prior analyses of a trio of "winners" in this universal contest. Those that tried but failed or are falling behind may be termed "global hopefuls." They are the subject of this chapter.

CITY RANKINGS

As Greg Clark writes, "With more than 200 indexes in circulation, global cities are now compared not just on business and investment performance. Quality of life, reputation and influence, infrastructure platforms, cultural amenities, knowledge assets, innovation potential, and resilience are all the subjects of objective and perception-based studies."[1] The *City Economic Capacity Index* is based on indicators measuring human capital, physical infrastructure, livability, and governance. Other rankings base their assessment of global cities on air connectivity, diversity, foreign direct investment, corporate headquarters, producer services, financial services, technology and media, and industry domination or hub status.[2] Knight Frank's *Prime Global Cities Index* assesses cities around the world against a set of metrics showing a city's global attractiveness in investment, wealth, and lifestyle.[3] The cities ranking at the top of the list have the highest numbers of high-net-worth individuals (HNWIs) and ultra-high-net-worth-individuals (UHNWIs), have the highest volume of private investment and the broadest international diversity of investors in real estate, possess the largest number of headquarters of major global firms, and have the most connected international airports.[4]

This approach establishes a tiered view of cities. They can be classified as belonging to one of three groups: established global cities, emerging global cities, and global hopefuls. Many of the global hopefuls acquired, at some point, a variety of transnational ingredients that placed them in visible positions with regard to the system's core.[5] While there are advantages to this approach, including the possibility of defining categories and metrics, it also has several disadvantages. Critiques of this hierarchical approach remark that a majority of studies on global cities tend to locate them in North America and Europe, with a few additional ones in Asia. These studies emphasize the "success" of these cities in terms of their central role in the organization of the world economy.[6] As noted in chapter 1, this literature has shown little interest in peripheral cities and their widespread failure to move beyond a dependent, subordinate position to the centers of power. According to this view, the group of truly global cities is extremely small.[7]

As Xuefei Ren and Roger Keil argue, "The term global city has entered everyday vocabulary, referring to an elite club of the most powerful and recognizable cities around the world."[8] They provide two distinct meanings of the term *global city*. Colloquially, it is "a descriptive, affirmative notion" frequently used by decision-makers "to draw attention to specific places." On the other hand, in its scholarly use, it is "a polysemic analytical term employed by critical urbanists to decipher the globalizing dimensions of contemporary urbanization."[9] According to these authors, in order to fully unpack the meaning of *global city*, it is first necessary to consider that the very use of the term "serves to glorify the status of particular cities in worldwide interurban competition."[10] The vision advanced by "growth coalitions"—private-public partnerships that aim to promote urban development—is largely the result of the "construction of 'models' of redevelopment and their circulation" through "global circuits of policy knowledge."[11] Models that are framed as success stories are reproduced in cities around the world, profoundly influencing their discursive practices, credentials, and networks of power.[12]

Dubai, Singapore, and Miami were able to combine an advantageous location—what Ruchir Sharma calls "geographic sweet spots"—with concrete actions that led them to open "their doors to the world, particularly to their neighbors."[13] All these cities had leaders who advanced policies that sought to transcend their city's regional and national economy, taking advantage of their strategic location and firmly grounding their efforts on political and economic stability. Moreover, they leveraged opportunities to gain a competitive edge thanks to their cities' comparative advantages and the presence of a legal system that was transparent, secure, and efficient.[14]

There is a rich literature that is critical of the use of global city hierarchies. Critiques emphasize the need to examine different kinds of cities, comparing, for instance, "the webs of relations which creatively draw cities into practical engagements with circulating policies, economic networks, transnational political influences or direct engagements with actors from specific other cities."[15] This body of literature has introduced the term *globalizing cities* to highlight "the diversity of pathways and the place- and region-specific patterns in and through which processes of globalization and urban restructuring were being articulated."[16] Studies have looked at the various ways in which transformations in the built environment have created "a new spatial order of cities" characterized by "a pattern of separate clusters of residential space, creating protective citadels and enclaves on the one side and constraining ghettos on the other, in a hierarchical relationship to each other."[17] Going beyond "city-centric assumptions," Neil Brenner and others talk about "planetary urbanization" and argue that we need to observe urbanization as a global process and understand that oceans, deserts, jungles, communications infrastructure, and so on are essential parts of the complex connections that represent the global fabric of urban life.[18]

Critics of the city hierarchy approach also argue against the assumption that a few cities serve as command-and-control nodes in the global economy, since the globalized economy is highly distributed and interconnected. Critics also argue that it is inaccurate to affirm that the emergence of global cities represents the disentanglement of urban growth from the development of national economies because, as cities such as Seoul demonstrate, the model of development used by nations plays a defining role in the relative importance of cities.[19] In China, where cities have also played a pivotal role in the country's economic miracle, urbanization grew and powerful city-centered economies emerged because the central government promoted the economic development of selected cities by assigning resources and advantageous politics to these places.[20] In brief, it is important to consider that not all globalizing cities have risen above their respective state governments as decision-makers in shaping economic policy and that the administrative, political, and regulatory role of the state is important in the evolution of the political economy of these cities.[21]

By comparing cities or studying various sectors and interconnectivities, without placing them in a global hierarchy, we gain a richer and more inclusive understanding of how cities are confronting current challenges with more options than merely attaining global status or taking unproductive approaches based on developmentalist metrics.[22] If we consider cities in developing countries such as those of the African continent "as dysfunctional, chaotic, failed, informal, or not globalized," we limit our understanding of them and help reinforce a frame of reference that "works to retain the Western city as the paradigmatic model against which all others are to be assessed."[23]

DUBAI, MIAMI, SINGAPORE—AND BEYOND

Despite these caveats in the academic critical literature, in the real world, urban elites struggle to achieve extraterritorial prominence by imitating those that have achieved this feat. In this context, Dubai, Miami, and Singapore are seen as extraterritorial entrepôts that have achieved central positions in the Middle East, Latin America, and Southeast Asia, respectively. These cities have moved beyond their national boundaries through a vast expansion of capital, trade, and talent. They have emerged as economic and financial hubs for entire regions.[24] Unlike established global cities like New York, London, and Tokyo, the emerging ones that occupy us here are restricted to certain regions of the world. They have risen from modest origins to play a strategic economic role, not as industrial centers but instead as logistical hubs that coordinate with production facilities located abroad and with the circulation of both commodities and capital in their respective regions.

These are cities "on the edge," not in the sense of the core-periphery model, but as emerging regions that intersect with the world in diverse ways. As Philip Kasinitz notes, these cities "remind us of a very important truth—that edges, where different networks, different cultures, different histories come together, is where a lot of the creative force of urban life happens."[25] Cities like Dubai, Miami, and Singapore are not defined by their size but by their function.[26] As Kasinitz suggests, they are not simply financial and commercial entrepôts, but examples of new trends in urban transformation, representing unique experiments that creatively use their geographical position. These cities have taken advantage of disjunctures in the global economy, harnessing "human movement, technological flow, and financial transfers" and positioning themselves in a global environment of "disorganized capitalism" where center-periphery models no longer apply.[27] There are much larger cities in the world today that do not have the same type of global connections because their economic and cultural influence is largely restricted to the nation-states in which they are situated.

Emerging global cities embody exceptional stories that challenge narratives on urban development because they run against dominant academic discussions that marginalize the kind of urban place that does not fit easily into existing hierarchies. As we discuss in the chapter on Miami and, at greater length in our book, *The Global Edge*, the confluence of diverse populations in this single geographic spot produced extensive change, leading to unexpected outcomes.[28] The present social, economic, and political character of Miami is the result of a process in which an immigrant minority, just recently arrived, laid claim to an American city and imposed itself politically. Cuban immigrants did not subordinate themselves to the preexisting social order, but instead laid claim to the city, ascending to positions of political and economic power that took generations for other foreign groups in other American cities to achieve. Their dominance in Miami resulted from the confluence of several factors: first, the wealth and power enjoyed by these Cuban exiles in their home country prior to the revolution; second, their vision, entrepreneurialism, and shrewdness in appreciating Miami's geographical advantages in ways not seen by its previous elites; and lastly, the geopolitics of the Cold War. Miami's rise as a relevant global player beyond its local setting is a good example of how a city that had been largely at the margins of key academic urban studies in the United States helps us make sense of fundamental cultural and demographic transitions in the twenty-first century.[29]

But it is still necessary to go beyond these exceptional stories to examine other cities with different realities. To repeat, we are not interested in building yet another hierarchy of global or globalizing cities, but instead focus on the unique dynamics that characterize different urban places today. Among them, the world-ranging competition for status and visibility among urban places must take center stage. Why should cities in so many countries and of such different sizes seek to call attention to themselves and imitate those that have achieved a measure of visibility? The phenomenon that we have termed "global hopefuls" was not foreseen or preordained. It has simply emerged as a feature of the modern world system, and we can analyze its implications for cities and their urban populations.

CITIES AND THEIR ASPIRATIONS

In our conversations and interviews with leaders in city government, economic development agencies, businesses, universities, and nonprofits throughout the world, we encountered striking similarities. These leaders want to attract banks, corporations, investors, young professionals, and entrepreneurs from around the world. They want to brand their places so that they acquire a global appeal, joining the top rank of global financial centers and occupying a "super-regional" position in the economy.[30] As Eugene McCann and Kevin Ward explain, local and national policymakers participate in global networks, "bringing certain cities into conversation with each other, while pushing others further apart."[31] These interactions, which we have observed firsthand in meetings held in São Paulo, Newcastle, Mumbai, Dubai, and Beijing, among other locations, "create mental maps of 'best cities'" that influence strategic planning at the local level. Urban policies are produced and circulated in networks of influencers, sustaining a process of "worlding" in which actors actively promote their cities as models of "best practices" while others seek to identify successful models of urban planning, marketing, and branding that can be transferred and adapted to their own cities.[32] Certain names appear frequently in these conversations: "Austin for quality of life and creativity, Barcelona and Manchester for urban planning and regeneration, Curitiba for environmental planning, Portland for growth management, Porto Alegre for participatory budgeting and direct democracy."[33]

While policies are grounded in specific locations, they are shaped by "global circuits of policy knowledge" that legitimize and empower "some interests at the expense of others, putting alternative visions of the future outside the bounds of policy discussion."[34] This is part of a process in which certain places aim to continuously reinvent themselves to acquire global status, seeking to implement lessons learned from metropolises that represent successful variations of the global city model.

Even Miami, already well established as a regional commercial and financial entrepôt, ceaselessly seeks to reinforce its position. On March 5, 2021, its Downtown Development Authority announced the arrival of eight high-tech firms coming from Silicon Valley, including investment giant Blackstone and Barry's Bootcamp, a favorite with start-up investors. Together these firms will add 700 jobs with salaries averaging $162,000 to the already large and complex Miami downtown mix.[35] A new facet of Miami's brand, or postpandemic rebranding, is its burgeoning tech scene. For example, the attractiveness of cryptocurrency allows the city to expand its brand, presenting its finance sector as forward thinking and the city on the cutting edge of technological innovation. Bitcoin 2021, billed as the biggest bitcoin event in history, was held in Miami's Wynwood neighborhood, attracting investors from around the world and solidifying Miami's rebranding effort. Miami is selling itself as "the crypto capital of the United States" and seeking to attract the attention of celebrities such as Elon Musk and Jack Dorsey.[36] In June 2021, Blockchain.com, the London-based cryptocurrency company, moved its U.S. headquarters from New York City to Miami.[37]

This is a worldwide trend that has uncertain implications because fast policy transfers embraced by cities aspiring to model themselves after the positive experience of others may not yield the expected results. North American and European centers have exercised worldwide influence as success stories, but the pool of existing models has increased in the last decades with the emergence of Chinese and other Asian cities as powerful players as well.[38]

Urban leaders compete in creating new imagery for their urban places—a goal seen in Delhi and Mumbai, Barcelona and Glasgow, and Panama City and São Paulo, among other examples. International locations have highly appealing fiscal incentives, an export-driven environment, and a hyper-modern urban landscape (office and residential high-rises, shopping malls, upscale gated communities, etc.).[39] Miami's Downtown Development Authority provides the latest example.

In some contexts, this effort also entails creating a safe space where stakeholders from the region can get together and negotiate on "neutral turf"; that is, it establishes and safeguards "an open house in a closed neighborhood."[40] This has worked well for cities in some locations. Miami and Dubai are good examples of places where leaders and businesspeople from widely diverse ideologies, political backgrounds, and nationalities can meet without the fear of violence, arrest, or indiscretions.[41] Such cities are considered premier centers for doing business beyond their immediate neighborhood because of their location, ease of international transportation, and safety. As a marketing specialist in Miami noted, "If an Argentine is going to meet with someone from Lima, Peru, chances are they will both fly to Miami."[42]

Property capital plays a key role in these plans. The city's aspiration to become a center of commerce and finance is interwoven with its positioning as a site for consumption. The local "growth machine" drives the expansion and segmentation of the built environment: builders and property managers determine the spatial distribution of different sectors of the population.[43] These cities seek to entice nonresidents to their real estate markets. Their "global status" determines the type of audience they can attract. Cities such as Delhi and Mumbai try to lure members of the Indian diaspora, while cities like Barcelona attract buyers from Europe and beyond, including new customers from Morocco, Russia, and China.[44]

While the policies may differ, North American cities' efforts to build and project the image of a "world-class city" are similar to the efforts of cities in the Global South, such as Delhi's plan to market its international image as a "global metropolis" in the early 2000s.[45] The particular brand of urbanism that attained widespread regard in the North set the tone for a global city model that is expanding to the South.[46]

More specifically, cities share an aspiration to become, at least partially, "super-regional champions," which means they must be all of the following: (1) a highly competitive financial center that serves as "a gateway for investment" for other regions; (2) a host for the world's top financial groups, leading global law firms, and biggest asset managers; (3) an international logistics hub with well-built trade and transport networks supported by the most advanced shipping ports and airports; (4) and finally, a desired destination that offers a high quality of life with a strong international real estate market and world-class shopping, eating, and entertainment.[47] Cities manage to develop some of these features with more or less success.

The challenge for cities striving to attain this position is to successfully combine several factors, namely, market attractiveness, livability, cultural diversity, and accessibility.[48] This is not an easy feat. Multinational corporations, law firms, and the world's top financial groups would not think of establishing their regional headquarters for Asia in Mumbai. Wealthy Mexicans in search of high-class real estate would not consider investing in São Paulo. Barcelona is not considered Europe's top choice as a financial hub. These are cities with certain global characteristics, aspiring to market themselves in the world scene, but their broad sphere of influence is largely limited to their own nations. Still, we observe significant variations among such cities. For example, Barcelona is not a global financial center, but it is a magnet for international talent, mainly as a result of its powerful city brand.

In the 1980s, the aspiration to gain international prominence was at the center of "urban reinvention" efforts undertaken by cities in the United States and Europe. The impetus for cities to remake themselves was particularly important in the context of high levels of deindustrialization that devastated large urban centers, such as in the Rust Belt states of the United States. The economies of cities such as Detroit, Milwaukee, Pittsburgh, New Orleans, and Buffalo, and those of European cities like Bilbao, Liverpool, Newcastle, Nantes, Rotterdam, and Turin, were usually concentrated on one or two key industries that suffered devastating declines in the last half of the twentieth century. For example, Pittsburgh was an "industrial cyclone" that produced a quarter of the world's total amount of steel at the beginning of the twentieth century, but it then experienced an unprecedented population exodus in the second half of the century. Subsequently, it sought to reinvent itself as a leader in science and technology at the turn of the twenty-first century.[49]

Folding itself primarily into the "eds-meds-tech" sectors, Pittsburgh strove to position itself at the cutting edge of these industries. Described as "America's most promising postindustrial experiment," Pittsburgh became a leader in biotechnology, healthcare, robotics, autonomous vehicles, and education.[50] The city charmed companies like Google, Uber, Facebook's Oculus, and Apple, and it has incubated several start-ups such as Krystal Biotech, a clinical stage gene therapy company; Argo, a self-driving technology company with a valuation of more than US$7 billion; and Duolingo, an e-learning start-up with 500 million app downloads.[51] In Pittsburgh, researchers work on an autonomous rover to help find life 40 million miles away on Mars; more locally, a project that pairs artificial intelligence with assistive technology has helped a patient with tetraplegia to become "the first person ever to experience the sensation of touch using a brain-controlled prosthetic limb."[52]

As more cities engaged in urban renewal programs, the global city as a policy goal became increasingly popular starting in the 1990s. In China, central state authorities promoted policies to raise a number of cities to the level of international centers, placing "the emphasis on infrastructure, signature buildings, and the built environment—namely on the visual image of a global city."[53] As we observed firsthand in Tianjin during 2008–2009, this metropolitan region developed a strategy for the twenty-first century to leverage its high-tech manufacturing and location as the "gateway to mainland China" in order to attract investors, professionals, and tourists. The creation of a free-trade zone, new joint ventures resulting in facilities such as Airbus's Final Assembly Line (the first one outside of Europe), and the construction of a high-speed train as part of the Beijing-Tianjin-Hebei "super-region" were among the many initiatives launched to compete internationally.[54]

Other cities around the world have embarked on major physical and economic restructuring efforts toward the same goal. Barcelona underwent a vast effort to reinvent itself into a technology and innovation hub, appealing to international talent and assertively promoting its brand to attract international tourism. São Paulo sprang from a regional center based on coffee production to be one of the world's fastest-growing megacities and a regional center of finance in Brazil. Mumbai morphed from a trading center centered on the textile industry into the richest city in India, with an economy rooted in the finance and service sectors, as well as one of the world's largest centers of film production, Bollywood. Examples could be multiplied. Former industrial cities the world over have put their sights on economic diversification—emphasizing technology, education, medicine, media production, tourism, and other knowledge and service-intensive sectors as the way forward in an increasingly interlinked global economy. No one wants to be left behind, but the race to the top has other less appealing paths, such as the marginalization of the working masses employed in the service industries and the attempt to conceal urban poverty behind glittering towers and fast superhighways.[55]

BRANDING THE GLOBAL CITY

Since the last century, branding has become an integral tool for urban growth and revitalization efforts. Often these strategies sell the city as an "utopia for young, well-educated professionals," and as such, they communicate a distinct message about which groups represent the ideal residents in the city.[56] Urban branding is intimately linked with the creative economic, financial, and tech sectors, and it purposely excludes groups and issues that challenge this sanitized narrative of success, integration, and harmony. In many cities that underwent processes of economic renovation, their industrial past is buried under the new layer of globalization and reconfigured as devoid of conflict or controversy. This is in stark contrast with the continuous conflict between social groups—across racial, ethnic, and other divides—that defines the city of the twenty-first century.

Mari Paz Balibrea, for example, vividly describes spaces in Barcelona that were once factories or industrial areas and that have been completely redeveloped for leisure, new industry, and services. Balibrea notes that fragments of old industry and factories have been left where textile factories were once located, such as chimneys in the Poble Nou district, and these are now the site of the 22@ Barcelona innovation district. Such objects could be seen as "symbols of bygone socio-economic activity, an allusion to the city's past," but, as Balibrea argues, "their spatial recontextualization disconnects them from the local history in which they originated . . . their disposition in the space conceals the complexity of an industrial past characterized by social struggles and human relationships that were lived out on that spot, replacing it with a new configuration of space which promises the absence of conflicts and equality through consumption and the market."[57]

This description evokes similar experiences in other postindustrial cities. In Pittsburgh, when one walks around the Waterfront development, one can see the large smokestacks from the steel mill that were left there as a tribute to the industrial past. In place of the mill, there is a new environment of leisure, shopping, and entertainment that has entirely replaced any remnants of the 1892 "Battle of Homestead," a quintessential moment in U.S. labor history.[58] Several of the cities discussed in this book, such as São Paulo and Lagos, exemplify efforts by governing elites to treat informal, poor settlements as disposable areas—inhabited by "capitalism's surplus humanity"—ignoring their histories and necessities while deploying militarized security forces to control these populations.[59]

For global hopefuls, urban branding is part of regional economic restructuring.[60] City leaders, economists, and consultants search for policy packages around the world—such as the "creative cities" package popularized by Richard Florida—and seek to replicate successful branding campaigns, particularly those designed for established cities.[61] As in the case of Pittsburgh and similar cities in the United States, Canada, and Europe, local elites have sought to control the city's image and physical design, "creating both a new global space and a new urban brand" to ensure a business and cultural climate that attracts white-collar workers in light industry, financial services, technology, and knowledge-based industries.[62]

As Véronique Dupont puts it, spectacle is "an integral part of the city marketing strategy."[63] Urban elites around the world yearn for their "Dubai moment"—a shorthand for the international attention a city gets that goes beyond the temporary visibility given by a global expo, an Olympiad, a World Cup, or the Commonwealth Games.[64] Having the tallest building in the world—like Dubai's Burj Khalifa—is not sufficient to confirm ascension to global city status, but it does help attract worldwide attention.[65] The vertical dimensions of cities around the world often evoke sci-fi imaginaries and represent a common aspiration for cities such as Dubai and Shanghai to become a "the global icon of urban futurity in the 21st century."[66] The confluence between the urban "growth machine" and the "spectacle machine" serves as a springboard in the quest to become prominent on the world scene. The leaders of these cities know that they cannot expect to become a New York or London. They thus need to create something unique that can charm, fascinate, and capture the imagination of a worldwide audience. Cities become "lifestyle producers," and the symbolic power of location turns them into a major "attraction factor."[67] When Dubai paid tribute to Diego Maradona following his death by adorning the Burj Khalifa with gigantic images of the soccer idol, the symbolism was evident. The spectacle appealed to a global audience, bringing together the tallest building and the most famous soccer player in the world.[68]

Globalized features of cities involve not only corporate, commercial, and financial services, but also media and cultural production. As Stefan Krätke explains, "The culture and media industry functions as a 'trend machine' that picks up on the trends developing primarily in the leading media cities, exploits them commercially in the form of a packaging and re-packaging of lifestyle elements and transmits them worldwide."[69] The positioning of cities on a global stage is often linked to their rise as sites for consumption. The growth machine and the spectacle machine operate in tandem to sell a location, molding the urban space around the desirability offered by a beautiful environment, safety, and proximity to shopping and entertainment.[70]

The city's brand is defined as the "city's intentional and organized story/proposition that differentiates it and seeks to drive demand."[71] Developing the city's brand requires urban elites to construct a narrative matrix that "can help apply the identity to different target audiences by linking it to practical applications for individual stakeholders."[72] There is a direct connection between late-twentieth-century branding strategies defining a postindustrial vision for cities in North America and Europe and branding for global hopefuls in the twenty-first century. Each embraced the notion of the city as a commodity. "A city's identity can be likened to that of a person," Greg Clark and his colleagues write in a report entitled "The Global Identity of Cities." "People have reputations based on how their brand is perceived by others. Their visibility refers to how many people know them and in what social circles."[73]

As with people, the image of cities is regularly tested by different types of crises, as well as by competition with others. Dubai is an example because its brand positioning has faced a number of challenges stemming from financial, political, and other problems. Studies tracking image and reputation trends have shown that Dubai has consistently maintained a positive buzz, even during crises and despite occasional surges of attention generated by other city-states in the competitive Persian Gulf region.[74]

In the case of the three emerging global cities discussed in the first part of this book, their brand narrative often defines success as ownership of expensive material possessions and control of social standing and style. Cities such as Miami cater to the wealthy and the middle class, but they are also attractive to the urban lower classes, which can relate to the lifestyle images produced by the city through the consumption of mass media and low-cost goods. Miami's place on the mental map of Latin Americans as a magnet for consumption reinforces its global status.[75]

There is a measure of irony in the fact that the symbolic value of a city can partially compensate for its rising inequality. Thus the working class laboring at low-wage jobs in construction, tourism, and other service sectors can still realize certain symbolic rewards by feeling part of the same urban community, even if the real material beneficiaries of its global status are a small minority of the population.[76]

The rapid rise of the world's ultra-rich has given impetus to the growth machine in globalizing cities. For example, "branded" residences are especially appealing to the wealthy. These residences result from a partnership between fashion brands and the real estate industry. Across the world, builders of high-end condominiums are teaming up with upscale brands in a bid to stand out in a crowded field and reach new consumers, especially international buyers. Just visit the Sunny Isles Beach district of North Miami Beach, where the new Residences by Armani Casa sold 80 percent of its units to international buyers, many of them from the U.S. Northeast, Mexico, and South America.[77] Next door to Armani, the Porsche Design Tower, which opened in 2016, allows residents to "drive their cars onto a private elevator that goes up directly to their apartments."[78] In a city characterized by a large transient population, the brand concept seeks to make non-Miamian investors feel that Miami is their home in the world. As development mogul Gil Dezer explains, "The idea is that when you live here, you really have no reason to leave."[79]

Real estate developers in cities with global aspirations seek to replicate this model, focusing on luxury construction to appeal to expatriates and locals who can afford this category of housing. In Lagos, Eko Atlantic is a major seaside development, "a city within a city," that is being built on land reclaimed from the Atlantic Ocean and that expects to house about 300,000 people in high-end residential units.[80] Promotional materials and media coverage on this mega development make frequent references to Lagos as the "Dubai of Africa." Despite these promotions, however, this luxury development has been plagued by major delays, financial challenges, corruption allegations, and controversies.[81] We will examine this story in detail in chapter 8.

Even if city government or private investors and developers seek to promote a brand, they still can face challenges if good governance practices are not present. Political and economic stability, a rock-solid protection of private property, and a good government bureaucracy are vital for economic growth and long-term strategic planning, as demonstrated by the cases of the emerging global cities examined in prior chapters. Population size and geographical climate advantages will not suffice if these three prerequisites plus an effective and committed political leadership are not present.

CONCLUSION

The twelve centuries since the rise of medieval cities from the ashes of feudalism and the emergence of the urban bourgeoisie as the new leading class spearheading the development of capitalism have culminated in the present scene, where, over the ashes of the industrial past, many cities struggle to rebrand themselves as privileged sites for consumption and where capitalism has evolved from the production of commodities for profit to the manipulation of money as a commodity and the endless accumulation of profit on the basis of novel forms of consumption.

Loyal to its historical role, the postindustrial city has become the locus for these new consumption opportunities as well as a vehicle for the endless accumulation of capital based on the commodity "exclusivity."

As urbanization continues to evolve as a process characterized by increasing integration of communication technology, the exclusive locations have become the prized goals for cities aspiring to a global status.[82] Trade and finance are no longer the sole drivers of the capital accumulation process. The concentration of global media firms, arts and recreation, and cultural production determines the attraction of cities and, hence, their profitability. Established global cities such as New York and emerging ones, such as Dubai and Miami, base their appeal not only on the density of corporate headquarters in finance, law, and technology, but also on the presence of international brands in sports, film, design, art, and architecture. From Barça in Barcelona and Art Basel in Miami to Bollywood in Mumbai and the Guggenheim in Bilbao, having a creative economy has become part of the race to join a highly selective group of places that appeal to the imagination of millions around the world.[83]

Developing a flashy international profile is closely linked to the buzz generated by exclusive events and transformations of the urban environment. In lieu of industrial plants, we have art fairs, and instead of affordable housing for the working masses, we get superprized places and condominium towers for the privileged few. This is how the intersection between capitalism and the city has evolved in the twenty-first century. The postpandemic world is likely to make mobility much more socioeconomically segmented, as the well-to-do face fewer travel restrictions thanks to their access to medical services, convenient testing options, and increasingly more sophisticated technology.

Ironically, the race for uniqueness and exclusivity eventually leads to homogenization. As Xiangming Chen and Ahmed Kanna have noted, "Despite local differences, homogenization reflects the strategic visions of urban growth that are shared by people with the cultural power to dream them up and the economic and political power to impose them."[84] Global cities and their imitations thus end up with similar cultural experiences conceived by and for the elites. There are Guggenheims across the world, restored waterfronts from Sydney to many Chinese cities, and iconic buildings designed by internationally famous architects dotting many cities on all continents.[85]

Miami, Dubai, and Singapore have succeeded in positioning themselves as places in which consumption, social aspirations, and a model of successful capitalism for some groups are effectively realized. The model represented by these emerging cities resonates powerfully with government and business leaders from other cities around the world vying for global preeminence.[86] It also appeals to the fantasies of many underpaid, exploited workers in developing countries who want to move to places that promise a better life. While these cities have been able to pin down the opportunities brought about by a world capitalism in crisis—they are global because they have succeeded in managing disorganized global flows of capital, technologies, culture, and people—they also represent another side of the capitalist world system. This side is embodied in the dormitory districts of immigrant working classes in Dubai and Singapore, which are placed in largely invisible locations, intentionally separated from the wealthy urban core. In Miami, the counterparts to the luxury residences and malls are the working classes who are servicing wealthy condominium towers and corporate skyscrapers, who earn meager salaries and must commute every day from the distant and often dilapidated districts where their residences are located. Those without a legal immigration status experience further vulnerability, constant fear, and abuse at the hands of employers, public officials, and security forces.

While income inequality continues to rise in emerging global cities, wealth inequality also increases as these urban centers become more appealing, driving up real estate prices. Corporations selling luxury wares and leaders of real estate "growth machines" team up in support of their respective interests. In addition, favorable tax laws promote real estate development, as in the case of Miami.[87] These benefits accrue mainly to the well-off, reinforcing a process in which wealth accumulation nurtures the expansion of luxury housing and commercial developments. This process leads to underinvestment in the housing and commercial needs of lower income groups.

We examine next the stories of the other cities seeking to position themselves in a similar place in the world economy or attempting to preserve a position of prominence that they once had. There is no set recipe for the transformation of hopefuls into actual global cities, but the hyperactive character of the capital accumulation process in this century, accompanied by the endless search for novelty and sources of distinction, may give some of the "hopefuls" the opportunity. As explained, there are significant costs associated with this global status. As centers of global capitalism, New York, London, and Tokyo are going nowhere, but there may arise new Singapores and Dubais that will take advantage of the decline of older centers, the global flows and disjunctures of the capitalist world system, and the ever-proliferating opportunities created by technological innovation.

CHAPTER 6

NEW ORLEANS

A Century of Decline

WITH THE COLLABORATION OF LARRY LIU

The ascent of Miami to the level of an emerging global city is not entirely due to the size of its economy. Although it has been growing quickly in recent years, in 2020 its GDP still ranked twelfth in the nation, at a par roughly with Seattle and slightly ahead of San Jose. Miami's GDP was still one-fifth that of New York, the paradigmatic global city.[1]

What has propelled Miami in the world ranks has not been the sheer size of its economy but its international character. As in other global cities, its various key economic sectors float above and ahead of the nation-state of which it is formally a part. Miami's Brickell banking district is not homegrown but is constructed from dozens of foreign multinational banks and financial corporations. The buyers of expensive units in the seemingly endless skyline of condominium towers are overwhelmingly well-heeled foreigners from South America, Russia, and Europe; the world-renowned Miami Beach art scene is not anchored by local galleries, but by a foreign concern, the Swiss-based Art Basel.

More surprising is the fact that, in its role as hemispheric commercial, financial, and cultural entrepôt, Miami usurped the place of another city in the same region that should have rightfully played this part, thus claiming a prominent place in the global urban hierarchy. By the mid-1800s, New Orleans was already gaining importance. A prominent historian of the period describes the situation: "Louisiana's most crucial economic contribution to the region was the enormous commercial traffic steered through the port of New Orleans, a city whose business and financial district constituted one of the most intensely concentrated sites of capital in the mid-nineteenth century Atlantic world."[2]

Indeed, by that time, New Orleans ranked third in size among American cities and was by far its most important port west of New York. That was the motivation for the Union army and navy to organize an expedition to capture the city early in the Civil War. By April 1862, the task had been accomplished and the conquest of the city spared it the heart-rending ravages meted out later on southern cities such as Atlanta and Vicksburg.[3] Yet what the Civil War itself did not accomplish, the end of slavery did. As the capital of a cotton and sugar plantation economy based on slave labor, the city could not prevent its own demise, especially since it did not follow its northern peers in transforming itself by industrializing: "Ultimately, the South's defeat would confirm New Orleans' standing as one of the last major outposts of an increasingly anachronistic trade-based Atlantic economy."[4]

THE EARLY YEARS

New Orleans was founded in 1718 by Jean-Baptiste Le Moyne de Bienville, governor of the French colony of Louisiana. After considering other alternatives, Bienville selected the site because it was on relatively high ground along a sharp turn of the Mississippi River, which provided a natural levee against its frequent floods. Bienville named his new city in honor of the Duke of Orleans, regent of France from 1715 to 1723. In time, it would become the capital of the territory, replacing Biloxi. The rise to prominence of the new city is remarkable because it was not on the Gulf of Mexico but 110 miles upriver. Ships bringing industrial goods from the American Northeast and Europe and those transporting cotton, sugar, and grain from the South and Midwest to these destinations had to travel that distance before reaching open water.[5]

Despite its inner location, New Orleans became the commercial entrepôt for this river traffic. Cotton balls and barrels of molasses, as well as grain from the interior, were warehoused there prior to their journey to New York, Boston, and Europe. Industrial imports from the more developed North arrived and were distributed throughout the vast Louisiana territory by New Orleans–based merchant houses. Less than a hundred years after its foundation, the economic importance of the city and the entire Mississippi valley drew the attention of the American government. Thomas Jefferson, in particular, was keen to annex it as a natural territorial extension of the young republic as it projected its economic might westward.[6]

As it turned out, history favored Jefferson's design. Despite its rising economic importance, "La Louisienne" was little more than a pawn in the Napoleonic struggle for European hegemony. It was actually ceded to Spain after the end of the Seven Years' War in 1763 to compensate the Spanish crown for the loss of Florida to the victorious British. The territory of which New Orleans was the capital became a Spanish colony until the early nineteenth century, when it was transferred back to French control. The transfer took place with Napoleon already in power and short of money to pursue his imperial designs in Europe. Unsurprisingly, the emperor acceded to the desires of Jefferson and the American republic and sold the vast Louisiana territory, New Orleans included, for a few million dollars.[7]

On December 20, 1803, the colony was formally transferred to American control by the French prefect Pierre Clement de Laussat, who had just taken control from Spain the month before only to hand over the city and entire colony to their new owners. In 1805, a census showed a city population of 8,500 comprising 3,550 whites, 1,556 free Blacks, and the rest slaves.[8] The eventful next decades saw rapid growth of this population, led both by an influx of American colonists and by the exodus of French planters after the successful slave revolt in Saint Domingue, rebaptized Haiti, which became the first Black-ruled independent country in the Americas. The mass arrival of both white French and mixed-race Creole refugees from Haiti greatly reinforced the French demographical and cultural presence in New Orleans, an influence that was to endure until well into the twentieth century.[9]

American control over the former French and Spanish colony was seriously challenged only a few years later when the British invaded New Orleans during the 1812–1815 war with the United States. The might of the rising British Empire and the still-feeble state of the new American republic left little doubt as to who the victor would be. The invaders came in force, an army of 9,000 infantry troops under the command of Major General Sir Edward Pakenham. They also brought a blockading fleet. The force advanced by way of Lake Borgne and on January 8, 1815, launched a direct attack on the city's defenders, who were led by Colonel Andrew Jackson. Jackson advised his troops to hold fire until the British troops were close. The tactic worked, and the attack was a disastrous failure. Two thousand British troops perished, including the commanding general. The invading force retreated, never to return. The victory in the Battle of New Orleans consolidated the American grip on the city and the Louisiana territory, ushering in a period of unprecedented expansion.[10]

The population of the city doubled by 1830, driven by the influence of French settlers from Saint Domingue, Americans from the Midwest and Northeast, and German and Irish immigrants from Europe. These diverse streams, added to the local Creole population, endowed New Orleans with a distinctly cosmopolitan flavor, almost anticipating its character as a global city. English and French were widely spoken in the streets, with the city also featuring Spanish- and German-speaking enclaves. By 1840, the population had reached 102,000, the third-largest in the country. New Orleans had become the unchallenged economic center in the South and, along with New York, the principal intermediary of commercial traffic with Europe.[11]

Given its geographic location and history, the city was expected to also become the economic and social capital of the hemisphere. It did not happen that way, and the reasons for this unexpected outcome are instructive.

POSTBELLUM NEW ORLEANS

In January 1862, the Union Western Gulf Squadron led by Captain D. G. Farragut sailed for New Orleans. The city was too important to be left in Confederate hands. The main defenses in the Mississippi consisted of two permanent forts, Fort Jackson and Fort St. Philip, which the Union Squadron duly bombarded and forced to surrender. Unlike with the British forty years earlier, Captain Farragut's ships and the Union army swiftly defeated the remaining defenses occupying the city, almost without a fight, in April 1862.[12]

New Orleans was thus spared the destruction meted out on Mobile and Atlanta. But the federal occupation did little to restore the economic status of the city. On the contrary, the occupying Union commander, General Benjamin Butler, regarded the city's merchant elite as almost personal enemies, co-conspirators in the South's attempt at secession and hence untrustworthy. His successor, General Nathaniel P. Banks, did try to improve relations with the local elite, but with little success given his ineffectiveness as an administrator and lack of interest in commercial affairs.[13] Cotton and midwestern grain ceased to arrive reliably at the port, and the city's financial dominance over Mississippi valley planters and farmers ended. By the conclusion of the Civil War, Confederate money was rendered worthless, impoverishing the city and severely constraining the resources of its commercial classes.[14]

The end of the Civil War also brought to prominence the "race question," created by the liberation of slaves and the attempts of northern leaders of the Reconstruction Era to integrate and promote Blacks into the circles of southern white society. For a while, those efforts appeared to work. In 1872, Lieutenant Governor P. B. S Pinchback took the place of Henry Clay Warmouth as governor of the state, becoming the first African American to occupy such a position in the country. In New Orleans itself, the city successfully operated an integrated public school system during the first Reconstruction decade.[15] Yet the policies of the federal government during the Banks governorship and beyond favored the arrival of swarms of northern speculators and entrenched a culture of corruption in South/North commercial affairs, alienating both the white elites and the common people from the Reconstruction effort: "Anxieties about 'carpetbaggers' and the cronyism favoring their interests formed another strand in the web of racial prejudices and anti-federal resentment that began elevating the hostilities felt by most local whites to pathological proportions."[16]

In September 1874, militias led by the White League and formed largely by former Confederate soldiers defeated the integrated metropolitan police in a pitched battle in the French Quarter and along Canal Street. The League forced Governor William P. Kellogg to flee the state, installing John McEnery as his replacement. Only the intervention of Union troops prevented this political coup, reinstalling Kellogg three days later. But even well into the twentieth century, segregationists would celebrate this short-lived victory, dubbing the conflict "The Battle of Liberty Place."[17]

The failure of northern-led Reconstruction and racial integration and the inability of the local commercial elites to restore the city to its former prominent place in the Atlantic trade system led northerners and Europeans to see the city as a colorful but near-chaotic place, not suitable to be the center of anything: "During Reconstruction, as endemic violence and cronyism cemented Louisiana's reputation as what one New York–based journal scornfully termed a 'South America republic,' New Orleans merchants found themselves relegated to the political sidelines."[18]

According to the historian Joe Gray Taylor, "The problem of race overrode all others in Louisiana, political or economic, during Reconstruction."[19] Unable to replace its prior commercial prominence with a new industrial base, the city's economy lapsed into seemingly irreversible decline. The fundamental problem of New Orleans during the postbellum period was that its preoccupation with internal politics and issues prevented any attempt to leap forward into a new role in the hemispheric and Atlantic trade based on its unique geographical position. The intrusive and misguided policies of the federal government, the battles for political hegemony within the state, and, above all, the "race question" kept the attention of both elites and commoners firmly focused on the internal scene, impeding any imaginative attempt to transcend it. Thus New Orleans entered the twentieth century as a secondary and declining urban center, still notable for its cosmopolitan character and lively street life but otherwise short of any significant financial or commercial role in the expanding American economy.[20]

THE TWENTIETH CENTURY

Miami was founded almost 180 years later than New Orleans. By the time the latter, also known as Crescent City because of its peculiar physical shape along a sharp turn of the Mississippi River, had experienced its period of glory and decline, Miami still did not exist. New Orleans was an established tourist destination for northerners at a time when Miami was no more than a village. What attracted tourists to Crescent City was not sun and sand, as was going to be the case in South Florida, but its lively street life, French-tinged history, and corruption. The city's red-light district, known as Storyville, opened in 1897 and soon became a major tourist attraction.[21]

Even though French-language instruction had been abolished after the Civil War and English became dominant thereafter, French still played a role. In the early twentieth century, the francophone character of the city, dating back to its origins and the subsequent heavy refugee migration out of Saint Domingue in the early nineteenth century, was still very much in evidence, with one-fourth of the population speaking French in ordinary conversations, while another half understood the language perfectly. As late as the 1940s, one still encountered elder Creoles who could not speak English at all. The last newspaper language in French, *Le Courier de la Nouvelle Orleans*, continued until 1955.[22]

In the absence of industrial development, the economic life of the city continued to pivot on commerce driven by the river. The significant problem posed by the distance of the New Orleans port from open sea access in the Gulf was met by a number of improvements over the years. As early as 1794, the Carondelet

Canal, connecting the back of the city with Lake Pontchartrain via Bayou St. John, opened. In 1838, the commercially important New Basin Canal created a shipping route from the lake to uptown New Orleans. The process culminated in 1963, when a new channel shortening the distance to the Gulf by forty miles was opened. About 5,000 oceangoing vessels docked in New Orleans every year, most bulk carriers of commodities such as cotton and grain. Forty countries had consular offices in the city.[23]

The economic life of New Orleans in the twentieth century continued to be centered on the interstate domestic system of the United States. Grains, cotton, and other commodities for export came from the interior of the country, while the flow of capital and visitors originated in the big metropolitan areas of the Northeast and Midwest, especially New York and Chicago. The Crescent City was never able to transcend this system and look abroad for its economic future. As far as its elites were concerned, the countries of the Caribbean and South America were as distant and basically as irrelevant as those in Asia.[24]

During the twentieth century, two major trends effectively prevented a leap forward. First, Crescent City never quite shook the legacy of Reconstruction, with its Black and mixed-race population confined to the lower classes and the poorest and less desirable physical areas. Blacks were banned from a range of employment opportunities, including the police and fire departments. No Black child was allowed an education in public high schools, and Black citizens were denied access to hotels, parks, museums, and restaurants by a rigid segregation system. A legal attempt to overthrow that system was made in 1892, and the case found its way to the Supreme Court. The final decision in *Plessy v. Ferguson* came in 1916, upholding segregation, which was then enforced with ever-growing strictness for the next half century.[25]

Racial segregation continued during the twentieth century as the city's population became increasingly Black. As shown in figure 6.1, the proportion of African Americans in New Orleans never went below 20 percent, but then it leapt to 45 percent in 1970 as school desegregation led to massive white flight toward the suburbs. By century's end the size of the Black population in the city had reached 67 percent.

Sitting atop this oppressive racial system, white elites evolved into a sort of semihereditary aristocracy with family roots in the city's antebellum past. Access to elite clubs and social circles was barred not only to colored citizens, but also to more recent migrants from other parts of the country. As late as

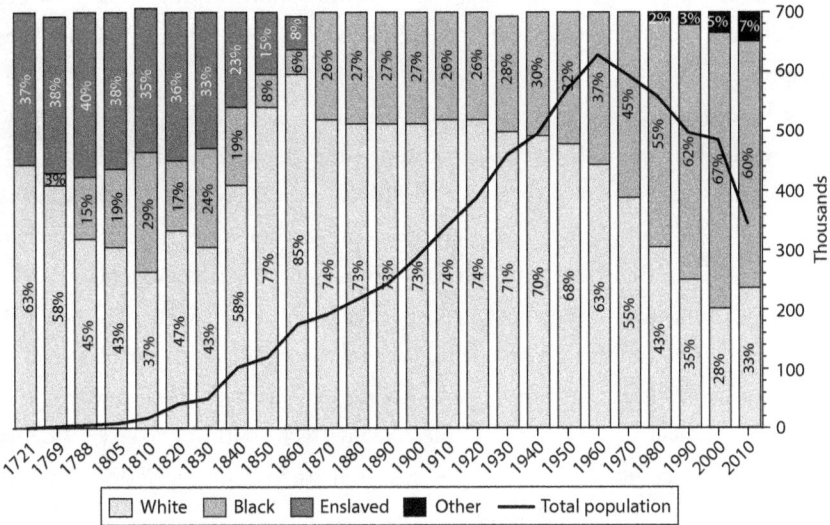

6.1 Share of the historical population of New Orleans by race.

Source: Data Center, https://www.datacenterresearch.org/reports_analysis/prosperity-index/; National Historical Geographic Information System, "New Orleans in the Era of Revolution: A Demographic Profile; Richard Campanella, *Bienville's Dilemma: A Historical Geography of New Orleans* (Lafayette: University of Lousiana Press, 2008); Gilbert C. Din and John E. Harkins, *New Orleans Cabildo: Colonial Louisiana's First City Government, 1769–1803* (Baton Rouge: Louisiana State University Press, 1996).

the 1970s, a study by University of Texas researchers contrasted the egalitarian practices of Junior League clubs in Connecticut and other New England cities with those in New Orleans, where membership was granted only to women with the right pedigrees and where a strict social hierarchy was enforced in favor of established families.[26]

Given this closed racial and social structure, it is not surprising that major migration flows—domestic or foreign—bypassed the city. No major migrant stream from elsewhere in the country or abroad targeted New Orleans. Cuban exiles escaping a communist revolution in their island never thought of settling in Crescent City, nor did subsequent large flows from Central America, Venezuela, or Colombia. As seen in chapter 3, such migrations going to South Florida eventually managed to overcome entrenched southern white elite rule, revolutionizing Miami's economic and social institutions. Nothing of the sort happened in Crescent City, where traditional southern elites continued to dominate the political landscape. Desegregation of schools and other institutions only started, under federal auspices, in the late 1960s, and it was implemented haltingly. In the absence of major population flows from elsewhere and confronted with white flight in the era of desegregation, the population of the city declined steadily, as seen in figure 6.2.

White flight and the extended Black franchise via the federal Voting Rights Act resulted in a political transformation: white segregationist leaders dominated until the mid-1960s, but the first Black mayor, Ernest "Dutch" Morial, was elected in 1978.[27] Morial's immediate predecessor, Moon Landrieu, had appointed more Black city officials to more closely reflect the majority population.[28] All mayoral successors to Morial, except Mitch Landrieu (2010–2018), have been Black, reflecting a broader U.S. trend toward Black political control in majority-Black cities. Despite this advancement in Black political power, every succeeding Black mayor has had to meet the needs of both inner-city residents and white-owned businesses fleeing to the suburbs, in addition to declining tax revenues, violent crime, and declining federal resources.[29]

The second factor negatively affecting the city is, ironically, its geographic location. Although Bienville studied the site carefully and selected it because of its natural levees, they did not prevent regular major flooding. The city has been regularly subjected to a one-two punch—flooding from the Mississippi and hurricanes from the Gulf. The 300-year history of New Orleans is regularly punctuated

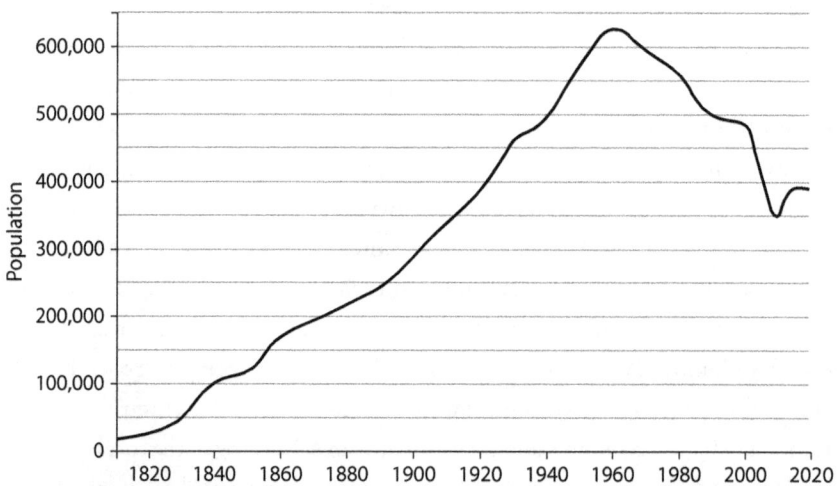

6.2 The population of New Orleans, 1820–2020.

Source: World Population Review, https://worldpopulationreview.com/us-cities/new-orleans-la-population.

by these natural catastrophes. While the city's leaders and population gallantly strove to rebuild on every occasion, the sense of déjà vu or "here we go again" has become almost too strong to overcome. Category V Hurricane Katrina in 2005 may have been the last straw. As of March 2006, more than half of the city's population ordered to evacuate prior to the storm had yet to return. The destruction directly affected the tourist industry, which had become the main and arguably only driver of this urban economy.[30] In the aftermath of Katrina, it lay in ruins.[31] Unsurprisingly, the effects of Katrina were most dramatic in the low-lying parishes of the city, which are also the ones inhabited by the poor, mostly African American population. Higher-lying areas, such as the French Quarter and the environs inhabited by high-income groups, were largely spared. The pattern is graphically portrayed in figure 6.3.

Historical predecessors of this disaster are numerous. In 1849, an upriver levee broke, creating the worst flooding the city has seen. The disaster, known as the *sauve crevasse*, left 12,000 people homeless.[32] The river again flooded dangerously in 1882 and 1927. The city was hit by major hurricanes in 1909 and again in 1915.

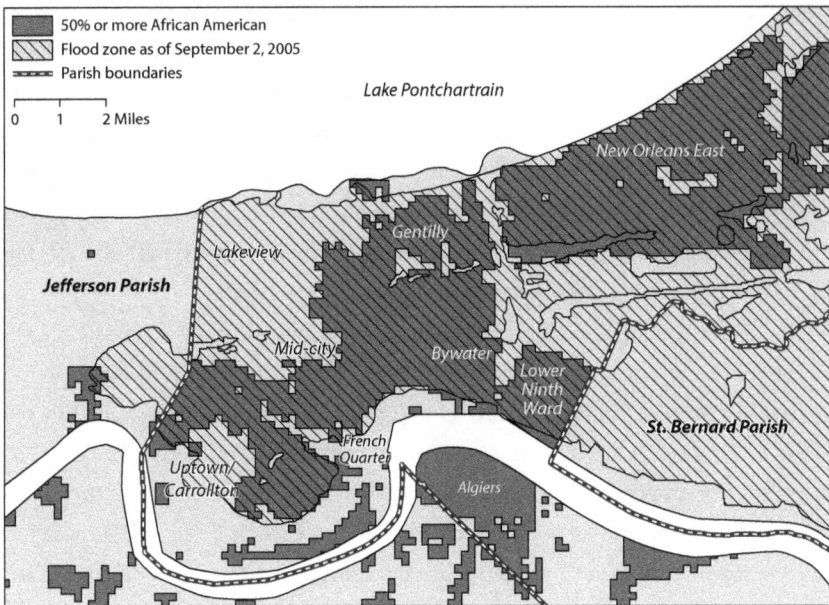

6.3 Racial characteristics of areas flooded by Hurricane Katrina in New Orleans.

Source: Jessica Marie Johnson, "Race and Katrina (map)," *Diaspora Hypertext, the Blog*, August 30, 2016.

In 1947, the Fort Lauderdale Hurricane arrived; while this time the pumps and levees succeeded in protecting the city proper, new suburbs in Jefferson Parish were deluged and the airport lay under two feet of water. Hurricane Betsy in 1965 was the direct predecessor of Katrina. This time a breach in the Industrial Canal connecting the city to Lake Pontchartrain produced catastrophic flooding in the Ninth Ward, as well as in neighboring towns. The devastation prompted President Lyndon Johnson to fly to Louisiana, promising federal reconstruction aid.[33] The effects of Betsy, like those of Katrina, were most deeply felt in the city's poorest parishes. In 2021, Hurricane Ida approached New Orleans dangerously, although this time it was largely spared.

In addition to hurricanes, New Orleans is threatened by the erosion of southern Louisiana's coastlines due to rising sea levels. With erosion, the city approaches the southern coastline and thereby becomes more susceptible to hurricane damage. Once the wetlands disappear, New Orleans will become an island surrounded by water. Only a small portion of southern Louisiana consists of solid land, while the majority consists of swamps, marshes, and wetland that lie underneath sea level. Local residents call New Orleans a "bowl" because the area between the Mississippi River and Lake Pontchartrain is up to fifteen feet below sea level. The soft ground causes subsidence and sinkholes in streets and neighborhoods. The bowl shape of the city also causes strong water pressure that threatens to overwhelm it during storm events. The Army Corps of Engineers has created levees and pumps to keep the water out of the bowl, which has been an enormous engineering achievement, but, given the trend toward rising sea levels, it is merely delaying the day of reckoning. Furthermore, pumping out the water causes the marshy soil to compact, which pushes the city further down, deepening the "bowl" and forcing the city to pump even more water in an endless vicious cycle.[34]

The challenges of water and wind on top of a closed social structure would be too much for any corporate planner thinking of siting global or hemispheric quarters in New Orleans. Few have come. Since oil rigs were established in the 1940s, New Orleans has become a site for oil tankers and refineries. In the 1960s to 1980s, skyscrapers were raised in the downtown area to house white-collar workers in the oil industry, although New Orleans took a secondary position to Houston. World War II induced the government to create a naval shipyard.[35] Shipping and oil industries have shed jobs since the 1980s, however.[36] Shipping declined with more automation in the containerization process,[37] while the oil industry has been threatened by declining oil prices.[38]

City leaders have been too preoccupied with internal squabbles and domestic problems to dream of transcending what had become by the mid-twentieth century an important, but decidedly provincial, urban economy. New Orleans remained the capital of its region, banking on the tourist attractions stemming from that distant French past and the cultural and musical traditions that flourished in the nineteenth century. The city basked in its memories, with no clear vision for its future, as other urban centers raced past it to establish themselves in the global economy.

THE PRESENT

Despite the allure of its history, New Orleans's present economic situation is not enviable. In the absence of other leading sectors, tourism became the main driver of the urban economy in the twenty-first century. In the 1990s, hotel capacity in the city grew to 37,000 rooms accommodating 10 million annual visitors. On the eve of Katrina, nearly one in four jobs in the metropolitan area was in the hospitality industry.[39] In contrast to Miami, where tourists often come to embark on their dream Caribbean cruise, tourists to New Orleans come for the city itself, attracted by its history, culture, and the lovely French Quarter music and street scene.

But anchoring an entire metropolitan economy on outside visitors is a risky proposition. As seen in prior chapters, tourism is one important sector of emerging global cities, but it acts as a supplement to other core activities in trade, finance and banking, and real estate. The flow of tourists is subject to unforeseen events. In the case of New Orleans, the devastation brought by Hurricanes Betsy and Katrina also did great damage to tourism, making the city increasingly dependent on federal assistance and private charity. The 2020 coronavirus pandemic worsened the situation, essentially stopping the flow of visitors (a situation shared with Miami and other tourist centers).[40]

But even before the 2020 catastrophe, the long-term economic trends for Crescent City were not bright. In 2019, the metropolitan GDP was $83.5 billion, third last among America's fifty largest metros and less than one-fourth that of Miami. While Miami's economy expanded by nearly $100 billion between 2010 and 2020, that of New Orleans remained stagnant (from $77.4 billion at the start of the decade). Average household income in New Orleans in 2015 was $36,964, compared with $53,482 nationwide. The city had the highest poverty rate among the fifty largest metros (18.6 percent). Average life expectancy in the metropolitan area in 2020 was 76.6 years, significantly lower than in the nation as a whole and in the bottom tenth of large cities. In the 20 percent poorer neighborhoods in the city, the figure was reduced to 71 years.[41]

In the aftermath of Katrina, city and state leaders have been casting about for industries and investments to move Crescent City out of its dependence on the tourist trade. Hopes center on massive warehousing and storage facilities and delivery services for Amazon and other large commercial corporations,[42] taking advantage of the strategic mid-South location of the city and its low-wage labor force. This is probably as it should be, since other leading economic actors are not likely to arrive anytime soon. Multinational banks and financial corporations do not regard New Orleans as the place to site their global headquarters; in the era of massive post-Panamax container vessels, a port site one hundred miles inland is unlikely to be competitive; repeated natural disasters and generalized poverty do not position it well to attract foreign real estate investors. There are a few points of light, though. In 2009, the city council approved the creation of a bioinnovation district that includes new hospitals (University Medical Center, Veterans Affairs Hospital).[43] Tulane University and Loyola University are significant research universities and an important source of employment.[44] This is in line with the "eds and meds" (education and healthcare industries) strategy of city revitalization common across declining mid-tier U.S. cities.[45] The city has also promoted the digital media, software, and filmmaking sectors.[46]

As a candidate for global status among world cities, New Orleans has a history of rapid rise and promise, followed by a century and a half of decline. Its significant rise in the nineteenth century was prompted by its incorporation into the American political economy, followed by flows of economically driven and talented migrants from the American North and of French exiles from the slave revolt in the Caribbean. The rise of the city to a prominent role in the transatlantic commercial trade was stopped in its tracks by the Civil War and its aftermath. New Orleans never recovered its antebellum important commercial and financial role in the American economy and never managed to attract another influx of determined and skilled migrants. Climate change, which brings soil erosion, rising sea levels, and susceptibility to floods and hurricanes, poses another existential threat to the city.

For reasons seen in this chapter, the city's economy and politics pivoted toward purely domestic concerns, dependent on an increasingly less important riverine trade. In the latest decades, the city has been compelled to rely on its past as a quaint center of attraction for northern visitors. This and plans to convert New Orleans into a giant warehousing center do not augur well for a future global role. Jean-Baptiste Bienville selected the site carefully and had great hopes for the city he founded three centuries ago. A difficult and near-tragic sequence of events has largely done away with this expectation, confining New Orleans to a secondary role in the American and global urban systems.

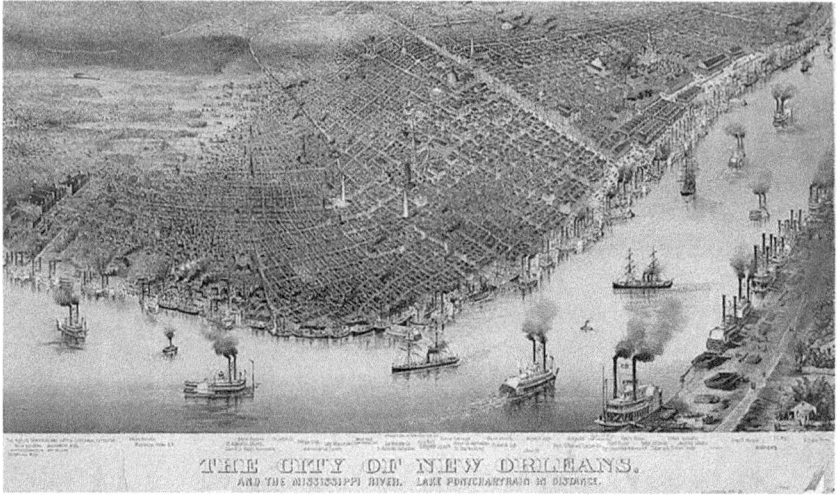

New Orleans in 1885, with the Mississippi River in the foreground.

Skyline of the Central Business District, New Orleans.

Streetcars have been an integral part of the New Orleans transportation network

Gallier House is a historic house museum on Royal Street in the French Quarter, New Orleans.

Ironwork Gallery on the corner of Royal and St. Peter Streets, New Orleans.

The annual Mardi Gras festival attracts thousands of people, thus forming an essential part of New Orleans tourism-driven economic model.

The flooded I-10/I-610/West End Boulevard interchange in northwest New Orleans after Hurricane Katrina made landfall on August 29, 2005.

CHAPTER 7

SÃO PAULO

Brazil's Always-Aspiring City

**WITH THE COLLABORATION OF ROSA HASSAN DE FERRARI
AND ANTHONY OCEPEK**

A number of cities in the world today have moved swiftly from humble beginnings to positions of global prominence. Dubai and Singapore, discussed in the first part of this book, exemplify this unique path. Some other cities were widely expected to assume a global role in their respective regions but never ascended to this position of prominence in the contemporary world economy. Such is the case of New Orleans. There are, finally, others that have been perennial aspirers to global prominence and that, at some points in their histories, closely approached this goal, only to fall back because of major institutional weaknesses. Of this last type of metropolis, none is more prominent than São Paulo, Brazil, a perennial global hopeful that, despite having failed in this quest, did succeed in consolidating a central position in its own country. São Paulo is today the real economic and cultural center of Brazil. How this city reached this position and how it failed to move beyond it is the story of this chapter.

São Paulo's transformation from a regional center supported by coffee production at the end of the nineteenth century to an international metropolis with an important role in global markets began within the context of rapid industrial development at the start of the twentieth century. Immigration policies controlled by São Paulo's elite and the expansion of public transportation—first railways and then trams and buses—allowed masses of workers to flow into the area, resulting in a population explosion. Today, São Paulo boasts the largest GDP among Latin American cities.[1] The city serves as a central node for Brazilian and South American commerce, trade, and financial transactions, as well as a center of wealth, luxury, arts, and culture.

Heavy immigration flows in the twentieth century accounted for more than 50 percent of the city's growth. Today the São Paulo metropolitan area is a megacity with over 22 million residents and the third-largest urban agglomeration worldwide (table 7.1).[2] New waves of immigrants have come from China, Senegal, and Angola, among other countries. Since 2010, there has been a growing influx of immigrants from Haiti and Venezuela as well (table 7.2).[3] Recent immigrants represent both low- and high-skilled professionals and often provide the city with new vibrancy, as they set up businesses and enrich the city's arts and culture.[4] São Paulo's government, noting the important role that immigrants play in helping the city economically, has tried to make the city a more welcoming destination, establishing legal, social, and psychological services to immigrants through the city's human rights office and passing legislation to improve working

TABLE 7.1 Population in São Paulo metropolitan area, 1872–2020

Year	Population	Growth, %
1872	31,385	
1890	64,934	106.90
1900	239,820	269.33
1910	346,410	44.45
1920	479,033	38.29
1930	1,060,120	121.30
1940	1,326,261	25.10
1950	2,334,038	75.99
1960	3,969,759	70.08
1970	7,620,490	91.96
1980	12,089,454	58.64
1990	14,775,840	22.22
2000	17,76,646	20.24
2010	19,659,808	10.66
2020	22,043,028	12.12

Source: United Nations, Department of Economic and Social Information and Policy Analysis, *Population Growth and Policies in Mega-Cities: São Paulo* (New York: UN Headquarters, 1993), https://www.un.org/development/desa/pd/fr/node/2016; World Population Review (2021).

TABLE 7.2 Total registered migrants by country of origin, São Paulo, 2019

Country	Number of registered migrants	Percent of population
Peru	11,111	3.1
Argentina	13,116	3.6
Korea	14,143	3.9
Spain	14,208	4.0
Haiti	16,291	4.5
Italy	17,128	4.7
Japan	24,631	6.8
China	27,414	7.6
Portugal	52,284	14.5
Bolivia	75,282	20.8
Others	95,592	26.5
Total	361,200	

Source: International Organization for Migration (2019).

conditions and an Amnesty Law (2009) to help with immigrant integration and to address xenophobia and discrimination.[5]

Today, São Paulo dominates Brazil's finance, insurance, real estate, and professional services sectors in terms of employment and is also the key acquirer and target for domestic mergers and acquisitions.[6] As of 2016, São Paulo possessed sixty-one of Brazil's eighty-one foreign credit institutions, as well as the fourth-largest stock exchange (B3—Brasil Bolsa Balcão) in the Americas. Itaú/ Unibanco and Santander Brasil, both based in São Paulo, are the second- and fifth-largest, respectively, private commercial banks in both Latin America and Brazil, with São Paulo–based HSBC, Safra, Votorantim, and Citibank Brasil rounding out the top ten commercial banks in Brazil.[7]

Fintechs, technology companies that provide financial services, are just some of the many groundbreaking and innovative developments that have propelled São Paulo into globalized digital frontiers. According to the 2020 Global Fintech Index (GFI), São Paulo is experiencing a swift rise as a financial center in Latin America due to its growing fintech ecosystem.[8] A recent Goldman Sachs report projects that the rise of fintechs will dramatically change the financial landscape in Brazil.[9] In the 2020 GFI, São Paulo ranked fifth globally when measuring competitive landscapes, enabling regulations, talent, and financial strength—following only behind Singapore, New York, London, and San Francisco.[10] São Paulo ranked ahead of cities such as Los Angeles, Chicago, and Miami.[11]

São Paulo's rapidly evolving innovation and tech ecosystem has not only helped the expansion of the fintech start-ups, but also aided the city's growth through a real estate boom. Nicknamed the "Brazilian capital of skyscrapers," São Paulo's skyline has filled with new office towers and soaring skyscrapers with internationally recognizable architecture. São Paulo is the tallest city in South America and sixty-ninth in the world—Miami by comparison is ranked twenty-fourth, while Singapore and Dubai rank eleventh and fourth, respectively.[12]

São Paulo is a center of culture in Brazil, with millions of tourists drawn to the city every year prior to the pandemic. The Bienal de São Paulo, or São Paulo Biennial, is held in the iconic 30,000-square-meter Ciccillo Matarazzo pavilion in the Parque do Ibirapuera and is the second-oldest art biennial in the world (after the Venice Biennial). Since its inception in 1951, it has drawn over 16,000 artists and attracted nearly 10 million tourists and visitors to São Paulo, increasing the global recognition of the city. In 2016, the biennial hosted thirty-three participating countries—a similar level of global engagement as the Art Basel Miami and other major art exhibitions in cities such as Hong Kong. The biennial is an international point of reference as a source of new ideas and debates in the international art world.[13]

The city has also sought to establish itself as a leading film center. The annual film festival, Mostra Internacional de Cinema em São Paulo, which is supported by the Ministry of Tourism and Government of the State of São Paulo through the Secretariat of Culture and Creative Economy, has promoted the Brazilian filmmaking industry globally since the 1970s. In 2016, the city government created the São Paulo Film Commission to help the city attract greater international investment for its domestic film industry.[14]

São Paulo hosts one of the top universities in Latin America, the Universidad de São Paulo (USP), and another major institution of higher education, the University of Campinas (UNICAMP), is located about sixty miles from the city. The work done by these universities, as well as by a significant number of technological institutes focusing on research and development (R&D) activities, positions São Paulo as a center for scientific activity. Technology parks complement a highly dynamic innovative economy with strong investment in R&D from both the public and private sectors. Scientific innovation encompasses research in areas ranging from infectious diseases to genomics and agricultural sciences.[15]

About fifty miles from São Paulo, São José dos Campos is a major R&D and innovation center located in the Paraíba Valley, with concentrations in aerospace and defense. The city, known as the "Brazil aeronautics capital," has developed leading technology centers such as the Instituto Tecnológico de Aeronáutica (ITA) and the Parque Tecnológico (TechPark).[16] Headquartered in São José dos Campos, Embraer is the third-largest commercial jet manufacturer after Boeing and Airbus, employing more than 18,000 people both within Brazil and internationally in cities such as Beijing, Singapore, Dubai, and Amsterdam.[17] Today Embraer is a leader in urban air mobility (UAM) products, and with the recently announced partnership with Eve Urban Air Mobility Solutions, Inc. (Eve) and Halo, the Brazilian manufacturer will produce 200 of Eve's electric vertical take-off and landing (eVTOL) aircraft. This partnership will expand its reach in the U.S. and UK markets and will position Embraer as a key player in the UAM industry.[18] Embraer also is looking to expand its global reach into the lucrative commercial aircraft market in Asia through the company's brand-new E2 series, leveraging its better fuel efficiency compared to other commercial aircraft on the market like the Airbus A320 or Boeing 737.[19]

São Paulo's other main economic sectors (service, commerce, and industry and construction) highlight the shift from the industrial engine that once drove the city to its current service economy, which is highly connected to global markets. Highly skilled professionals work mostly in the FIRE (finance, insurance, real estate), information technology, and R&D sectors. These professionals typically spend their leisure time, live, and work in São Paulo's newest commercial center, which lies on and around Itaim Bibi. This center expands into Avenida Brigadeiro, Faria Lima, Avenida Luiz Carlos Berrini, and the suburb of Brooklin. From this center, headquarters of national companies and branches of international companies conduct business, and ultra-chic designer restaurants and European-style clubs make a lively nightlife scene. This area of São Paulo serves as the most important command-and-control center of the entire country, controlling the national economy and being highly integrated into the global financial network.[20]

São Paulo's role as a service, commerce, and tourist center helped to make the city a strategic hub for transportation. São Paulo/Guarulhos International

Airport is the busiest in South America, with millions of passengers annually. The airport industry brings in jobs and revenues from tourism and supply chain commerce.[21] The nearby port of Santos continues to experience growth in container traffic and cargo tonnage.[22] Principal export markets for São Paulo centered earlier on the United States, Argentina, Mexico, Germany, and Chile, but China has become an increasingly important export market for the region (table 7.3). It became the second-largest export market for São Paulo in the late 2010s, jumping from an estimated $128 million in 1997 to $6.13 billion by 2020. With imports, the principal markets since the 1990s have largely consisted of the United States, Germany, Japan, South Korea, and (however decreasingly) Argentina. China has now displaced the United States as the main import market, increasing from $630 million in 1997 to $10.8 billion in 2020.[23]

TABLE 7.3 State of São Paulo's largest export and import markets, 5-year totals (billion $)

	1997–2001		2002–2006		2007–2011		2012–2016		2017–2020	
	Exports rank									
1	United States	22.36	United States	36.14	Argentina	39.47	United States	39.07	United States	35.45
2	Argentina	15.76	Argentina	16.75	United States	33.37	Argentina	33.92	China	23.03
3	Netherlands	3.904	Mexico	9.22	Mexico	9.44	China	16.18	Argentina	20.97
4	Mexico	3.779	Chile	5.741	Venezuela	8.77	Netherlands	11.27	Mexico	6.99
5	Germany	3.218	Germany	5.223	Netherlands	8.64	Mexico	9.24	Chile	6.8
	Imports rank									
1	United States	37.14	United States	31.11	United States	60.67	United States	64.4	China	44.3
2	Germany	13.09	Germany	14.8	China	39.26	China	57.46	United States	39.24
3	Argentina	10.46	Argentina	9.02	Germany	32.23	Germany	32.28	Germany	20.21
4	Japan	7.58	China	7.382	Japan	15.37	Nigeria	17.398	South Korea	10.23
5	Italy	5.398	Japan	6.524	Argentina	14.88	South Korea	15.94	Japan	8.28

Source: OEC, https://oec.world/en/profile/subnational_bra_state/sao-paulo, 2021.

Despite its spectacular population and economic growth, as well as its integral function in global financial systems, São Paulo is a profoundly unequal city, a common trait among cities that play a significant role in the global economy. Its GINI index (0.577 in 2019) has steadily increased in the last decade.[24] Legacies of slavery have resulted in sociospatial disparities that are heavily racialized. Unequitable access to sanitation, water, housing, urban amenities, employment, and security defines the unequal nature of this city. Continuous internal migration in search of economic opportunities and long-standing social tensions manifest spatially, making São Paulo a highly segregated city. The poor are clustered in either peripheral areas or isolated locations within the central city that lack basic services, while the elite and middle classes are concentrated in new commercial areas and business districts.[25]

The following historical review of São Paulo demonstrates the city's status as a global hopeful, with regional but not global influence.

EARLY HISTORY

The area where São Paulo exists today was originally inhabited by the Tupi peoples of the Tupinikin and Guaianà groups. Early European settlers took advantage of the shifting alliances and kinship ties within these groups, leveraging and encouraging intervillage warfare and rivalries. These rivalries, combined with the spread of new diseases, gave European settlers control of the territories and the ability to enslave the local population. Colonial enterprises—including the nascent sugar industry—created a constant demand for labor, which was forcibly filled by indigenous peoples. Mortality rates were extremely high within this population, and so Portuguese and Brazilian-born settlers began the practice of *bandeirantes*, or expeditions and raids for the sole purpose of capturing and enslaving indigenous peoples. Between 70,000 and 80,000 were enslaved in the early 1600s, making São Paulo a main center for enslavement well into the mid-1700s.[26]

The labor of indigenous slaves supported São Paulo's mining boom in the 1690s. The growing economy of São Paulo attracted Portuguese merchants in the early 1700s, and within a few decades these newcomers were well integrated into the São Paulo elite. By the early 1800s the city of São Paulo had a small but growing domestic and foreign immigrant population. The demographics also changed as Africans were brought in as slaves to replace the enslaved indigenous population, which was liberated by royal decree in 1758.[27]

Until the mid-1800s, São Paulo remained a provincial town with little access to the rest of the colony of Brazil. Although one of the poorest colonial centers, São Paulo was strategically situated at the crest of Serra do Mar, an intermediary point between the coast and the hinterlands. Its nodal location and African slave labor came to sustain the region's first major export industry—sugar.[28]

The collapse of Haiti's sugar production as a result of that country's revolution led to a shortfall in global sugar markets, creating an incentive for the planter elite to produce increasingly larger quantities of sugar for export. The expansion of this industry was facilitated by the crown's decision to allow Portuguese ships to trade with any of the ports of Brazil and, subsequently, to engage in free trade with any friendly nation. The financial capital acquired by São Paulo's elite families during the mining era allowed them to invest in the expansion of the road to Santos in the late 1700s, eventually establishing the town as an international port a century later. Sugar remained the dominant cash crop through the 1830s, to be replaced by coffee.[29] Coffee production led to growth in infrastructure building—new rail lines connecting the interior with the coast—and the coffee barons consolidated as an influential interest group with increasing political ambitions and extraordinary economic power.[30]

THE NEW POWER BALANCE AND
THE ORIGINS OF INDUSTRIALIZATION

São Paulo's coffee barons campaigned for decentralization under a federal system to further consolidate their regional power and keep profits from the coffee industry within the regional government's coffers. These profits would, in turn, quickly make their way back into the pockets of the coffee oligarchy.[31] In 1852, the federal government passed a law that created special incentives to draw in foreign and domestic private capital for the expansion of the coffee complex and plantation economy. Investment in railroads that extended to the core of the region's coffee production area dramatically lowered transportation costs. As part of the government's incentives, the private railways owned thirty kilometers on either side of a rail line, resulting in an increase in land value and development of the lines. The growth of the railroad system fostered international trade, domestic industrialization, and the rise of national capitalism.[32]

Important demographic changes for São Paulo and its surroundings, and for Brazil as a whole, occurred during the last quarter of the 1800s. Slavery was abolished, and both domestic and international immigration provided the labor force for the growing economy in the region. The planter elite, through their political influence, obtained state subsidies for the transatlantic transportation of immigrants, mostly from northern Italy, to work on coffee plantations. The new workers provided cheap labor while simultaneously helping the elites intentionally whiten the population. In the last few decades of the nineteenth century, the city's economic opportunities attracted not only immigrants from other countries but free Blacks as well. Black communities lived in *cortiços* (inner-city, overcrowded tenements with inadequate public utilities and services) in close proximity to major sources of employment, primarily working as domestic laborers in white households and in textile factories.[33]

The white elite narrative of regional identity was centered on modernity and progress, and Blacks were seen as antithetical to those concepts. Therefore, immigration stayed relatively open, albeit stratified, until the 1920s, and São Paulo remained a strong magnet for new immigrants, particularly from Europe. Subsequent migration schemes in the 1920s and 1930s brought over immigrants from Asia. For instance, roughly 200,000 Japanese farmers settled in rural areas of São Paulo State under a government-directed agricultural program. However, under the Getúlio Vargas regime of the 1930s and 1940s, domestic politics and a reevaluation of a national identity rooted in racism led to discrimination against the Japanese and many other "nonwhite" immigrant communities.[34]

THE RISE OF A METROPOLIS

The period known as *café com leite*—or "coffee with milk"—dominated national politics beginning in 1889, with the coffee barons of São Paulo and the dairy producers of Minas Gerais serving alternatively as presidents until 1930.[35] New legislation and regulations facilitated the rise of industry and companies during this period. Hundreds of new businesses were formed, with the new immigrants entering the business environment in large numbers. The São Paulo bond market and stock market, established in 1890, soared. In 1905, there were 28 joint-stock companies listed, and by 1913 that number had increased to 185. During this period, capital investment in the industrial sector doubled, while the market for corporate business formation broadened and created conditions for economic diversification that spurred industrialization. New state-financed public utilities and infrastructure and the rapid industrialization of production made São Paulo home to some of Brazil's largest industrial ventures.[36]

Industrialization enabled capitalist growth and development of the city. Areas of dense urbanization emerged next to rural land as infrastructure expanded. An irregular system of streets, few public spaces, and public utilities and services signaled the growth of the city. The emerging capitalist class—a rural and urban elite composed of plantation and factory owners, the native Brazilian aristocracy, and the immigrant nouveau riche—built European-styled mansions, creating the Garden neighborhoods of Higienópolis, Pacaembu, Jardin Europa, Jardin America, and Jardin Paulistano. These and other developments marked the origins of the sociospatial segregation of the city that is still present today.[37]

São Paulo's population grew rapidly at the turn of the twentieth century, and demand for housing climbed sharply. An urban plan modeled after French prefect Georges-Eugène Haussmann's urban renovation in Paris created grand boulevards and plazas—a trend followed in other large Latin American cities at the time.[38] Critics disparaged the city for spending vast amounts of money on projects that replicated French aesthetics while the demand for public housing was still not met. In response, the city government granted tax concessions for large-scale projects. Developers sought profit above all else and built affordable, though poorly designed, units to house the city's new residents.[39]

The first decades of the twentieth century represented an era of state budget deficits, labor protests, and an overproduction of coffee, but also of flourishing industry, which cemented São Paulo as Brazil's leading manufacturing center. At this time, the local elites began promoting the city on the world stage as a rising metropolis. They sought external endorsement and hosted a range of foreign officials, businessmen, technical personnel, and journalists to increase the city's international recognition. These visits would often result in books and magazine articles describing São Paulo as "Brazil's leading manufacturing center," projecting the image of a metropolis with national, regional, and international aspirations.[40]

Political reshuffling in the 1920s and the emergence of Getúlio Vargas in the 1930s brought an end to café com leite politics, especially after Vargas assumed near-absolute powers in 1937. Despite these major changes, the Paulistas' economic power continued to play a strong role in Brazilian politics for decades to come.[41] The Great Depression of the 1930s had a damaging impact on the economy of the state and the city, forcing a restructuring of the relationship with international markets. As the city continued to accelerate its industrialization—incentivized by the emergence of import substitution policies—rural migration to cities increased dramatically.

The Vargas government's import substitution strategy eventually led to a second industrial revolution. Brazil became one of the fastest-growing economies in the world. São Paulo emerged as a leader in the automobile industry through government-supported industrialization. A major influx of foreign capital during these decades strengthened São Paulo's position in Brazil's manufacturing efforts. State expenditure on infrastructure supported the new industrial dynamism and reinforced the city's nodal character.[42]

The military dictatorship that took power in 1964 focused on political stability while dismantling the populist and leftist movements through demobilization and heightened control of the elite political class.[43] The regime implemented a new model of economic growth to strengthen the domestic market for consumer durables and to encourage exports and inflows of foreign capital. Government subsidies aimed at integrating different regions through protected industrial zones led to the decentralization of industry in São Paulo. Contingents of the city's workers and residents resisted the dictatorship and mobilized for human, civil, political, economic, and social rights. In São Paulo's peripheries, women championed the "right to the city" movement, adding to the growing demand for democratization.[44] As the resistance gathered momentum, many sectors of society coalesced against the dictatorship, including the urban middle class and industrial and business groups who decried their lack of political power.[45]

Despite the social problems and spurred by profits from the industrialization boom of the preceding decades, the city continued to grow well into the 1970s. New large-scale developments by private developers, mainly for the elites, created exclusive neighborhoods designed by foreign architects and accompanied by new zoning and land use policies. However, the oil shock of 1979 curbed economic growth nationally. The 1980s were marred by unemployment, poverty, and in São Paulo, deindustrialization. High internal migration from the countryside (mostly from the northeast) led to a massive growth of the cortiços within the city and of peripheral, informal settlements.[46] As in other cities around the world—Mumbai, Manila, Dhaka, and others—migration to the cities offered substantial improvements in well-being, particularly in the quality of healthcare and education, when compared to conditions in rural areas.[47] However, the lack of adequate housing and infrastructure resulted in deepening economic inequalities and spatial segregation in urban settings. Financial, management, and cultural services remained concentrated in the city's center, where classes with greater purchasing power continued to reside.[48]

By the end of the 1980s, it is estimated that two-thirds of the city's population lived in substandard housing.[49] As Teresa Caldeira has argued, cities like São Paulo illustrate that "inequalities cannot always be mapped out in simple dualistic oppositions, such as regulated versus unregulated, legal residencies versus slums, formal versus informal, and so forth. Rather, these are cities of multiple formations of inequality, and categories such as formal and regulated are always shifting and unstable."[50] In São Paulo, as in other cities of the Global South, the poor include auto workers, consumers, borrowers, and activists. Contestation between organized citizens and the government over policies that regularized and legalized the situation of poor residents shaped the urban dynamic in São Paulo.[51]

Urban expansion propelled by the local "growth machine" was not only horizontal but vertical as well. Starting in the 1940s, São Paulo saw an explosion of high-rises, much earlier than Miami. New vertical developments expanded rapidly in the 1960s and 1970s for middle- and high-income residents. By the end of the 1970s, almost 80 percent of districts with the greatest vertical development were in the wealthy southwest. Head offices and management further concentrated within the city, while manufacturing industries became increasingly decentralized.

As urbanization expanded while spatial segregation deepened, the city acquired a new global image as modern buildings replaced old coffee mansions along Paulista Avenue to house movie theaters, designer shops, bank head offices, and specialized services. The area of Faria Lima attracted the city's elite, where real estate developers constructed more offices, retail buildings, and luxury apartment buildings. New buildings housed the headquarters of multinational corporations in the financial and manufacturing sectors.[52] The iconic Avenida Paulista evolved into the principal public space for the city, where massive gatherings took place (such as the world's largest LGBTQIA+ pride parade) and where the diverse peoples of the city, along with its deep cleavages, converged in multiple ways as people came to work, shop, protest, celebrate, and also live on the street. As Francesco Perrotta-Bosch wrote: "From the poorest on the pavements to the wealthiest in the offices, [Avenida Paulista] is a concentration of contrasts, a microcosm of urban Brazil, with all its dynamism and its divisions."[53]

ECONOMIC DEVELOPMENT, HOUSING, AND INFRASTRUCTURE

Following the tumultuous period of the 1980s, São Paulo, and Brazil writ large, entered a new period centered on neoliberal economic policy. While import substitution industrialization fueled the expansion of São Paulo's economy in previous decades, neoliberal policies took over as a recipe to solve social ills and to prepare the city for the economic challenges ahead, under the assumption that free markets would result in the "emergence of a trickle-down effect of sustained growth leading to better employment, higher incomes, and a stronger basis for social peace and order."[54] Neoliberalism aimed to remove trade barriers, reorienting the economy toward new export markets. The unintended consequence, however, was that it diminished the attraction of cities such as São Paulo, which were now confronted by secondary cities located within and outside Brazil that were able to effectively compete for new export industries, services, and tourism.

As the twentieth century drew to a close, São Paulo's deindustrialization continued as more industries moved to the hinterlands, leaving behind the tightening environmental controls and the growing power of the industrial labor movement.[55] Federal, state, and municipal policy responses to pollution began in the mid-1970s. The establishment of São Paulo's Environmental Protection Agency in 1975 fostered state and local legislation targeting air and water quality standards. In 1978, municipal governments used a new law to set out land use zones for industry that barred major polluting industries from opening in greater São Paulo.[56]

At the same time, the labor movement was growing in the industrial belt of São Paulo. Prior to the coup of 1964, industrial relations inherited from the Estado Novo had prevented labor unions from being autonomous and independent of the state apparatus. Toward the end of the 1970s, a new type of unionism took shape, eventually organized around the Workers' Party (PT). This "new unionism" relied on heavy grassroots participation, with organizing taking place on the shop floor and in neighborhoods. This movement was deeply tied to class consciousness and coalesced in response to repressive tactics used by the military regime to exert control over the industrial working class.[57]

In 1980, over 300,000 metalworkers from the industrial belt of São Paulo went on strike for forty-one days. During this period workers maintained the strike mainly from the neighborhoods in which they lived. From this close interaction of communities and unions, workers expanded their demands from solely monetary issues to encompass full socioeconomic rights for the working class. These struggles would eventually spread throughout the rest of the state and country, winning the support of the business community and ultimately heavily influencing Brazil's political structure.[58]

These transformations occurred against a background of relentless deindustrialization. The São Paulo metropolitan region's share of national industrial production decreased from 43 to 25 percent from 1970 to 2000. The loss of industrial jobs and the decrease in family income forced many middle-class families to the peripheries of the city and residents of the outskirts to cortiços in the city's center, exacerbating sociospatial segregation.[59] The number of people engaged in the informal workforce increased, just as tertiary-sector jobs were replacing manufacturing and industrial jobs.[60] This context framed São Paulo's economic transition from an industrial to financial center as banks, both national and international, expanded, along with finance services, advertising and consulting companies, and information technology firms.

While the city became Brazil's capital of services, the area was faced with increased unemployment, a growing share of workers in the informal sector, an expansion of slums, and rising inequality, with wealth concentrated in a smaller segment of the population.[61] Spatially, São Paulo continued to reflect a polycentric growth structure; multiple clusters of economic activity developed around the city that reflected different historical periods, with Faria Lima/Vila Olímpia and Berrini/Nações Unidas expanding and considered a part of a "new corporate axis" for the city. These two hubs were developed primarily through public-private partnerships, with large public investments in infrastructure used by local authorities to develop the areas.[62] The periphery also continued to grow, fueled by the need for cheap housing.

Neoliberalism led to a pattern of residential segregation that came to define the city in similar ways to other large cities. The development of condominiums and gated areas reinforced the isolation of high-income residents, the expansion of cortiços and *favelas* (informal settlements) defined a different form of isolation, and continued peripheralization of the metropolitan region left many areas in the central city abandoned and blighted.[63] Housing developed in an unplanned manner, forcing the poor to illegally occupy land due to the impossibility of obtaining affordable land or public housing.[64]

Government programs such the Minha Casa Minha Vida (MCMV), launched in the first decades of the 2000s, promoted construction of new housing, roughly 1 million homes, to allow those living in the favelas and cortiços to move into new, planned housing that provided adequate sanitation and housing amenities. However, while the goal was to improve and expand the housing stock for underprivileged citizens, high land costs in São Paulo, coupled with political corruption resulting in well-connected construction companies being awarded contracts, meant that most new construction excluded lower-income residents of the city. Meanwhile, in 2010 there were more than 290,000 empty residential units within São Paulo's municipal borders, a number that excluded the multiple derelict factories, shops, and office buildings within the city limits.[65] The phenomenon of structural poverty—expressed in the city's dilapidated built environment—became a defining factor in a city that struggled to cope with increasing inequality, pervasive social deprivation, and endemic violence.

Like several of the cities examined in this book, São Paulo has struggled with issues around inequality, social deprivation, rule of law, and endemic violence. Miami, for example, has grappled with these issues at different points in its history, most notably in the 1980s. Even today, a long-standing record of brutality, misconduct, abuse, and deadly violence against Blacks in the Miami Police Department is still prevalent.[66] Another city, New Orleans, still faces increasing inequality and has one of the highest poverty rates of large metro areas in the United States.[67] In Brazil, state governments have little control over the highly autonomous police force. Organized crime, the arbitrary power of police, and high levels of police impunity reinforce the (un)rule of law in São Paulo, where the high numbers of civilians killed by military and civilian police forces have not changed significantly since the early 1990s.[68]

While sharing some similarities, particularly structural racism, São Paulo's overall experience is distinct from that of Miami and New Orleans. Over 300 years of slavery and the country's authoritarian legacy have embedded violence, racial discrimination, weak citizenship rights, and deep inequalities into the fabric of Brazilian life. Endemic violence continues partly because state institutions have difficulty addressing the correlation between violence and social deprivation. Intense social and urban inequalities manifest spatially, making São Paulo a highly segregated city. The technologies of security in São Paulo are significantly more militarized than those in Miami. From the 1980s onward, gated communities and areas of exclusive consumption such as shopping malls—where only the well-to-do and elites are welcomed—have become, much like the gated communities of cities such as Lagos, privatized spaces for work, leisure, and residence.[69] As Martin Coy has argued, "Altogether, gated communities deepen the fragmentation of urban society and urban space. Due to their totally privatized organization, they form new extraterritorial spaces beyond public management and control and, consequently, they render the boundaries between public and private space increasingly irreconcilable."[70]

The central justification for these exclusive, private, and secured gated communities and other spaces of exclusive consumption is the fear—whether real or not—of crime. As a counterpart to gated communities, informal settlements are the target of militarized policing.[71] These sections of the urban space are conceived by elites as a threat to "the city's goal of being regarded as global, high-tech, modern or attractive to the wider world."[72] Informal settlements in cities like São Paulo and Lagos are "frequently bulldozed by government planners, police forces or militaries, whether to clear the way for modern infrastructure or real-estate development, to address purported threats of crime or disease, or simply to push the marginalized populations out of sight of the enclaves."[73]

Excessive decentralization, a legacy of the 1988 constitution, and remnants of authoritarianism in Brazil have prevented civilian governments from reforming key institutions like the police. Although the history of São Paulo and its role today as the economic powerhouse of Brazil afford the city global recognition, low trust in government, cronyism, and corruption have created conditions in which the rule of law, policing, and endemic poverty continue to hinder the city's positioning as a globalizing city of the twenty-first century. Similar to cities such as New Orleans, São Paulo continues to face poverty, inequality, and racial, ethnic, and socioeconomic disparities. In this Brazilian city, the globalized enclaves of finance, real estate, and conspicuous consumption exist along with "poor peripheries," which are sites of permanent conflict and contestation.[74]

Attempts to revitalize the inner-city core of São Paulo did not help alleviate structural problems and instead benefited the elites and middle classes. Urban renewal programs followed trends in many other cities in that they chased a model of the global city as a policy goal, stressing among other things the importance of the built environment. For example, streets in Centro Velho and Centro Novo were made into pedestrian districts, the Vale do Anhangabaú was renovated to reestablish a green space, the Edifício Martinelli was renovated to accommodate the city's administration, and the Sala São Paulo Concert Hall was constructed, among other projects. These schemes, while representing attempts by the city government toward revitalization, led to the development of "islands of restauration" within a city characterized by a blighted and decaying environment.[75]

São Paulo's geographical spread, housing deficit, and spatial segregation placed immense pressure on authorities to address the city's infrastructure challenges. Mobility in the city further illustrates urban inequalities. Elites avoid the inconveniences of living in a sprawling metropolis by using other means of transportation; for instance, in the early 2000s, the number of helicopters registered in São Paulo was second only to that of New York. City officials have looked to public-private partnerships for the capital needed to fund large-scale infrastructure projects that benefit the middle and lower classes, such as with new metro lines to connect different parts of the city and alleviate chronic traffic congestion.[76] There has also been a concerted effort to expand and upgrade the existing road networks in the State of São Paulo. Private companies, often located outside Brazil, have been lured to bid on road projects, offered concession fees, and guaranteed investments in upgrades and maintenance.[77] These partnerships have traditionally lacked oversight, have not succeeded in maintaining road conditions, and are seen as extremely advantageous to the interests of private companies. The high degree of corruption in Brazil's political system has been often mentioned as a systemic problem that prevents authorities from implementing effective solutions that address pressing infrastructure needs in major urban conglomerates.[78] This corruption is a major factor that has set back or prevented São Paulo from aspiring to become a global city.

GLOBAL BEYOND BRAZIL?

São Paulo is an aspiring global city, a regional powerhouse in Latin America, perhaps only second to Miami in the hemisphere. Today, its technology companies are comparable to those in major tech hubs around the world, and its cultural industries, centered on advertising and the arts, rank high globally, outcompeting cities such as Singapore and Barcelona.[79] The codirector of the BRICLab at Columbia University, writing of the city's strengths and its renewal, notes that the "city has succeeded in its metamorphosis. Its complex of hospital centres makes it the leading destination in Latin America for health services, its theatres are a small-scale Broadway, and it is a centre for fashion, design and technology.

All major multinationals have their Brazil offices in São Paulo."[80] As presented throughout this book, branding promotes the city by attracting international talent and investors, empowering economic performance, strengthening global connections, and simultaneously creating areas of luxury. São Paulo as an aspiring global city has taken steps to brand itself as an arts, cultural, and innovation center for Brazil and the region. This is pursued, for example, through the construction of iconic, internationally recognizable buildings with global aesthetics and the use of cultural events and mega events like music festivals as part of a strategy of "cultural urbanism" that seeks to boost the city image, branding the city as a global player.[81]

However, São Paulo has not yet joined the group of cities that have reached a position of prominence beyond their immediate region in the capitalist world economy. Even with strengths in technology and finance and a push toward expanding its international cultural productivity, the challenges preventing São Paulo's full ascendency as a global city are manifold and largely a result of the city's evolution. Like other Latin American cities, São Paulo has vast economic inequalities and urban poverty, an informal sector that comprises a large proportion of the labor market, sociospatial segregation, persistent and destructive government corruption, and high crime and victimization rates.[82]

During the last years, São Paulo has slipped in several performance metrics. The 2020 Global Cities Index, which ranks cities in terms of business activity, human capital, information exchange, cultural experience, and political engagement, shows an overall decline for São Paulo between 2017 and 2020, from 73rd to 123rd place.[83] Respondents to a survey listed security, unemployment, education, corruption, air pollution, and public transport as top concerns.[84] São Paulo also slipped from 120th to 298th place in the Brookings economic performance ranking of the world's 300 largest metro areas, with significant decreases in employment and economic growth rates.[85]

While São Paulo performs better than Singapore, Hong Kong, and Miami in some of its efforts to mitigate environmental issues, the city ranks low in terms of waste-management practices and accessibility for city residents, with such problems as traffic congestion and other transportation-related issues.[86] Poor air quality, intensified by the rise of single motor vehicle use, is a serious problem as well. The ability to protect oneself and one's family from these negative environmental impacts is directly correlated with socioeconomic status, as working-class and poor residents spend longer times commuting to and from work than their wealthier counterparts, live in substandard housing, and use cooking and heating devices that expose them to unhealthy air pollutants.[87] The effects of climate change exacerbate issues of air pollution and water scarcity and quality. As temperatures rise, droughts and flooding become more frequent, and mortality rises in the city's overcrowded, poorer areas, in particular those without vegetation.[88] Even though São Paulo has more doctors per capita than major cities in the Global North and some of its hospitals are among the best in the world, healthcare coverage is not readily available to a large proportion of its population.[89]

Basic to São Paulo's various structural challenges is the city's long-standing sociospatial segregation. Both physical and social structures have turned this metropolis into a "city of walls," as Caldeira describes it, where the elite and the poor live side-by-side but are separated by high security fortifications and where access to services, public spaces, and claims to effective rights, rule of law, and security differ markedly across the classes.[90] This bifurcation of the city manifests itself in high levels of crime and victimization, police violence, organized crime, and a resulting deterioration in the quality of urban life. These features significantly lessen the appeal of the city to international investors, potential new residents, and buyers of real estate from around the world.[91]

Fear of crime is significantly accompanied by widespread corruption, which mars the democratic process and causes precarity in legal and financial systems. Ubiquitous among all levels of government and the corporate elite, corruption poses barriers to strengthening the economy, as well as significantly reducing public trust in elected officials and democratic institutions. Reforms are unlikely to succeed in an environment in which it is difficult to garner enough support "to overcome likely elite opposition" to changes in the status quo and "where narrow, fragmented patterns of organization prevail in society and inside the state."[92] At a national level, widespread distrust of government and institutions in general, resulting from repeated corruption scandals, paved the way for the victory of far-right candidate Jair Bolsonaro in 2018, who ran on a populist platform of anticorruption.[93]

Sectors of the middle class and the wealthy have increasingly sought protection from economic and social instability outside the country's borders. For many, Miami is the haven of choice; its solid legal system, orderliness, rule of law, and familiar language and culture attract Brazilians who want to safely invest their resources and display their affluence, a luxury not always available in Brazil.[94] Many Brazilians view Miami as a place of glamour, sophisticated consumption, and above all, safety. For many, Miami is "the safest city of Brazil"—an aspirational destination and a market for optimism. Those with savings choose Miami as a place to invest the money that they have earned at home.[95] Consequently, São Paulo's influence among Brazilians is dwarfed by that of Miami, which is the one city in the Western Hemisphere that exercises attraction over the entire Latin American region.[96]

São Paulo's leaders have advanced citywide initiatives that attempt to address violent crime, law enforcement practices, and accessibility and sustainability, seeking to improve the quality of life for all residents. Some of these efforts have yielded positive results, such as a dramatic drop in homicides in the last two decades.[97] Other initiatives, such as urban renewal efforts, especially those driven by globalizing agendas, have largely transformed the city for tourism, conspicuous consumption, and recreation for the elites. Similar to the strategies adopted in other cities that have sought to reinvent themselves through urban renewal and city branding, São Paulo's growth coalition, along with elites and public institutions, has emphasized the importance of beautification efforts to enhance the aesthetical appeal of the urban environment. Such efforts commonly result in the forced displacement of people in central city areas.[98]

Public space is reconfigured through rules, spatial transformations, and police enforcement. In São Paulo, displacement is better captured by the concept of "hygienization," which is sensitive to legacies of racism and socioeconomic stigma and which "highlights the state's role in systematically and violently removing low-income housing, people, and informal economies from certain areas."[99] Agendas of urban development are thus forcibly imposed on the poor and justified by a civilizing narrative. The "hygienization" of São Paulo has occurred as elites attempt to take possession of the long-abandoned core of the city. As this area deteriorated and became a magnet for low-income residents, growth coalitions utilized the status quo as an excuse to justify the development of new residential and commercial areas elsewhere.[100] In turn, when forces championing urban redevelopment in the city's core decided to reclaim dilapidated and decayed areas, "hygienization" provided a rationale for gentrification and further spatial segregation.

The global Covid-19 pandemic and local patterns of inequality have made more apparent the deep social and political problems that define São Paulo. Social-distancing guidelines have been nearly impossible to exercise in the densely populated favelas, where overcrowding and minimal government support create an environment conducive to the spread of illness. Informal work, compounded by the systemic difficulties characteristic of underserved neighborhoods, has left many city residents in very vulnerable positions. Many poor die at home, and inadequate models for tracing the spread of the illness have made the true toll of the virus in low-income communities difficult to calculate.[101]

CONCLUSION

In 2017, Portes and Nava published the results of a comparative study of institutional quality and national development in five Latin American countries plus Portugal. The conclusions of their study singled out "immunity to corruption" and "proactivity" toward key actors in their respective fields of activity as the major factors characterizing real developmental institutions.[102] These findings aligned well with an earlier analysis of "embedded autonomy" as the key factor promoting national development.[103] Opposed to these beneficial factors are the mortal effects of widespread corruption and the capture of the state apparatus by private interests. Countries and cities that fall prey to this last situation condemn themselves to permanent subordination in the highly competitive contemporary world economy. The experience of São Paulo vividly reflects this trend.

In the global cities of today, the exclusivity of location drives real estate growth, business investment, and the spatial concentration of trade and finance. These sectors give rise to major centers of arts, culture, recreation, and tourism. Cities seek recognition on a global stage through global branding, including international events and urban renewal initiatives. Growth coalitions often seek to heighten, through the transformation of the urban environment, the city's presence in the minds of investors, home buyers, and consumers around the world. However, these transformations frequently exacerbate existing inequalities and further the city's physical and socioeconomic bifurcation.

In Latin America, the implementation of a neoliberal economic model in the 1990s deepened inequalities and contributed to the expansion of a vast informal sector that provides little relief in times of economic uncertainty and very limited opportunities for those aspiring to higher wages, better housing conditions, and, eventually, access to a middle-class lifestyle.[104] Additionally, despite efforts to create an environment more conducive for entrepreneurs to thrive, excessive regulations continue to hinder their economic potential, failing to nurture an ecosystem supportive of formal business activities.[105]

The case of São Paulo illustrates two important points. First, megacities are not guaranteed a place among urban centers that have reached the status of key players in the fields of international commerce, finance, real estate, arts, and sports. São Paulo's position of national prominence and economic power in Brazil does not necessarily make it a coordinating center where multiple forms of investment, mergers, and acquisitions operate on an international scale, where international banks and global corporations feel sufficiently confident to site their regional headquarters, and where the wealthy in their respective regions (and often in other parts of the world) come to make real estate purchases and other investments to protect their capital from the insecurity in their own countries.

Second, cities that serve as regional centers in the world economy have risen to this status through different paths, indicating that there is no set path for cities aspiring to this position. São Paulo benefited from a strategic geographic location and was connected to an international port for the trade of commodities, which made possible the booming coffee industry at the end of the nineteenth century and enabled the city and region to emerge as a manufacturing powerhouse in the twentieth century under import substitution policies. However, São Paulo never implemented the institutional measures necessary to obtain the confidence of capital—both corporate and private—from around the world so that it could establish itself as a player beyond its immediate region and Brazil. São Paulo is no different from other Latin American cities where "improvement in the institutional quality of the state and more decisive action in support of the classes and sectors most victimized" by highly exclusionary economic models have failed to materialize.[106] Deep economic inequality, fear and insecurity, systemic racism, and pervasive corruption are not a viable recipe for global positioning. Academics, entrepreneurs, and civil society leaders agree on the imperative to "get the political system in order," address the deep-rooted "promiscuous relationship between the state and private firms," strengthen checks and balances, and address the country's staggering socioeconomic divide.[107]

The transformation of São Paulo since colonial times can be conceived as a multilayered history of exploitation, racism, and violence, but also of cultural diversity, industrialization, innovation, and economic regeneration. Here is a city built over a complex and rich past that continues to hope for a global future.

In contrast, the evolution of a much smaller urban center like Miami into an emerging global city cannot be traced to an industrial past or an era of plentiful trade—this is a city built from scratch.

Seeing São Paulo, a global hopeful, in light of Miami—a city that adjusted to the opportunities and challenges of a globalized economy and the allure of cosmopolitan culture and social life—helps us understand that the stages of urban history are not predetermined or inevitable. Miami, which did not exist for most of the nineteenth century and was a seasonal beach resort for more than half of the twentieth century, is an improbable case of a new type of global city. São Paulo, South America's economic powerhouse, is a confounding case of a premier industrial metropolis that has not attained its global destiny. The contrasting trajectories of these cities serve as compelling examples that history is not without a sense of irony.

View of Vale do Anhangabaú (Anhangabaú Valley), São Paulo, in the 1920s.

The Octavio Frias de Oliveira Bridge, commonly known as "Ponte Estaiada," is a cable-stayed bridge in São Paulo over the Pinheiros River.

The Paraisópolis slum next to luxury apartments of Morumbi, São Paulo, 2004.

Street in the República district of São Paulo.

Avenida Paulista is one of the most important avenues in São Paulo.
(*Source*: Pixabay)

Monumento Bandeirantes, São Paulo, commemorating *bandeirantes* (settlers carrying out expeditions into Brazil's interior) by the Italian Brazilian sculptor Victor Brecheret (1894–1955) at the entrance of Ibirapuera Park.

Liberdade, a neighborthood of São Paulo. It is the entrance to the Japanese neighborhood with many shops, bars, and restaurants.

CHAPTER 8

LAGOS

Africa's New Dubai?

WITH THE COLLABORATION OF ROSA HASSAN DE FERRARI AND ANTHONY OCEPEK

Cities such as Miami and Singapore, as well as Gulf cities such as Dubai, have moved to positions of global influence following transformational paths that break from established models of development.[1] Other cities have recently improved their status as influential metropolises in their own regions and seek to utilize this position as a platform to enhance their global standing. These cities may not have attained a position of preeminence in the world economy, but they are linked in multiple ways to global economic and political activities.[2] Although they continue to struggle with structural problems that range from institutional fragilities to informal economies, poverty, and stark inequalities, they represent examples of creative, diverse, and unique forms of urban life.

Lagos is a changing city in a rapidly urbanizing continent that has the potential to move to new levels of economic and geopolitical prominence in the coming decades. Similar to Dubai, which saw unprecedented growth from a small town with an important port to a city that caters to global elites, Lagos too has grown rapidly and seeks to replicate many of Dubai's successes, though with a different development model. Understanding Lagos's evolution and the creative force of its urban life requires a perspective that goes beyond paradigmatic models of "global cities" or North American and western European archetypes. Like other cities in the Global South, Lagos has distinctive forms of local, global, and transnational connections. To understand the city's aspirations, we must look at both the city's unique identity and its many links to global processes.[3]

AFRICA'S DUBAI? AN OVERVIEW

Lagos's strategic location made it a main trade route on the waterway along the Bight of Benin, which transformed it from a small crossroads of regional trade to one the most important international ports on the western coast of Africa. The city's original source of wealth—the transatlantic slave trade—and British colonialism shaped Lagos's urban history. Drawn to the city because of its strategic location, the British forcibly destroyed local forms of rule, imposing institutional, legal, and commercial changes that transformed the local society. British colonial domination represented a comprehensive social, political, and economic project to secure control over a vast system of people and territory.[4] While the Lagos of today cannot be tied solely to the history of colonialism and postcolonialism, these periods left deep and profound marks on the city.

Throughout the twentieth century and into this century, Lagos became the largest seaport in West Africa and Nigeria's premier economic and transportation hub, channeling over 70 percent of the country's foreign commerce.[5] During this time, the city's growth into a megacity led to disorganized, unplanned expansion. Governance standards declined under the military regimes that ruled the country from the 1960s until the end of the century, except for a brief democratic hiatus between 1979 and 1983. This time was also marked by an oil boom, and the ensuing prosperity attracted an unprecedented number of migrants from Nigeria's rural areas, as well as Ghanaians, Togolese, Dahomeyans, and other groups. More recently, migrants from mainland China have settled in Lagos, where some have arrived as employees of Chinese state-owned companies (such as those in the oil and gas, telecommunications, electronics, and cement sectors) and others are engaged in trade and small-business activity.[6] The rapid demographic growth of the city is portrayed in table 8.1.

The transition to democratic rule in 1999 helped breathe new life into the city, setting up its aspirations as a global hopeful as the many problems confronting the city due to previous government mismanagement were tackled. Starting under State Governors Bola Tinubu and Babatunde Fashola, Lagos embarked on plans to remake itself into a global metropolis. City and state officials viewed these efforts as an attempt to make the Lagos metropolitan area "a global economic and financial hub that is safe, secure, functional and productive."[7]

Reflecting the global narrative in recent decades, the Lagos State Development Plan for 2012–2025 proposed a pathway of strategic change that purported

TABLE 8.1 Estimated historical and projected population of Lagos, 1950–2035

Year	Population	Growth (percent)
1950	325,218	
1955	468,460	44.04
1960	762,418	62.75
1965	1,135,439	48.93
1970	1,413,528	24.49
1975	1,889,802	33.69
1980	2,572,218	36.11
1985	3,500,464	36.09
1990	4,764,093	36.10
1995	5,982,680	70.91
2000	7,280,706	21.70
2005	8,859,399	21.68
2010	10,441,182	17.85
2015	12,239,206	17.22
2020	14,368,332	17.40
2025	17,156,392	19.40
2030	20,600,156	20.07
2035	24,418,768	18.54

Source: "Lagos Population 2021," World Population Review.

to make Lagos into Africa's model city, inspired by Singapore and Dubai, among others.[8] According to Lagos state governor Akinwunmi Ambode, this is happening "when you see us reclaim fifty hectares of land at the Oworonshoki end of our lagoon; when you see us clear a whole stretch at the Badagry and Epe Marina; when we insist that our prime waterfront must not be taken over by shanties and slums; when you see us embark on some ambitious road, flyover and modern bus terminal constructions; we are preparing the grounds for a major source of employment and prosperity."[9] Like Governor Ambode, elected officials know all too well that branding their cities as centers of consumption is key to their global image. Cities must sell success, social standing, and pleasure to reinforce their allure and serve as magnets for investors, both domestic and international. This agenda is exclusionary, as cities direct their limited resources to attract well-to-do consumers and investors with places that offer physical beauty, safety, security, and functionality.[10]

Population and economic growth are essential to becoming a model megacity. Global consulting firms advise investors to think of cities when mapping potential strategies to finance new projects and ventures in the African continent. As a Brookings report put it, "Rapid urbanization is one good reason why companies should make cities a central focus of their African growth strategies."[11] By 2030 there will be seventeen cities in Africa with more than 5 million residents and five cities with a population larger than 10 million.[12] With a population estimated at over 14 million in 2020, Lagos is already the most populated city on the African continent and is projected to become one of the most populated cities in the world, with 32.6 million residents, by 2050.[13]

Moreover, a large percentage of the urban population in Africa is under the age of twenty-five. Cities will benefit greatly from the ingenuity and drive of this younger generation, which is emerging with tremendous force. This generation includes millions who have the knowledge and skills to replace an older and conventional cohort of leaders and to swiftly help move the continent to a new future with massive job creation, innovation and sustainability, and government-led efforts against poverty and inequality.[14]

Immigration is also helping to grow Lagos and provide new economic networks and opportunities. Every day, approximately 3,000 migrants arrive in Lagos in search of economic opportunities. Furthermore, rapid urbanization, combined with industrialization, infrastructure investment, expansion of digital and mobile access, and innovation in the fields of energy and food production, has the potential to create extraordinary development for the city and broader region. The area's economic acceleration has been accompanied by improvements in the ease of doing business and promising growth in technological and creative industries.[15]

Lagos's rapid economic growth is reflected in the city's major role in the country's economy, contributing 30 percent to Nigeria's GDP in 2017.[16] It is estimated that by 2030 the economy in Lagos will surpass that of Johannesburg, making it the richest African city. Lagos's economy is the seventh largest on the continent, putting it ahead of entire countries. If Lagos were its own country, it would rank as Africa's fifth richest.[17] The city is the historical entry point for foreign investment as well. Sixty percent of industrial investment in Nigeria is in Lagos. The two major ports serving the Lagos area, Apapa and Tin Can Island, function as the key logistical hubs for the transport of imports and exports in the country.[18] The concentration of manufacturing, banking, financial, and trade activity has benefited and provided further stimulus to sea, land, and air transport facilities. Lagos has also become a tourist center and a highly educated city, with over 20 percent of citizens holding at least one degree from a tertiary institution.[19]

With this rapid demographic and economic expansion have come new challenges. Lagos, like other global hopefuls, is a city of contrasts. Two-thirds of the population live in precarious settlements that house the "poorest of the poor."[20] Daily, hundreds of thousands of citizens are stuck in the city's infamous traffic gridlocks as a few wealthy residents traverse the city in private helicopters.[21] As in other megacities, "spectacular wealth and grinding hardship" define the extremes of life in this urban setting.[22] Both the poor and the rich often seek refuge from political and economic instability, crime, and violence by venturing to safer and more predictable locations abroad—the destitute through dangerous journeys across the Sahara Desert and the Mediterranean Sea, the wealthy through "golden visas" obtained by investments.

In the bustling Otigba Computer Village, traders working out of umbrella stands on the street sell used hardware imported from the United States, where it is considered junk, while fancy tech companies sell the latest iPhones to affluent customers.[23] Formal and informal economies coexist and interconnect in multiple ways, encompassing a broad range of sectors, from consumer goods to transportation.[24]

THE CHALLENGE OF ASPIRING TO GLOBAL STATUS

The city's dramatic growth has put a massive burden on urban infrastructure. Lack of government funding has worsened this and other challenges because the metropolitan area lags behind other comparable megacities in its budget allocation relative to its population. Deficient housing, substandard healthcare facilities, pollution, overcrowding, traffic congestion, and environmental and infrastructure degradation continue to define life in Lagos, despite the many government policies focused on advancing public-private partnerships.[25] There is currently a deficit of 2 to 5 million housing units; as a result, informal dwellings continue to expand.[26] In the Makoko floating settlements, emblematic of deprived settlements elsewhere in the city, residents lack access to clean water, sanitation, electricity, and transportation. As depicted in table 8.2, lack of access to decent housing and services is common among households in Lagos State (reliable data for the Lagos metropolitan area are not available). Crucially, urban residents also lack rights of occupancy, placing them at constant risk of eviction and other forms of abuse or harassment by developers and state officials. In fact, evictions are common, and thousands of people are dislodged from their homes every year, sometimes violently.[27]

As in the case of São Paulo and other cities in the Global South, these impoverished communities are continuously engaged in mobilization "to acquire the basic necessities of their lives, to get access to collective resources (land, shelter, piped water, electricity) and to public space (street pavements, intersections, street parking places)."[28] The absence of public policies and sustained investments to address the needs of the urban poor does not mean that these communities, and their intermediaries, are not regularly confronting and bargaining with local authorities and political leaders to obtain needed resources. Still,

TABLE 8.2　Quality of housing and access to urban services in Lagos State, 2012 and 2014

	Percent of households, 2012	Percent of households, 2014
Lack of access:		
Adequate housing	70	*NA*
Water	84	88
Sanitation	69	67
Solid waste collection	28	28
Transportation	52	*NA*
Sustainable electricity	88	76
Rights of occupancy	37	40

Source: Fabienne Hoelzel, ed., *Urban Planning Processes in Lagos: Policies, Laws, Planning Instruments, Strategies and Actors of Urban Projects, Urban Development, and Urban Services in Africa's Largest City* (Abuja, Nigeria, and Zürich, Switzerland: Heinrich Böll Stiftung Nigeria and Fabulous Urban, 2018), https://ng.boell.org /sites/default/files/160206_urban_planning_processes_digital_new.pdf.

precarious settlements continue to be regularly cleared to make way for middle- and upper-income housing, forcing the poor into ever more distant locations. The Covid-19 pandemic exacerbated the problem of displacement in cities such as Lagos.[29]

Even though the government has set up programs to help people buy homes, these government-backed mortgages have high interest rates and such restrictive terms and conditions that most new residences being built are affordable only by the well-to-do. For a metropolis that is expected to add tens of millions of new residents in an area slightly smaller than the entire territory of Hong Kong, underinvestment in housing for those in the lower income brackets represents one of the greatest challenges for the future.[30] As shown in table 8.3, when compared to other cities considered in this study (plus Mumbai, another global hopeful), Lagos has some of the least affordable housing. Luxury and higher-income housing is largely out of reach for a majority of Lagos's growing population.

Even amid these challenges, Lagos continues to grow as a center of commerce, technology, tourism, and creativity. Nigeria receives a quarter of the continent's funding for tech start-ups, and many of these companies are concentrated in Lagos.[31] A thriving hospitality industry contributes a significant portion of Nigeria's wealth, and tourism is expected to grow in the next decade.[32] Luxury apartments, shopping malls, and majestic new urban developments, such as Eko Atlantic (an exclusive "city within a city" in coastal Lagos that is being built on land reclaimed from the Atlantic Ocean), are part of Lagos's aspiration to become "Africa's new Dubai."

The city has become a point of convergence for businesses throughout the region and beyond, with the Murtala Muhammed International Airport generating the majority of international airline connections in West Africa.[33] In addition, Lagos has evolved into a major educational center, hosting a flourishing university environment that benefits from a significant number of professionals trained abroad.[34] As mentioned already, new waves of migration and commercial activity—from China in particular—are shaping the urban environment, from the wholesale shops selling textiles in the Ojota shopping complex to the offices of Chinese companies.[35]

Lagos's dramatic growth in recent decades, its economic diversification, and its expanding global brand have consolidated the city as the economic and cultural center of Nigeria and as one of the most important cities on the continent. Like São Paulo and a few other cities around the world, Lagos stands as a significant

TABLE 8.3 Housing affordability: Lagos in comparative perspective

City	Average housing cost/salary ratio
Miami	3.90
Dubai	3.94
Singapore	13.37
Hong Kong	17.09
Mumbai	20.47
Lagos	44.77

Source: Average housing cost from CBRE Research (2020), https://www.cbreresidential.com/uk/sites/uk-residential/files/CBRE-Global%20Living_2020_Final.pdf; Nigeria Property Centre (2021), https://nigeriapropertycentre.com/market-trends/average-prices/for-sale/houses/lagos; Average salary from Average Salary Survey (2021), https://www.averagesalarysurvey.com.

Data:

Dubai:

Average home price: $329,003. Source: CBRE Global Living 2020 report, https://www.cbreresidential.com/uk/sites/uk-residential/files/CBRE-Global%20Living_2020_Final.pdf.

Average salary: 306,579 AED, $83,464 USD. Source: https://www.averagesalarysurvey.com/dubai-united-arab-emirates.

Hong Kong:

Average home price: $1,254,442 USD. Source: CBRE Global Living 2020 report, https://www.cbreresidential.com/uk/sites/uk-residential/files/CBRE-Global%20Living_2020_Final.pdf.

Average salary: HK$568,927, $73,383 USD. Source: https://www.averagesalarysurvey.com/hong-kong.

Lagos:

Average home price: ₦89,530,000, $217,835 USD. Source: https://nigeriapropertycentre.com/market-trends/average-prices/for-sale/houses/lagos.

Average salary: ₦2m, $4866 USD. Source: https://www.payscale.com/research/NG/Location=Lagos/Salary.

Miami:

Average home price: $367,249. Source: CBRE Global Living 2020 report, https://www.cbreresidential.com/uk/sites/uk-residential/files/CBRE-Global%20Living_2020_Final.pdf.

Average salary: $94,137. Source: https://www.averagesalarysurvey.com/miami-united-states.

Mumbai:

Average home price: $504,785. Source: CBRE Global Living 2020 report, https://www.cbreresidential.com/uk/sites/uk-residential/files/CBRE-Global%20Living_2020_Final.pdf.

Average salary: 1,791,059 INR, $24,666 USD. Source: https://www.averagesalarysurvey.com/mumbai-india.

Singapore:

Average home price: $915,601 USD. Source: CBRE Global Living 2020 report, https://www.cbreresidential.com/uk/sites/uk-residential/files/CBRE-Global%20Living_2020_Final.pdf.

Average salary: SGD 90,490, $68,464 USD. Source: https://www.averagesalarysurvey.com/singapore.

example of a global hopeful—a city with both tremendous potential and dramatic challenges. In the rest of this chapter, we describe the evolution of the city, from Lagos's emergence as a major port in the slave trade and the transformation of its urban networks to the postcolonial process of state formation and the city's eventual positioning as a metropolis aspiring to global prominence.[36]

ENSLAVEMENT, COLONIALISM, AND URBAN TRANSFORMATION

Lagos was originally founded by the Awori people in the mid-thirteenth century as a fishing village that paid levies to the Kingdom of Benin. Its geography and waterways played a strategic role in the area's growth. The 400-mile inland waterway and river system along the Bight of Benin was a major trade area long before the Portuguese arrived in the mid-1400s, and the village served as a crossroads of peoples and cultures. A complex system of roads accompanied the river routes, and items produced in and around Lagos were traded throughout East and West Africa and reached Europe and the Middle East.[37] In the second half of the 1500s, the Kingdom of Benin established a military camp on Lagos Island, but less than a century later the powerful kingdoms of Yoruba and Aja rivaled Benin for military and political power. The ensuing conflict between neighboring kingdoms drove many migrants to Lagos, solidifying its position as a multicultural hub in the region.

The transatlantic slave trade, initially dominated by Portuguese merchants, altered the course of the city. For three centuries, starting in the fifteenth century, the slave trade was the single most important economic activity in and around what is now Nigeria. The British, French, and Dutch participated in the slave trade along the Bight of Benin, but it was the Portuguese who played a dominant role in the export of enslaved Africans to sugar plantations in Brazil and the Caribbean, which supplied European markets. After the legal abolition of slavery in the nineteenth century, repatriated slaves began arriving in Lagos, bringing with them the traditions, languages, and religions acquired during their time in bondage. Bolstered by profitable exports of palm oil and other cash crops, Lagos continued to grow as a trade center in the nineteenth century as it benefited from the stability, security, and protection offered by its lagoon.[38]

By the late 1800s, Lagos was known as "the Liverpool of West Africa," having established its preeminence in the region's maritime economy. The expansion of the railroad in the 1880s connected the city with the hinterlands, and the deep-water port built in 1907 increased Lagos's vital role in international trade routes. Lagos continued to grow thanks to the successive waves of migrants and the arrival of returnees from the African Atlantic diaspora.[39]

Britain's colonial system of governing through indigenous institutions solidified a model of "indirect rule" that allowed domestic elites to exercise local authority while submitting to British central power. The British manipulated indigenous populations to ensure the colonial government a loyal workforce, employing many European-educated Lagosians in lower-level government positions while preserving a racist structure that denied them opportunities for social and political mobility. In 1914, the borders of the modern state of Nigeria were established, encompassing regions where the large, centralized states of Kanem-Bornu, Benin, Oyo, and the Sokoto Caliphate had ruled before.[40] The new borders, the conglomeration of diverse ethnic groups, and changes in traditional power structures would have long-standing implications for Nigeria's state formation.

The city's growth in the early twentieth century led to advances in sewage control, health, electricity, and tramways. After a plague in the 1920s, the government founded the Lagos Executive Development Board (LEDB), which helped create a medical department, the police service, and a public works agency. The LEDB was also responsible for the replanning and development of Lagos, which was already at this time suffering from overcrowding and poor living conditions in certain areas. The LEDB led efforts on clearing and demolishing precarious settlements, and in the 1930s hundreds of homes were destroyed on the premise that they were structurally unsound and breeding grounds for disease. New houses were built, but there was a continued shortage of adequate housing for displaced residents.[41]

Following World War II, the colonial government engaged in massive capital expenditures to promote economic and social improvements in the city. The plan called for expansive public spending on social services, including education and health, and new infrastructure intended to cultivate manufacturing and the extractive economy. Several iterations of planning and development schemes were implemented in subsequent decades, but the results were suboptimal because of a mismatch between goals and the needs of the population, the mismanagement of funds, and outright corruption.[42]

Demolitions of poor settlements continued through the 1950s under the Lagos Central Planning Scheme. Local leaders and residents protested these demolitions, but a growing population resulted in increased demand for land and housing and therefore a significant upsurge in the price of real estate. From 1950 to the early 1960s, the population of Lagos rose from about 325,000 to over 760,000.[43] Villages surrounding Lagos began to be absorbed into the metropolis as agricultural land became inhabited. Poorer residents were forced to seek housing in less desirable, inland locations where inexpensive, uncontrolled, and illegal dwellings expanded the footprint of the city.

The expansion of the railway and road system helped increase exports and trade in Lagos by connecting the capital to the hinterland. By 1912 the Lagos rail line joined the Kano line, and by 1920 it reached the northern border with Niger, enabling faster transport and facilitating the rapid movement of people and goods. The reduced cost of shipping and faster transport allowed European companies to make enormous profits in the commodities market. In the late 1930s, only seven European firms controlled two-thirds of all Nigeria's export trade. The largest firm was the United African Company, which accounted for 40 percent of the export economy at the time.[44] Because of the ports, the system of roads, and the railway network, the value of exports grew exponentially from 1900 to the 1960s. Commercial activity and the city's position as a major transportation hub continued to attract both foreign and domestic immigrants, leading to significant population growth in the first half of the twentieth century.[45]

NATIONALISM, INDEPENDENCE, AND CIVIL STRIFE

As the colonial government encouraged segregation, racial divisions deepened in the early twentieth century. A growing nationalist political front, led by figures such as Herbert Macaulay, Eyo Ita, and Nnamdi Azikiwe, rallied against British authorities, criticizing the regime and calling for greater participation and representation of Lagosians in government.[46] Local Black newspapers amplified a message of African pride and resistance against the racist ideology of the colonial government, and nationalist politics rose as an important force in Lagos in the first half of the century.

The emergence of the Lagos Youth Movement represented a new phenomenon driven by the surging number of young Lagosians now receiving a Western education—not only in the United Kingdom but also in historically Black colleges and universities (HBCUs) in the United States. Lagos had the highest concentration of Western-educated Nigerians, and their efforts sustained a rise in indigenous participation in politics, organized education, and labor unions and increased women's presence in the colonial civil service. The Lagos Youth Movement was the most powerful pan-Nigerian nationalist organization in the country, uniting a diverse group of ethnic groups against the colonial government, and Lagos established itself as the nucleus of nationalist activity in Nigeria.[47]

The National Council of Nigeria and the Cameroons (NCNC), created in 1945, was to become a driving force behind Nigeria's independence. This political party was a conglomeration of many different ethnic and social groups from various parts of the country whose activities were concentrated in Lagos. Communism and socialism found a home in the nationalist movement, which promoted anti-imperialism and the empowerment of the working class. The enactment of new constitutions gave Nigerians greater legislative power, paving the way for the country's independence.[48] On October 1, 1960, Nigeria became a fully sovereign state within the British Commonwealth.

Ethnic divides, as well as the regionalism and factionalism that had simmered under the independence movement, generated serious rifts for the new nation. Regional differences continued despite important initiatives such the First National Development Plan, which proposed nationwide advances in agriculture, manufacturing, and education and the growth and diversification of the economy through an import substitution strategy. Demands for a dismantling of the federal system culminated in the overthrow of the civilian democratic regime in 1966 and a bloody three-year civil war between the Nigerian government and Biafran separatists.

The 1970s were fraught with civil unrest and violence. A thriving economy, thanks to the booming oil business, did not benefit the overall population, and socioeconomic inequality grew, creating a deeply divided society. Oil delivered "wealth and means of patronage to the rentier state and its joint venture partners, the transnational oil companies."[49] Control of government funds by corrupt politicians allowed them to grow wealthy, breeding electoral fraud, political manipulation, and violence. In turn, fluctuations in the price of oil—alongside state corruption and mismanagement of public funds—contributed to recurrent cycles of economic instability.

The oil boom affected Lagos in several ways. The oil bonanza drove further urban development, but the city grew with a logic of its own. The car assembly plants (Mercedes, Volkswagen, and Peugeot) established in the 1950s and 1960s encouraged the expansion of thoroughfares, and the oil boom subsidized fuel. Tens of thousands of people continued to arrive to the metropolis to work in both the formal and informal sectors. By 1970, Lagos had a population of just under 1.5 million. A decade later, its population had grown to over 2.5 million.[50] Shantytowns grew rapidly, while the business district moved from the south side of Lagos Island to Victoria Island. The concentration of economic activity there drove the need for housing, and the city's footprint expanded into the suburbs through new developments for the middle class. In 1991, the federal capital moved out of Lagos to Abuja. The move was proposed because of overcrowding—Lagos now had a population of over 5 million—and the decision to locate Nigeria's seat of power closer to other regions in an attempt to promote national unity.[51] This political shift led to a drop in federal funding for Lagos, which gradually reduced its reliance on investment from the central government, relying instead on revenue from its ports and industries and an expansion in its taxation rate to help fund infrastructure and other projects.[52]

CORRUPTION, THE INFORMAL SECTOR, AND URBAN REFORM

In the 1990s, uncontrolled spending and the civil war in Liberia, which became known as "Nigeria's Vietnam," led to large budget deficits. Government corruption and investment in "white elephant" projects, in addition to improper accounting of the country's oil revenues and economic mismanagement by the military junta, are cited as the principal causes of the economic troubles, leading to increased unrest in the country. While presidential elections were meant to take place in 1993, crackdowns against government critics and prodemocracy elements led to protracted political conflict. President Ibrahim Babangida ultimately stepped down and put in place an interim government, which was soon overthrown in a coup by General Sani Abacha, who would rule the country until 1999.[53] The ensuing general elections were marked by serious procedural shortcomings, and many elected and appointed public officials became involved in corruption scandals, further debilitating the legitimacy of democratic institutions and the rule of law.[54]

As in other countries around the world, Nigeria adopted a neoliberal economic model under the "Washington Consensus" in the 1980s. The resulting process of deindustrialization impacted key industries. For instance, the opening of the country's markets to global competition, a lack of investment in infrastructure, and the rise of Chinese textile imports decimated the domestic textile industry, which, at its peak, employed over a million workers and was the second largest in Africa behind Egypt.[55]

Nigerian governments relied heavily on oil production as the dominant export commodity.[56] While Lagos State did not possess oil reserves comparable to other regions in Nigeria, the area attempted to position itself as a key energy provider for the nation. As for the city of Lagos, deindustrialization, economic decline, and lack of federal investment led to a severe deterioration in the quality of infrastructure and services and a steady growth in the city's already vast informal sector.[57]

In the early 2000s, successive administrations created or reorganized a few agencies to increase public safety and services and to promote major capital investments in infrastructure. For example, reforms and capital spending in the Lagos Waste Management Authority expanded waste collection in the city, investment in the police force aimed to increase its effectiveness and overall security in the city, and a public mass transit system was developed with a focus on bus rapid transit lines and the LAGBUS[58] to tackle traffic congestion. Yet today the private *danfos* minibuses still dominate the city's public transportation.[59]

With these reforms under way, the government shifted toward revitalizing the city's historical core on Lagos Island, focusing on redeveloping the area to make the city attractive to foreign investors. The Lagos State Urban Renewal Agency was established under the Lagos State Ministry of Physical Planning and Urban Development with the principal goal of revitalizing the Lagos Island central business district, developing the Marina district, and upgrading residential areas. With growing demand for commercial space, many residential areas on Lagos Island were converted to commercial purposes, decreasing the available housing stock in the area and contributing to rising traffic congestion as workers commuted to the Lagos Island district.[60]

In the 2000s, a public-private partnership involving the Lagos State Government, with federal government support, set in place a massive development project: Eko Atlantic. Mirroring the grand projects of Dubai, Eko Atlantic is designed to house 250,000 people in luxury and upper-middle-class housing as well as the corporate headquarters of Nigerian and foreign firms. The lavish project will also create restaurants and shops along a boulevard modeled after Paris's Champs-Élysées.[61] Eko Atlantic is emblematic of the way the local growth machine responds to the desires of the well-to-do, as investors have hedged their bets against the rising sea and decided to build a massive urban development over what was once the most popular beach in Lagos. These real estate developments enable the wealthy to shield themselves from poverty, crime, and rising waters while being protected by private guards, surveillance cameras, and other security measures.[62]

Eko Atlantic is part of a broad trend whereby city planners and private developers are spending billions on developmentalist initiatives, including seaside business districts, smart tech hubs, and futuristic residential cities. Like Eko Atlantic, these initiatives are being sold as high-end, smart, and sustainable communities, with the goal of emulating the ostensible success of other urban centers to help their cities position themselves as premier centers in the global competition for talent and capital.[63] On the African continent, similar real estate developments have been designed in Kenya, Ghana, Mauritius, and the Democratic Republic of the Congo. These projects evoke images of Dubai's own economic growth model, emphasizing luxury consumerism through transformative megaprojects. Many architects worldwide advocate against an "imposing" form of urbanism, questioning the Dubai model as focused on appearance and impression, and not on a people-centered approach.[64]

In Lagos, as in many of the cities examined in this book, luxury developments and gated communities have become a critical part of the urban landscape. As we have discussed in the chapter on São Paulo, these communities become self-contained cities within the city for the elite, islands for the wealthy, that provide amenities and security, in stark contrast to their surrounding neighborhoods. Indeed, when viewed from above in São Paulo, walls separate leafy gated communities with tennis courts and swimming pools from crowded, cramped dwellings that lack access to sanitation and other basic services. These islands of privilege promise to insulate the wealthy from the city's urban poor, who are criminalized and often abandoned by the city's urban management and planning apparatus.[65]

The gated communities in these global hopefuls are a double-edged sword. On one hand, they are viewed favorably by elites as being capable of "reducing crime temporarily or permanently; decreasing the fear of crime or mak[ing] available psychological respite," and they increase property values by creating a sense of community and exclusivity. On the other hand, these developments produce "a false sense of privacy and safety; relocating crime; segregating communities; decreasing response times of emergency vehicles; causing tension and conflict between urban residents; enhancing the fear of crime; triggering social segregation; increasing urban separation and fragmentation; causing problems with regards to services and maintenance."[66]

A literal island of wealth in Lagos, for example, is Banana Island (referring to the shape of the island). A "1.63-million-square-meter sand-filled island in Lagos Lagoon" that opened in 2000, it is located "a little more than 5 miles east of Tafawa Balewa Square, the commercial and ceremonial heart of Lagos," and offers "security, tranquility and privacy" to its wealthy residents within minutes of the business, financial, and arts districts in the city.[67] Eko Atlantic and other projects on Lekki peninsula are the latest iteration of planned residential developments geared towards the region's upper classes along a peninsula that includes gated communities, an airport, a seaport, and areas reserved for a free-trade zone.[68] They are part of a history of displacement, a pattern of eliminating long-existing indigenous communities by replacing them with new residential complexes, business districts, and transportation hubs.

Urban developments such as Eko Atlantic and Banana Island will only continue to exacerbate Lagos's wealth and income inequalities and further marginalize the poor.[69] As in São Paulo and other global hopefuls, "the Lagos State government often sees the urban poor, particularly in informal settlements, as obstacles to the attainment of sustainable urban development and urban modernity."[70] On behalf of such an agenda, "the state government often manipulates planning and urban development regulatory frameworks," and the resulting policies and regulations cause further distress to the poor, already in a vulnerable position, who are exposed to economic injustices, police violence, and environmental hardship.[71]

Examples such as Eko Atlantic in Lagos embody another dimension of global cities: the phenomenon of "land reclamation," a process of urban transformation that entails manufacturing territory by moving massive amounts of coastal area materials from one location to another. Lagos follows the examples of Hong Kong, Dubai, Singapore, and Tokyo, which in turn followed the path of Rotterdam and, in the eighteenth and nineteenth centuries, the remaking of the shorelines of New York and San Francisco. The urban centers that we have labeled emerging global cities and global hopefuls are all major players in the global demand for landfill and concrete to support unprecedented rates of urban expansion. The grandiose construction projects that have come to define a city's global aspirations cannot be fully understood without noting the massive dredging and movement of sand and gravel from coasts, oceans, seas, estuaries, and islands.[72]

In places such as Singapore, creating new territory by importing sand and other materials has been vital for the city's growth machine. In Dubai, appreciating the city from the ground, marveling at the futuristic high-rises and skylines, is not enough—one must have coastal properties such the "Palms" and the "World," which are "instantly recognizable through the satellite-mediate gaze of Google Earth."[73] These islands are the result of massive movements of land to maximize the appeal and value of coastal areas. It is not surprising that global hopefuls such as Lagos combine the militarized security and exclusivity of the gated community with the construction of artificial islands and other land reclamation projects. These areas sell global elites an individualist version of paradise. Spatial segregation, population growth, massive infrastructure projects, and a powerful global branding machine drive a worldwide demand for natural resources such as sand and gravel, whose massive extraction has major environmental, economic, and geopolitical impacts.[74]

TECHNOLOGY AND CREATIVE INDUSTRIES

The technology sector in Lagos is one of the strongest in Africa, and the city is ranked third in Africa behind Johannesburg and Nairobi in fintech concentration. According to the GSMA Ecosystem Accelerator Programme, which measures the number of active tech hubs,[75] there are over eighty-five such hubs in Nigeria, with Lagos being the top innovative city, possessing more than forty of these hubs. This number places it at the forefront when compared to other cities in Africa such as Cairo and Cape Town. It is hoped that the creation of new hubs such as the recent Tech Experience Centre will help Lagos lead the way to "technological emancipation"[76] for the region, which aspires to emerge as Africa's Silicon Valley.[77] Lagos is also considered a global fintech growth hub—one of nine such hubs rapidly emerging as alternative fintech destinations, including among cities such as Dubai. Going forward, Lagos aims to position itself as the gateway for financial and technological activity in Nigeria and the broader West African region.[78] Other cities in the continent are "dreaming of becoming

Africa's Singapore." Kigali in Rwanda, for instance, is trying to create a financial ecosystem that would position it as a new financial hub in continental Africa. For players such as Lagos and Kigali, the competition for preeminence in the continent's financial market "is not only African. . . . It is global."[79]

Lagos features a vibrant art scene with art fairs, international festivals, high-end art auctions, and art galleries and museums. The city's up-and-coming fashion industry and hip-hop music have gained worldwide attention. Above all, the creative economy is bolstered by Nollywood, one of the world's largest film industries in terms of number of movies and the country's second-largest employer after agriculture.[80]

Lagos's film industry has a tremendous potential to serve as anchor for the city's global branding.[81] The local film industry was born from a grassroots collective effort and the rugged entrepreneurship of Lagos. It is commonly explained that Nollywood began in the 1970s when an Igbo trader began recording traveling Yoruba theater performances. Seeing the initial success in the market, other traders and entrepreneurs soon began producing popular videos.[82] These were inexperienced, self-taught directors and producers. With more and more Lagosians and Nigerians owning televisions and VHS equipment and devoting more leisure time to home entertainment, the country developed a voracious appetite for locally produced films. The industry's popularity was founded in stories that were inherently African, appealing to and resonating with people across the continent and in the diaspora.[83]

Unlike the film industry in francophone Africa, which receives grants from the European Union and France, Nollywood has not relied on financial involvement from abroad until recently. The commercial success of *Living in Bondage*—Nollywood's first big hit in 1992—encouraged businesspeople from Lagos to invest in the burgeoning industry. Early Nollywood was characterized by low-value, home video production. This pattern continues today, as the cost of production is overall fairly low when compared to other film industries globally, between $10,000 and $70,000 per film.[84] Averaging fifty movies a week, Nollywood produces more films per year than Hollywood, and the industry is nearing Bollywood's annual number of films.[85]

Nollywood has become increasingly international and an important branding tool for Nigeria, promoting its self-proclaimed regional exceptionalism and acting as a visible form of cultural machinery in Africa and the African diaspora. Nollywood films are now broadcast on satellite and cable TV. In 2012, a satellite channel was launched for francophone countries in Africa, where viewers could watch Nollywood films in French. Nollywood's films are also screened at film festivals around the world, and the industry has its own film festival, Nollywood Week, the first and only Nigerian film festival held in Paris.[86]

In 2020 Netflix launched its streaming platform in Nigeria, Netflix Naija, which aims to feature increasing numbers of Nigerian movies and TV series, emphasizing the importance of producing content that features African voices—as the launching campaign emphasized, "Made by Africans, watched by the world." Nollywood's output is essential to this strategy of expansion in the African market. Netflix's head of Africa Originals and Acquisitions has stated, "We are aiming to become a strong part of the local ecosystem in terms of growing the capacity and talent in the market."[87] There is a surge in interest on the part of streaming services such as Netflix to capture audiences in the continent, where the number of subscriptions is expected to reach almost 13 million by 2025. For instance, Netflix and Sony Pictures TV, as well as Will Smith's Westbrook Studios, have partnered with Nigerian producer Mo Abudu's EbonyLife to coproduce original films and TV series emphasizing African storytelling. The need to generate Black content is manifested in a rush to invest millions into local productions, bolstering a new generation of African authors, filmmakers, actors, and producers.[88]

These partnerships bring together major players in the global entertainment industry and build new alliances that connect local and diasporic content and production, global streaming platforms, and international investors. These connections create a transnational cultural space that is viewed by some as *Afropolitanism*, a term used to depict "the kinds of transnational fissures through which cultures flow throughout Africa, transporting and transforming material like fashion, music and art."[89] The African city is seen as vital to these transnational flows because it serves "as a hub for exchange while simultaneously generating much of its bricolaged content."[90] It is in this context that Lagos stands as a place of "worlds in movement" where the globalizing city becomes intimately linked to Afropolitanism.[91]

As in the case of Bollywood and Mumbai, Nollywood has the potential to further expand the cultural influence of Lagos, and Nigeria more broadly, throughout Africa and around the world. As an "expression of boundless Nigerian entrepreneurialism," Nollywood gives Nigeria a platform to speak on behalf of Africa and articulate a compelling message about the continent's reality to global audiences.[92]

CONCLUSION

Lagos's future is tied to a number of challenges, including exclusionary urban planning and deficient infrastructure, environmental problems, public-sector corruption, and a vast informal sector. These challenges illustrate the complex scenario faced by cities aspiring to position themselves in the global economy. The key issue for Lagos lies in the arduous balance between achieving its global aspirations and meeting the needs of millions of existing residents and the millions more slated to populate the city in the coming decades.[93]

Urban planning practices have failed to effectively address social and economic exclusion and to provide solutions to alleviate the long-standing problem of access to basic services. There is also a deficit in city and regional planning around transportation, food production and delivery, and the management of health, among other areas. Infrastructure planning has not focused on integrating the "grey (such as treatment facilities and sewers), green (trees, lawns and parks) and blue (wetlands, rivers and flood plains) systems."[94] The consequences of poor urban planning have deepened spatial inequalities and contributed to environmental damage, unstable supply chains, and recurrent health crises.[95]

A relevant component of the city's global aspirations is the development of new means to satisfy the desires of wealthy residents, who expect to have access to opportunities for consumption that are like those offered in other globalizing cities. Like affluent consumers in emerging global cities such as Dubai as well as global hopefuls such as São Paulo, these individuals "in high-up levels are a new form of citizen. . . . Consumption fixes a day-to-day good life and gives substance of a sort for daydreams and aspirations." They are concerned with "what to buy, where to get it, and how to deploy its use," and they seek the necessary safety and security to enjoy their consumer lifestyle. This is a common pattern that defines a fundamental aspect of globalizing cities and that highlights "the significance of consumption as intricately connected with governance and stability."[96] The well-to-do place a premium on legal and political stability, and they are ready to take advantage of opportunities to transfer their capital and invest elsewhere to seek protection from political instability or economic turmoil in their countries. Lagos is no exception.[97]

While the need to upgrade and expand urban infrastructure is vast, the importance of international trade has exposed the inability of Lagos's ports to meet the demands of a rapidly urbanizing Nigerian population. Lagos is not making the necessary infrastructure investments and structural reforms in the operation of its ports that will solidify its role as a commercial and transportation hub. The ports' capacity has not increased since the 1990s, with many operators looking to other ports in neighboring countries as operating costs rise. The cost of transportation into the mainland and traffic congestion in and out of the ports are major obstacles to the city's competitiveness, resulting in millions of dollars lost in economic activity and, as noted, a growing preference for other ports in the region.[98] As shown in the chapters on Miami, Dubai, and Singapore, physical and intangible investments in port facilities and operations are critical economic engines for the global city, helping to integrate it within both its regional and global economies.

Coastal erosion and flooding, in addition to major problems such as air pollution, create uncertainties about the city's future and the well-being of its residents. A recent study by the World Bank on the cost of coastal zone degradation estimates that such degradation costs the city and the state billions of dollars per year. Of particular concern is the cost of flooding, which is "high in Lagos (US$4 billion per year) due to its relatively large, flooded area, and to high value assets and large population at risk."[99] Rising sea levels and coastal erosion have already caused a decline in water quality, damage to drainage infrastructure, and a higher incidence of water- and vector-borne diseases.[100] Solutions to mitigate the flooding from ocean surges and to help reduce coastal erosion, such as the "Great Wall of Lagos" in Victoria Island, have been mired in controversy because they have failed to consider the potentially devastating impact—worsening floods, for instance—on less affluent communities.[101]

Another concern is the high level of air pollution in the city. The main sources of pollution are road transportation, industrial emissions, and power generation, as well as poor waste management and the ports. The number of vehicles has quadrupled in the last decade, and the average commute times have increased to four hours, the longest in the world.[102] According to a recent World Bank study, air pollution caused $2.1 billion in economic losses in 2018 and an estimated 11,200 premature deaths. Children under the age of five are affected the most, accounting for 60 percent of total deaths.[103]

Widespread public-sector corruption is endemic and affects many sectors, including port operations, public transit, construction, and waste collection, among others. The 2020 Corruption Perceptions Index ranked Nigeria 149th out of 180 surveyed countries on the perceived corruption in society and politics, grouping the country with Mozambique and Guatemala.[104] Average residents are, "paradoxically, active participants in the social reproduction of corruption, even as they are also its primary victim and its primary critics." The phenomenon of corruption shapes everyday life, with citizens having to navigate the institutional system and adjust themselves to its rules and dynamics.[105]

Other cities covered in our study were able to make significant inroads in the fight against corruption. The city-state of Singapore, for example, established a strong legal framework to enforce robust anticorruption laws like the Prevention of Corruption Act, which makes corruption and bribery a high-risk, low-rewards activity, establishing severe punishments for those found guilty.[106] Unlike Singapore, which is ranked third on Transparency International's corruption index, Nigeria does not have a comprehensive and effective anticorruption framework or an independent, well-funded, and properly paid and rewarded judiciary and police force.[107]

One of the last remaining challenges for Lagos pertains to its economic structure and its reliance on the informal economy. The vast informal sector is integral to the functioning of the city, and, while the interconnection between formal and informal markets exhibits a great deal of innovation and creativity, the reality is that informality impairs the opportunity to create the level of trust and legal certainty that attracts foreign investment and international partnerships. As the state proliferates rules and controls that hamper regular transactions, it creates more incentives for informality.[108]

Today, the informal sector maintains a strong presence in Lagos's economy. In 2015, for example, over 95 percent of new jobs were informal (representing 65 percent of all workers), compared to 5.5 percent in the formal sector. For both citizens and migrants, the informal economy is often the only employment opportunity. The informal sector is key to the city's economic life, worth an estimated US$48.2 billion compared to the formal sector's US$90 billion. The informal sector runs on its own system of rules, with industry-specific administration, sanitation, security personnel, and apprentice programs, among other services.[109]

Considering Lagos as a global hopeful entails assessing the many challenges that it confronts as well as the opportunities that it presents. Such an analysis should eschew the tendency of studies of global urbanization that dismiss peripheral cities "as dysfunctional, chaotic, failed, informal, and not globalized" and that pose models of "success" built on the experience of cities in North America, Europe, and some parts of Asia.[110] Cities such as Lagos need to find new models of urban development that allow them to harness their economic, social, and creative capacity while also mitigating their most urgent social, infrastructural, and environmental challenges and working collectively to create more just and sustainable cities.

Resorting to existing blueprints modeled on "the Western city as the paradigmatic model against which all others are to be assessed" is perilous for the developing world. As Jennifer Robinson cogently argued, "To aim to be a 'global city' in the formulaic sense may well be the ruin of most cities."[111] A viable alternative entails, among other things, avoiding a vision of urban development that leads to homogenization (for example, by emphasizing urban models exclusively formulated by and for the elites) and, in turn, having the audacity to define alternative futures that reflect a city's history, geography, culture, and networks and that leverage its unique characteristics and potential.

The Lekki-Ikoyi Link Bridge is a 1.36-kilometer (0.84-mile) cable-stayed bridge in Lagos State that opened May 29, 2013.

Aerial view of the Makoko community in Lagos, 2018.

Two-thirds of Lagos's millions of residents live in precarious conditions, like the Makoko informal settlement pictured here, which is home to over 85,000 people.

Idumota Market in Lagos, one of the largest markets in western Africa.

An aerial view of "Eko Atlantic," a megaproject under construction in Lagos.

PART III

CHAPTER 9

HONG KONG

A Threatened Global City

LARRY LIU

The case of Hong Kong is included in this book not as an instance of a rising global city, but as one whose status and prominence as such are now threatened by its unique geographical and geopolitical position. With a GDP, adjusted to reflect purchasing power parity, of US$439.46 billion and a GDP per capita of US$58.165, Hong Kong vies with Singapore for regional hegemony. Both islands are part of the Asian Tiger group (along with South Korea and Taiwan). The two islands have similar populations (5.3 million in Singapore; 7.5 million in Hong Kong) and a similar land area. They also share a past of British rule that infused both with an efficient legal system undergirded by British common law. Their economies evolved in a similar direction, from labor-intensive industry to maritime and air commerce and then to high finance. But Hong Kong got there first, and, until recently, Singapore could only dream of reaching the centrality and economic importance of the British colony.

In addition to British rule, Hong Kong had the advantages of an ethnically homogeneous population of over 90 percent Han Chinese and of proximity to the large Guangzhou region, from which it could draw unlimited labor. By contrast, Singapore had to meet its labor needs by importing workers from more distant places such as China, India, Pakistan, and the Philippines. With recent innovations in transportation technology, workers residing in the city of Shenzhen can travel to their Hong Kong offices in fifteen minutes.[1]

By the early twentieth century, all these advantages had given Hong Kong a position of global centrality rivaling Tokyo. The city had the largest number of skyscrapers in the world and the highest concentration of ultra-high net worth individuals. In 2000, the Hong Kong stock exchange had a market capitalization of US$3.87 trillion, seventh in the world and right below those of established global cities like New York, London, and Tokyo.[2] In terms of a global economic index that takes into account stock exchanges, sites of multinational corporations, banks, and financial institutions, Hong Kong ranked right below the largest global cities and on a par with Chicago and Zurich.[3]

There have been internal problems, as we will see, such as vast economic inequalities and a housing market that excludes most of the working population, but the overriding issue has been the increasingly aggressive stance of the Chinese Communist Party (CCP) toward the civil and political freedoms in its "special administrative region" (SAR). Unlike Singapore, Hong Kong never achieved independence, moving from the status of a British colony to that of a SAR after its return to Chinese control. For a while, the Chinese government tolerated the "one country, two systems" arrangement agreed upon with Great Britain, but in recent years it has asserted greater political control. This move has been prompted by the declining significance of Hong Kong relative to the rest of the Chinese economy and by the increasing restlessness of the city's young people, who are driven by the lack of economic opportunities and fear of authoritarian control. The two factors operated as a pincer: Hong Kong's share of Chinese commercial trade declined from 50 percent in 1997 to just 13 percent in 2015, while efforts of the central government to assert its authority triggered increasingly violent confrontations with a population fearful over the loss of its British-style rule of law and nascent democracy.[4]

HISTORICAL OVERVIEW

Becoming a British Colony

The area that we recognize as Hong Kong was settled by the Hundred Yue tribes of southern China 6,000 years ago. In 111 BC, the Han dynasty conquered the southern region of China, including the territory of Hong Kong. Early settlers in Kowloon and Hong Kong Island were farmers and, due to the coastal location, fishermen and pirates. Under the Qing dynasty, Hong Kong became increasingly connected to the mainland as magistrates collected taxes and registered fishing vessels.[5] Western influence in the region goes back to the sixteenth century, when the Portuguese colonized Macau (1557). When the Qing dynasty temporarily banned Chinese overseas trade to suppress coastal piracy (1647–1684),

Macau became the major port city for trading purposes. Realizing the delete-rious economic effects of the trade ban, the Qing lifted it but restricted trade with foreigners to the port of Canton (Guangzhou), where the British East India Company set up a post for trade in 1771.[6] The British traders earned fortunes selling Chinese goods (silk, porcelain, and tea) to the West, but they were also losing a lot of silver to the Chinese. To help balance the trade account, the British began selling opium to the Chinese. The result for China was widespread opiate addiction and a widespread perception of social decay. The Qing imposed a ban on opium in 1796, which the British traders effectively ignored.[7] In 1839, Lin Zexu, the viceroy of Hunan and Jiangxi, decided to confiscate opium and destroy it. While the value of the opium confiscated was low, Britain regarded this act as hostile and declared war on China, sending the Royal Navy to block the port of Canton.

The Opium War (1839–1842) resulted in a resounding victory for Britain, which allowed it to impose a major indemnity against the Qing and seize Hong Kong Island as a colonial possession by the Treaty of Nanking (Nanjing).[8] The treaty also forced five more ports to be opened to trade with the West. It was a humiliating and unequal treaty for the Qing and for the Chinese in general, who came to regard reunification with Hong Kong over 150 years later as a restoration of national pride and as an end to their colonial humiliation.[9]

Britain's territorial interest was not confined to Hong Kong Island. While the British had no explicit desire to formally colonize the whole of China, they extended their hold beyond Hong Kong. The Second Opium War (1856–1860) resulted in the Treaty of Tientsin (Tianjin) and the Convention of Peking (Beijing), which extended British possession to Kowloon peninsula and Stonecut-ters Island; in addition, foreign diplomatic missions opened in Beijing, and ten more ports opened to Western powers.[10] A final territorial addition occurred in 1898, when Britain received a ninety-nine-year lease for the New Territories. The British military was looking for more space for troop exercises, and speculators wanted more land. But, most importantly, other European powers and Japan were intent on carving out spheres of influence in China, and the British were concerned that these powers could threaten Hong Kong by seizing the New Ter-ritories first.[11] The lease was handed out for free, mainly because the Chinese gov-ernment did not want to give the impression that it was "selling out" the country to foreigners.[12] But because the lease was time limited, the British had to reckon with the possibility of having to surrender the colony later on.

The Nineteenth Century: Setting Up Colonial Rule

What was the motivation for Britain to have a colony in China? Britain did not trust the Chinese government to uphold the interests of British traders. It wanted to ensure that its merchants were safe and could enforce trade arrangements between the two countries. When the British began to settle Hong Kong Island in 1841, only 5,000 individuals lived there, primarily local farmers and fishermen, but the British legal environment promoted commerce and quickly attracted merchants and missionaries from Europe.[13] Hong Kong also attracted Chinese migrants, but the Canton authorities restricted the movement of wealthy Chinese, being open only to emigration by vagabonds, thieves, and the lower classes.

By the 1850s, more and more Chinese were attracted to Hong Kong because Western competition for cotton products was causing high unemployment among the Cantonese, who found migration to Hong Kong or another Western country (e.g., to California to build railroads) a more attractive option.[14] The Chinese became an important source of labor for the bustling colony. In the middle of the nineteenth century, China was afflicted by the Taiping Rebellion, which brought substantial political turmoil and gave many Chinese another reason to move to Hong Kong.[15] Hong Kong also attracted overseas Chinese traders (living in America, Canada, and Southeast Asia), who used the city as a central node for trade.[16] Hong Kong developed a service- and trade-based entrepôt economy, creating vibrant banking, insurance, shipping, shipbuilding, and ship repair sectors. Hong Kong also profited substantially from the continued trade in opium, which was brought in from India and, via Hong Kong, exported to mainland China.[17] A secondary industry was assisting Chinese people in their voyage of emigration to other destinations, since they departed from Hong Kong.[18]

The social structure of Hong Kong reflected the racial hierarchy typical of a European colony: the white British (only 2 percent of the population) were at the top of this hierarchy, being the colonial officials, missionaries, merchants, and professionals. They also filled middle-class positions as supervisors in factories and workshops, policemen, government inspectors, soldiers, mechanics, and artisans. The vast majority of the population were Chinese, primarily lower-class laborers and artisans. A smaller group of Chinese merchants founded a network of voluntary associations and became Chinese community leaders.[19] Chinese temples like Man Mo Temple, founded in 1847, were the main institutions that guaranteed social control of the Chinese population, aside from providing for religious festivals and rituals. The District Watch Force was organized by the Chinese to police themselves. There were voluntary associations for mutual assistance, bank and insurance services, and a fire brigade.[20]

The British minimally interfered in Chinese affairs, practicing "benign neglect," which might explain why they maintained their rule for so long. Aside from these two main groups, there were the Portuguese (who were mostly government clerks), the Parsi traders, the Indian soldiers (Sikhs, Punjabis, and Muslims), and the Eurasians (usually the offspring of British men and Chinese women), who were junior government officials and clerks.[21] Eurasians had a fragile identity because the Chinese did not recognize individuals as Chinese if their father was not Chinese and the British disapproved of miscegenation. On the other hand, the British had greater trust in Eurasians than in full-blooded Chinese and appointed many Eurasians to the civil service.[22]

The British and Chinese tended to live in naturally segregated areas, although the British explicitly excluded the Chinese from the posh neighborhood of Victoria Peak. The British upper class had their elite social clubs, such as the Hong Kong Club, the Cricket Club, the Jockey Club, and the Ladies Recreation Club, which did not admit Chinese or non-Europeans. The Chinese businessmen formed their own clubs, such as the Chinese Club, founded in 1899.[23] In addition to housing segregation, the early colonial period was marked by the colonial authorities' use of harsh methods to repress crime, which included flogging and frequent curfews. Flogging was not abolished until 1880. Crime, gambling, and prostitution were rampant. Governor Richard Graves MacDonnell attempted to regulate gambling, but witnessing a series of negative side effects, he abandoned the attempt.[24] Prostitution was common, in part, because of the skewed gender ratio (seven Chinese men and five European men for every woman). The colonial authorities strictly regulated prostitution that served European men, forcing prostitutes to frequently undergo medical checks. Chinese prostitutes were girls who were either abandoned by poor parents or abducted by human traffickers.[25] While colonial rulers retained a laissez-faire attitude on Chinese affairs, they made an exception during the 1894 plague pandemic, which resulted in the death of 2,500 people. Since the Chinese community was skeptical of Western medicine, the British dispatched a hospital ship and sent health inspectors to sanitize the infected areas.[26]

The Twentieth Century: The Formation of a Hong Kong Identity

The early twentieth century was marked by substantial political turmoil in main-land China. In 1911, the Qing dynasty was toppled and replaced by a weak republican government under Yuan Shi-kai (who previously crowned himself the last emperor), who had to contend with political instability and regional warlords in the various provinces. The consequence for Hong Kong was an increase in immigrants and refugees from the mainland, which was reflected in the growing population (table 9.1). The population has since been continuously expanding, with the exception of the 1940s during the Japanese occupation. Hong Kong increasingly attracted entrepreneurs, who came to purchase real estate. Economic integration with the mainland continued with the completion of the Kowloon-Canton Railway.[27] The economy diversified, including industries in boatbuilding, glassmaking, ropemaking, tobacco, cosmetics, electronics, textiles, pharmaceutical goods, and automobile parts.[28] As the economy diversified, the working class became increasingly assertive, launching labor strikes especially in the 1920s, which was a period of high inflation and stagnant wages.[29]

A second political issue was that Hong Kong harbored political refugees, who could use Hong Kong as a safe haven to launch political schemes against mainland parties, including the CCP. Hong Kong merchants used their wealth to fund the Nationalist Kuomintang (KMT), which seized political power in China during the 1920s. The free press (suppressed on the mainland) allowed for the circulation of political opinions. Despite relative freedom, the British colonial government did impose limits on Chinese political activity by suppressing the CCP's student recruitment drives in Hong Kong and deporting political activists back to the mainland (including Sun Yat-sen, the leader of the Nationalist Party).[30]

Another major political event was World War I, which forced many British colonials to move back to Europe for the war effort. It was a boon for the Chinese, because many higher-ranking positions in banking and shipping became vacant and were filled by Chinese.[31] Until then, the British had excluded the Chinese population from high corporate and political positions. This was the beginning of the gradual indigenization of the Hong Kong political economy. In 1926, Chow Shouson was the first ethnic Chinese person to be appointed to the powerful executive council, the ruling colonial administration.[32] The foundation of the University of Hong Kong (1912) to train highly skilled Chinese technicians created an English-speaking professional class of Chinese people, who resented British

TABLE 9.1 Population of Hong Kong, 1872–2016

Year	Population
1872	121,985
1881	160,402
1891	221,441
1901	368,987
1911	456,739
1921	625,166
1931	840,473
1941	1,639,337
1945	650,000
1951	2,020,000
1961	3,129,648
1971	3,936,630
1986	5,495,488
1996	6,412,937
2006	6,864,346
2016	7,336,585
2021	7,403,100

Source: 1872–1971: Fan Shuh Ching, *The Population of Hong Kong* (Geneva: Committee for International Coordination of National Research in Demography, 1974), http://www.cicred.org/Eng/Publications/pdf/c-c21.pdf; 1941–1951: Saw Swee-Hock and Chiu Wing Kin, "Population Growth and Redistribution in Hong Kong, 1841–1975," *Southeast Asian Journal of Social Science* 4, no. 1 (1975): 123–131; 1986–2021: Hong Kong Census and Statistics Department. https://www.censtatd.gov.hk/en/web_table.html?id=1A#.

discrimination in hiring.[33] Henry Lethbridge noted the gradual formation of a Hong Kong identity: "Hong Kong had come of age in 1925: it was no longer simply a congeries of various groups, composed of acquisitive, rootless, transient individuals, but was beginning to coalesce into a community and, if all racial divisions are included, into a plural society, its members bound together, as it were, in a network of contractual arrangements. It had begun to acquire an identity."[34]

The Hong Kong identity, which combined a commitment to British rule of law with Chinese culture, became more pronounced in response to two further traumatic events: the Japanese occupation (1941–1945) and the final victory of the CCP in the Chinese Civil War (1949). The first event undermined Hong Kong people's faith in the power of their white British colonial overlords, and the second event abruptly reduced (but did not halt) the hitherto free flow of people and commerce across the border, creating a growing rift in political and cultural values between Hong Kong and the CCP's authoritarian rule.[35]

Japan's interest in seizing Hong Kong came from its desire to strangle China's supply routes during World War II. The surrounding Guangdong and Fujian provinces had already been occupied by Japan prior to the capture of Hong Kong in 1941.[36] Hong Kong people chafed under Japanese rule because of the high inflation created by the forced requisition of essential goods to sustain the Japanese war effort. The occupiers also shot or beheaded the Chinese for failing to bow in the required manner.[37] In these and many other ways, the fate of Hong Kong's population under the Japanese was quite similar to that experienced in Singapore (see chapter 4).

After World War II Hong Kong was restored to British rule, but the British experienced a further indigenization of the political and economic structure. Britain realized that anticolonial sentiment had become widespread throughout all its colonies, so it became necessary to offer participation to the indigenous population in order to retain legitimacy and prevent an independence movement.[38] An important qualification in the Hong Kong case was that there was no strong independence movement because Hong Kong's fate was tied up with the relationship between Britain and China. China's Nationalist leader Chiang Kai-shek briefly considered Hong Kong's reunification, but he faced a bigger threat in fighting the communists. The CCP under Mao Zedong, in turn, was little interested in recapturing Hong Kong as long as the British treated the Chinese well. Without a strong challenge from China, Britain restored colonial rule by relying principally on Chinese community allies, such as Chow Shouson and the Eurasian businessman Robert Kotewall.[39]

In 1946, the colonial government opened the civil service to the Chinese, although it took until the 1980s for most positions to be filled by Chinese. The general chamber of commerce was not opened to Chinese participation until the 1980s.[40] The reluctance to cede control to the indigenous population reflected the British paternalistic attitude, which was only challenged when the British faced pressure to return Hong Kong to China. The British initially argued that Hong Kong must not be democratized because communist China would not tolerate it.[41]

Hong Kong's industrialization, which began in the early twentieth century, accelerated in the 1950s and 1960s. A contributing factor was the migration of Shanghai industrialists to Hong Kong, as they saw no future for themselves in a communist China that was rapidly moving to nationalize the means of production and expropriate capitalists. Furthermore, the CCP takeover resulted in an American-led economic embargo that substantially reduced (but did not eliminate) the trade flows between China and the world, threatening the entrepôt-based economic model of Hong Kong.

Hong Kong needed an industrial base to thrive economically, which was made possible by its political stability, a good port, and a stable supply of cheap labor from China. Industrial production included diverse sectors such as textiles, clothing, plastic toys, flowers, flashlights, batteries, aluminum, enamel, and rattan ware.[42] Industrial expansion was buttressed by increasing demand for financial services. Hong Kong could attract foreign capital because it had a stable currency regime (in contrast to mainland China). Shanghai bankers who moved to Hong Kong were also adept at garnering loans from British banks.[43] Employment became more dependent on manufacturing: it increased from 5 percent industrial workers in 1950 to a peak of 40 percent in 1980.[44] Industrialization was a largely indigenous Chinese process rather than a deliberate British colonial policy, although it cannot be denied that the British rule-of-law framework served as a precondition for its development.

Rising prosperity was associated with more leisure time, more international travel, and a flourishing cultural environment that included the Cantonese opera (revived from an earlier era) and the opening of Hong Kong's Arts Festival (1973), Arts Centre (1979), Academy for the Performing Arts (1984), and the Hong Kong Museum of Art (1985).[45] From the mid-1970s to the 1980s, Hong Kong–based Cantopop (Cantonese pop music) became an important source of entertainment for the local population, although it has been supplanted by Mandarin pop in the 2000s. The movie industry flourished with leading actors that included Bruce Lee and Jackie Chan.[46]

The postwar era was also marked by social reforms. In 1946, the ordinance on housing segregation was repealed, which was followed by a greater mixing of races in the real estate market. In a sharp departure from the previous laissez-faire policies, the British also invested in a welfare state. The change included public housing to address squalid living conditions; primary education; public assistance for low-income individuals; transportation, including a new subway and a tunnel connecting Kowloon and Hong Kong Island; and health services.[47] This social welfare legislation was passed in reaction to the major riots and labor strikes that occurred in 1967. The upheaval can partly be explained by distributional struggles in industry, but also by CCP infiltration and incitement to anticolonial activity. The colonial administration reacted to these protests with swift punishment and the incarceration of 5,000 individuals, often without trial.[48] Ultimately, the insurgency failed because protesters had no interest in supporting communist rule. The general population opposed the CCP, as many Hong Kong people were refugees from the communist regime.[49]

In addition to expanding the welfare state, the colonial government took measures to control corruption. After high-profile corruption cases became known to the public, the colonial government introduced an independent commission against corruption in 1974, which was tasked with investigating and punishing official crimes. This measure swiftly increased the legitimacy of the colonial government.[50]

In the early 1980s, Chinese economic reforms under Chairman Deng Xiaoping substantially improved China–Hong Kong relations. Bilateral trade flows increased. Hong Kong had ample capital, while China had ample labor. Hong Kong's business owners had been facing increasing labor costs at home and took advantage of the cheap Chinese labor by building up factories in the nearby city of Shenzhen, which the CCP declared a special economic zone.[51] Hong Kong banks were also important originators of loans for China. Subsequently, the Hong Kong business community became enthusiastic supporters of reunification with China.[52]

As for the working classes, the labor market increasingly split as stable blue-collar occupations disappeared in favor of college degree–based, high-skilled positions and menial low-skilled jobs in the service sector.[53] Recent data suggest that educational attainment has been increasing: the share of college graduates increased from 23 percent to nearly 33 percent from 2006 to 2016. Nonetheless, one-fifth of the population still lacked a high school diploma. Individuals with only a primary school education experienced only a HK$2,000 increase in salary from 2012 to 2020, while college degree holders received an increase of HK$5,200.[54] Hence not every Hong Kong resident benefited from economic development and globalization, with increasing inequality evident between winners and losers.

While Hong Kong's economic fate became increasingly tied to mainland China, it faced an uncertain political future because Britain's lease on the New

Territories was expiring. Real estate tycoons giving out fifteen-year leases needed certainty for their plans and wanted the colonial government to clarify Hong Kong's political status. Governor Murray MacLehose had the impression that Deng Xiaoping would accept a continuation of Hong Kong's British colonial status, as China already was receiving tremendous economic benefits from the status quo. He was mistaken. Deng insisted on Hong Kong reverting to China's sovereignty under a "one country, two systems" regime that should become a role model for later reunification with Taiwan.[55] Britain relented and accepted the handover under the condition that Hong Kong would retain the British rule of law, which Chinese negotiators formally agreed to. The Sino-British Joint Declaration of 1984 stated that Hong Kong would be returned to China in 1997. China would immediately assume control over defense and foreign policy, but Hong Kong would have autonomy in economic and social affairs.[56]

According to the agreement, Hong Kong would become a special administrative region (HKSAR) with its own government, free port status with a separate customs territory, free flow of capital, autonomous currency, no taxation from China, and an unchanged political status for fifty years after the handover. In 1990, China formulated Hong Kong's basic law with the input of Hong Kong community and political leaders. The basic law of 1990 codified Hong Kong's legal autonomy (including rule of law and personal freedoms) but affirmed the power of the Beijing government to amend and overrule Hong Kong's laws as it saw fit.[57] The latter point became a major source of contention during subsequent prodemocracy protests years after reunification.

During these Sino-British negotiations, Hong Kong citizens were not consulted. There were concerns that their freedom and way of life would be threatened by reunification, and this sense of insecurity created a popular desire for more democratic participation. Between 1984 and 1997, 10 percent of the Hong Kong population voted with their feet by leaving the island for Western countries. For many Hong Kong people the departure was not necessarily permanent: "parachute kids" (who lived overseas, but whose parents remained in Hong Kong) and "astronaut" parents (who traveled back and forth between Hong Kong and Western countries) became commonplace.[58] As for the colonial rulers, they were fairly restrained before the handover and willing to work with the Chinese government to agree on common policies. This included the 1987 agreement to raze the walled city of Kowloon, a low-income neighborhood where crime, drugs, gambling, and prostitution flourished. The walled city was replaced by a public park in 1994.[59] This development may be read as a sign that the old, colonial laissez-faire regime was no longer to be tolerated.

The public mood swiftly shifted during the 1989 Tiananmen protests, where prodemocracy protests gathered steam in Beijing precisely at the time that eastern European communism was being toppled. Deng Xiaoping recognized the threat to the CCP and sent tanks into the capital streets to crush the antigovernment protests.[60] Prodemocracy activists in Hong Kong were helpless, unable to face the communist crackdown. The Hong Kong lawmaker Martin Lee claimed at that time that Britain's transfer of Hong Kong to China was like surrendering Jews to Nazi Germany.[61] The British responded to Tiananmen by more explicitly favoring democratic reforms, which they had never previously entertained. First, Britain increased the number of elected legislative council seats, raising them to thirty (see figure 9.1). In the first democratic elections for eighteen legislative seats, the prodemocracy faction won twelve. This result greatly displeased the CCP, which henceforth opposed further democratization.[62] Hong Kong also adopted, at this time, the International Covenant on Civil and Political Rights, the International Covenant on Economic, Social and Cultural Rights, and the International Labour Convention.[63]

In 1992, the British government appointed the last colonial governor, Chris Patten, a former member of Parliament and chairman of the United Kingdom's Conservative Party. He was a political appointee, not a diplomat or technocrat as was the practice; hence he was more open to confrontation with Beijing. Patten introduced fresh political reforms, increasing the number of elected legislative

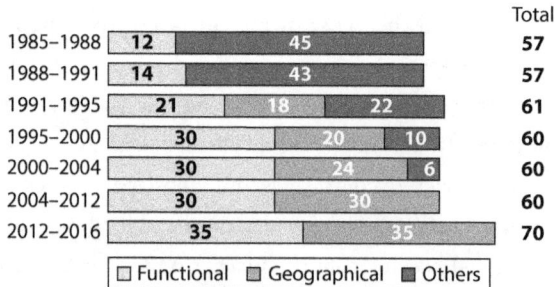

9.1 Legislative seats by type in Hong Kong.

Source: Tanna Chong, "Legco Election 2016: How a Handful of Voters Elect 30 Hong Kong Lawmakers," *South China Morning Post*, February 6, 2014, https://www.scmp.com/news/hong-kong/article/1421613/legco-election-2016-how-handful-voters-elect-30-hong-kong-lawmakers.

seats, widening the base of the functional constituencies (council seats that are given to professional groups, such as real estate, finance, healthcare, and education), and barring legislative council members from being in the executive council in order to strengthen the power and autonomy of the latter.[64] China highly disapproved of the Patten reforms, fearing that an expansion of democracy could advance Hong Kong's independence movement and increase democratization demands on the mainland, which had just been suppressed during the Tiananmen confrontations. The British push toward democratization of Hong Kong between 1991 and 1997 may have been modest, but it generated political expectations among younger citizens that the Chinese government could not tolerate. On the other hand, the common view is that democracy in Hong Kong is "young and has shallow roots" that could easily be undone by China.[65]

The British formally departed Hong Kong on June 30, 1997, bringing a century and a half of colonial history to an end. Steve Tsang praised the British legacy, noting that "Britain was leaving behind a vibrant modern economy with a higher per capita GDP than that of the metropolitan country itself, a well-educated population admired for its resourcefulness and entrepreneurial drive, a law-abiding and human rights-respecting society, as well as a stable, liberal and efficient government."[66] The mainland Chinese academic Sun Haichao took a decidedly less charitable view of British colonization: "The rule of colonial countries over colonies includes cruel repression, cultural colonization and economic plunder. After the British occupied Hong Kong following the First Opium War, they successively adopted unequal treaties . . . to control Hong Kong until June 30, 1997."[67] From China's perspective, the restoration of sovereignty in Hong Kong marked the end of a century of humiliation inflicted by Western imperialism that began with the unequal treaties in the 1840s.[68] Reunification via the "one country, two systems" model was China's way of realizing "socialism with Chinese characteristics."[69]

INTO THE TWENTY-FIRST CENTURY: POSSIBLE REUNIFICATION WITH CHINA AND DISCONTENTS

The Hong Kong "special administrative region" (HKSAR) faced early challenges involving the Asian financial crisis (1997–1998) and the severe acute respiratory syndrome (SARS) virus (2003). Hong Kong pegged its currency to the U.S. dollar after 1983 even as it had a higher rate of inflation than the United States. Speculative attacks attempted to force Hong Kong to devalue, but given its huge financial reserves, it maintained the peg. It also raised the interest rate from 8 percent to 23 percent, and the Hong Kong Monetary Authority purchased company stock market shares to halt their downward slide. Thus, Hong Kong fared better than other Asian economies, who were faced with high unemployment, currency devaluation, and nonperforming loans.[70] SARS had begun in nearby Guangdong province and between March and June 2003 infected 1,750 persons and killed 298 in hospitals and housing estates in Hong Kong. The administration introduced contact tracing, isolation of infected patients, school closures, temperature checks in public places, cleansing campaigns, and public information campaigns to bring the disease under control.[71]

Regarding politics, China's first priority was to undo Patten's political reforms. China created an unelected provisional legislative council, which replaced the legislative council approved by the Patten reforms in 1995. A year later this provisional council was replaced by an elected council, but only twenty of the sixty seats were elected in geographic constituencies. The remaining seats were appointed via functional constituencies, which ensured that prodemocracy factions could never gain a majority (see figure 9.1). Before the handover by Britain, a 400-member selection committee voted for the first chief executive, Tung Chee-hwa, to rule the HKSAR. Prodemocracy activists, believing that the process would ensure the appointment of a pro-Beijing candidate, protested against Tung's election and were dragged away by police.[72] Tung promptly ruled out further steps toward democratization.

China ensured the domination of HKSAR's political institutions via its business community. Hong Kong's economy is dominated by four big families who control a vast empire of real estate, shopping malls and retail stores, utilities, garbage collection, and airports.[73] The HKSAR government uses profits from the land tax and land sales to fund major infrastructure projects that benefit the four families, while public services (welfare, housing, etc.) are neglected. Domination by big business (real estate, finance) tends to prevent start-ups and holds down small businesses with high rent. The HKSAR government has invested HK$100 billion via the innovation and technology bureau to foster technology start-ups, but it has failed to compete with industry leaders in Silicon Valley or Singapore. A business park named Cyberport that was launched in 1999 to foster technology companies is now struggling as a "ghost town" with low occupancy rates.[74]

Domination by big businesses creates extreme income and wealth inequality. While 18 percent of Hong Kong residents lived under the poverty line in 2016, 35 percent of the city's GDP was owned by the top ten billionaires.[75]

The economic disparities are even more apparent in the housing sector. While the government approved new skyscrapers to serve the business community, private-sector housing became increasingly unaffordable. The 2017 ratio of house prices to income was 18.1.[76] Thirty percent of the city's population live in the Public Rental Housing Estates, with waiting lists longer than three years. The rising real estate prices are caused by the very high demand for Hong Kong property by affluent residents of mainland China, who can easily outbid locals.[77] Unaffordable housing hits young adults particularly hard: a whopping 60 percent of people between ages thirty and thirty-five live with their parents, often in cramped apartments.[78]

With reunification, Hong Kong opened the doors to mainland immigration, issuing 150 daily one-way entry permits, which amount to 550,000 every decade. The number of mainland tourists increased from 4.3 million in 2004 to 47 million in 2014. The entry of mainland money and people bid up not only residential housing and rental properties, but also retail rents. Luxury boutiques service the rising demands of rich Chinese customers, thus pushing out small retail stores that service local residents. Another development has been the entry of pregnant mainland women to Hong Kong to give birth to children there, which entitles the children to Hong Kong permanent residency. This pattern creates resentment among locals, who experience diminishing hospital resources.[79]

As noted earlier, with the disappearance of industrial jobs because of off-shoring to the Chinese hinterland, there emerged an increasingly skewed labor market with high demand for both high-skilled and low-skilled jobs. Furthermore, self-employment as an alternative to regular jobs declined. The HKSAR government introduced a minimum wage in 2010, which was raised to HK$34.50 an hour by 2017.[80] Foreign domestic helpers from the Philippines were especially disadvantaged as their pay was cut during the Asian financial crisis and the deflationary period in the early 2000s.[81]

Economic discontent (unaffordable housing, extreme inequality, and business and real estate domination) was reinforced by political discontent (lack of democracy and threat to personal freedoms). The CCP decided to ally itself with the business community of Hong Kong, while neglecting the poor and the young.

This decision reduced the legitimacy of the HKSAR administration. Nonetheless, China remained intent on strengthening its grip on Hong Kong's politics: in 2003, the HKSAR government proposed a new national security bill (to criminalize treason, subversion, secession, and sedition), which caused mass protests and had to be withdrawn under public pressure.[82]

In 2014, The Chinese National People's Congress promulgated a selection process for the Hong Kong chief executive elections in 2017 and beyond. The election committee, overwhelmingly staffed with probusiness and pro-Beijing representatives, would appoint two or three candidates. The people of Hong Kong would vote for the chief executive, who would then have to be approved by the Chinese central government. Prodemocracy activists thought that this electoral reform was undemocratic and had to be opposed. This announcement caused the September–December 2014 protests by the Umbrella Movement (as protesters used umbrellas to shield themselves from police pepper spray). Student leaders such as Joshua Wong and Agnes Chow, as well as older leaders (university, religion, and civil society leaders) such as Benny Tai, Chan Kin-man, and Chu Yiu-ming, were instrumental in these prodemocracy protests.[83] While the government crushed the demonstrations, the legislature finally voted down the election reform bill.[84]

After the 2014 protests, more prodemocracy candidates were emboldened to run for office, but some of the prodemocracy lawmakers were prevented from being sworn in for holding "unconstitutional" (seditious, antigovernment) political views. In 2016, student leaders founded Demosisto, a prodemocracy political organization.[85] The youth in Hong Kong have become politicized with the waves of protest, as more and more of them self-identify as "Hong Konger" rather than Chinese.

In 2019, the HKSAR government led by Carrie Lam proposed an extradition bill with China and Taiwan, which prodemocracy activists claimed would result in the extradition of anti-Beijing activists to the nondemocratic mainland justice system. Mass protests occurred again, ultimately forcing the HKSAR government to suspend and then withdraw the bill. The protesters were emboldened and further demanded the release and exoneration of protesters, the prosecution of cops who used violence, and the resignation of Chief Executive Lam. The HKSAR government rebuffed these demands. In the November 2019 district council elections (which tend to be nonpolitical), the prodemocracy parties won a landslide.[86]

Beijing had enough and took advantage of the Covid-19 lockdowns, which prevented social and political gathering for public health reasons. On June 30, 2020, the government passed a national security law that criminalized any act it deemed subversive or seditious, with serious penalties ranging between ten years and life in prison. This was done without any input by HKSAR officials. Demosisto promptly disbanded, as members feared prosecution.[87] Much smaller protests in response to the passage of the new law promptly resulted in the imprisonment of some protesters, citing the provisions of the new law. The student leaders Joshua Wong, Agnes Chow, and Ivan Lam were sentenced to jail in December 2020, while Nathan Law fled to exile in Britain.[88]

In July 2020, the HKSAR government made a dozen prodemocracy candidates ineligible for running in the next election and delayed the legislative election, officially because of safety concerns relating to Covid-19 but, in reality, because of fear of an election victory by the prodemocracy camp. In November, the HKSAR government ejected four opposition lawmakers, which resulted in the mass resignation of all remaining fifteen opposition lawmakers, leaving a third of the legislative seats vacant and giving the pro-Beijing politicians full rein.[89] The legislature then passed laws to drop references to democratic institutions from school textbooks, criminalize Chinese flag burning, and require the singing of the Chinese national anthem in schools. Prodemocracy academics were fired. China accomplished political peace, albeit an unhappy one. It could afford this harsh repression because, despite its reliance on Hong Kong as a window for foreign investment, the size of Hong Kong's economy has diminished steadily in relation to the mainland's.

The national security law has substantially altered foreign attitudes toward Hong Kong. Many Western countries have suspended their extradition agreements. The United States imposed sanctions on eleven Chinese and HKSAR officials. As of July 2020, the United States ended preferential visiting rights for HKSAR passport holders, placing them on a par with Chinese passports.[90] On the flipside, Britain, citing breach of the Sino-British agreement of 1984, has eased restrictions on 3 million Hong Kong residents who applied for a BNO (British National Overseas) status to acquire a British passport without quota restrictions.[91]

The protests were damaging to the economy, leading to the recession of 2019. The number of tourists declined by 40 percent even before the Covid-19 pandemic. Demand for real estate, a central pillar of the Hong Kong economy, declined by 24 percent.[92] Yet Chinese businesses have largely supported the national security law, citing the prospects of greater political stability. JD.com, an e-commerce retailer, raised $3.9 billion selling shares in the stock exchange in August 2020, mainly because U.S. sanctions had made it more difficult for Chinese companies to raise money in America. Chinese businesses are signing rental leases for new office space in Hong Kong.[93] The Hong Kong Monetary Authority published a pitchbook in June 2020 to invite foreigners to continue investing in Hong Kong, citing the continued benefits of common law and of being the "dominant gateway to China." Foreign reserves more than doubled, from nearly US$200 billion to US$440 billion from 2008 to 2020.[94] On the other hand, net capital flows that were relatively balanced and a deficit of not more than HK$50 billion prior to 2020 turned more negative, reaching nearly HK$100 billion by the second quarter of 2021.[95]

CONCLUSION

As of 2021, Hong Kong's status as a stable and reliable financial center was under threat as it struggled through political instability and the Covid-19 pandemic. On the one hand, prudent public health measures (with over 87 percent of the population vaccinated as of April 2022),[96] large capital inflows from Chinese companies, and strict national security laws have stabilized the political economy for now. As China's economy continues to grow, Hong Kong may be able to ride that wave. On the other hand, Hong Kong is facing the same sanctions regime from the Western developed countries as China and is highly exposed to the U.S.-China geopolitical rivalry. These sanctions further threaten Hong Kong's position as a global financial center, even as it might remain a national financial center. Other large countries, such as India, have recently passed regulations further restricting Chinese investments.[97] Many young Hong Kong people, chafing in an oppressive political climate and with few opportunities, might leave Hong Kong, resulting in a brain drain. The underlying socioeconomic and political discontent arising from an unaffordable cost of living and housing, a government under the thumb of big business and the CCP, and the diminution of political rights for a restive youth do not augur well for the future. The more restrictive environment is not limited to commerce and politics, but also affects the art world: the newly opened M+ contemporary art museum has had to remove politically sensitive art exhibits critical of the CCP.[98]

The present drama of Hong Kong represents a case study of what happens when one of the preconditions for an emerging global city disappears: reliable rule of law under a stable judicial system. The island rose to prominence under British rule when financial operations were predictable and investors felt secure in their investments. The decision of the CCP to take back effective political control of the former British colony has removed these guarantees. While the present island government has been making noises about the continuation of British-style common law in the governance of mercantile transactions, no sane leader of a multinational corporation would currently decide to establish its regional Asian headquarters in Hong Kong.[99]

The movement of multinational businesses and offices from Hong Kong to Singapore, which today appears minor, may turn into a flood if present political conditions worsen. Hong Kong still counts in its favor two factors. The first is the inertial weight of past investments and practices when the city was the effective regional business capital. The second is its role as a key gateway into the vast Chinese market. The operation of path dependence—the past determining the future—may encourage international firms to adopt a wait-and-see attitude toward the CCP's growing presence and control. Western banks like Morgan Stanley indicated in July 2021 that they wanted to expand their office footprint in Hong Kong despite the national security law.[100] But this pattern may not last.

On the other hand, the increasing presence in Hong Kong of Chinese banks and large firms will have two effects. First, it will increasingly compromise Hong Kong's role as a legally impartial regional center; second, it will justify new investments by global corporations only for the purpose of gaining entry into the Chinese market. Already new investments by Hong Kong–based firms in other countries of the region, especially India, are being treated and regulated as no different from other Chinese firms.[101] The increasingly apparent role of the island as an economic gateway to the mainland puts it in direct competition with other coastal cities vying for the same role, primarily Shanghai. Already a multinational firm doing business in China, Procter and Gamble, has decided to move its headquarters to Shanghai to avoid the continuing instability and turmoil on the island.[102]

Hong Kong will remain an important commercial port and financial center for China, but its past role as regional entrepôt for the world economy in the Asian theater is increasingly threatened. That role will almost inevitably devolve to what had been, until recently, a much lesser competitor—the island-nation of Singapore.

Victoria Harbor and Hong Kong Island in the 1860s.

Kowloon City and Victoria, Hong Kong in the 1960s.

Southern Kowloon and Victoria, Hong Kong in 2014.

A residential building in Quarry Bay, Hong Kong.

Wong Tai Sin Temple, which is dedicated to the Taoist deity Wong Tai Sin.

CONCLUSION

Theoretical Implications, Climate Change,
and Future Challenges

S o what have we learned from this journey into the past and present of cities? In this final chapter, we seek to synthesize the major themes of our study as they bear on existing urban theories and likely trends in the future. This effort at synthesis answers three main questions. First, how does the evolution of the capitalist system in the last half century leading to the emergence of global cities fit within classic accounts of urbanization and urban history? Second, what bearing do contemporary events, especially what we have baptized as "emerging global cities," have on extant theories of urbanization and the derived policies? Third, what is the future of these cities, and what effects will looming major challenges to their prominence and their very existence have? These include fissures in political systems that have so far emerged in leading cities, postpandemic socioeconomic inequalities, and the effects of global climate change and sea-level rise (SLR). The history of urbanization under capitalism has been full of surprises, and the rise of global cities may not represent its end point but open up a new chapter whose reach and consequences are, at present, incalculable.

THE GREAT U-TURN

Since its unpromising beginning in the ninth century, the marriage between capitalism and the city continued relentlessly, although with multiple vicissitudes, for the next eleven centuries. From their pitiful appearance and constrained circumstances in the "century of no markets,"[1] urban centers gradually regained their commercial functions, attracting new classes of people—artisans and merchants—to themselves. Two centuries later, the battle was fully engaged between these free urban burghers and the servile-based feudal order centered in the noble castles and abbeys in the countryside. Chapter 1 summarized this evolution of the urban-capitalist relationship, including both the changing functions of the city and the changing character of the class struggle within and beyond it.

This was not a straightforward story, for the centuries-old struggle against feudalism did not see it replaced by capitalism, in the modern sense, but by an alliance of enriched merchants, carefully guarding their monopolies, and sovereigns bent on expanding their lands while subjugating an unruly and warlike feudal nobility. During this period, roughly associated with the late Middle Ages and the Renaissance, cities fully regained their economic function as marketplaces while gaining political freedoms from their feudal overlords. Urban autonomy was short-lived, however, as the urban merchant class, locked in a struggle with the artisan guilds, willingly surrendered city liberties in exchange for royal protection. The nation-state, not the city, emerged from the process as the dominant encompassing political unit.[2]

It took major revolutions in Britain and France and countless other struggles to bring an end to the absolutist monarchies of Europe and their allied entrenched mercantile elite. These developments led to the first steps toward free trade and the definite ascent of the industrial bourgeoisie to the top of the class structure. The process was well under way before the Industrial Revolution, but the latter consolidated it and led to the century-old *Pax Britannica* and free-trade imperialism.[3]

Cities were transformed; while fulfilling their traditional functions as administrative centers and marketplaces, they also became sites for capitalist production. The industrial city became the model and culmination of the process of capitalist urbanization and the paradigm for other cities to imitate. Theories of urbanization in the late nineteenth and early twentieth centuries followed suit, assuming that industrial production in the cities of the capitalist centers represented the end point of the history of urbanization.[4]

History, however, had other designs, for as Marx and Engels presciently saw, what industrialism mainly did was to bring the antagonists in the evolving class struggle—this time the bourgeoisie and the proletariat—into the same restricted urban space. If the industrial city was primarily a machine for capitalist accumulation, it was not a peaceful one because the workers, victims of surplus extraction, reacted vigorously and tenaciously to their exploitation. Endless strikes and confrontations followed, all invariably centered in the cities.[5] These culminated in proletarian uprisings of various sorts, the consolidation of industrial trade unions, the rise of communist and socialist parties, and the eventual Bolshevik triumph in Russia. The Bolshevik triumph, added to the decline of the major industrial economies during the Great Depression, led to the assumption that capitalism as a global system had come to an end.[6]

Again, it did not happen that way, thanks to the extraordinary innovations introduced by Franklin Roosevelt's New Deal in America and to the rise of a new brand of heterodox economics led by John Maynard Keynes. Both saw that the only avenue for rescuing capitalism from itself was massive deficit spending sponsored by the state. That policy was to see its culmination during World War II. The war had two key consequences. First, it generated the largest economic stimulus implemented so far, eliminating, in a few years, the worst effects of the Great Depression. Second, it consolidated the position of the United States as the world's hegemonic capitalist power.[7]

As seen in chapter 1, major American corporations made use of their unchallenged global control to launch a historic pact with their trade unions with the support of the state. Rising labor costs brought about by higher wages and a package of new benefits for workers could be met because these costs could be passed on to the final price of goods, as these corporations enjoyed oligopolistic control of their markets. The result was two decades of labor peace under *Pax Americana* and the consolidation of a privileged sector of the working class known as the "primary" labor market.[8]

This relatively happy state of affairs did not last for reasons discussed in chapter 1. Confronted with an onslaught of competition from abroad, American manufacturing corporations reacted by, in effect, jettisoning the historical pact with labor as they moved the bulk of industrial production abroad. This is what Bluestone and Harrison baptized "the Great U-Turn."[9] This turn was experienced not only by the industrial working class as the primary labor market and stable jobs disappeared, but also by entire cities that lost their principal economic function and reverted to their prior role as marketplaces and administrative centers.

Services replaced industry as the major employer. But these services varied greatly among deindustrializing cities. Many resorted to "eds and meds" complexes as their chosen option and, wherever possible, dressed up their historic past as tourist attractions. In every case, the result was a bifurcated labor market where professional and technical personnel with advanced credentials benefited from the new division of labor, while the displaced, industrial proletariat became marginalized.[10]

A few cities gained from the Great U-Turn, however, by attracting the leading service sectors involved in financing and coordinating the capitalist economy. While industrial production facilities could be decentralized worldwide, their capitalization and coordination could not. The major actors performing these functions had to concentrate in physically restricted spaces. These were the global cities. New York, London, Tokyo, and to a lesser extent Paris, Frankfurt, and Chicago were generally glad to shed their industrial past and assume their new hegemonic status.[11] This transformation did not bring the class struggle to an end but transformed it in unexpected ways, creating, among other things, a growing physical segregation between spaces inhabited by the beneficiaries of the new economy and the working classes servicing them. Not only the labor market, but also the physical structure of global cities, became increasingly bifurcated.

Despite these and other unappealing features, global cities turned out to be a model that urban elites elsewhere sought to imitate. The heightened need for coordination, finance, and administration brought about by the Great U-Turn could not be satisfied by just a few cities; it required regional platforms as well. This need created a new opportunity for global hopefuls, although, as we have seen, few succeeded in achieving these goals. Emerging global cities as well as the more established ones left an industrial past behind, or never had one, concentrating instead on large-scale commerce, real estate, and producer services. In that sense, they were also reflections and beneficiaries of the great economic U-Turn.

THEORETICAL IMPLICATIONS

Despite their disparate historical origins and other differences, emerging global cities possess three common characteristics that differentiate them from others: (1) a reliable legal system capable of inducing confidence among both corporate and individual investors; (2) an efficient probusiness government bureaucracy that is generally immune to corruption; and (3) leaders who are determined to make their city succeed against the global competition. In the cases of Dubai and Singapore, that role was assumed by motivated political leaders, while in Miami it fell to a class of single-minded exile bankers and financiers. These converging experiences have four main implications for urban theory and policy.

The first, and most obvious, is that they have done away with the past divide between global cities—all situated in the advanced world—and "Third World" cities victimized by decisions taken by the hegemonic powers. This divide, denounced in eloquent terms by Robinson and Brenner, is now qualified by the experiences of cities that, once peripheral in the global system, have managed to ascend to strategic positions.[12] This achievement implies that there is a measure of flexibility within that system, provided that the conditions listed previously are met.

The second theoretical implication is that industrialism and development are no longer synonymous. The decision of economic elites in the advanced nations to physically separate production from administration, coordination, and design led to the emergence of successful cities that do not produce anything tangible. Instead of things, they deal in symbols and innovative ideas—from financial derivatives to novel ways to channel and profit from consumer demand. In the process, past attempts by governments in Latin America and elsewhere in the periphery to develop their countries through import substitution industrialization fell by the wayside. Factories engaged in the production of material things no longer represent "development," insofar as the design for such things and the ways and means to market them are controlled from elsewhere. The "creative classes" engaged in this symbolic work do not commonly live near the peripheral proletariat that actually produce the physical commodities.[13] Investment in the intangible economy—digitization, technology, artificial intelligence—is central to the future of these cities, and the global competition for high-skilled talent is continuously intensifying.

The third theoretical implication of the industrial U-Turn is that cities no longer serve as passive marketplaces, providing a physical site for buyers and sellers to come together. That classic Weberian image stands in need of modification as the city itself becomes an actor in the global competition for recognition and dominance. Governing elites dress up their cities, adorning them with multiple festivals, art shows, and sports competitions and branding them as secure and chic places to live and work. Brand Dubai has worked wonders under Sheik Maktoum's leadership, culminating in the Heart of Europe complex built on a set of man-made islands four kilometers from shore and imitating, at great cost, themes borrowed from the Old Continent.[14] Singapore promotes its new tourist complex in Sentosa Island, while continuing to bill itself as a stable and secure investment venue that is profiting, most recently, from Hong Kong's loss of global status. The combination of ease of business, rule of law, and respect for multiculturalism places Singapore in a strong position to benefit as a destination for the transfer of financials and migration of talent from Hong Kong. Miami elites have turned the Art Basel fair in December into the centerpiece of year-round events that buttress the city's standing as the cultural capital of the Americas. The mayor's office has resorted to the allure of new techs to rebrand the city as the world's cryptocurrency capital. In contrast with traditional images of the city as the passive physical site for political and economic events to happen, the city itself is the event.[15] People are encouraged to be part of it—living, visiting, and investing there. A business or a residential address in the Heart of Europe, Sentosa Island, or Brickell Avenue is a desirable status symbol, marketed as such the world over.

The fourth main implication for urban theory is the novel ways in which migration and the city have become intertwined. As has been noted in the past by urban scholars, migration and the development of cities have been but two sides of the same coin during the history of capitalism.[16] From the near disappearance of European cities through population loss in the "century of no markets" to their revival after the reconquest of the Mediterranean and the inflow of new classes of people, migration was a key element of the cities that were to become the cradles of capitalism. That relationship endured over the centuries as heavy labor migration became a necessary condition for the rise of industrial centers, first in Britain and then in France, Germany, and North America. The decline of the industrial era, marked by the Great U-Turn, was reflected in population outflows from formerly prosperous industrial centers that went on to form the new Rust Belts in America, the English Midlands, and elsewhere.[17]

The migration-urbanization link has assumed a new form in the present era, in which, it is safe to assert, new global cities would not have emerged without heavy and diversified migration toward them. The relationship is most clearly seen in the cases of Dubai and Singapore. A native population of a few hundred thousand could not have launched the miraculous rise of these cities, were it not for a heavy foreign inflow. That inflow included a class of expatriates—professionals and technicians—coming initially from Britain and then from elsewhere in Europe and North America, followed by heavy labor movements from nearby peripheral countries. India and, to a lesser extent Pakistan, Bangladesh, and the Philippines, were prime sources of these migrations, which last to our day.[18]

Miami is different because the initial migration flows that triggered its transformation were not prompted by local leaders, but foreign ones. Fidel Castro's communist revolution in Cuba was the event most responsible for this transformation. As seen in chapter 3, it led to the departure of tens of thousands of well-educated and experienced business leaders and professionals, most of whom made their new home in South Florida. Their experience of migration and resettlement then served as a template for tens of thousands of additional escapees from other Latin American revolts and dictatorships, as well as for impoverished populations in Haiti and elsewhere in the Caribbean that made Miami their chosen destination. Before it became the economic and cultural "capital" of the Americas, Miami was the place of refuge for the victims of many institutional failures and political convulsions in the countries to its south.[19]

Today, as seen in the respective chapters, over 80 percent of Dubai's population, 30 percent of Singapore's, and the majority of the population of Miami's metropolitan area are of foreign origin. Without this foreign component, it is quite doubtful that these cities would have achieved their present position of global prominence. Once again, migration became an indispensable condition for the novel turn that the evolution of global capitalism has taken.

A NEW TURN: CITIES AND CLIMATE CHANGE

History never stops, and the story told previously would be incomplete without at least touching on what may be its next chapter. For as the capitalist system created the socioeconomic conditions for the rise of global cities and then emerging cities, its consequences for the planet may be altogether different. Put simply, if immigration was a precondition for the emergence of global cities, as just noted, the relentless warming of the planet, and the SLR created by the same system, may cause an exodus from these and other urban centers in the future.

Forty-five percent of the world's population live in urban areas, and this figure is expected to grow to 68 percent by 2050. While cities are the most affected by the consequences of climate change, they are simultaneously the most important contributors to global warming. Cities occupy less than 2 percent of the planet's surface, yet they generate 60 percent of all carbon emissions, and their energy consumption represents 78 percent of the world's total output.[20]

As climate change has increased, so too has the occurrence of extreme weather events: droughts, extreme heat, extreme precipitation, hurricanes, tornados, and wildfires. Of the top ten costliest weather disasters in the United States, all but one were the result of hurricanes and extreme precipitation events. The costliest disaster was Hurricane Katrina, which hit Louisiana and New Orleans in 2005. The storm caused over $170 billion in estimated damages and, with a thirty-foot storm surge, collapsed levees that left 1,833 dead.[21]

Extreme weather events like Hurricane Katrina are forecasted to occur and continue to impact coastal cities with increasing frequency. A significant surge from heavy storms in the last seventy years is causing more flooding on the Mississippi River, which shuts down river traffic and threatens the operations and facilities at the Port of New Orleans.[22] With half of New Orleans falling three to twelve feet below sea level, multibillion-dollar investments in storm surge barriers and flood walls, among other infrastructure projects, are critical for mitigating threats of flooding to the city, especially as the area continues to lose wetlands to coastal erosion.[23] Already, many residents have begun to seek places further inland to establish new communities as their homes fall into the Gulf of Mexico.[24]

Flooding is not the only risk facing urban areas. Heat stress is one of the most potentially deadly effects of climate change.[25] Heat stress ranges from milder conditions like heat rash and cramps to exhaustion and heat stroke in the most serious cases. Extreme heat and humidity are projected to impact areas where currently 1.2 billion people live.[26] By 2050, New Orleans is expected to have on average 120 days with a heat index above 105°F.[27] In South America, the metropolitan area of São Paulo, with its extensively built environment and lack of vegetation, is experiencing a heat island effect that results in warmer temperatures for longer periods of time.[28] High temperatures lead to a greater incidence of dengue fever, higher rates of cardiovascular and respiratory disease, and increased mortality rates. Furthermore, rising temperatures and other effects of climate change are likely to increase the frequency of pandemics and the emergence of new diseases.[29] The heat effect also raises the intensity of severe weather. Rainfall is many times higher in São Paulo than in less urbanized areas of the region, resulting in greater injuries and fatalities, damage to buildings, and enormous financial losses due to frequent flooding.[30]

SLR is one of the most important concerns for many of the coastal cities included in this study, as well as for cities such as Mumbai, Jakarta, Bangkok, and Shanghai. In 2019, the global mean sea level was 3.4 inches (87.6 millimeters) above the 1993 average and rose an additional 0.24 inch (6.1 millimeters) between 2018 and 2019. Globally, the mean water level rose by 0.14 inch (3.6 millimeters) per year from 2006 to 2015, 2.5 times the average rate during the twentieth century. Tens of millions of city dwellers are exposed to the consequences of these rising waters. In the United States, over 40 percent of the population live in coastal zones that are prone to flooding, shoreline erosion, and extreme weather events.[31]

Rising temperatures are also accelerating climate-induced migration around the world. A report by the World Bank estimates that, by 2050, there will be 86 million climate migrants—internally displaced—in sub-Saharan Africa, 40 million in South Asia, and 17 million in Latin America if current climate projections hold true.[32] Lagos, for example, is one of the cities where SLR is expected to create between 3 and 8 million climate migrants.[33] A recent study that examines climate migration patterns in the United States concludes that "the southeast portion of the United States will experience disproportionately high effects from SLR-driven flooding due to the large vulnerable populations in New Orleans and Miami."[34] Repeated climate disasters have been a major cause of New Orleans's decline, as seen in chapter 6. Miami—an emerging global city—may well be next, negating its past economic and cultural rise.

Dubai, situated in a coastal arid region where most of the population lives in low-lying areas, is also expected to become a source of refugees as the effect of climate change worsens.[35] In 2019, the population of Dubai reached 3,331,420, an increase of 74.8 percent in ten years, with an additional 1,146,000 people temporarily located in the city for work or tourism.[36] Beyond the precarious situation of many of Dubai's famous coastal real estate investments, the growing population and aridity of the region increase water stress, leading Dubai to invest heavily in technologies such as desalination to create enough fresh water to meet its growing demand.[37] In early 2018, Dubai launched the Gulf Cooperation Council's first commercial vertical farm using hydroponic technology, which cut water usage by 90 percent relative to traditional farming. Private-public partnerships have spurred the proliferation of smart water technology, which aims to increase water productivity and the reuse of treated water to 95 percent, as part of the United Arab Emirates' ambitious Water Security Strategy for 2036.[38]

The impact of SLR is not limited, however, to urban agglomerations near coastal areas. Relocating millions of climate migrants will place unprecedented strains on noncoastal urban systems, especially larger cities closer to affected coastal areas, such as Houston and Austin in the United States.[39] As Mathew Hauer explains, "With millions of potential future migrants in heavily populated coastal communities, SLR scholarship focusing solely on coastal communities endorses a narrative that characterizes SLR as primarily a coastal issue, obscuring the potential impacts in landlocked communities created by SLR-driven migration."[40] Future waves of climate migrants, whether they are crossing national borders or migrating internally, can shape the reality of urban communities around the world.[41]

To understand the impact of climate change on cities, we must consider not only the disruption of the physical environmental but also its psychological effect on people. Growing research is focusing on "ecological grief," defined as "intense feelings of grief as people suffer climate-related losses to valued species, ecosystems and landscapes."[42] This approach to climate change draws attention to people's attachment to place as a fundamental aspect of urban life. The notion of place attachment is vital to understanding globalizing cities, where a large portion of the population is foreign born, transience is common, and a significant number of people live in more than one country.[43] People-place bonds will be affected by environmental changes. If we observe urbanization as a global process, as Brenner and others posit, and conceive of ecosystems and landscapes as essential components of the urban fabric, then it is evident that environmental disruptions can dramatically affect people's sense of place, their emotional and psychological relationships, and the ways in which they construct identity.[44]

Many of the cities that have emerged as global hubs—Miami, Singapore, Dubai, and Hong Kong—and others that represent different aspects of global aspirations—Lagos, São Paulo, New Orleans, Mumbai, Barcelona, and Jakarta—are directly exposed to environmental distress. Cities like Jakarta are "collapsing in slow motion"; the sleek malls, high-end condos, container ports, tropical vegetation, waterways, garbage, boats, and people create a spectacle where the most real but often ignored truth is the existential threat to the city. "If we don't do something, we're doomed," says the city's deputy governor. "We will be leaving Jakarta."[45] In fact, the Indonesian government announced in 2019 that it planned to move the capital to eastern Borneo, building a planned city there that is less affected by rising sea levels.[46]

A DIRE FUTURE?

The threat of rising waters is ever increasing for our trio of emerging global cities. For Miami, with a 5.9-inch SLR since 1996 alone and with the city sitting on average about 16 inches above flood stage, any further rise will put it at increasing risk. The potential economic loss is immense, with estimates of $5.7 billion in residential property values by 2050 in Miami Beach alone and $8.7 billion across all of Miami-Dade County.[47] Moreover, if the prediction of a five- to nine-foot SLR by 2100 is accurate, then 2.5 million residents in Miami could be displaced and require relocation—five times the number of climate migrants projected for New Orleans.[48]

As we consider the future of cities, it is important to understand that the impact of climate change will go far beyond damage to buildings and infrastructure. These cities are at risk of losing their identity. What will happen to Mumbai—a city built on what was once a group of islands—if its historic downtown is wiped out? How will Shanghai's identity change if the core of the city disappears under water?[49] Can we imagine a Miami brand without Miami Beach? Climate change, as discussed, is expected to drive migration in ways that differ from "business as usual." For cities such as Miami, Dubai, and Singapore, people are at risk of losing their attachment to the city and their connection to a place that has become home—part of the "ecological grief" mentioned earlier.

Its blue waters and sandy beaches draw tourists to Miami by the millions, projecting a global image that attracts foreign investment in the city's numerous condominiums and attractions. This image will be disrupted if flooding leads to murky, polluted waters and creates increasing uneasiness about safety. There are concerns about the structural soundness of buildings on the coast—following the collapse of the Champlain Towers South near Miami Beach in June 2021[50]—and concerns about the Turkey Point nuclear power plant located on Biscayne Bay south of Miami. With millions living near the plant, any rise in sea level places the population and surrounding environment at risk of having a disaster like the 2011 Fukushima Daiichi nuclear accident.[51]

Climate change also increases urban inequality. In Miami, the rise in sea level has turned higher elevations into valued real estate. Real estate developers are eyeing this higher ground, where poorer and underprivileged populations historically lived, and beginning to market it to the well-off.[52] With the sharp divisions that characterize Miami along socioeconomic and racial lines, there are signs of "climate gentrification," where only two things, money and elevation, will matter.[33] While previously the well-off resided along the coasts and lower-income individuals were located inland, there has been a shift. In coastal regions that are anticipated to be prone to flooding in coming decades, property values are declining, while the higher-elevated real estate inland along the Atlantic coastal ridge is seeing an appreciation. The wealthy have been moving into previously economically distressed areas close to Little Haiti or Liberty City, increasing property values there and forcing lower-income individuals and businesses out.[54]

Efforts to build a more resilient city and plan for the sheltering of the most vulnerable sectors of the population are stalled because "nobody owns the risk" when it comes to collective action. So far, improvements have centered on wealthier neighborhoods such as in Miami Beach, where hundreds of millions have been spent to install pumps and raise streets.[55] In a city where international investors interact with a large portion of the real estate market, there are few incentives to turn away from what has been so far a safe investment. Real estate markets such as Miami are expected to receive new waves of overseas buyers—eager to invest in U.S. property—as the government eases travel restrictions for vaccinated visitors.[56] The answers proposed to the impending crisis range from simple denial to the belief that science and technology will somehow provide a solution against the rising seas.[57]

Cities are dynamic entities in constant flux. History provides numerous examples showing that cities do not collapse but gradually decline. Social cohesion erodes when the return on investment in urban living is no longer an attractive proposition for residents.[58] That is a point at which people decide to leave.

It would be the height of tragedy that a city of immigrants where global prominence was largely built by the energy and talents of population inflows now becomes the stage for massive climate outmigration. It may still not happen, but at present there is nothing to prevent South Miami's mayor Philip Stoddard's gloomy prediction: "In the end, we all leave."[59]

While rising sea levels represent an existential threat for many cities, including global ones, it is also a fact that over the last three decades more land has been gained than lost worldwide. As we saw in chapter 4, Singapore has increased its land area by the simple expedient of importing sand from neighboring countries and draining the sea, using Dutch-engineered methods. Cities with global aspirations have embarked on bold projects to expand their built environment.

As Jeff Goodell writes, "On coasts and in shallow bays around the world, enormous dredging machines are pumping sand and gravel out of the bottom of the sea and creating new land."[60] In established global cities, emerging ones, and global hopefuls, the redesign of coastal areas represents a key component of urban development. From the Palm Jumeirah archipelago in Dubai to the reclaimed land in front of Victoria Island in Lagos—where Eko Atlantic is rising—cities around the world are creeping further into the sea, building islands and new real estate developments. The new urbanization comes at a high cost to the environment because the creation of new land destroys coral reefs and disrupts coastal ecosystems, endangering the life of the seas.[61]

The outcome of this race is uncertain. Yet it is clear that while local growth machines obstinately continue to market new artificial marvels to the very wealthy, the victims of the relentless rising seas will be counted among the everyday citizenry, in particular, poor and vulnerable populations. Just as there have been winners and losers in the era of globalization—both among people and among cities—the new race against planetary warming and rising seas may not mark the end of the human race but a quantum leap in the gap between those able to survive and prosper and those unable to do so. The glaring economic and social disparities that we have highlighted as a mark of the global city may offer a first glimpse of that inevitable future.

OTHER CHALLENGES

Other major concerns for emerging global cities are the fragmentation of the political leadership, uncertainties in the transmission of power, and the absence of decisive leadership coming from the top. These are challenges shared by Dubai, Singapore, and Miami. Each of them faces a difficult future if political fragmentation becomes their dominant feature.

These cities also face the challenge of guaranteeing political inclusion and freedoms for their citizenry. These protections would strengthen the migration-urbanization link, which, as seen previously, has been vital for the emergence of these cities. As they face stronger competition in their regions and globally, they will need to attract new talent that helps solidify their role in the world economy. The case of Hong Kong demonstrates how political instability, contraction of political rights, and the weakening of the rule of law can damage a city's reputation and have deleterious consequences on the retention of global talent, international investors, and the ability to effectively compete.

A related, important dimension of these cities' futures is how they can include marginalized communities in their economic prosperity. As historic global cities such as New York and London have demonstrated, global centers of finance and trade struggle with a continuous rise in inequality. While cities are becoming generators of wealth and innovation, they are also becoming more unequal. Among cities aspiring to attain an influential position in their continent, Lagos is a case of a major urban center attempting to be a center for innovation and cultural creativity—with booming and internationalizing sectors such as the film industry—where simultaneously inequality and poverty are rapidly rising.[62] As seen in chapter 8, luxury apartments, shopping malls, and majestic new urban developments are part of Lagos's aspiration to become "Africa's new Dubai," yet the city's informal dwellings and the informal economy continue to expand.[63] In New Orleans, it is yet to be seen if the city will remove or retrofit highways that, in the name of modernization of regional transportation and economic progress, were built through African American communities in the 1960s, demolishing homes and businesses and affecting the vibrancy of these communities.[64]

The postpandemic world adds other challenges. Covid-19 has irrevocably disrupted the workforce in distinct and diverging ways. The shape and use of office space look drastically different, employee engagement is emerging as one of the most important aspects of a company's success, skills in metacognition and critical thinking are now in high demand, and the digital divide will put low-wage workers with less formal education at a greater disadvantage.[65] As companies move to embrace employee engagement by focusing more on learning, development, creativity, and collaboration and by offering upskilling and advancement opportunities, and as the adoption of automation and artificial intelligence grows exponentially, the movement of talent is becoming more and more fluid in a postpandemic world.[66]

Cities are seeking to adapt to the future of work. Among other initiatives, they are now offering co-living areas, or communities of like-minded professionals that offer the social interactions that in-person work used to offer. New Orleans is one of cities selected by the co-living company Common to host a "Remote Work Hub," leveraging its low cost of living and the commitment to diversify its employment mix.[67] The continued decline in population in New Orleans makes inflow migration, including the movement of high-skilled talent, an imperative if the city is going to develop the services that are important for emerging global cities.

Dubai and Singapore illustrate the importance of aggressive programs to attract individuals as part of efforts to continually bolster the quality of talent and the range of investors drawn to these cities. The current geopolitical conditions in Eastern Europe and Asia, the role of the Chinese Belt and Road Initiative, and the economic effects of the pandemic offer new opportunities for these cities as they compete for preeminence in their regions. Singapore, for example, has invested heavily in optimizing port operations through integrated terminal and marine operations systems so that it can retain its dominance in the region.[68] Through these investments, Singapore is striving to not only expand the capacity of its ports, but also to position itself as a global leader in maritime technology.[69]

City governments around the world are interested in people-centered planning, adaptable and sustainable environments, green technologies and green spaces, and a reduced transportation footprint.[70] The concept of the "smart city," which was at the forefront of many city planners' agendas, is now being replaced by the idea of the "fifteen-minute city," in which neighborhoods are designed so that residents can access all essential services and work within a small radius of their home. The intention is to break down areas of mono-activity—work, leisure, and residential—and to instead support a polycentric city with proximity, diversity, density, and equity as the key pillars.[71]

We are thus seeing a watershed moment in cities around the world as they address legacies that often led to the discrimination and exclusion of members of their communities. In the years to come, these conversations will continue and will likely lead to different types of cities. Some may become more inclusive places that guarantee the rights of their citizens, incorporating their needs into development goals and lessening the achievement gaps. Others may clamp down against calls for inclusion and exert greater control over specific communities.

Emerging global cities were built from scratch. Audacity played a fundamental part in their evolution from low-end manufacturing centers or regional drug-trafficking cores into strategic commercial, financial, and transportation hubs, magnets for international real estate investors, and branded cultural and artistic centers. Leaders with diverse ethnic backgrounds in very different settings showed a common affinity to Western-style capitalism and a significant tolerance for risk—unusual for locations originally marked by a high degree of parochialism. Leaders in these cities engaged in a decisive transformational effort whose consequences—visibly displayed in their stunning skylines—were unthinkable only a few decades ago.

Still, history moves fast. The growing importance of other cities—"global hopefuls"—can create serious challenges to the dominance of the trio of emerging global cities explored in this book. In the financial sector, for example, São Paulo may leverage its innovative strengths in the fintech industry and usurp the financial position of Miami in Latin America.[72] Kuala Lumpur and Bangkok are two regional rivals striving for preeminence vis-à-vis Singapore. Riyadh, bolstered by decisive backing from the Saudi government, is challenging Dubai's economic dominance in the region, making large investments in innovative technologies and the urban environment to entice investors, professionals, and tourists. In late 2021, Abu Dhabi restarted construction of the Guggenheim Abu Dhabi (GAD) museum, designed by Frank Gehry. With GAD, the emirate emphasizes culture to distinguish Abu Dhabi "from the shopping malls and glitz of Dubai, an hour down the road."[73]

The stories told in this book show that, in an age when Silicon Valley is glorified and major awe-inspiring engineering feats are completed, it is possible to create innovative urban projects in the periphery. The cities we have focused on are not New York or London. They should not be measured against these global cities. They are a very different type of entity, and as such they deserve their own nomenclature.

These urban case studies—of emerging global cities and hopefuls—remind us that the development of the twenty-first-century city reflects not only the transformations of the capitalist system but also the manifold impacts of a world of images. These peripheral cities were not destined to achieve financial and commercial centrality, but they did. We cannot predict whether emerging global cities can maintain and strengthen their status or whether global hopefuls can ascend to positions of preeminence. The future of these cities is the subject of an unfolding story to be told in years to come.

NOTES

INTRODUCTION

1. Alejandro Portes and Ariel C. Armony, *The Global Edge: Miami in the Twenty-First Century* (Berkeley: University of California Press, 2018).

2. Eugene McCann and Kevin Ward, "Relationality/Territoriality: Toward a Conceptualization of Cities in the World," *Geoforum* 41, no. 2 (March 2010): 175–184.

3. Richard Florida, *The Rise of the Creative Class: And How It's Transforming Work, Leisure, Community, and Everyday Life* (New York: Basic Books, 2002).

4. Annalee Newitz, *Four Lost Cities: A Secret History of the Urban Age* (New York: Norton, 2021), epilogue.

5. Mark Abrahamson, *Global Cities* (New York: Oxford University Press, 2004), chap. 4.

6. Saskia Sassen, *The Global City: New York, London, Tokyo* (Princeton, NJ: Princeton University Press, 1991).

7. Sassen, *The Global City*; Abrahamson, *Global Cities*.

8. Charles Tilly, *Durable Inequality* (Berkeley: University of California Press, 1998); Douglas S. Massey, *Categorically Unequal: The American Stratification System* (New York: Russell Sage Foundation, 2007).

9. Florida, *The Rise of the Creative Class*; Abrahamson, *Global Cities*.

10. William J. Wilson, *The Truly Disadvantaged: The Inner City, the Underclass, and Public Policy* (Chicago: University of Chicago Press, 1987); Mitchell Duneier, *Sidewalk* (New York: Farrar, Strauss, and Giroux, 2000); Patricia Fernandez-Kelly, *The Hero's Fight: African-Americans in West Baltimore* (Princeton, NJ: Princeton University Press, 2017); Matthew Desmond, *Evicted: Poverty and Profit in the American City* (New York: Crown, 2016); Alice Goffman, *On the Run: Fugitive Life in an American City* (Chicago: University of Chicago Press, 2014).

11. Jorge E. Hardoy, "Two Thousand Years of Latin American Urbanization," in *Urbanization in Latin America: Approaches and Issues*, ed. J. E. Hardoy, 4–55 (Garden City, NY: Anchor Books, 1975); Richard Morse, "Trends and Issues in Latin American Urban Research, 1965–1970," *Latin American Research Review* 6, no. 1 (Spring 1971): 3–52; Janet Abu-Lughod, *Third World Urbanization* (New York: Routledge, 1977).

12. Alejandro Portes and John Walton, *Urban Latin America: The Political Condition from Above and Below* (Austin: University of Texas Press, 1976); Bryan Roberts, *Cities of Peasants: The Political Economy of Urbanization in the Third World* (London: Edward Arnold, 1978); Talton Ray, *The Politics of the Barrios of Venezuela* (Berkeley: University of California Press, 1969).

13. Ash Amin and Stephen Graham, "The Ordinary City," *Transactions of the Institute of British Geographers* 22, no. 4 (1997): 416.

14. Amin and Graham, "The Ordinary City," 417.

15. Amin and Graham, "The Ordinary City," 417–418.

16. See Arjun Appadurai, "Disjuncture and Difference in the Global Cultural Economy," *Theory, Culture, and Society* 7, no. 2–3 (1990): 295–310.

17. Harvey Molotch and Davide Ponzini, *The New Arab Urban* (New York: New York University Press, 2019); Portes and Armony, *The Global Edge*.

18. Xavier Cortada, chair of the Miami-Dade Cultural Affairs Council, interview by Portes, February 2020; Alejandro Portes and Brandon Martinez, "Emerging Global Cities: Structural Similarities and Historical Differences," supplement, *Spanish Sociological Review (RES)* 28, no. 3 (2019).

19. Molotch and Ponzini, *The New Arab Urban*.

20. Lee Kwan Yew, *From Third World to First: The Singapore Story, 1965–2000* (New York: HarperCollins, 2000); Jon S. T. Quah, "Why Singapore Works: Five Secrets of Singapore Success," *Public Administration and Policy* 21, no. 1 (2018).

21. Jonathan Haskel and Stian Westlake, *Capitalism Without Capital: The Rise of the Intangible Economy* (Princeton, NJ: Princeton University Press, 2018), 15.

22. Haskel and Westlake, *Capitalism Without Capital*, 5, 21, 35.

23. Haskel and Westlake, *Capitalism Without Capital*, 215.

24. On Singapore's patent grants, see M. Szmigiera, "Ranking of the 20 Countries with the Most Patent Grants 2019," Statista, March 30, 2021, https://www.statista.com/statistics/257152/ranking-of-the-20-countries-with-the-most-patent-grants/.

25. Haskel and Westlake, *Capitalism Without Capital*, 3–4, 35, 144, 155–156.

1. THE ROLE OF CITIES IN THE CAPITALIST ECONOMY: AN OVERVIEW

1. Georg Simmel, "The Metropolis and Mental Life," in *The Sociology of Georg Simmel*, ed. Kurt H. Wolff (New York: Free Press, 1969); Scott Greer, *The Emerging City: Myth and Reality* (New York: Free Press, 1962); Louis Wirth, "Urbanism as a Way of Life," *American Journal of Sociology* 44, no. 1 (1938): 1–21.

2. William F. Whyte, *Street Corner Society* (Chicago: University of Chicago Press, 1943); Gerald Suttles, *The Social Order of the Slum: Ethnicity and Territory in the Inner City* (Chicago: University of Chicago Press, 1968); Mitchell Duneier, *Slim's Table: Race, Respectability, and Masculinity* (Chicago: University of Chicago Press, 1992).

3. Immanuel Wallerstein, *The Modern World-System I: Capitalist Agriculture and the Origins of the European World-Economy in the Sixteenth Century* (New York: Academic Press, 1974).

4. Henri Pirenne, *Medieval Cities: Their Origins and the Revival of Trade* (Princeton, NJ: Princeton University Press, 1969).

5. Max Weber, *The City*, ed. Don Martindale and Gertrud Neuwirth (New York: Free Press, 1958).

6. Pirenne, *Medieval Cities*; Maurice Dobb, *Studies in the Development of Capitalism* (New York: International Publishers, 1963).

7. Giovanni Arrighi, *The Long Twentieth Century: Money, Power and the Origins of Our Times* (London: Verso, 1994); Dobb, *Studies in the Development of Capitalism.*

8. Arrighi, *The Long Twentieth Century.*

9. Pirenne, *Medieval Cities.*

10. Karl Marx, *Capital, a Critical Analysis of Capitalist Production* (Moscow: Foreign Languages, 1959); Karl Marx and Friedrich Engels, *The Communist Manifesto* (New York: Penguin, 1967); Arrighi, *The Long Twentieth Century.*

11. Weber, *The City*, chap. 2.

12. Weber, *The City*; Pirenne, *Medieval Cities*, chap. 4; Dobb, *Studies in the Development of Capitalism.*

13. Max Weber, *The Protestant Ethic and the Spirit of Capitalism*, trans. T. Parsons (London: Unwin, 1985); Weber, *The City*, chap. 2; Pirenne, *Medieval Cities*, chap. 2; Steven E. Ozment, *The Reformation in the Cities* (New Haven, CT: Yale University Press, 1975).

14. Dobb, *Studies in the Development of Capitalism*, chap. 2.

15. Dobb, *Studies in the Development of Capitalism*, 88.

16. Weber, *The City*, chap. 3; Dobb, *Studies in the Development of Capitalism*, chap. 3.

17. Dobb, *Studies in the Development of Capitalism*, 157.

18. Dobb, *Studies in the Development of Capitalism*, chap. 4; Weber, *The City*, chap. 3.

19. Weber, *The Protestant Ethic*; Dobb, *Studies in the Development of Capitalism*, chap. 4.

20. Charles Tilly, *The Contentious French: Four Centuries of Popular Struggle* (Cambridge, MA: Harvard University Press, 1986), chap. 7; Immanuel Wallerstein, *The Modern World-System III: The Second Era of Great Expansion of the Capitalist World-Economy, 1730s–1840s* (San Diego, CA: Academic Press, 1989), chap. 1.

21. Dobb, *Studies in the Development of Capitalism*, 172.

22. Dobb, *Studies in the Development of Capitalism*, 176.

23. Tilly, *The Contentious French*, chap. 9; Karl Marx, *The Eighteenth Brumaire of Louis Bonaparte* (New York: International Publishers, 1963).

24. Friedrich Engels, *The Condition of the Working Class in England*, trans. W. O. Henderson and W. H. Chaloner (Stanford, CA: Stanford University Press, 1968), chap. 3.

25. Marx, *Capital*, vol. 1.

26. Dobb, *Studies in the Development of Capitalism*, chap. 7; Arrighi, *The Long Twentieth Century*, chap. 3; Brinley Thomas, *Migration and Economic Growth*, 2nd ed. (Cambridge: Cambridge University Press, 1973).

27. Thomas, *Migration and Economic Growth*; Gerald Rosenblum, *Immigrant Workers: Their Impact on American Labor Radicalism* (New York: Basic Books, 1973); Matthew Josephson, *The Robber Barons* (New York: Harcourt Brace, 1934); Thorstein Veblen, *The Theory of the Leisure Class* (New York: MacMillan, 1899), chaps. 3, 4.

28. Engels, *The Condition of the Working Class*; Marx, *Capital*, vol. 1; Arrighi, *The Long Twentieth Century*, chap. 3.

29. Arrighi, *The Long Twentieth Century*; Wallerstein, *The Modern World-System I.*

30. Robert Heilbroner, *The Worldly Philosophers*, 7th ed. (London: Penguin, 1999), chap. 9.

31. Arrighi, *The Long Twentieth Century*, chap. 4; Saskia Sassen, *The Global City: New York, London, Tokyo* (Princeton, NJ: Princeton University Press, 1991).

32. Richard Edwards, *Contested Terrain: The Transformation of the Workplace in the Twentieth Century* (New York: Harper Torchbooks, 1979); Michael Piore, "Notes for a Theory of Labor Market Segmentation," in *Labor Market Segmentation*, ed. R. C. Edwards, M. Reich, and D. Gordon (Lexington, MA: D.C. Heath, 1975), 125–171.

33. Sassen, *The Global City*, 9. See also Douglas S. Massey, *Categorically Unequal: The American Stratification System* (New York: Russell Sage Foundation, 2007), 34–35.

34. Sassen, *The Global City*, chap. 1; Edwards, *Contested Terrain*; Alejandro Portes, *Economic Sociology: A Systematic Inquiry* (Princeton, NJ: Princeton University Press, 2010), chap. 5; David Harvey, *The Condition of Postmodernity* (Cambridge, MA: Basil Blackwell, 1989).

35. Barry Bluestone and Bennett Harrison, *The Deindustrialization of America* (New York: Wiley, 1982); Bennett Harrison and Barry Bluestone, *The Great U-Turn: Corporate Restructuring and the Polarizing of America* (New York: Basic Books, 1990).

36. Sassen, *The Global City*, chaps. 1, 9.

37. Bluestone and Harrison, *The Deindustrialization of America*; Harvey, *The Condition of Postmodernity*; Alejandro Portes and Ruben G. Rumbaut, *Immigrant America: A Portrait*, 4th ed. (Berkeley: University of California Press, 2014), chap. 1.

38. Bluestone and Harrison, *The Deindustrialization of America*; Harvey, *The Condition of Postmodernity*; Massey, *Categorically Unequal*; Sassen, *The Global City*, chaps. 2, 9; Sharon Zukin, *Naked City: The Death and Life of Authentic Urban Places* (New York: Oxford University Press, 2010).

39. Zukin, *Naked City*; John R. Logan and Harvey Molotch, *Urban Fortunes: The Political Economy of Place* (Berkeley: University of California Press, 1987), chaps. 2, 3.

40. Douglas S. Massey and Nancy Denton, *American Apartheid: Segregation and the Making of the Underclass* (Cambridge, MA: Harvard University Press, 1993); Massey, *Categorically Unequal*.

41. Sassen, *The Global City*, chaps. 8, 9; Portes, *Economic Sociology*, chaps. 5, 7; Harvey, *The Condition of Postmodernity*; Robert Wuthnow, *The Left Behind: Decline and Rage in Small Town America* (Princeton, NJ: Princeton University Press, 2018).

42. Pirenne, *Medieval Cities*; Weber, *The City*; Reinhard Bendix, *Max Weber: An Intellectual Portrait* (Berkeley: University of California Press, 1960).

43. Bendix, *Max Weber*; see also Ozment, *The Reformation in the Cities*.

44. Wallerstein, *The Modern World-System*; Alejandro Portes and John Walton, *Urban Latin America: The Political Condition from Above and Below* (Austin: University of Texas Press, 1976); Brandon Martinez and Alejandro Portes, "Latin American Cities," *Sociology of Development* 7, no. 1 (March 2021): 25–51.

45. Jorge Enrique Hardoy, "Two Thousand Years of Latin American Urbanization," in *Urbanization in Latin America: Approaches and Issues*, ed. J. E. Hardoy (Garden City, NY: Anchor Books, 1975); Portes and Walton, *Urban Latin America*.

46. Hardoy, "Two Thousand Years"; Martinez and Portes, "Latin American Cities."

47. Arrighi, *The Long Twentieth Century*; Dobb, *Studies in the Development of Capitalism*.

48. Arrighi, *The Long Twentieth Century*; Wallerstein, *The Modern World-System*; Yaw Nyarko, "The United Arab Emirates: Some Lessons in Economic Development" (working paper, World Institute for Economic Development, Helsinki, 2010).

49. Arrighi, *The Long Twentieth Century*; Dobb, *Studies in the Development of Capitalism*; Wallerstein, *The Modern World-System I*.

50. Fernando H. Cardoso and Enzo Faletto, *Dependency and Development in Latin America* (Berkeley: University of California Press, 1984); Alejandro Portes and John Walton, *Labor, Class and the International System* (New York: Academic Press, 1981), chap. 3; Hardoy, "Two Thousand Years."

51. Arrighi, *The Long Twentieth Century*; Stanley Lebergott, *Manpower in Economic Growth: The American Record Since 1800* (New York: McGraw-Hill, 1964); Portes and Rumbaut, *Immigrant America*, chap. 1.

52. Raúl Prebisch, "A Critique of Peripheral Capitalism," *CEPAL Review* 1 (1976): 9–76.

53. Cardoso and Faletto, *Dependency and Development*; Alejandro Portes, "Neoliberalism and the Sociology of Development: Emerging Trends and Unanticipated Facts," *Population and Development Review* 23 (June 1997): 229–259; Anibal Quijano, "La Colonialidad del Poder y la Experiencia Latinoamericana," in *Pueblo, Época y Desarrollo*, ed. R. Briceño-Leon and H. R. Sonntag (Caracas: Nueva Sociedad, 1998), 27–38; Prebisch, "A Critique."

54. Hardoy, "Two Thousand Years"; Portes and Walton, *Urban Latin America*; Alejandro Portes and Bryan Roberts, "La Urbanización en América Latina durante los Años del Experimento Neoliberal," in *Ciudades Latinoamericanas*, ed. Alejandro Portes, Bryan R. Roberts, and Alan Grimson (Buenos Aires: Prometeo, 2005), 19–74.

55. Portes, "Neoliberalism and the Sociology of Development"; Osvaldo Sunkel, "The Unbearable Lightness of Neoliberalism," in *Rethinking Development in Latin America*, ed. C. Wood and Bryan Roberts (University Park: Pennsylvania State University Press, 2005), 55–78.

56. Harrison and Bluestone, *The Great U-Turn*; William Robinson, *Promoting Polyarchy: Globalization, U.S. Intervention, and Hegemony* (Cambridge: Cambridge University Press, 1996); Marina Ariza and Juan Carlos Ramírez, "Urbanización, Mercados de Trabajo, y Escenarios Sociales en el México Finisecular," in *Ciudades Latinoamericanas*, ed. Alejandro Portes, Bryan R. Roberts, and A. Grimson (Buenos Aires: Prometeo Editores, 2005), 299–362; Bela Balassa, Gerardo Bueno, and Pedro Pablo Kuczynski, *Toward Renewed Economic Growth in Latin America* (Washington, DC: Institute for International Economics, 1986).

57. Ariza and Ramirez, "Urbanización"; Portes and Roberts, "La Urbanización"; Raul Delgado-Wise, "Replanteando la cuestion del Desarrollo y su Relación Dialéctica con la Exportación de la Fuerza de Trabajo" (paper presented at the conference "Immigration and Development at a Global Turning Point," University of Miami, October 22, 2020).

58. Peter Evans, *Embedded Autonomy: States and Industrial Transformation* (Princeton, NJ: Princeton University Press, 1995); Alejandro Portes and Bryan R. Roberts, "The Free Market City: Latin American Urbanization in the Years the Neoliberal Experiment," *Studies in Comparative and International Development* 40 (Spring 2005): 43–82.

59. Robert Sampson, *Great American City: Chicago and the Enduring Neighborhood Effect* (Chicago: University of Chicago Press, 2013); Douglas S. Massey and Nancy Denton, *American Apartheid: Segregation and the Making of the Underclass* (Cambridge, MA: Harvard University Press, 1993).

60. Sassen, *The Global City*, chaps. 1, 2.

61. Sassen, *The Global City*, chaps. 3, 4.

62.   Alejandro Portes and Ariel C. Armony, *The Global Edge: Miami in the Twenty-First Century* (Berkeley: University of California Press, 2018); Yasser Elsheshtawy, "Real Estate Speculation and Transnational Development in Dubai," in *The New Arab Urban*, ed. H. Molotch and D. Ponzini (New York: New York University Press, 2019), 235–255.

63.   Richard Florida, *The Rise of the Creative Class* (New York: Basic Books, 2002); Richard Florida, *The Flight of the Creative Class* (New York: Collins, 2007).

64.   Neil Brenner and Christian Schmid, "The Urban Age in Debate," *Latin American Urban and Regional Studies* 127 (2016): 307–339; Neil Brenner, *Urban Theory and the Scale Question* (New York: Oxford University Press, 2019).

65.   Jennifer Robinson, "Global and World Cities: A View from off the Map," *International Journal of Urban and Regional Research* 26, no. 3 (September 2002): 531–532.

66.   Brenner, *Urban Theory*; Neil Brenner, "Theses on Planetary Urbanization," *New Society* 243 (2013): 38–66.

67.   Brenner, *Urban Theory*. See also Jean-Paul Addie, "Review of New Urban Spaces: Urban Theory and the Scale Question by Neil Brenner," *Regional Studies* (October 2019).

68.   Bryan Roberts, *Cities of Peasants: The Political Economy of Urbanization in the Third World* (London: Edward Arnold, 1978); Portes and Walton, *Urban Latin America*.

69.   Evans, *Embedded Autonomy*; Alejandro Portes and Lori D. Smith, *Institutions Count: Their Role and Significance in Latin American Development* (Berkeley: University of California Press, 2012).

70.   Portes and Armony, *The Global Edge*, chap. 4; Joan Henderson, "Destination Development: Singapore and Dubai Compared," *Journal of Travel and Tourism* 20, no. 3–4 (2006): 33–45; Elsheshtawy, "Real Estate Speculation."

71.   Lee Kuan Yew, *From Third World to First: The Singapore Story, 1965–2000* (New York: HarperCollins, 2000).

2. DUBAI: FROM MARGINAL GULF TOWN TO REGIONAL HUB

1.   "Expo 2020 Dubai Will Yield an AED 122 Billion Investment Windfall for the UAE," Expo 2020 Dubai, April 15, 2019, https://www.expo2020dubai.com/en/whats-new/20190415 -economic-impact-study.

2.   James Swanston, "Is Dubai Facing Another Debt Crisis?," *Capital Economics*, April 20, 2020, https://www.capitaleconomics.com/publications/middle-east-north-africa-economics /middle-east-economics-focus/is-dubai-facing-another-debt-crisis/.

3.   Simeon Kerr and Andrew England, "Dubai Contemplates a Downsized Future After the Pandemic," *Financial Times*, May 10, 2020, https://www.ft.com/content/5ff1cc05-64eb-4e1a -bf53-62c7e62d5a2c.

4.   Martin Hvidt, "Economic and Institutional Reforms in the Arab Gulf Countries," *Middle East Journal* 65, no. 1 (2011): 85–102.

5.   Alex Boodrookas and Arang Keshavarzian, "Giving the Transnational a History: Gulf Cities Across Time and Space," in *The New Arab Urban: Gulf Cities of Wealth, Ambition, and Distress*, ed. Harvey Molotch and Davide Ponzini (New York: New York University Press, 2019), 35–57.

6.   See Adam Hanieh, *Capitalism and Class in the Gulf Arab States* (New York: Palgrave Macmillan, 2011); Ahmed Kanna, *Dubai: The City as Corporation* (Minneapolis: University of

Minnesota Press, 2011); Arang Keshavarzian, "Geopolitics and the Genealogy of Free Trade Zones in the Persian Gulf," *Geopolitics* 15, no. 2 (May 2010): 263–289; Roland Marchal, "Dubai: Global City and Transnational Hub," in *Transnational Connections and the Arab Gulf*, ed. Madawi Al-Rasheed (London: Routledge, 2005); Stephen J. Ramos, *The Blueprint: A History of Dubai's Spatial Development Through Oil Discovery* (Dubai Initiative working paper, Harvard Kennedy School, 2010).

7. Adam Hanieh, *Money, Markets, and Monarchies: The Gulf Cooperation Council and the Political Economy of the Contemporary Middle East* (Cambridge: Cambridge University Press, 2018), 15.
8. Hanieh, *Capitalism and Class*, 14.
9. Hanieh, *Capitalism and Class*, 14.
10. Hanieh, *Capitalism and Class*, 16.
11. "Trucial States" refer to the tribal entities in the Gulf, ruled by sheikhs, that signed truce treaties with the British government in return for protection. These treaties began in 1820 and continued until they were officially annulled in 1971. Among those sheikhdoms were the seven emirates that form the United Arab Emirates today, along with Bahrain.
12. Kiren Chaudhry, "The 'Uncanny' Writ Regional: New and Recurring Forms of Poverty and Inequality in the Arab World," in *Rebuilding Devastated Economies in the Middle East*, ed. Leonard Binder (New York: Palgrave Macmillan, 2007), 24.
13. Stephen Ramos and Peter G. Rowe, "Planning, Prototyping, and Replication in Dubai," in *The Superlative City: Dubai and the Urban Condition in the Early Twenty-First Century*, ed. Ahmed Kanna (Cambridge, MA: Harvard University Press, 2013), 18–33.
14. Christopher M. Davidson, *Dubai: The Vulnerability of Success* (New York: Columbia University Press, 2008), 12.
15. Davidson, *Dubai*, 12.
16. Yasser Elsheshtawy, "Redrawing Boundaries: Dubai, an Emerging Global City," in *Planning Middle Eastern Cities: An Urban Kaleidoscope in a Globalizing World*, ed. Yasser Elsheshtawy (London: Routledge, 2004), 169–200.
17. Jim Krane, *City of Gold: Dubai and the Dream of Capitalism* (New York: St. Martin's, 2009), 15.
18. Krane, *City of Gold*, 16.
19. Davidson, *Dubai*, 14.
20. Davidson, *Dubai*, 17
21. Davidson, *Dubai*, 24–27.
22. Hanieh, *Capitalism and Class*, 5.
23. Davidson, *Dubai*, 23.
24. Davidson, *Dubai*, 52.
25. Davidson, *Dubai*, 68.
26. Ramos and Rowe, "Planning, Prototyping, and Replication in Dubai," 22.
27. Davidson, *Dubai*, 73.
28. Davidson, *Dubai*, 74.
29. Davidson, *Dubai*, 74.
30. Ramos and Rowe, "Planning, Prototyping, and Replication in Dubai," 23.
31. Ramos and Rowe, "Planning, Prototyping, and Replication in Dubai," 23.
32. Kristian Coates Ulrichsen, *The United Arab Emirates: Power, Politics, and Policy-Making* (Oxford: Routledge, 2017), 92; Syed Ali, ed., *Dubai: Gilded Cage* (New Haven, CT: Yale University Press, 2010).

33. Ramos and Rowe, "Planning, Prototyping, and Replication in Dubai," 23.

34. Ulrichsen, *The United Arab Emirates*, 92.

35. Keshavarzian, "Geopolitics and the Genealogy of Free Trade Zones," 272.

36. Keshavarzian, "Geopolitics and the Genealogy of Free Trade Zones," 273.

37. Ramos, *The Blueprint*, 14.

38. Davidson, *Dubai*, 106.

39. Ulrichsen, *The United Arab Emirates*, 92.

40. Mina Akhavan, "Gateway: Revisiting Dubai as a Port City," in *The New Arab Urban*, 175–193.

41. Hanieh, *Money, Markets, and Monarchies*, 6.

42. Keshavarzian, "Geopolitics and the Genealogy of Free Trade Zones," 270.

43. Elsheshtawy, "Redrawing Boundaries," 173.

44. Ramos and Rowe, "Planning, Prototyping, and Replication in Dubai," 21.

45. Fatma Al-Sayegh, "Merchants' Role in a Changing Society: The Case of Dubai, 1900–90," *Middle Eastern Studies* 34, no. 1 (2019): 87–102.

46. Arang Keshavarzian, "From Port Cities to Cities with Ports: Toward a Multiscalar History of Persian Gulf Urbanism in the Twentieth Century," in *Gateways to the World: Port Cities in the Persian Gulf*, ed. Mehran Kamrava (Oxford: Oxford University Press, 2016), 8.

47. Al-Sayegh, "Merchants' Role in a Changing Society," 88.

48. Elsheshtawy, "Redrawing Boundaries," 175.

49. Elsheshtawy, "Redrawing Boundaries," 175.

50. Krane, *City of Gold*, 23.

51. Davidson, *Dubai*, 76.

52. Davidson, *Dubai*, 77.

53. Davidson, *Dubai*, 85.

54. Ramos, *The Blueprint*.

55. Hazem Beblawi, "The Rentier State in the Arab World," in *The Rentier State*, ed. Hazem Beblawi and Giacomo Luciani (London: Routledge, 2016).

56. Omar AlShehabi, "Histories of Migration to the Gulf," in *Transit States: Labour, Migration and Citizenship in the Gulf*, ed. Abdulhadi Khalaf, Omar AlShehabi, and Adam Hanieh (London: Pluto, 2014), 6.

57. This trend was reversed after Iraq's invasion of Kuwait in 1990.

58. AlShehabi, "Histories of Migration to the Gulf," 7.

59. Abdulhadi Khalaf, "The Politics of Migration," in *Transit States*, 47.

60. Marchal, "Dubai," 104.

61. Department of Economic Development, Government of Dubai, *Dubai Economic Report 2019*, https://ded.ae/page_report/en/report_2019.

62. Martin Hvidt, "The Dubai Model: An Outline of Key Development-Process Elements in Dubai," *International Journal of Middle East Studies* 41, no. 3 (August 2009): 403.

63. Yasser Elsheshtawy, "Resituating the Dubai Spectacle," in *The Superlative City*, 104–121.

64. ASDA'A BCW, *A Call for Reform: 11th Annual ASDA'A BCW Arab Youth Survey 2019*, https://www.chathamhouse.org/sites/default/files/2019%20Arab%20Youth%20Survey.pdf.

65. Adam Hanieh, *Money, Markets, and Monarchies*; Ahmed Kanna, "Introduction," in *The Superlative City*, 15.

66. Embassy of the UAE, Washington, DC, "How the UAE Became the Center for Art in the Middle East," *Smithsonian.com*, April 3, 2018, https://www.smithsonianmag.com /sponsored/uae-center-for-art-middle-east-180968375/.

67. Krane, *City of Gold*, 76.

68. Keshavarzian, "Geopolitics and the Genealogy of Free Trade Zones," 277.

69. Ulrichsen, *The United Arab Emirates*, 93.

70. Christopher Davidson, "Dubai: Foreclosure of a Dream," *Middle East Report*, no. 251 (Summer 2009): 8–13.

71. Michelle Buckley and Adam Hanieh, "Diversification by Urbanization: Tracing the Property-Finance Nexus in Dubai and the Gulf," *International Journal of Urban and Regional Research* 38, no. 1 (2014): 155–175.

72. Akhavan, "Gateway," 177.

73. Ramos and Rowe, "Planning, Prototyping, and Replication in Dubai," 23–27.

74. Krane, *City of Gold*, 139.

75. Krane, *City of Gold*, 139.

76. Hvidt, "The Dubai Model," 409.

77. Kanna, *The Superlative City*, 131.

78. Keshavarzian, "Geopolitics and the Genealogy of Free Trade Zones," 263.

79. Keshavarzian, "Geopolitics and the Genealogy of Free Trade Zones," 270.

80. Keshavarzian, "Geopolitics and the Genealogy of Free Trade Zones," 269.

81. Hanieh, *Money, Markets, and Monarchies*, 16.

82. Yasser Elsheshtawy, "Real Estate Speculation and Transnational Development in Dubai," in *The New Arab Urban*, 235–255.

83. Ramos, *The Blueprint*, 14.

84. Davidson, *Dubai*, 115.

85. Keshavarzian, "Geopolitics and the Genealogy of Free Trade Zones," 274.

86. Davidson, *Dubai*, 115.

87. Akhavan, "Gateway," 178.

88. Davidson, *Dubai*, 182.

89. Ahmed Kanna, "The Trajectories of Two 'Asian Tigers': The Imperial Roots of Capitalism in Dubai and Singapore," in *Rethinking Global Urbanism: Comparative Insights from Secondary Cities*, ed. Xiangming Chen and Ahmed Kanna (New York: Routledge, 2012), 48.

90. The Dubai Industrial Strategy 2030 aims to elevate Dubai into a global platform for knowledge-based, sustainable, and innovation-focused businesses. Five key objectives will serve as the foundation for Dubai's industrial future. See UAE, "Dubai Industrial Strategy 2030," https://u.ae/en/about-the-uae/strategies-initiatives-and-awards/local -governments-strategies-and-plans/dubai-industrial-strategy-2030.

91. Hvidt, "The Dubai Model," 404.

92. "Dubai Moves to Attract World's Remote Workers with New Residency Programme," *The National*, October 14, 2020, https://www.thenationalnews.com/uae/government/dubai -moves-to-attract-world-s-remote-workers-with-new-residency-programme-1.1093699.

93. Rory Reynolds, Nick Webster, and Anam Rizvi, "UAE to Expand 10-Year Golden Visa System to All Doctors, PhD Holders and Highly Skilled Workers," *The National*, November 17, 2020.

94. Simeon Kerr and Andrew England, "Saudi Arabia Tries to Lure Multinationals from Dubai," *Financial Times*, January 10, 2021.

95. Natasha Turak, "'Dramatic and Risky'—and a Shot at Dubai? Saudi Arabia Issues Bold Business Ultimatum to Pull Regional HQ Offices into the Kingdom," *CNBC*, February 16, 2021.

96. Aziz Yaakoubi, Marwa Rashad, and Davide Barbuscia, "Saudi Arabia Amends Import Rules from Gulf in Challenge to UAE," Reuters, July 5, 2021.

3. MIAMI: FROM WINTER RESORT TO HEMISPHERIC CAPITAL

1. Miami-Dade County, *Comprehensive Annual Financial Report, 2019*, www.miamidade.gov /finance/library/CAFR201-completePDF.

2. Alejandro Portes and Alex Stepick, *City on the Edge: The Transformation of Miami* (Berkeley: University of California Press, 1993), chap. 1.

3. Julio Frenk, opening address to the External Advisory Council of the University of Miami Advanced Institute of the Americas, March 2019.

4. Alejandro Portes and Ariel Armony, *The Global Edge: Miami in the Twenty-First Century* (Berkeley: University of California Press, 2018), chap. 1.

5. Polly Redford, *Billion-Dollar Sandbar: A Biography of Miami Beach* (New York: E. P. Dutton, 1970).

6. Redford, *Billion-Dollar Sandbar*; Portes and Stepick, *City on the Edge*, chap. 4.

7. Field interviews in Miami with the leader of Liberty City's Urban League (March 2017) and with the senior partner of a major downtown law firm (February 2020). See also T. D. Allman, *Miami: City of the Future*, rev. ed. (Gainesville: University of Florida Press, 2013).

8. Portes and Stepick, *City on the Edge*, chaps. 1, 5.

9. Interview with head of the Florida International Bankers Association in Miami, January 2020; Marcos Kerbel and Richard Westlund, *Leading the Way: A Comprehensive History of International Banking in South Florida* (Miami: Florida International Bankers Association, 2004).

10. Joan Didion, *Miami* (New York: Simon and Schuster, 1987); David Rieff, *Going to Miami: Exiles, Tourists, and Refugees in the New America* (Boston: Little, Brown, 1987).

11. Field interview with Black community activist in Liberty City, 1987. Cited in Portes and Stepick, *City on the Edge*, 14.

12. Rieff, *Going to Miami*; Luis Botifoll, "How Miami's New Image Was Created," Occasional Papers Series, Institute of Inter-American Studies, University of Miami, 1985.

13. Cited in Portes and Stepick, *City on the Edge*, 26.

14. Yohel Camayd-Freixas, "Crisis in Miami," special report to the project "Help-Seeking and Services, Use Among Latin American Refugees" (Baltimore, MD: Department of Sociology, Johns Hopkins University, 1988); cited in Portes and Stepick, *City on the Edge*, 26.

15. Cited in Portes and Stepick, *City on the Edge*, 35, based on field interviews in Miami, January 1982.

16. Portes and Armony, *The Global Edge*, chap. 1; Didion, *Miami*; Botifoll, "How Miami's New Image Was Created."

17. Portes and Armory, *The Global Edge*, chaps. 1, 4; Allman, *Miami*.

18. Field interviews with white business executives and *Miami Herald* publishers conducted in Miami in 1987, cited in Portes and Stepick, *City on the Edge*, 10–11, 14–15.

19. Kerbel and Westlund, *Leading the Way*; Botifoll, "How Miami's New Image Was Created"; interview with head of Florida International Bankers Association, January 2020.

20. Kerbel and Westlund, *Leading the Way*; Portes and Armory, *The Global Edge*, chap. 4.

21. Allman, *Miami*; Botifoll, "How Miami's New Image Was Created."

22. Jan Nijman, *Miami: Mistress of the Americas* (Philadelphia: University of Pennsylvania Press, 2010), 80, 89–90.

23. Field interviews in Miami with head of Florida International Bankers Association and senior partner of Greenberg Traurig law firm, January and February 2020; Nijman, *Miami*.

24. Miami-Dade Planning Metropolitan Organization, *Miami-Dade County Compendium of Transportation: Facts and Trends Report*, July 2014, http://miamidadetpo.org/library/studies/compendium-of-transportation-facts-and-trends-report-2014-07.pdf; "Port Asian Service Volume Rises, 11 Percent," *Miami Today*, April 20, 2017, 1.

25. Miami-Dade Aviation Department, *Miami International Airport Cargo Hub*, 2014; Miami-Dade Planning Metropolitan Organization, *Miami-Dade County Compendium of Transportation*; "Flying Goldmine," *Miami Today*, April 20, 2017, 1.

26. Allman, *Miami*, 393.

27. Ernest Hemingway, *A Moveable Feast* (New York: Simon and Schuster, 1961).

28. Knight Foundation, "Evolving Arts Ecosystem: A Study of Miami," Knight Foundation Arts Division, December 2018; field interview with artist Xavier Cortada, chair of Miami-Dade Arts Council, February 11, 2020.

29. Interview with Xavier Cortada, February 11, 2020.

30. Knight Foundation, "Evolving Arts Ecosystem"; Jane Woodridge, "Art Basel Parent Committed to Art Fairs," *Miami Herald*, December 8, 2019, 26.

31. Field interview with chair of Miami-Dade Arts Council, February 11, 2020.

32. Linda Robertson, "The Battle for Wynwood," *Miami Herald*, March 9, 2020.

33. Field interview in Miami with senior executive of Greenberg Traurig law firm, February 21, 2020.

34. This section draws on selected passages in chapters 2 and 8 of Portes and Armory, *The Global Edge*.

35. United States Census Bureau, *American Community Survey*, 2021; Wikipedia, s.v. "Miami-Dade County," https://en.wikipedia.org/wiki/Miami-Dade_County,_Florida.

36. Portes and Stepick, *City on the Edge*, chap. 8; Allman, *Miami*, 131–132.

37. "QuickFacts: Miami-Dade County, Florida," United States Census Bureau, https://www.census.gov/quickfacts/fact/table/miamidadecountyflorida/POP060210.

38. N. D. B. Connolly, *A World More Concrete: Real Estate and the Remaking of Jim Crow South Florida* (Chicago: University of Chicago Press, 2014).

39. John A. Stuart and John F. Stack, *The New Deal in South Florida: Design, Policy, and Community Building, 1933–1940* (Gainesville: University of Florida Press, 2008).

40. D. Francis and A. Harris, "Introduction: Looking for Black Miami," *Anthurium: A Caribbean Studies Journal* 16, no. 1 (2020): 2.

41. "Opa Locka: Breakdown of Families in Poverty," United States Census Bureau, *American Community Survey*, 2015.

42. N. Williams, *All Power to All People*, 2019, sculpture on display at Adrienne Arsht Center, Miami, https://www.olcdc.org/post/allpower.

43. Wikipedia, s.v. "Miami Gardens," https://en.wikipedia.org/wiki/Miami_Gardens, _Florida; *General Statistical Data*, Miami-Dade County Department of Planning, 2020, https://www.miamidade.gov/finance/library/genstat03.pdf; "QuickFacts: Miami Gardens City, Florida," United States Census Bureau, *American Community Survey*, 2020.

44. Wikipedia, s.v. "Miami Gardens"; field interview with Miami African American lawyer and community leader, February 2017.

45. Field interview with Miami African American lawyer and community leader, February 2017.

46. Field interview with director of the Urban League of Miami in Liberty City, February 2017.

47. Field interview with Miami African American lawyer and community leader, February 2017.

48. Portes and Stepick, *City on the Edge*, chap. 8.

49. Charles Rabin, "Art Acevedo Sworn in as Miami Police Chief," *Miami Herald*, April 29, 2021, 1; Portes and Armony, *The Global Edge*, chaps. 5, 8.

50. Alex Stepick, "The Refugees Nobody Wants: Haitians in Miami," in *Miami Now! Immigration, Ethnicity, and Social Change*, ed. Alex Stepick and Guillermo Grenier (Gainesville: University of Florida Press, 1992); Portes and Stepick, *City on the Edge*, chap. 8.

51. Stepick, "The Refugees Nobody Wants."

52. Portes and Armony, *The Global Edge*, chap. 4.

53. Stepick, "The Refugees Nobody Wants"; Portes and Stepick, *City on the Edge*, chap. 8.

54. Stepick, "The Refugees Nobody Wants"; Portes and Stepick, *City on the Edge*, chap. 8.

55. Field interview in Miami with Haitian community leader M. Bastien, March 2017; Susan Danseyar, "Jean Monestime Wants Details," *Miami Today*, May 11, 2017, 23.

56. Field interview in Miami, March 2017.

57. Portes and Stepick, *City on the Edge*, chap. 7; Patricia Fernandez-Kelly and Sara Curran, "Nicaraguans: Voices Lost, Voices Found," in *Ethnicities: Children of Immigrants in America*, ed. R. G. Rumbaut and Alejandro Portes (New York: Russell Sage Foundation, 2001).

58. Margarita Rodriguez, "Navigating Uneven Development: The Dynamics of Fractured Transnationalism," in *The State and the Grassroots*, ed. Alejandro Portes and Patricia Fernandez-Kelly (Oxford: Berghahn, 2015); field interview in Miami with former editor of *La Estrella de Nicaragua*, April 2017.

59. Portes and Stepick, *City on the Edge*, chap. 7.

60. Fernandez-Kelly and Curran, "Nicaraguans"; Rodriguez, "Navigating Uneven Development."

61. Portes and Stepick, *City on the Edge*, chap. 7.

62. Portes and Stepick, *City on the Edge*, 163–166.

63. Portes and Stepick, *City on the Edge*, 163–166.

64. Wikipedia, s.v. "Nicaraguan Adjustment and Central American Relief Act," https://en.wikipedia.org/wiki/Nicaraguan_Adjustment_and_Central_American_Relief_Act; field interview with former editor of *La Estrella de Nicaragua*, April 2017.

65. Rodriguez, "Navigating Uneven Development."

66. Portes and Armony, *The Global Edge*, 16; interview with former newspaper editor, April 2017.

67. Rodriguez, "Navigating Uneven Development"; field trip to East Little Havana, April 2017.

68. Interview with former mayor of Doral, April 2017.

69. Interview with former mayor of Miami, April 2016; see also Elizabeth Aranda, Sally Hughes, and Elena Sabogal, *Making a Life in Metropolitan Miami* (Boulder, CO: Lynne Rienner, 2014).

70. Field interview with Miami African American lawyer and community leader, February 2017.

71. The above quotation is from an interview with Alberto Ibargüen in Miami, April 2017.

72. Aranda, Hughes, and Sabogal, *Making a Life*; Fernandez-Kelly and Curran, "Nicaraguans"; field trip to East Little Havana, April 2017.

4. SINGAPORE: FROM FISHING VILLAGE TO WORLD-CLASS METROPOLIS

1. Kuan Yew Lee, *From Third World to First: The Singapore Story, 1965–2000* (New York: HarperCollins, 2000), 2:230; Sock-Yong Phang, "Strategic Development of Airport and Rail Infrastructure: The Case of Singapore," *Transport Policy* 10 (2003): 5.

2. Lee, *From Third World to First*, 2:231.

3. Phang, "Strategic Development"; Rachel Bok, "Airports on the Move? The Policy Mobilities of Singapore Changi Airport at Home and Abroad," *Urban Studies* 52 (2014): 2724–2740.

4. World Bank Database, https://data.worldbank.org/indicator/NY.GDP.MKTP.CD?locations=SG

5. John Leyden, *Malay Annals* (London: Longman, Hurst, Rees, Orme and Brown, 1821), 37–44.

6. John N. Miksic, *Singapore and the Silk Road of the Sea, 1300–1800* (Singapore: National University of Singapore Press, 2013), 183–185.

7. Susan Tsang and Audrey Perera, *Singapore at Random* (Singapore: Didier Millet, 2011), 120.

8. Peter Borschberg, *The Singapore and Melaka Straits: Violence, Security and Diplomacy in the 17th Century* (Singapore: National University of Singapore Press, 2010), 157–158.

9. Dennis DeWitt, *History of the Dutch in Malaysia* (Petaling Jaya, Malaysia: Nutmeg, 2007).

10. Mun Cheong Yong and V. V. Bhanoji Rao, *Singapore-India Relations: A Primer* (Singapore: National University of Singapore Press, 1995), 3.

11. Barbara Leitch Lepoer, *Singapore: A Country Study* (Washington, DC: Government Printing Office, 1989), http://countrystudies.us/singapore/.

12. Saw Swee-Hock, "Population Trends in Singapore, 1819–1967," *Journal of Southeast Asian History* 10, no.1 (1969): 38.

13. Michael D. Barr, *Singapore: A Modern History* (London: I. B. Tauris, 2019), 185.

14. Lepoer, *Singapore*.

15. Jason Lim, "The Dynamics of Trans-Regional Business and National Politics: The Impact of Events in China on Fujian-Singapore Tea Trading Networks, 1920–1960," in *Singapore*

in Global History, ed. Derek Heng and Syed Muhd Khairudin Aljunied (Amsterdam: Amsterdam University Press, 2009), 135–150.

16.   Lepoer, *Singapore*.

17.   Barr, *Singapore*, 181.

18.   Swee-Hock, "Population Trends in Singapore," 40.

19.   Lepoer, *Singapore*.

20.   "Population and Population Structure," Singapore Department of Statistics, accessed November 1, 2021, https://www.singstat.gov.sg/find-data/search-by-theme/population /population-and-population-structure/latest-data.

21.   Lepoer, *Singapore*.

22.   Lepoer, *Singapore*, 12–13.

23.   James S. Olson and Robert Shadle, *Historical Dictionary of the British Empire, K–Z* (Westport, CT: Greenwood, 1996), 710.

24.   Lepoer, *Singapore*.

25.   "First Rubber Trees Are Planted in Singapore: 1877," *History SG*, last updated August 1, 2019, http://eresources.nlb.gov.sg/history/events/a8ceea4c-1c8b-4c9a-885c-b85038b39e4c.

26.   Barr, *Singapore*, 98.

27.   Barr, *Singapore*, 29.

28.   Lepoer, *Singapore*.

29.   Barr, *Singapore*, 197.

30.   Lepoer, *Singapore*.

31.   Diane K. Mauzy and R. S. Milne, *Singapore Politics Under the People's Action Party* (London: Routledge, 2002), 16.

32.   Barr, *Singapore*, 115.

33.   Matthew Jones, "Creating Malaysia: Singapore Security, the Borneo Territories, and the Contours of British Policy," *Journal of Imperial and Commonwealth History* 28, no. 2 (2000): 85–109.

34.   Lepoer, *Singapore*.

35.   Jon S. T. Quah, "Why Singapore Works: Five Secrets of Singapore's Success," *Public Administration and Policy* 21, no. 1 (2018): 5–21.

36.   Lee said that:

> China "is the product of a civilization which has gone through all its ups and downs, of floods and famine and pestilence, breeding a people with very intense culture, with a belief in high performance, in sustained effort, in thrift and industry. And [Malay] people, more fortunately endowed by nature, with warm sunshine and bananas and coconuts, and therefore not with the same need to strive so hard. Now, these two societies really move at two different speeds, It's like the difference between a high-revolution engine and a low-revolution engine. I'm not saying that one is better or less good than the other. But I'm, just stating a fact that one was the product of another environment, another history, another civilization, and the other is a product of another different climate, different history.

> Interview with Alan Ashbolt in ABC studios, Canberra, March 24, 1965. See Michael D. Barr, "Lee Kuan Yew: Race, Culture and Genes," *Journal of Contemporary Asia* 29, no. 2 (1999): 145–166.

37.   Mauzy and Milne, *Singapore Politics*, 22.

38.   Asma Abdullah and Paul B. Pedersen, *Understanding Multicultural Malaysia: Delights, Puzzles and Irritations* (Petaling Jaya, Malaysia: Pearson, 2003), 59.

39.   Barr, *Singapore*, 118.

40.   Kuan Yew Lee, *The Singapore Story* (Singapore: Times Editions, 1998), 1:24.

41.   Alejandro Portes, *Economic Sociology: A Systematic Inquiry* (Princeton, NJ: Princeton University Press, 2010), chap. 6.

42.   "Focus: Singapore '80," *Far Eastern Economic Review*, August 1, 1980, 161.

43.   L. A. Mills, *Southeast Asia: Illusion and Reality in Politics and Economics* (Minneapolis: University of Minnesota Press, 1964), 268.

44.   W. G. Huff, "The Developmental State, Government, and Singapore's Economic Development Since 1960," *World Development* 23, no. 8 (1995): 1421–1438.

45.   Kuan Yew Lee, "Prime Minister's Press Conference," Singapore, August 26, 1965. https://www.nas.gov.sg/archivesonline/data/pdfdoc/lky19650826.pdf.

46.   Kuan Yew Lee, *Hard Truths to Keep Singapore Going* (Singapore: Straits Times Press, 2011), 27.

47.   Lee, *Hard Truths*, 10–12.

48.   Chua Beng Huat, *Liberalism Disavowed: Communitarianism and State Capitalism in Singapore* (Singapore: National University of Singapore Press, 2017).

49.   Lee, *Hard Truths*, 33.

50.   Lepoer, *Singapore*.

51.   Huff, "The Developmental State"; "Housing for All (Singapore Survey)," *The Economist*, December 29, 1979.

52.   Syed Muhd Khairudin Aljunied, "Beyond the Rhetoric of Communalism: Violence and the Process of Reconciliation in 1950s Singapore," in *Reframing Singapore*, ed. Derek Heng and Syed Muhd Khairudin Aljunied (Amsterdam: Amsterdam University Press, 2009), 69–87.

53.   Valerie Chew, "Public Housing in Singapore," National Library Board Singapore, 2009, https://eresources.nlb.gov.sg/infopedia/articles/SIP_1585_2009-10-26.html.

54.   Lee, *Hard Truths*, 95.

55.   William Koh, Richard M. Steers, and James R. Terborg, "The Effects of Transformational Leadership on Teacher Attitudes and Student Performance in Singapore," *Journal of Organizational Behavior* 16 (1995): 319–333; Li-Ching Ho, "Global Multicultural Citizenship Education: A Singapore Experience," *Social Studies* 100, no. 6 (2009): 285–293.

56.   Pak Tee Ng, "The Evolution and Nature of School Accountability in the Singaporean Educational System," *Educational Assessment, Evaluation, and Accountability* 22 (2010): 275–292; Eugene Kheng-Boon Tan, "Law and Values in Governance: The Singapore Way," *Hong Kong Law Journal* 30 (2005): 91–102.

57.   Huff, "The Developmental State"; Garry Rodan, "Singapore Exceptionalism: Authoritarian Rule and State Transformation," in *Political Transitions in Dominant Party Systems: Learning to Lose*, ed. J. Wong and E. Friedman, 231–251 (New York: Routledge, 2008).

58.   John Aglionby, "A Tick in the Only Box," *The Guardian*, October 26, 2001.

59.   Sally Andrews, "'Soft' Repression: The Struggle for Democracy in Singapore," *The Diplomat*, February 6, 2015.

60.   Barr, *Singapore*, 129.

61. "All liberalizing autocrats believed that they can, like Lee, achieve modernity but delay democracy. But they can't. Other than the oil-rich Gulf states, Singapore is the only country with a per capita GDP of over $10,000 that is not a democracy. . . . It is an obvious exception to the rule and one that will not last." Fareed Zakaria, cited in Lee, *Hard Truths*, 43.

62. Lee, *Hard Truths*, 45.

63. Lee, *Hard Truths*, 54.

64. Lee, *Hard Truths*, 100.

65. "We know that if our foe wins, we die, and die painfully. But when we win, our foes live comfortably even in prison, with butter and eggs and meat according to special rations which the rules of the game lay down upon us. This is in part an unequal conflict; because on the one side is terror that is absolute; on the other side terror which is not really terror. It is just a deterrent, and often no more than a soporific. You put a man in, you feed him, he studies, he writes memoirs, he comes out and he fights. If his side wins, he pulls your fingernails out and you are dead." Cited in Peggy Durdin, "Lee Kuan Yew and Singapore: A Profile," *Asian Affairs* 1, no. 3 (1974): 166.

66. Lepoer, *Singapore*.

67. Lee, *Hard Truths*, 319.

68. Lepoer, *Singapore*.

69. Mauzy and Milne, *Singapore Politics*, 31.

70. "2012 Investment Climate Statement—Singapore," U.S. Department of State, Bureau of Economic and Business Affairs, 2012, https://2009-2017.state.gov/e/eb/rls/othr/ics/2012/191233.htm.

71. Lepoer, *Singapore*.

72. Rongxing Guo, *Intercultural Economic Analysis: Theory and Method* (New York: Springer, 2009), 145.

73. Lepoer, *Singapore*.

74. Lee, *From Third World to First*, 2:89–102.

75. Huff, "The Developmental State."

76. Huff, "The Developmental State," 1428.

77. Lepoer, *Singapore*.

78. Lepoer, *Singapore*.

79. Lee, *From Third World to First*, 2:64.

80. "Bankers Shocked by 45% China Tax Rate Mull Leaving Hong Kong," *Bloomberg News*, July 14, 2020; "A Night at the Cathay," *The Economist*, July 4, 2020, 74–75.

81. David Ramli and Lulu Chen, "The Super Rich Are Choosing Singapore as the World's Safest Haven," *Bloomberg*, May 26, 2021.

82. Raúl Prebisch, "Notes on Trade from the Standpoint of the Periphery," *CEPAL Review* 28 (1986): 203–216; Giovanni Arrighi, Beverly J. Silver, and Benjamin D. Brewer, "Industrial Convergence and the Persistence of the North-South Divide," *Studies in Comparative International Development* 38, no. 1 (2003): 3–31.

83. Tsao Yuan Lee, *Growth Triangle: The Johor-Singapore-Riau Experience* (Singapore: Institute of Southeast Asian Studies and Institute of Policy Studies, 1991); Huff, "The Developmental State," 1435.

84. Huff, "The Developmental State," 1428.

85. Alejandro Portes and Lori D. Smith, *Institutions Count: Their Role and Significance in Latin American Development* (Berkeley: University of California Press, 2012); Alejandro Portes and Jean C. Nava, "Institutions and National Development: A Comparative Study," *Spanish Sociological Review* 26 (2017): 1–23.

86. Lee, *Hard Truths*, 168.

87. Lee, *Hard Truths*, 269.

88. Lee, *Hard Truths*, 267. Fertility rate from https://www.singstat.gov.sg/modules/infographics/total-fertility-rate.

89. Steven Vertovec, "Low-Skilled Migrants After COVID-19: Singapore Futures?," Compas, April 21, 2020.

90. Brenda Yeoh and Weiqiang Lin, "Rapid Growth in Singapore's Immigrant Population Brings Policy Challenges," Migration Policy Institute, April 3, 2012.

91. "My definition of Singaporean, which will make us different from any others, is that we accept whoever joins us. And that's an American concept. You can keep your name, whatever it is, you have come, join me, you are American. We need talent, we accept them. That must be our defining attribute." Lee, *Hard Truths*, 292.

92. Max Weber, *The Sociology of Religion*, trans. E. Fistchoff (1922; Boston: Beacon, 1964).

93. Sandra Upson, "Singapore's Water Cycle Wizardry," *IEEE Spectrum*, May 28, 2010.

94. Jun Sen Ng, "New Ideas to Feed a Growing Island," *Straits Times*, February 4, 2018.

95. Alejandro Portes and Ariel Armony, *The Global Edge: Miami in the Twenty-First Century* (Berkeley: University of California Press, 2018).

96. Jason Fan, "PM Lee's 1st Big Speech to S'pore Featured Casinos, 5-Day Work Week & Slayed Other Sacred Cows," *Mothership*, August 12, 2019; "PM Lee Talks About Casinos, Population, Family, in Part 2 of Chinese TV Interview," *Straits Times*, November 30, 2014.

97. Fan, "PM Lee's 1st Big Speech"; Alejandro Portes and Brandon Martinez, "Emerging Global Cities: Structural Similarities and Historical Differences," *Spanish Sociological Review* 28, no. 3 (2019): 9–21.

98. John Berthelsen, "A Lee Dynasty in Singapore After All?," *Asia Sentinel*, May 4, 2021.

99. Max Weber, "The Sociology of Charismatic Authority," in *From Max Weber: Essays in Sociology*, ed. H. H. Gerth and C. Wright Mills (1922; New York: Oxford University Press, 1946), 245–264.

100. Reinhard Bendix, *Max Weber: An Intellectual Portrait* (New York: Anchor, 1962).

101. Yuen-C Tham, "Good Governance Eroding, Says Tan Cheng Bock," *Straits Times*, July 27, 2019.

5. GLOBAL HOPEFULS: AN OVERVIEW

1. Greg Clark, *Global Cities: A Short History* (Washington, DC: Brookings Institution, 2016), 111.

2. Joel Kotkin, *Size Is Not the Answer: The Changing Face of the Global City* (Singapore: Civil Service College, 2014). Other indexes: "New Priorities for a New World: 2020 Global Cities Index," Kearney, https://www.kearney.com/global-cities/2020; *Global Power City Index*, Institute for Urban Strategies, https://mori-m-foundation.or.jp/english/ius2/gpci2

/2018.shtml; "IESE Cities in Motion Index 2020," IESE Business School, https://blog.iese
.edu/cities-challenges-and-management/2020/10/27/iese-cities-in-motion-index-2020/;
Alan Berube, Jesus Leal Trufillo, Tao Ran, and Joseph Parilla, "Global Metro Monitor,"
Brookings, https://www.brookings.edu/research/global-metro-monitor/.

3. "Prime Global Cities Index—Q1 2021," Knight Frank, https://www.knightfrank.com
/research/report-library/prime-global-cities-index-q1-2021-8017.aspx.

4. *Branded Residences Report, 2019*, Knight Frank, https://content.knightfrank.com/research
/1617/documents/en/global-branded-residences-2019-5874.pdf.

5. Clark, *Global Cities*, 100–101, 104–105, 117.

6. Xuefei Ren and Roger Keil, eds., *The Globalizing Cities Reader*, 2nd ed. (New York: Routledge, 2018).

7. Richard Schaedel, Jorge Hardoy, and Nora Scott-Kinzer, "Two Thousand Years of Latin
American Urbanization," in *Urbanization in the Americas from Its Beginning to the Present*,
ed. Richard P. Schaedel, Jorge E. Hardoy, and Nora Scott-Kinzer (Berlin: De Gruyter
Mouton, 2011); Alejandro Portes and Bryan Roberts, "The Free-Market City," *Studies in
Comparative International Development* 40, no. 1 (2005).

8. Ren and Keil, *The Globalizing Cities Reader*, xxiii.

9. Ren and Keil, *The Globalizing Cities Reader*, xxviii.

10. Ren and Keil, *The Globalizing Cities Reader*, xxviii.

11. On "growth coalitions," see John Logan and Harvey Molotch, *Urban Fortunes: The Political
Economy of Place* (Berkeley: University of California Press, 1987).

12. Eugene McCann and Kevin Ward, "Relationality/Territoriality: Toward a Conceptualization of Cities in the World," *Geoforum* 41, no. 2 (March 2010): 175–184.

13. Ruchir Sharma, *The Rise and Fall of Nations: Forces of Change in the Post-Crisis World* (New
York: Norton, 2016).

14. These successful cases were also helped by geopolitical factors, particularly Cold War
dynamics, as the chapter on Dubai shows.

15. Jennifer Robinson, "New Geographies of Theorizing the Urban: Putting Comparison to
Work for Global Urban Studies," in *The Globalizing Cities Reader*, 457; see also Richard G.
Smith, "The Ordinary City Trap," *Environment and Planning* A, no. 45 (2013): 2290–2304;
Richard G. Smith, "The Ordinary City Trap Snaps Back," *Environment and Planning* A,
no. 45 (2013): 2318–2322.

16. Ren and Keil, *The Globalizing Cities Reader*, xxvii.

17. Peter Marcuse and Ronald van Kempen, eds., *Globalizing Cities: A New Spatial Order?*
(Malden, MA: Blackwell, 2000), 3–4.

18. Neil Brenner and Christian Schmid, "Planetary Urbanisation," in *Urban Constellations*,
ed. Mathew Gandy (Berlin: Jovis, 2011); Neil Brenner, "Global Cities, Glocal States:
Global City Formation and State Territorial Restructuring in Contemporary Europe,"
Review of International Political Economy 5, no. 1 (1998).

19. Brenner, "Global Cities, Glocal States"; Richard Child Hill and June Woo Kim, "Global
Cities and Developmental States," *Urban Studies* 37, no. 12 (2000).

20. Xuefei Ren, *Urban China* (Cambridge: Polity, 2013).

21. Ren, *Urban China*; Xuefei Ren, "Global City Building in China and Its Discontents,"
in *The Globalizing Cities Reader*; Fulong Wu, "From 'State-Owned' to 'City Inc.': The Case

of Shanghai," in *The Making of Global City Regions: Johannesburg, Mumbai/Bombay, São Paulo, and Shanghai*, ed. Klaus Segbers (Baltimore, MD: Johns Hopkins University Press, 2007).

22. Nick Schuermans, review of *Ordinary Cities: Between Modernity and Development*, by Jennifer Robinson, in *Belgeo: Revue Belge de Géographie*, March 31, 2009.

23. Laurent Fourchard, "Between World History and State Formation: New Perspectives on Africa's Cities," *Journal of African History* 52, no. 2 (July 2011): 247.

24. "Can Dubai Enter the Premier League of Financial Centres?," *The Economist*, August 22, 2020, https://www.economist.com/finance-and-economics/2020/08/22/can-dubai-enter-the-premier-league-of-financial-centres.

25. Philip Kasinitz, "The Global Edge: Miami in the Twenty-First Century" (remarks at the University of Miami Institute for Advanced Study of the Americas, Miami, FL, April 15, 2019).

26. See Clark, *Global Cities*, 126–127.

27. Arjun Appadurai, "Disjuncture and Difference in the Global Cultural Economy," *Theory, Culture, and Society* 7 (1990): 296–298.

28. Portes and Armony, *The Global Edge*.

29. Portes and Armony, *The Global Edge*, 196.

30. "Can Dubai Enter the Premier League?"

31. McCann and Ward, "Relationality/Territoriality," 175.

32. McCann and Ward, "Relationality/Territoriality," 176; see also Aihwa Ong, "Worlding Cities, or the Art of Being Global," in *Worlding Cities: Asian Experiments and the Art of Being Global*, ed. Anaya Roy and Aihwa Ong (West Sussex, UK: Wiley-Blackwell, 2011).

33. McCann and Ward, "Relationality/Territoriality," 175.

34. McCann and Ward, "Relationality/Territoriality," 177.

35. Rob Wile, "700 Jobs Are Coming to Downtown, Some with Barry's Bootcamp and Steve Cohen's Hedge Fund," *Miami Herald*, March 5, 2021, https://www.miamidda.com/wp-content/uploads/3.5.21-Miami-Herald-700-Jobs-are-Coming-to-downtown-some-with-Barrys-Bootcamp-and-Steven-Cohens-hedge-fund.pdf.

36. Akane Otani, "Elon Musk Has Become Bitcoin's Biggest Influencer, Like It or Not," *Wall Street Journal*, May 23, 2021, https://www.wsj.com/articles/elon-musk-has-become-bitcoins-biggest-influencer-like-it-or-not-11621762202.

37. Ashley Portero, "Cryptocurrency Company Blockchain.com Chooses Brickell for US Headquarters," *South Florida Business Journal*, June 3, 2021, https://www.bizjournals.com/southflorida/news/2021/06/03/crypto-company-blockchaincom-chooses-brickell-for.html.

38. Ren, *Urban China*; McCann and Ward, "Relationality/Territoriality," 175; see Clark, *Global Cities*, 100–101, 104–105, 107–108, 117; Véronique Dupont, "The Dream of Delhi as a Global City," *International Journal of Urban and Regional Research* 35, no. 3 (2011): 533–554.

39. Dupont, "The Dream of Delhi"; Clark, *Global Cities*, 107–108.

40. Sharma, *The Rise and Fall of Nations*, 168.

41. Sharma, *The Rise and Fall of Nations*, 168.

42. As quoted in Portes and Armony, *The Global Edge*, 129.

43. Portes and Armony, *The Global Edge*, 22.

44.   Dupont, "The Dream of Delhi"; Greg Clark and Tim Moonen, *The 10 Traits of Globally Flu-ent Metro Areas* (Washington, DC: Brookings Institution, 2013), https://www.brookings.edu/wp-content/uploads/2016/06/TenTraitsIntnl.pdf; Greg Clark and Tim Moonen, "The 10 Traits of Globally Fluent Metro Areas: Barcelona's Compelling Global Identity," Brookings Institution, 2013, https://www.brookings.edu/blog/the-avenue/2013/09/03/the-10-traits-of-globally-fluent-metro-areas-barcelonas-compelling-global-identity/. Real estate broker, conversation with Ariel Armony, Barcelona, October 25, 2017.

45.   Dupont, "The Dream of Delhi"; Prahalad Singh, "DDA: Master Plan for Delhi, 2021," CommonFloor, April 26, 2020, https://www.commonfloor.com/guide/dda-master-plan-for-delhi-2021-56810; Tracy Neumann, *Remaking the Rustbelt: The Postindustrial Transfor-mation of North America* (Philadelphia: University of Pennsylvania Press, 2016).

46.   See Clark, *Global Cities.*

47.   "Can Dubai Enter the Premier League?"; "Dismantling Pittsburgh: Death of an Airline Hub," *USA Today*, October 16, 2007, https://abcnews.go.com/Travel/story?id=3724036&page=1.

48.   See San Nguyen, "The Modern Image of Global City," Medium, June 23, 2017, https://medium.com/@sannguyen/the-modern-image-of-global-city-13b8eae96a49.

49.   Alan Mallach, *The Divided City: Poverty and Prosperity in Urban America* (Washington, DC: Island Press, 2018), 51.

50.   Neumann, *Remaking the Rustbelt*, 201.

51.   Ingrid Lunden, "Language Learning App Duolingo Confirms It Has Raised $35M on a $2.4B Valuation," TechCrunch, November 18, 2020, https://techcrunch.com/2020/11/18/language-learning-app-duolingo-confirms-it-has-raised-35m-on-a-2-4b-valuation/.

52.   Byron Spice, "CMU's Zoë Rover Shows Robots Can Find Subterranean Organisms," *Carnegie Mellon University News*, February 28, 2019, https://www.cmu.edu/news/stories/archives/2019/february/rover-finds-subterranean-organisms.html; quotation from "The White House at Our House," PITTMED, Fall 2016, https://www.pittmed.health.pitt.edu/story/white-house-our-house.

53.   Ren, "Global City Building in China," 308.

54.   Mark Preen, "China's City Clusters: The Plan to Develop 19 Super-Regions," *China Brief-ing News*, August 14, 2018, https://www.china-briefing.com/news/chinas-city-clusters-plan-to-transform-into-19-super-regions/; "Airbus' Assembly Facility Marks 10 Years of Quality Manufacturing for A320 Family Jetliners," AIRBUS, September 28, 2018, https://www.airbus.com/en/newsroom/news/2018-09-airbus-china-assembly-facility-marks-10-years-of-quality-manufacturing-for; *The Future of Urban Development Initia-tive: Dalian and Zhangjiakou Champion City Strategy* (Geneva: World Economic Forum, 2014), www3.weforum.org/docs/WEF_IU_FutureUrbanDevelopment_DalianZhangjiakou_ChampionCityStrategy_2014.pdf. Armony lived in Tianjin in 2008–2009 and frequently visited the city and region for fieldwork over the following decade.

55.   Sharon Zukin, *Naked City: The Death and Life of Authentic Urban Places* (Oxford: Oxford University Press, 2009); Alejandro Portes and Brandon Martinez, "Emerging Global Cities: Structural Similarities and Historical Differences," *Spanish Review of Sociology* 28, no. 15 (2019).

56.   Neumann, *Remaking the Rustbelt*, 176.

57. Mari Paz Balibrea, "Urbanism, Culture and the Post-Industrial City: Challenging the 'Barcelona Model,'" *Journal of Spanish Cultural Studies* 2, no. 2 (September 2001): 190.

58. Fieldwork, Pittsburgh, PA, October 2020.

59. Loïc Wacquant, "The Militarization of Urban Marginality: Lessons from the Brazilian Metropolis," *International Political Sociology* 2, no. 1 (2008): 56.

60. Neumann, *Remaking the Rustbelt*, 176.

61. Neumann, *Remaking the Rustbelt*, 174, 190–191, 193, 200–201, 213–214; Mallach, *The Divided City*; Richard Florida, *The Rise of the Creative Class* (New York: Basic Books, 2002).

62. Neumann, *Remaking the Rustbelt*, 175; Sharon Zukin, "Competitive Globalization and Urban Change: The Allure of Cultural Strategies," in *Rethinking Global Urbanism: Comparative Insights from Secondary Cities*, ed. Xiangming Chen and Ahmen Kanna (New York: Routledge, 2012), 19.

63. Dupont, "The Dream of Delhi," 544.

64. Mark Byrnes, "Revisiting Pittsburgh's Era of Big Plans," *Bloomberg CityLab*, June 25, 2019, https://www.bloomberg.com/news/articles/2019-06-25/-imagining-the-modern-in -postwar-pittsburgh.

    Ren and Keil discuss the "mega-event fever" experienced by cities in the Global South in the early 2000s: "The high-profile mega-events attracted global spotlight to the host cities, helping to realize their global city ambitions, but also intensifying patterns of polarization and contestation in the local society." Ren and Keil, *The Globalizing Cities Reader*, xxiv. On the theme of Sydney's 2000 Olympic bid and the relationship between mega events and multiculturalism and environmental issues in the postmodern city, see G. Waitt, "Playing Games with Sydney: Marketing Sydney for the 2000 Olympics," *Urban Studies* 37, no. 7 (1999): 1055–1077. On the local impact of the Olympic Games in Sydney, particularly in terms of social and political legacies, see K. A. Owen, "The Sydney 2000 Olympics and Urban Entrepreneurialism: Local Variations in Urban Governance," *Australian Geographical Studies* 40, no. 3 (2002): 323–336.

65. As Sharma writes, "Public architecture as spectacle—a hotel shaped like a sail, the world's biggest mall," is an important symbol of Dubai's transformation. Sharma, *The Rise and Fall of Nations*, 166–167.

66. Stephen Graham, "Vertical Noir: Histories of the Future in Urban Science Fiction," *City* 20, no. 3 (2016): 399.

67. Stefan Krätke, "'Global Media Cities': Major Nodes of Globalising Culture and Media Industries," in *The Globalizing Cities Reader*, 352.

68. Minaam Ansari, "Dubai's Iconic Burj Khalifa Honours Argentine Great Maradona with Dazzling Gesture," *Republic World*, December 1, 2020, https://www.republicworld.com /sports-news/football-news/dubais-iconic-burj-khalifa-honours-argentine-great -maradona-with-dazzling-gesture.html.

69. Krätke, "Global Media Cities," 352.

70. Portes and Armony, *The Global Edge*; Dupont, "The Dream of Delhi."

71. Greg Clark, Marek Gootman, Max Bouchet, and Tim Moonen, "The Global Identity of Cities: Seven Steps to Build Reputation and Visibility for Competitiveness and Resilience," Brookings Institution, July 28, 2020, 7, https://www.brookings.edu/research/seven-steps -build-reputation-visibility-for-competitiveness/.

72. Clark et al., "The Global Identity of Cities," 26.

73. Clark et al., "The Global Identity of Cities," 8.

74. R. Govers, "Brand Dubai and Its Competitors in the Middle East: An Image and Reputation Analysis," *Place Branding and Public Diplomacy* 8 (2012).

75. Portes and Armony, *The Global Edge*, chap. 7.

76. Portes and Armony, *The Global Edge*; Zukin, *Naked City*.

77. Shivani Vora, "Luxury Living in Miami Moves North," *New York Times*, June 18, 2019, https://www.nytimes.com/2019/06/18/realestate/luxury-living-miami-north-beach-sunny-isles.html.

78. Vora, "Luxury Living."

79. Not surprisingly, the growing global phenomenon of branded residences responds to a sustained growth in real estate investment by wealthy individuals, who look for opportunities in emerging global cities. For instance, according to the Miami Association of Realtors, "the Miami Mega Region is the No. 1 U.S. destination for global consumers and home to diversified foreign homebuyers." Chris Umpierre, "International Home Sales Totaled $6.9 Billion in the Miami Mega Region in 2019; According to Latest MIAMI Realtors International Report," Miami Realtors, June 10, 2020, https://www.miamirealtors.com/2020/06/10/international-home-sales-totaled-6-9-billion-in-the-miami-mega-region-in-2019-according-to-latest-miami-realtors-international-report/.

80. Paul Wallace and Tope Alake, "Lagos Building Luxury Homes in Face of Affordable Housing Crisis," *Bloomberg*, December 20, 2019, https://www.bloomberg.com/news/articles/2019-12-20/lagos-building-luxury-homes-in-face-of-affordable-housing-crisis; Yinka Ibukun, Sophie Mongalvy, and Antony Sguazzin, "Dream of a Lagos Champs-Élysées Banks on Nigerian Recovery," *Bloomberg*, May 29, 2018, https://www.bloomberg.com/news/articles/2018-05-29/eko-atlantic-city-eyes-2023-finish-as-nigeria-economy-rebounds.

81. Taibat Lawanson, "Lagos' Size and Slums Will Make Stopping the Spread of COVID-19 a Tough Task," The Conversation, April 1, 2020, http://theconversation.com/lagos-size-and-slums-will-make-stopping-the-spread-of-covid-19-a-tough-task-134723; "Nigeria Housing: 'I Live in a Floating Slum' in Lagos," *BBC News*, March 5, 2020, https://www.bbc.com/news/world-africa-51677371; Adebayo Akesanju Kester, "Emerging 'New Cities' in Africa and Socio-Spatial Inequality: A Case Study of the Eko Atlantic City Project in Lagos, Nigeria" (MA thesis, University of Amsterdam, 2014). On Eko Atlantic, see Jeff Goodell, *The Water Will Come: Rising Seas, Sinking Cities, and the Remaking of the Civilized World* (New York: Little, Brown, 2017), 213–221.

82. Portes and Armony, *The Global Edge*.

83. Florida, *The Rise of the Creative Class*; Krätke, "Global Media Cities"; Donald Carter, ed., *Remaking Post-Industrial Cities: Lessons from North America and Europe* (London: Routledge, 2016).

84. Chen and Kanna, *Rethinking Global Urbanism*, 18.

85. Chen and Kanna, *Rethinking Global Urbanism*, 18–19.

86. Chen and Kanna, *Rethinking Global Urbanism*, 131–132. Most of the global growth in consumption in the next decades will come from about one hundred cities, and a third of those cities will generate a quarter of the world's total growth for the period 2015–2030; Portes and Armony, *The Global Edge*, 132.

87. See Jonathan Haskel and Stian Westlake, *Capitalism Without Capital: The Rise of the Intangible Economy* (Princeton, NJ: Princeton University Press, 2018), 136–138.

6. NEW ORLEANS: A CENTURY OF DECLINE

1. Wikipedia, s.v. "List of U.S. Metropolitan Areas by GDP," https://en.wikipedia.org /wiki/List_of_U.S._metropolitan_areas_by_GDP.

2. Scott P. Marler, *The Merchants' Capital: New Orleans and the Political Economy of the Nineteenth-Century South* (New York: Cambridge University Press, 2013), 119.

3. Justin A. Nystrom, *New Orleans After the Civil War* (Baltimore, MD: Johns Hopkins University Press, 2010), chap. 1.

4. Marler, *The Merchants' Capital*, 120.

5. Richard Campanella and Tulane University Center for Bioenvironmental Research, "Economic Timeline: Selected Historical Events That Shaped the New Orleans Economy, 1700–2010," The Data Center, August 4, 2010, https://www.datacenterresearch.org /reports_analysis/economic-timeline/; John S. Kendall, *History of New Orleans* (Chicago: Lewis, 1922).

6. Marler, *The Merchants' Capital*, chap. 1; Campanella et al., "Economic Timeline."

7. Kendall, *History of New Orleans*; Wikipedia, s.v. "The Louisiana Purchase," https://en .wikipedia.org/wiki/Louisiana_Purchase.

8. Kendall, "History of New Orleans"; Wikipedia, s.v. "History of New Orleans," https:// en.wikipedia.org/wiki/History_of_New_Orleans.

9. Campanella et al., "Economic Timeline"; Kendall, *History of New Orleans*.

10. Martin Siegel, *New Orleans: A Chronological and Documentary History, 1539–1970* (Dobbs Ferry, NY: Oceana, 1975); Ory Mazar Nergal, "New Orleans," in *Encyclopedia of American Cities* (New York: Dutton, 1980); Kendall, "History of New Orleans."

11. Marler, *The Merchants' Capital*, chap. 1; Leonard Huber, *New Orleans Architecture* (New Orleans, LA: Pelican, 1975); Campanella et al., "Economic Timeline."

12. Marler, *The Merchants' Capital*, chap. 4; Kendall, *History of New Orleans*; Robert Reinders and John Duffy, *End of an Era: New Orleans, 1850–1860* (New Orleans, LA: Pelican, 1964).

13. Nystrom, *New Orleans After the Civil War*; Siegel, *New Orleans*; "History of New Orleans."

14. Marler, *The Merchants' Capital*, chap. 4; Nystrom, *New Orleans After the Civil War*.

15. "History of New Orleans"; Reinders and Duffy, *End of an Era*.

16. Marler, *The Merchants' Capital*, 193.

17. Campanella et al., "Economic Timeline"; "History of New Orleans"; Nystrom, *New Orleans After the Civil War*.

18. Marler, *The Merchants' Capital*, 206.

19. Joe Gray Taylor, *Louisiana Reconstructed, 1863–1877* (Baton Rouge: Louisiana State University Press, 1974), 279.

20. "Over a century before Hurricane Katrina, New Orleans was pummeled by the economic equivalent of a 'perfect storm': a deadly combination of short-sighted commercial hubris, corrupt and reactionary government, and overacting changes to both the internal structure of Southern agriculture and the . . . external trade flows that constituted the American urban system." Marler, *The Merchants' Capital*, 208.

21. "History of New Orleans," Wikipedia; Siegel, *New Orleans*.
22. Nergal, "New Orleans"; Campanella et al., "Economic Timeline"; "History of New Orleans"; Walter Cowan, *New Orleans Yesterday and Today: A Guide to the City* (Baton Rouge: Louisiana State University Press, 1983).
23. Albert A. Fossier, *New Orleans: The Glamour Period, 1800–1840* (New Orleans, LA: Pelican, 1957); Siegel, *New Orleans*.
24. Marler, *The Merchants' Capital*, chap. 6, epilogue.
25. Taylor, *Louisiana Reconstructed*; Reinders and Duffy, *End of an Era*; "History of New Orleans."
26. Charles M. Bonjean, Bernic M. Moore, and Adreain A. Ross, "The Junior League of New Orleans: A Profile of Member Attitudes and Orientations," Report for National Association of Junior Leagues (Austin, TX: Hogg Foundation for Mental Health, 1976).
27. Frederick D. Wright, "The Voting Rights Act and Louisiana: Twenty Years of Enforcement," *Publius* 16, no. 4 (1986).
28. Wikipedia, s.v. "Moon Landrieu," https://en.wikipedia.org/wiki/Moon_Landrieu.
29. David R. Colburn and Jeffrey S. Adler, eds., *African-American Mayors: Race, Politics, and the American City* (Champaign: University of Illinois Press, 2005).
30. "History of New Orleans," Wikipedia.
31. Campanella et al., "Economic Timeline"; "History of New Orleans"; Robert Habans et al., "Placing Prosperity: Neighborhoods and Life Expectancy in New Orleans Metro," The Data Center, August 13, 2020.
32. Cowan, *New Orleans Yesterday and Today*; Fossier, *New Orleans*; "History of New Orleans."
33. Campanella et al., "Economic Timeline"; Habans et al., "Placing Prosperity"; "History of New Orleans."
34. Elizabeth Kolbert, "Louisiana's Disappearing Coast," *New Yorker*, March 25, 2019, https://www.newyorker.com/magazine/2019/04/01/louisianas-disappearing-coast.
35. Richard Campanella, "New Orleans: A Timeline of Economic History," New Orleans Business Alliance, 2012, https://richcampanella.com/wpcontent/uploads/2020/02/article_Campanella_New-Orleans-Timeline-of-Economic-History_NOBA.pdf.
36. Steve Olson, *Increasing National Resilience to Hazards and Disasters: The Perspective from the Gulf Coast of Louisiana and Mississippi: Summary of a Workshop* (Washington, DC: National Academies Press, 2011), 19.
37. Justin A. Nystrom, "The Vanished World of the New Orleans Longshoreman," *Southern Spaces*, March 5, 2014, https://southernspaces.org/2014/vanished-world-new-orleans-longshoreman/.
38. Kathy Finn, "Oil Boom and Bust," *My New Orleans*, May 1, 2017, https://www.mynewCorleans.com/oil-boom-and-bust/.
39. Google Search, "New Orleans Economy," n.d.; New Orleans Business Alliance, "Doing Business in New Orleans," New Orleans.com., https://www.neworleans.com/business/.
40. Campanella et al., "Economic Timeline"; Habans et al., "Placing Prosperity."
41. "List of U.S. Metropolitan Areas by GDP"; Google Search, "New Orleans Economy," n.d.; Habans et al., "Placing Prosperity."
42. Anthony McAuley, "Amazon Is Expanding in New Orleans with Its 'Last Mile' Delivery Partners," Nola.com, August 10, 2020.
43. Campanella, "New Orleans."

44.   Amy Liu and Allison Plyer, *The New Orleans Index at Five: Measuring Greater New Orleans' Progress Toward Prosperity* (New Orleans, LA: Brookings Metropolitan Policy Program and Greater New Orleans Community Data Center, 2010).

45.   Alan Mallach, *The Divided City: Poverty and Prosperity in Urban America* (Washington, DC: Island Press, 2018).

46.   Campanella, "New Orleans."

7. SÃO PAULO: BRAZIL'S ALWAYS-ASPIRING CITY

1.   United Nations, Department of Economic and Social Information and Policy Analysis, *Population Growth and Policies in Mega-Cities: São Paulo* (New York: UN Headquarters, 1993), https://www.un.org/development/desa/pd/fr/node/2016.

2.   Tobias Töpfer, "São Paulo: Big, Bigger, Global? The Development of a Megacity in the Global South," in *Globalization and the City: Two Connected Phenomena in Past and Present*, ed. Günter Bischof, Andreas Exenberger, James Mokhiber, and Phillip Strobl (Innsbruck, Austria: Innsbruck University Press, 2016). The population of the city of São Paulo was 12.33 million in 2019: Ariel C. Armony, Bruno Massola Moda, and Lucilene Cury, "A Discussion on Global Cities and Immigration: The Case of São Paulo and Miami" (conference paper, IPSA World Congress of Political Science, July 10–15, 2021).

3.   Carolina Rossetti de Toledo, "Population Flows in São Paulo," *Pesquisa FAPESP* 215 (2014). According to the Brazilian Federal Police, immigrants living in São Paulo city represented 2.37 percent of the total city population in 2019: Armony et al., "A Discussion on Global Cities."

4.   Simon Romero, "Immigrants Stir New Life into São Paulo's Gritty Old Center," *New York Times*, April 14, 2014, https://www.nytimes.com/2014/04/15/world/americas/immigrants -stir-new-life-into-sao-paulos-gritty-old-center.html.

5.   Armony et al., "A Discussion on Global Cities"; X. I. León Contrera, "Projeto inovador: Comitê Paulista para Imigrantes e Refugiados foi lançado," *Jornal da CMDH—Informativo Bimestral da Comissão Municipal de Direitos Humanos* (January 2008): 3–4; Teressa Juzwiak, "Sao Paulo, Brazil, a Case Study from 'Migrant and Refugee Integration in Global Cities—The Role of Cities and Businesses,'" The Hague Process on Refugees and Migration, 2014, 18–19, https://thp.merit.unu.edu/migrant-refugee-integration-global -cities-role-cities-businesses/; José Roberto de Melo, "Superintendência Regional do Trabalho e Emprego em São Paulo, SRTE/SP 92," June 10, 2010, http://www.normaslegais .com.br/legislacao/portariasrtesp92_2010.htm; *Migration Governance Indicators, City of São Paulo* (Geneva: United Nations, International Organization for Migration, 2019), 16. Despite these initiatives, immigrants in São Paulo face many problems. For example, 90 percent of São Paulo's 300,000 Bolivians work within the textile industry, and many reports highlight the unethical labor policies of the industry, which are said to be akin to modern-day slavery. Human trafficking is another serious problem that renders many individuals susceptible to exploitation. Jefferson Puff, "Racismo contra imigrantes no Brasil é constante, diz pesquisador," *BBC News*, August 26, 2015; Paulo Illes, Gabrielle Louise Soares Timóteo, and Elaine da Silva Fiorucci, "Human Trafficking for Labour Exploitation in the City of São Paulo," *Cadernos Pagu* 31 (2008); "Global Slavery Index:

Brazil," Global Slavery Index, https://www.globalslaveryindex.org/2018/findings/country
-studies/brazil/.

6. Fabio Betioli Contel and Dariusz Wójcik, "Brazil's Financial Centers in the Twenty-First
Century: Hierarchy, Specialization, and Concentration," *Professional Geographer* 71, no. 4
(2019): 684–685, 688–689.

7. Fabio Betioli Contel, *The Financialization of the Brazilian Territory: From Global Forces to
Local Dynamisms* (Cham, Switzerland: Springer, 2020), 41–47.

8. Carlos Macedo et al., *Fintech's Brazil Moment*, Goldman Sachs, May 12, 2017, https://www
.gspublishing.com/content/research/en/reports/2017/05/12/f21e671e-dad0-4ef4-ba07
-d694211b0c94.pdf.

9. Macedo et al., *Fintech's Brazil Moment*.

10. *The Global Fintech Index 2020*, Findexable, 2019, https://findexable.com/wp-content
/uploads/2019/12/Findexable_Global-Fintech-Rankings-2020exSFA.pdf.

11. Andres Schipani, "Nubank Shakes Up Brazil's Banking Bureaucracy," *Financial Times*,
March 30, 2020, https://www.ft.com/content/c0014ce4-6273-11ea-abcc-910c5b38d9ed.

12. "São Paulo," Council on Tall Buildings and Urban Habitat, accessed February 15, 2021,
https://www.skyscrapercenter.com/city/sao-paulo.

13. "São Paulo Biennial (Brazil)," Biennial Foundation, https://www.biennialfoundation
.org/biennials/sao-paolo-biennial/. Art Basel Miami presented work from twenty-nine
countries in the 2019 show, and during the 2019 Hong Kong Exhibition of Art HK,
thirty-five countries participated. More than 90,000 events are organized in the city
of São Paulo annually, including one of the world's most important auto shows. Ricardo
Geromel, "All You Need to Know About Sao Paulo, Brazil's Largest City," *Forbes*, June 12,
2013, https://www.forbes.com/sites/ricardogeromel/2013/07/12/all-you-need-to-know
-about-sao-paulo-brazils-largest-city/?sh=7defcd6121ad.

14. "São Paulo International Film Festival," Mostra, accessed February 18, 2021, https://44
.mostra.org/; "São Paulo Film Commission," Spcine, accessed February 18, 2021, http://
spcine.com.br/spfilmcommission/; "Brazil Corner: How São Paulo Intends to Become
a Center of Film Production," portada, April 8, 2017, https://www.portada-online
.com/latin-america/brazil-corner-how-sao-paulo-intends-to-become-a-center-of
-film-production/; John Hopewell, "São Paulo Launches Production Incentive to Grab
Post-COVID Shoots," *Variety*, May 18, 2020, https://variety.com/2020/film/spotlight
/brazil-city-incentives-productions-1234607311/.

15. "Technology Parks," InvestSP, 2021, https://www.en.investe.sp.gov.br/why-sao-paulo
/innovation-science-and-technology/technology-parks//; Gustavo Faleiros, "How Science
Supports São Paulo," *Nature*, November 28, 2018, https://www.nature.com/articles/d41586
-018-07536-1; John Cohen, "An Intriguing—but Far from Proven—HIV Cure in the 'São
Paulo Patient,'" *ScienceMag*, July 7, 2020, https://www.sciencemag.org/news/2020/07
/intriguing-far-proven-hiv-cure-s-o-paulo-patient.

16. J. H. de Sousa Damiani et al., "The Innovation System of Sao Jose dos Campos: Main
Institutions, Architecture, Contributions to Economic and Social Development, Per-
spectives and Future Challenges" (paper presented at Portland International Conference
on Management of Engineering and Technology (PICMET), Portland, OR, 2018), 1–17;
"Welcome to One of the Largest Innovation and Entrepreneurship Hubs in Brazil,"
Parque Tecnológico, accessed June 28, 2021, https://pqtec.org.br/en/.

17.   "About Us," Embraer, accessed June 28, 2021, https://embraer.com/global/en/about-us.

18.   "Eve Announces Halo as Launch Partner in the Urban Air Mobility Market with an Order for 200 eVTOL Aircraft," Embraer, June 1, 2021, https://embraer.com/global/en /news?slug=1206878-eve-announces-halo-as-launch-partner-in-the-urban-air-mobility -market-with-an-order-for-200-evtol-aircraft.

19.   Pranjal Pande, "Why Asia Is a Big Market for Embraer's E2 Series," *Simple Flying*, May 9, 2021, https://simpleflying.com/asia-embraer-e2-series/.

20.   Alejandro Portes and Bryan R. Roberts, "The Free-Market City: Latin American Urbanization in the Years of the Neoliberal Experiment," *Studies in Comparative International Development* 40, no. 1 (2005): 43–82. The city's stock exchange, BM&F Bovespa, although low compared to the stock exchanges of both traditional major finance centers like New York, Tokyo, and London and emerging centers like Mumbai and Shanghai, had a 2.4 percent share of worldwide capitalization as of 2019, up from 0.1 percent in 1990, making it the most significant in all of Latin America.

21.   Marcelo Cantor, *Market Analysis—Airport Sector Brazil* (The Hague: Netherlands Enterprise Agency, 2020), 7, https://www.rvo.nl/sites/default/files/2020/06/Airport-Sector-in -Brazil.pdf; Elzbieta Visnevskyte, "Situation in South America's Busiest Airports," Aerotime Hub, November 20, 2020, https://www.aerotime.aero/26482-situation-in-south-america -s-busiest-airports; "Busiest Airports in South America," AirMundo, accessed June 30, 2021, https://airmundo.com/en/blog/busiest-airports-in-south-america/; *The Importance of Air Transport to Brazil*, IATA, https://www.iata.org/contentassets/bc041f5b6b96476a80 db109f220f8904/brazil-the-value-of-air-transport.pdf.

22.   "Santos Port Authority Statistics," Porto de Santos, accessed February 18, 2021, http://www .portodesantos.com.br/informacoes-operacionais/estatisticas/relatorio-de-analise-do -movimento-fisico/.

23.   "São Paulo," Observatory of Economic Complexity (OEC), last modified March 2021, https://oec.world/en/profile/subnational_bra_state/sao-paulo.

24.   *Índice de Gini da distribuição do rendimento domiciliar per capita, segundo as Grandes Regiões, as Unidades da Federação e os Municípios das Capitais*, IBGE, 2019, https://ftp.ibge.gov.br /Indicadores_Sociais/Sintese_de_Indicadores_Sociais/Sintese_de_Indicadores_Sociais _2020/indice_das_tabelas_sis2020.pdf.

25.   Eduardo Marques, "Governing a Large Metropolis: São Paulo—Urban Policies and Segregation in a Highly Unequal Metropolis" (conference paper, Second ISA Forum of Sociology, Buenos Aires, Argentina, August 1–4, 2012).

26.   John Monteiro, *Blacks of the Land*, trans. James Woodward and Barbara Weinstein (Cambridge: Cambridge University Press, 2018), 18.

27.   Elizabeth Anne Kuznesof, *Household Economy and Urban Development: São Paulo, 1765 to 1836* (Boulder, CO: Westview, 1986); Francisco Vidal Luna and Hebert Klein, "Slave Economy and Society in Minas Gerais and São Paulo, Brazil in 1830," *Journal of Latin American Studies* 36, no. 1 (2004): 1–28.

28.   Kuznesof, *Household Economy*.

29.   Brian Godfrey, "Modernizing the Brazilian City," *Geographical Review* 81, no. 1 (1991): 18–34.

30.   Thomas E. Skidmore, *Brazil: Five Centuries of Change*, 2nd ed. (Oxford: Oxford University Press, 2010); Werner Baer, *The Brazilian Economy: Growth and Development* (London: Lynne Rienner, 2008).

31. Barbara Weinstein, *The Color of Modernity: São Paulo and the Making of Race and Nation in Brazil* (Durham, NC: Duke University Press, 2015).

32. Benicio Viero Schmidt, "Modernization and Urban Planning in 19th-Century Brazil," *Current Anthropology* 23, no. 3 (1982): 255–262.

33. Kim D. Butler, "Up from Slavery: Afro-Brazilian Activism in São Paulo, 1888–1938," *The Americas* 49, no. 2 (1992): 179–206.

34. Weinstein, *The Color of Modernity*; Andre Kobayashi Deckrow, "São Paulo as Migrant -Colony: Pre-World War II Japanese State-Sponsored Agricultural Migration to Brazil" (PhD diss., Columbia University, 2019); C. R. Cameron, "Colonization of Immigrants in Brazil," *Monthly Labor Review* 33, no. 4 (1931): 36–46; Butler, "Up from Slavery"; Jeffrey Lesser, "Immigration and Shifting Concepts of National Identity in Brazil During the Vargas Era," *Luso-Brazilian Review* 31, no. 2 (1994): 23–44.

35. Campos et al., "Political Instability, Institutional Change and Economic Growth in Brazil Since 1870," *Journal of Institutional Economics* 16, no. 6 (2020): 883–910.

36. Anne Hanley, "Is It Who You Know? Entrepreneurs and Bankers in Sao Paulo, Brazil, at the Turn of the Twentieth Century," *Enterprise and Society* 5, no. 2 (2004): 187–255.

37. Ariel C. Armony, Lucilene Cury, and Bruno Massola Moda, "As Cidades Globais e Seus Habitantes: Uma Reflexão Transdisciplinar" (unpublished manuscript, 2020), typescript; Godfrey, "Modernizing the Brazilian City."

38. Armony et al., "As Cidades Globais."

39. Warren Dean, *The Planter as Entrepreneur: The Case of São Paulo* (Austin: Institute of Latin American Studies, University of Texas, 1966).

40. Weinstein, *The Color of Modernity*.

41. Weinstein, *The Color of Modernity*; Butler, "Up from Slavery."

42. Peter Marcuse and Ronald van Kempen, eds., *Of States and Cities: The Partitioning of Urban Space* (Oxford: Oxford University Press, 2002).

43. Ignacy Sachs et al., *Brazil: A Century of Change* (Chapel Hill: University of North Carolina Press, 2009).

44. Teresa Caldeira, "Social Movements, Cultural Production, and Protests: São Paulo's Shifting Political Landscape," *Current Anthropology* 56, no. 11 (2015): S126–S135.

45. Sachs et al., *Brazil*.

46. Marques, "Governing a Large Metropolis"; Leslie Bethell, "Brazil: The Last 15 Years," *Index on Censorship* 8, no. 4 (1979): 3–7.

47. See Ben Wilson, *Metropolis: A History of the City, Humankind's Greatest Invention* (New York: Doubleday, 2020), 373. Paulo Freire, world-renowned educator and author of the acclaimed *Pedagogy of the Oppressed*—who became secretary of education of São Paulo in 1989—led an effort to address inequalities in educational access and outcomes. Freire and his team worked on a new model of education and implemented major changes to the curriculum via school councils, broader literacy training outside of K–8 education, and participatory planning and delivery supported by nongovernment organizations and social movements. The results of Freire's reforms were swift. The city experienced a consistent rise in student retention rates, from 77.81 percent in 1985 to 87.7 percent in 1991. Freire secured public funds for reconstructing and rebuilding schools, and teachers' salaries increased. Furthermore, by offering extra compensation—often up to

50 percent of baseline salaries—the administration was able to attract the most quali-fied teachers to work in the city's traditionally neglected areas. Carlos Alberto Torres, "Paulo Freire as Secretary of Education in the Municipality of São Paulo," *Comparative Education Review* 38, no. 2 (1994): 181–214; "Why Is the Brazilian Right Afraid of Paulo Freire?," Open Democracy, https://www.opendemocracy.net/en/democraciaabierta/why-is-the-brazilian-right-afraid-of-paulo-freire/.

48. Armony et al., "As Cidades Globais." Following the democratic transition in 1985, political divides reflected a polarized environment in which the political preferences of important sectors of the highly educated population and business elite vastly diverged from those of the low-income population. The left, namely, the Brazilian Labor Party (Partido Trabalhista Brasileiro [PTB]) had greater traction among the poor, and the right, specifically the Democratic Social Party (Partido Democrático Social [PDS])—later called the Brazilian Social Democracy Party (Partido da Social Democracia Bra-sileira [PSDB])—had greater traction among the wealthy and moderate voters. Fernando Limongi and Laura Mesquita, "Estratégia Partidária e Clivagens Eleitorais: As Eleições Municipais pós Redemocratização," in *São Paulo: Novos Percursos e Atores*, ed. Lúcio Kowarick and Eduardo Marques (São Paulo: Editora 34, 2011).

49. United Nations, *Population Growth and Policies.*

50. Caldeira, "Social Movements," 127.

51. Teresa Caldeira describes autoconstructors as residents who "build their houses and cities step-by-step according to the resources they are able to put together." Teresa Caldeira, "Peripheral Urbanization: Autoconstruction, Transversal Logics, and Politics in Cities of the Global South," *Society and Space* 35, no. 1 (2016): 3–20.

52. United Nations Human Settlements Programme, *São Paulo: A Tale of Two Cities* (Nairobi: UN Habitat, 2010).

53. Francesco Perrotta-Bosch, "Electric Avenue: Avenida Paulista as a Microcosm of Urban Brazil," *Architectural Review* (blog), October 21, 2019, https://www.architectural-review.com/essays/electric-avenue-avenida-paulista-as-a-microcosm-of-urban-brazil.

54. Portes and Roberts, "The Free-Market City," 46.

55. Francisco Vidal Luna and Herbert S. Klein, *An Economic and Demographic History of São Paulo, 1850–1950* (Stanford, CA: Stanford University Press, 2018).

56. United Nations, *Population Growth and Policies.*

57. Paulo Fontes and Larissa R. Corrêa, "Labor and Dictatorship in Brazil: A Historiograph-ical Review," *International Labor and Working-Class History* 93 (2018): 27–51; John Markoff and Silvio R. Duncan Baretta, "Economic Crisis and Regime Change in Brazil: The 1960s and the 1980s," *Comparative Politics* 22, no. 4 (1990): 421–444.

58. Paulo Fontes and Francisco Barbosa de Macedo, "Strikes and Pickets in Brazil: Work-ing-Class Mobilization in the 'Old' and 'New' Unionism, the Strikes of 1957 and 1980," *International Labor and Working-Class History* 83 (2013): 86–111.

59. United Nations, *Population Growth and Policies.*

60. São Paulo city experienced an increase of 28.8 to 46.2 percent of total value in tertiary jobs, and a decrease from 69.1 to 49.1 percent in manufacturing; Marcuse and van Kem-pen, *Of States and Cities.*

61. Portes and Roberts, "The Free-Market City," 50–66.

62. Roberto Rocco, "Towards a Polycentric Metropolis: Global Strategies and Unequal Development in São Paulo," *Urbani Izziv* 17, no. 2 (2006): 196.

63. Haroldo da Gama Torres, "Residential Segregation and Public Policies: São Paulo in the 1990's," *Revista Brasileria de Ciências Sociais* 2 (2006): 41–55.

64. Caldeira, "Social Movements," 127; Lucy Earle, *Transgressive Citizenship and the Struggle for Social Justice* (London: Palgrave Macmillan, 2017), 68.

65. Earle, *Transgressive Citizenship*, 85–88.

66. Erica Goode, "Miami Police Department Is Accused of Pattern of Excessive Force," *New York Times*, July 9, 2013.

67. "QuickFacts: New Orleans City, Louisiana," United States Census, https://www.census .gov/quickfacts/fact/table/neworleanscitylouisiana/PST120219.

68. Cintia Acayaba and Leo Arcoverde, "Batalhões da Grande SP matam 60 percent mais em 2020; na capital, aumento de mortes por policiais militares chega a 44 percent," *O Globo*, https://g1.globo.com/sp/sao-paulo/noticia/2020/06/23/batalhoes-da-grande-sp-matam -60percent-mais-em-2020-na-capital-aumento-de-mortes-por-policiais-militares-chega -a-44percent.ghtml.

69. Teresa Caldeira, *City of Walls* (Berkeley: University of California Press, 2000).

70. Martin Coy, "Gated Communities and Urban Fragmentation in Latin America: The Brazilian Experience," *GeoJournal* 66 (2006): 122.

71. Loïc Wacquant, "The Militarization of Urban Marginality: Lessons from the Brazilian Metropolis," *International Political Sociology* 2, no. 1 (2008): 56–74.

72. Stephen Graham, *Cities Under Siege: The New Military Urbanism* (London: Verso, 2010), 112.

73. Graham, *Cities Under Siege*, 9.

74. Graham, *Cities Under Siege*, 9.

75. Martin Coy and Tobias Töpfer, "Inner-City Development in Megacities Between Degradation and Renewal: The Case of São Paulo," in *Megacities: Our Urban Global Future*, ed. F. Kraas, S. Aggarwal, M. Coy, and G. Mertins (Dordrecht: Springer, 2014), 113–116.

76. Brian Winter, "On Sao Paulo Subway, a Leap for Brazil Infrastructure," Reuters, February 1, 2013, https://www.reuters.com/article/brazil-infrastructure-subway/on-sao -paulo-subway-a-leap-for-brazil-infrastructure-idUKL1NoB11EC20130201?edition-redirect =uk; Geromel, "All You Need to Know."

77. Richard Mann, "São Paulo Governor Plans R$18 Billion Infrastructure Investments by 2022," *Rio Times*, February 15, 2021, https://riotimesonline.com/brazil-news/sao-paulo /politics-sao-paulo/brazils-sao-paulo-governor-plans-r18-billion-investments-by -2022/; "Public-Private Partnership Stories, Brazil: São Paulo Roads," International Finance Corporation, February 2019, https://www.ifc.org/wps/wcm/connect/6a30d7b8-99e0-4425 -809d-6749b843ef56/PPP-Stories-Brazil-SP+Roads.pdf?MOD=AJPERES&CVID =mz3AneC.

78. Leslie Elliott Armijo and Sybil D. Rhodes, "Explaining Infrastructure Underperformance in Brazil: Cash, Political Institutions, Corruption, and Policy Gestalts," *Policy Studies* 38, no. 3 (2017): 231–247.

79. "HSE Global Cities Innovation Index," HSE University, 2020, https://gcii.hse.ru/en/.

80. Marcos Troyjo, "São Paulo Offers Blueprint for What Brazil Could Achieve," *Financial Times*, March 13, 2018, https://www.ft.com/content/5138c8e4-2127-11e8-8d6c-a1920d9e946f.

81.   Brizotti-Pasquotto et al., "Iconic Buildings and City Marketing: The Central Area of São Paulo," *Bitácora Urbano Territorial* 24, no. 2 (2014): 21–30. The proposal of a new cultural center, the Complexo Cultural Teatro da Dança, is an example of the city's urban branding efforts, which involve hiring a famous Swiss architecture firm and private corporations commissioned with the area's development.

82.   See Brandon Martinez and Alejandro Portes, "Latin American Cities: Their Evolution Under Neoliberalism and Beyond," *Sociology of Development* 7, no. 1 (2021): 25–51.

83.   "New Priorities for a New World: 2020 Global Cities Index," Kearney, https://www.kearney.com/global-cities/2020.

84.   "IMD Smart City Index 2019," IMD World Competitiveness Center, October 2019, 172–173, https://www.imd.org/research-knowledge/reports/imd-smart-city-index-2019/.

85.   Max Bouchet, Sifan Liu, Joseph Parilla, and Nader Kabbani, *Global Metro Monitor 2018*, Brookings Institution, June 2018, https://www.brookings.edu/wp-content/uploads/2018/06/Brookings-Metro_Global-Metro-Monitor-2018.pdf.

86.   "Citizen Centric Cities: The Sustainable Cities Index 2018," Arcadis Global, 10–17, 29, https://www.arcadis.com/campaigns/citizencentriccities/index.htm; "Global Power City Index 2020," Mori Memorial Foundation, January 15, 2021, 11, http://mori-m-foundation.or.jp/english/ius2/gpci2/index.shtml.

87.   Paulo Hilario Nascimento Saldiva, "Opening Roundtable: Applying Research to Address Community Health Disparities and Wellness" (paper presented at Place-Based Conference: The Role of Universities in Sustainable, Just and Inclusive Cities, Pittsburgh, PA, January 21–22, 2021).

88.   Daniel Aldana Cohen, "The Rationed City: The Politics of Water, Housing, and Land Use in Drought-Parched São Paulo," *Public Culture* 28, no. 2 (2016): 261–289; Helena Ribeiro Sobral, "Heat Island in São Paulo, Brazil: Effects on Health," *Critical Public Health* 15, no. 2 (2005): 147–156; Felipe Vemado and Augusto José Pereira Filho, "Severe Weather Caused by Heat Island and Sea Breeze Effects in the Metropolitan Area of São Paulo, Brazil," *Advances in Meteorology* 3 (2016): 1–13; Saldiva, "Opening Roundtable: Applying Research"; Gabriela Marques Di Giulio et al., "Mainstreaming Climate Adaptation in the Megacity of São Paulo, Brazil," *Cities* 72, Part B (2018): 238–239.

89.   "Building Globally Competitive Cities: The Key to Latin American Growth," McKinsey Global Institute, August 1, 2011, https://www.mckinsey.com/featured-insights/urbanization/building-competitive-cities-key-to-latin-american-growth.

90.   Caldeira, *City of Walls*.

91.   Marques, "Governing a Large Metropolis"; Acayaba and Acroverde, "Batalhões da Grande SP."

92.   Kurt Weyland, *Democracy Without Equity* (Pittsburgh, PA: University of Pittsburgh Press, 1996), 15, 211.

93.   Anthony Boadle and Gabriel Stargardter, "Far-Right Bolsonaro Rides Anti-corruption Rage to Brazil Presidency," Reuters, October 28, 2018, https://www.reuters.com/article/us-brazil-election/far-right-bolsonaro-rides-anti-corruption-rage-to-brazil-presidency-idUSKCN1N203K; Wendy Hunter and Timothy Power, "Bolsonaro and Brazil's Illiberal Backlash," *Journal of Democracy* 30, no. 1 (2019): 68–82.

94.   Alejandro Portes and Ariel C. Armony, *The Global Edge: Miami in the Twenty-First Century* (Berkeley: University of California Press, 2018); Nancy Beth Jackson, "Miami Real Estate

Market Embraces Brazilians," *New York Times*, December 29, 2011, https://www.nytimes .com/2011/12/30/greathomesanddestinations/30iht-remiami30.html.

95. Portes and Armony, *The Global Edge*, 133–138.

96. Aside from Miami's luxury property market, which Brazilians dominated in 2015, the city's influence over Latin America extends to business. Miami's location, ease and speed of transportation to and from Latin America, and the fact that most personal and professional communication is conducted in Spanish make it the premier center for doing business in the Western Hemisphere.

97. "Can a New Master Plan Fix What Ails São Paulo, Brazil?," Planetizen, February 16, 2016, https://www.planetizen.com/node/84067/can-new-master-plan-fix-what-ails-s %C3%A3o-paulo-brazil; Robert Muggah and Ilona Szabó de Carvalho, "Violent Crime in São Paulo Has Dropped Dramatically. Is This Why?," World Economic Forum, March 7, 2018, https://www.weforum.org/agenda/2018/03/violent-crime-in-sao-paulo-has-dropped -dramatically-this-may-be-why/.

98. Xuefei Ren and Roger Keil, eds., *The Globalizing Cities Reader*, 2nd ed. (New York: Routledge, 2018), chaps. 17, 43, 44, 50, 52.

99. Jeff Garmany and Matthew Richmond, "Hygienisation, Gentrification, and Urban Displacement in Brazil," *Antipode* 52, no. 1 (2020): 129.

100. Flavio Villaça, "São Paulo: Urban Segregation and Inequality," *Estudos Avançados* 25, no. 71 (2011): 37–58.

101. Shannon Sims, "How One of Brazil's Largest Favelas Confronts Coronavirus," *Bloomberg*, May 3, 2020, https://www.bloomberg.com/news/features/2020-05-03/how-one-of-brazil -s-largest-favelas-confronts-coronavirus. On Covid-19 and inequalities, see Josiah Kephart et al., "COVID-19, Ambient Air Pollution, and Environmental Health Inequities in Latin American Cities," *Journal of Urban Health* 98, no. 3 (2021): 1–5; Roberta Gondim de Oliveira et al., "Racial Inequalities and Death on the Horizon: COVID-19 and Structural Racism," *Cadernos de Saúde Pública* 36, no. 9 (2020): 1–14.

102. Alejandro Portes and Jean C. Nava, "Institutions and National Development: A Comparative Study," *Spanish Review of Sociology* 26, no. 1 (2017): 1–23.

103. Peter Evans, *Embedded Autonomy: States and Industrial Transformation* (Princeton, NJ: Princeton University Press, 1995).

104. Martinez and Portes, "Latin American Cities."

105. "Building Globally Competitive Cities."

106. Martinez and Portes, "Latin American Cities," 48.

107. "A Dream Deferred," *The Economist*, June 5, 2021, https://www.economist.com/special -report/2021/06/05/a-dream-deferred. According to a 2018 study by the OECD ("A Broken Social Elevator? How to Promote Social Mobility: Overview and Main Findings"), a Brazilian family from the poorest 10 percent of earners would have to spend nine generations to reach the average income.

8. LAGOS: AFRICA'S NEW DUBAI?

1. Harvey Molotch and David Ponzini, eds., *The New Arab Urban: Gulf Cities of Wealth, Ambition, and Distress* (New York: New York University Press, 2019), 3.

2.   Jennifer Robinson, "New Geographies of Theorizing the Urban: Putting Comparison to Work for Global Urban Studies," in *The Globalizing Cities Reader*, 2nd ed., ed. Xuefei Ren and Roger Keil (New York: Routledge, 2018), 453–458.

3.   Robinson, "New Geographies"; Laurent Fourchard, "Between World History and State Formation: New Perspectives on Africa's Cities," in *The Globalizing Cities Reader*, 257–263.

4.   Ambe J. Njoh, "Urban Planning as a Tool of Power and Social Control in Colonial Africa," *Planning Perspectives* 24, no. 3 (June 16, 2009): 301–317.

5.   Umar Lawal Dano, Adbul-Lateef Balogun, Ismaila Rimi Abubakar, and Yusuf Adedoyin Aina, "Transformative Urban Governance: Confronting Urbanization Challenges with Geospatial Technologies in Lagos, Nigeria," *GeoJournal* 85, no. 4 (August 2020): 1039–1056; Ben Wilson, *Metropolis: A History of the City, Humankind's Greatest Invention* (New York: Knopf Doubleday, 2020), 375.

6.   Allen Hai Xiao, "Interfered Rhythms, Navigating Mobilities: Chinese Migrants on the Roads in Lagos, Nigeria," in *Transport, Transgression and Politics in African Cities*, ed. Daniel E. Agbiboa (New York: Routledge, 2019), 99–118.

7.   Oluwafemi Ayodeji Olajide, Muyiwa Elijah Agunbiade, and Hakeem Babatunde Bishi, "The Realities of Lagos Urban Development Vision on Livelihoods of the Urban Poor," *Journal of Urban Management* 7, no. 1 (2018): 22.

8.   *Lagos State Development Plan 2012–2025*, Lagos State Government, September 2013, https://dokumen.tips/documents/lagos-state-development-plan-2012-2025.html?page=1.

9.   Ayodeji Rotinwa, "Lagos: The Taxman Cometh," *The Africa Report*, July 2, 2018, https://www.theafricareport.com/600/lagos-the-taxman-cometh/.

10.   See Alejandro Portes and Ariel C. Armony, *The Global Edge: Miami in the Twenty-First Century* (Berkeley: University of California Press, 2018), 132.

11.   Acha Leke and Landry Signé, *Africa's Untapped Business Potential: Countries, Sectors, and Strategies* (Washington, DC: Brookings, 2019).

12.   Fred Dews, "Charts of the Week: Africa's Changing Demographics," *Brookings*, January 18, 2019, https://www.brookings.edu/blog/brookings-now/2019/01/18/charts-of-the-week-africas-changing-demographics/.

13.   Daniel Hoornweg and Kevin Pope, "Socioeconomic Pathways and Regional Distribution of the World's 101 Largest Cities," Global Cities Institute Working Paper No. 4 (2014), 9; R. Bassett, P. J. Young, G. S. Blair, F. Samreen, and W. Simm, "The Megacity Lagos and Three Decades of Urban Heat Island Growth," *Journal of Applied Meteorology and Climatology* 59, no. 12 (2020): 2041–2055.

14.   Gabriella Sierra, *The Future Is African* (podcast), Council on Foreign Relations, December 11, 2020, 33:09, https://www.cfr.org/podcasts/future-african#:~:text=Projections%20show%20that%20by%202050,young%20people%20in%20the%20world.

15.   L. N. Chete, J. O. Adeoti, F. M. Adeyinka, and O. Ogundele, *Industrial Development and Growth in Nigeria: Lessons and Challenges*, Africa Growth Initiative at Brookings, 2016, https://www.brookings.edu/wp-content/uploads/2016/07/l2c_wp8_chete-et-al-1.pdf.

16.   Olajide et al., "The Realities of Lagos."

17.   See *Global Cities 2030*, Oxford Economics, December 2016, https://resources.oxford economics.com/global-cities-2030. Nchimunya Hamukoma, Nicola Doyle, Sara Calburn, and Dickie Davis, "Lagos: Is it Possible to Fix Africa's Largest City?," Brenthurst

Foundation, March 2019, https://www.thebrenthurstfoundation.org/downloads/discussion -paper-03-2019-lagos-is-it-possible-to-fix-africa-s-largest-city-.pdf; Wilson, *Metropolis*, 375.

18. *Nigerian Port Statistics 2012–2017*, National Bureau of Statistics, 2018, https://nigerianstat. gov.ng/elibrary.

19. Hamukoma et al., "Lagos."

20. "Lagos Population 2021," World Population Review, accessed April 14, 2021, https:// worldpopulationreview.com/world-cities/lagos-population.

21. Mfonobong Nsehe, "The Black Billionaires 2018," *Forbes*, https://www.forbes.com/sites /mfonobongnsehe/2018/03/07/the-black-billionaires-2018/; Daniel Agbiboa, ed., *Transport, Transgression and Politics in African Cities: The Rhythm of Chaos* (New York: Routledge, 2019).

22. Molotch and Ponzini, *The New Arab Urban*.

23. Wilson, *Metropolis*.

24. The informal sector can be defined as the "economic actions that bypass the costs of, and are excluded from the protection of, laws and administrative rules." Alejandro Portes and William Haller, "The Informal Economy," in *The Handbook of Economic Sociology*, ed. Neil J. Smelser and Richard Swedberg (Princeton, NJ: Princeton University Press, 2010), 403.

25. Oka Obono, "A Lagos Thing: Rules and Realities in the Nigerian Megacity," *Georgetown Journal of International Affairs* 8, no. 2 (Summer/Fall 2007): 31–37.

26. Hamukoma et al., "Lagos."

27. "Nigeria Housing: 'I Live in a Floating Slum' in Lagos," *BBC*, March 5, 2020, https:// www.bbc.com/news/world-africa-51677371; Fabienne Hoelzel, ed., *Urban Planning Processes in Lagos* (Abuja, Nigeria, and Zürich, Switzerland: Heinrich Böll Stiftung Nigeria and Fabulous Urban, 2018), 17. Roughly 19,000 people were evicted in a two-year period from Badia East in central Lagos (2013–2015), and in early 2020, 10,000 residents were ordered to evacuate with short notice from Tarkwa Bay, a popular beachfront community for Lagosians. See Mathias Agbo, "The Tragic Human Cost of Africa's New Megacities," ArchDaily, May 24, 2017, https://www.archdaily.com/872025/the-tragic-human -cost-of-africas-new-megacities.

28. Fourchard, "Between World History and State Formation," 261.

29. Rebecca Enobong Roberts, "Displaced and Isolated: The Realities of Covid19 for Internally Displaced People in Lagos, Nigeria," Internal Displacement Monitoring Centre (IDMC), April 2020, https://www.internal-displacement.org/expert-opinion/displaced -and-isolated-the-realities-of-covid19-for-internally-displaced-people-in.

30. Paul Wallace and Tope Alake, "Lagos Building Luxury Homes in Face of Affordable Housing Crisis," *Bloomberg*, December 20, 2019, https://www.bloomberg.com/news /articles/2019-12-20/lagos-building-luxury-homes-in-face-of-affordable-housing-crisis.

31. Topsy Kola-Oyeneyin, Mayowa Kuyoro, and Tunde Olanreqaju, "Harnessing Nigeria's Fintech Potential," McKinsey & Company, September 23, 2020, https://www.mckinsey .com/featured-insights/middle-east-and-africa/harnessing-nigerias-fintech-potential.

32. Simona Varrella, "Direct Tourism Contribution of Lagos to the Gross Domestic Product of Nigeria from 2006 to 2026," Statista, February 22, 2021, https://www.statista.com /statistics/795082/nigeria-lagos-tourism-contribution-to-gdp/; "Tourism Holds Positive

Growth for Business in Nigeria," *ATTA*, February 7, 2020, https://www.atta.travel/news/2020/02/tourism-holds-positive-growth-for-business-in-nigeria/.

33. Thomas Kolawole Ojo, "Passenger Movements Development and Structure at Murtala Muhammed International Airport, Lagos," *Public Transport* 7, no. 2 (2015): 223–234.

34. Husein Abdul-Hamid, Donald Baum, Oni Lusk-Stover, and Huge Wesley, "The Role of the Private Sector in Lagos, Nigeria," World Bank Group, June 30, 2017.

35. Xiao, "Interfered Rhythms."

36. Moloch and Ponzini, *The New Arab Urban*, 304; Fourchard, "Between World History and State Formation."

37. Toyin Falola and Matthew M. Heaton, *A History of Nigeria* (Cambridge: Cambridge University Press, 2008).

38. Falola and Heaton, *A History of Nigeria*; Kristin Mann, *Slavery and the Birth of an African City: Lagos 1760–1900* (Bloomington: Indiana University Press, 2007); Kaye Whiteman, *Lagos* (Oxford: Signal Books, 2012).

39. Ayodeji Olukoju, "The Port of Lagos, 1850–1929: The Rise of West Africa's Leading Seaport," in *Atlantic Ports and the First Globalisation, c. 1850–1930*, ed. M. S. Bosa (London: Palgrave Macmillan, 2014).

40. Njoh, "Urban Planning"; Whiteman, *Lagos*; Falola and Heaton, *A History of Nigeria*.

41. Larne Davies, "Gentrification in Lagos: 1929–1990," *Urban History* 45, no. 4 (2018): 712–732.

42. R. O. Ekundare, "Nigeria's Second National Development Plan as a Weapon of Social Change," *African Affairs* 70, no. 279 (1971): 146–158.

43. Bright Alozie, "Space and Colonial Alterity: Interrogating British Residential Segregation in Nigeria, 1899–1919," *Ufahamu: A Journal of African Studies* 41, no. 2 (2020): 1–26.

44. Falola and Heaton, *A History of Nigeria*.

45. Whiteman, *Lagos*. See Alozie, "Space and Colonial Alterity."

46. Falola and Heaton, *A History of Nigeria*.

47. Falola and Heaton, *A History of Nigeria*.

48. Falola and Heaton, *A History of Nigeria*.

49. Falola and Heaton, *A History of Nigeria*; Kenneth Omeje, "The Rentier State: Oil-Related Legislation and Conflict in the Niger Delta, Nigeria," *Conflict, Security, and Development* 6, no. 2 (2006): 211.

50. "Lagos, Nigeria Metro Area Population 1950–2021," Macrotrends, accessed April 22, 2021, https://www.macrotrends.net/cities/22007/lagos/population; Whiteman, *Lagos*.

51. "Lagos, Nigeria Metro Area Population."

52. Fourchard, "Between World History and State Formation."

53. Amadu Sesay and Charles Ugochukwu Ukeje, "The Military, the West, and Nigerian Politics in the 1990s," *International Journal of Politics, Culture, and Society* 11, no. 1 (1997): 30–38.

54. Dhikru Adewale Yagboyaju, "Nigeria's Fourth Republic and the Challenge of a Faltering Democratization," *African Studies Quarterly* 12, no. 3 (2011): 93–106.

55. Olumide Victor Ekanade, "The Dynamics of Forced Neoliberalism in Nigeria Since the 1980s," *Journal of Retracing Africa* 1, no. 1 (2014): 1–24; Sola Akinrinade and Olukoya Ogen, "Globalization and De-Industrialization: South-South Neo-Liberalism and the Collapse of the Nigerian Textile Industry," *The Global South* 2, no. 2 (2008): 159–170.

56. See, for example, Obasesam Okoi, "The Paradox of Nigeria's Oil Dependency," Africa Portal, January 21, 2019, https://www.africaportal.org/features/paradox-nigerias-oil -dependency/; Folayan Ojo, "Nigeria's Export Performance: Trends, Problems and Prospects," *Pakistan Economic and Social Review* 15, no. 3–4 (1977): 174–188.

57. Olajide et al., "The Realities of Lagos."

58. LAGBUS is a state-owned company launched by Lagos State that leases large buses and franchises bus routes.

59. Diane de Gramont, "Governing Lagos: Unlocking the Politics of Reform," Carnegie Endowment for International Peace, January 12, 2015, 15–23. See Xiao, "Interfered Rhythms."

60. I. C. Ezema, O. J. Ediae, and E. N. Ekhaese, "Prospects, Barriers and Development Control Implications in the Use of Green Roofs in Lagos State, Nigeria," *Covenant Journal in Research and Built Environment* 4, no. 2 (2016): 54–70.

61. Yinka Ibukun, Sophie Mongalvy, and Antony Sguazzin, "Dream of a Lagos Champs-Élysées Banks on Nigerian Recovery," *Bloomberg*, May 29, 2018, https://www.bloomberg.com /news/articles/2018-05-29/eko-atlantic-city-eyes-2023-finish-as-nigeria-economy -rebounds.

62. Martin Lukacs, "New, Privatized African City Heralds Climate Apartheid," *The Guardian*, January 21, 2014, https://www.theguardian.com/environment/true-north/2014/jan/21/new -privatized-african-city-heralds-climate-apartheid.

63. Robinson, "New Geographies."

64. Agbo, "The Tragic Human Cost"; Anatxu Zabalbeascoa, "Los arquitectos quieren menos Dubái y más Venecia," *El País*, June 16, 2018, https://elpais.com/cultura/2018/06/16 /actualidad/1529159142_487847.html?rel=listapoyo.

65. Stephen Graham, *Vertical: The City from Satellites to Bunkers* (London: Verso, 2016), 159–166; Olusola Oladapo Makinde, "Typological Analysis of Gated Communities Characteristics in Ibadan, Nigeria," *IntechOpen*, October 5, 2020, https://www.intechopen .com/online-first/76444.

66. Makinde, "Typological Analysis of Gated Communities," 2.

67. Nancy Ruhling, "Banana Island in Lagos Is a Billionaire's Paradise," *Mansion Global*, February 2, 2019, https://www.mansionglobal.com/articles/banana-island-in-lagos-is-a -billionaire-s-paradise-120592.

68. Iroham Chukquemeka Osmond, Durodola Olufemi Daniel, Ayedum Caleb Abiodum, and Ogunbola Mayowa Fadeke, "Comparative Study of Rental Values of Two Gated Estates in Lekki Peninsula Lagos," *Journal of Sustainable Development Studies* 5, no. 2 (2014): 221.

69. Olajide et al., "The Realities of Lagos," 21.

70. Olajide et al., "The Realities of Lagos," 30.

71. Olajide et al., "The Realities of Lagos," 30.

72. Graham, *Vertical*, 159–166.

73. Stephen Graham, "Vertical Noir: Histories in the Future of Urban Science Fiction," *City* 20, no. 3 (2016): 389–406; Graham, *Vertical*, 163.

74. Aurora Torres, Jodi Brandt, Kristen Lear, and Jianguo Liu, "A Looming Tragedy of the Sand Commons," *Science* 357, no. 6355 (2017): 970–971.

75. Tech hubs are defined as "those with a physical local address, offering facilities and support for tech and digital entrepreneurs." Dario Giuliani and Sam Ajadi, "618 Active Tech Hubs: The Backbone of Africa's Tech Ecosystem," *GSMA Blog*, July 10, 2019, https://www.gsma.com/mobilefordevelopment/blog/618-active-tech-hubs-the-backbone-of-africas-tech-ecosystem/.

76. Adeyemi Adepetun, "New Tech Experience Center Debuts in Lagos," *The Guardian NG*, September 23, 2020, https://guardian.ng/technology/tech/new-tech-experience-centre-debuts-in-lagos/.

77. Charlie Sammonds, "Lagos: The Heart of Africa's Tech Scene," Medium, March 27, 2019, https://medium.com/primalbase/lagos-a-cluster-of-booming-tech-hubs-3e633058ad4c.

78. *The Global Fintech Index 2020*, Findexable, December 2019, https://findexable.com/wp-content/uploads/2019/12/Findexable_Global-Fintech-Rankings-2020exSFA.pdf; Kola-Oyeneyin et al., "Harnessing Nigeria's Fintech Potential." Lagos is home to Jumia, Africa's largest e-commerce company, and in 2019 Nigerian tech start-ups received $663 million in venture capital, with a majority of those receiving funding being based in Lagos. Most tech companies either have their start or are based in the Yaba suburb, situated between the University of Lagos and the Yaba College of Technology. This prime location for innovation and the presence of incubators such as Co-Creation Hub (Cc-Hub) have helped the area to be labeled "Yabacon Valley." "Beyond Silicon Valley: The Six Cities Building the Future of the Global Tech Industry," *Rest of World*, July 16, 2021, https://restofworld.org/2021/beyond-silicon-valley/.

79. "Capital Cities: The Countries Dreaming of Becoming Africa's Singapore," *The Economist*, October 23, 2021, 47.

80. Norimitsu Onishi, "Nigeria's Booming Film Industry Redefines African Life," *New York Times*, February 18, 2016, https://www.nytimes.com/2016/02/19/world/africa/with-a-boom-before-the-cameras-nigeria-redefines-african-life.html; Alyssa Maio, "What Is Nollywood and How Did It Become the 2nd Largest Film Industry?," StudioBinder, https://www.studiobinder.com/blog/what-is-nollywood/.

81. Rebecca Moudio, "Nigeria's Film Industry: A Potential Gold Mine?," *Africa Renewal*, May 2013, https://www.un.org/africarenewal/magazine/may-2013/nigeria%E2%80%99s-film-industry-potential-gold-mine.

82. Maio, "What Is Nollywood?"; Onookome Okome, "Nollywood: Spectatorship, Audience, and the Sites of Consumption," *Postcolonial Text* 3, no. 2 (2007): 1–21.

83. Onishi, "Nigeria's Booming Film Industry."

84. "What's Nollywood?," NollywoodWeek, accessed April 21, 2021, http://www.nollywood week.com/en/whats-nollywood/; Adekeye Adebajo, "Nollywood as a Pan-African Cultural Phenomenon," Institute for Pan African Thought and Conversation, May 25, 2017, https://ipatc.joburg/nollywood-as-a-pan-african-cultural-phenomenon/; Moudio, "Nigeria's Film Industry."

85. Stephan Heyman, "Hurray for Nollywood," *New York Times*, October 22, 2014, https://www.nytimes.com/2014/10/23/arts/international/hurray-for-nollywood.html.

86. Adebajo, "Nollywood as a Pan-African Cultural Phenomenon"; Françoise Ugochukwu, "Why Nigerians Living Abroad Love to Watch Nollywood Movies," The Conversation, March 22, 2020, https://theconversation.com/why-nigerians-living-abroad-love-to

-watch-nollywood-movies-132983. See Françoise Ugochukwu, "Nollywood in Diaspora: A Cultural Tool" (paper for Reading and Producing Nollywood: An International Symposium, March 23–25, 2011, Lagos, Nigeria); Françoise Ugochukwu, "Language and Identity: Nigerian Video-Films and Diasporic Communities," *African Renaissance* 13, no. 3–4 (2016). 57–76; African Press Organization, "The 8th Edition of the Nollywood-Week Film Festival Goes Global," Newswires, April 27, 2021, https://www.einnews.com/pr_news/539540099/the-8th-edition-of-the-nollywoodweek-film-festival-goes-global-selection-includes-films-from-other-african-countries-and-the-african-diaspora/.

87.   Christina Goldbaum, "South African Filmmakers Move Beyond Apartheid Stories," *New York Times*, May 10, 2021, https://www.nytimes.com/2021/05/10/world/africa/south-african-filmmakers-move-beyond-apartheid-stories.html.

88.   Goldbaum, "South African Filmmakers"; Bernard Dayo, "Netflix Is Launching in Nigeria, but Not Everyone Is Happy," *Vice*, December 28, 2020, https://www.vice.com/en/article/k7agzn/netflix-naija-launch-nigeria; Andreas Wiseman, "Will Smith & Jada Pinkett Smith's Westbrook Teams with Nigeria's EbonyLife on Film & TV Slate," *Deadline*, February 16, 2021, https://deadline.com/2021/02/jada-pinkett-smith-will-smith-westbrook-nigeria-ebonylife-film-tv-slate-1234694457/.

89.   Achille Mbembe and Laurent Chauvet, "Afropolitanism," *Nka: Journal of Contemporary African Art* 46 (2020): 56–61.

90.   Sarah Balakrishnan, "The Afropolitan Idea: New Perspectives on Cosmopolitanism in African Studies," *History Compass* 15, no. 2 (2017): e12362. See Emilia María Durán-Almarza, Ananya Jahanara Kabir, and Carla Rodríguez González, eds., *Debating the Afro-politan* (New York: Routledge, 2019).

91.   Mbembe and Chauvet, "Afropolitanism"; Okome, "Nollywood"; Sidra Lawrence, "Afro-politan Detroit: Counterpublics, Sound, and the African City," *Africa Today* 65, no. 4 (Summer 2019): 19–37; Balakrishnan, "The Afropolitan Idea."

92.   Onishi, "Nigeria's Booming Film Industry." Although Nollywood generated roughly $600 million in annual revenues as of 2016, its box office revenues do not come close to those of the other "woods." In 2012, Hollywood had $10.8 billion in box office revenues and Bollywood $1.6 billion. Nollywood trailed far behind, at $91 million. On the impact of Bollywood on India's economy and the role of the Indian diaspora in Bollywood's globalization, see, for instance, Theodore Metaxas, Eleni Bouka, and Maria-Marina Merkouri, "Bollywood, India and Economic Growth: A Hundred Year History," *Journal of Economic and Social Thought* 3, no. 2 (2016): 285–301.

93.   Daniel Hoornweg and Kevin Pope, "Population Predictions for the World's Largest Cities in the 21st Century," *Environment and Urbanization* 29, no. 1 (2016): 195–216.

94.   Patrick Brandful Cobbinah, Ellis Adjei Adams, and Michael Odei Erdiaw-Kwasie, "Can COVID-19 Inspire a New Way of Planning African Cities?," The Conversation, September 20, 2020, https://theconversation.com/can-covid-19-inspire-a-new-way-of-planning-african-cities-145933.

95.   Cobbinah et al., "Can COVID-19 Inspire a New Way?"

96.   Molotch and Ponzini, *The New Arab Urban*, 304, 308–309.

97.   Portes and Armony, *The Global Edge*, 17, 73, 162. According to our conversations with Nigerian businesspeople and entrepreneurs based in Lagos and those who live abroad,

low levels of interpersonal and institutional trust are the most important factor hindering investment and innovation in Nigeria. For a study that explores the process of trust development in Nigeria's financial sector, conducted in Lagos in 2016, see Damilola Mary Joseph, "An Exploration of Trustworthiness in the Nigerian Investment Field: Perspective of Financial Advisors and Investors" (PhD diss., University of Portsmouth, UK, 2019).

98. Neil Munshi, "Nigeria's Port Crisis: The $4,000 Charge to Carry Goods Across Lagos," *Financial Times*, December 28, 2020, https://www.ft.com/content/a807f714-7542-4464 -b359-b9bb35bdda10.

99. Lelia Croitoru, Juan José Miranda, Abdellatif Khattabi, and Jia Jun Lee, "The Cost of Coastal Zone Degradation in Nigeria: Cross River, Delta and Lagos States," World Bank Group, October 2020, ix, x.

100. Chinedum Uwaegbulam, "How Rising Seas May Wipe Off Lagos, Others by 2050," *The Guardian*, November 6, 2019, https://guardian.ng/news/how-rising-seas-may-wipe-off -lagos-others-by-2050/.

101. Emmanuel Akinwotu, "Waves of Change: Nigeria's Lagos Battles Erosions," *Phys.org*, July 10, 2019, https://phys.org/news/2019-07-nigeria-lagos-atlantic-erosion.html.

102. "Quick Study: Ricky Burdett on Changing Cities: Man Versus City," September 30, 2014, *The Economist*, https://www.economist.com/prospero/2014/09/30/man-v-city.

103. Croitoru et al., "The Cost of Coastal Zone Degradation in Nigeria," ix.

104. "2020 Corruption Perceptions Index," Transparency International, https://www.transparency .org/en/cpi/2020/index/nga.

105. Xiao, "Interfered Rhythms," 110.

106. W. G. Huff, "The Developmental State, Government and Singapore's Economic Development Since 1960," *World Development* 23, no. 8 (August 1995): 1435; "Singapore's Corruption Control Framework," Corrupt Practices Investigation Bureau (CPIB), June 2, 2020, https://www.cpib.gov.sg/about-corruption/prevention-and-corruption/singapores -corruption-control-framework/. On Miami's efforts to fight corruption, see Portes and Armony, *The Global Edge*, 68–69.

107. Nigeria's corruption is highlighted in the country's fall from 136 in 2015 to 149 in 2020 in the index, despite President Buhari's signature campaign promise to fight corruption. "2020 Corruption Perceptions Index"; Munshi, "Nigeria's Port Crisis." In 2021, the Lagos State government announced the creation of an anticorruption agenda to combat instances of corruption by public officials. Oolasunkanmi, "Lagos to Establish Anti-Corruption Agency, as Sanwo-Olu Signs Bill Deepening Accountability in Governance," Lagos State Government, April 19, 2021, https://lagosstate.gov.ng/blog/2021/04/19/lagos-to-establish-anti -corruption-agency-as-sanwo-olu-signs-bill-deepening-accountability-in-governance/.

108. Portes and Haller, "The Informal Economy," 406–413.

109. Hoelzel, *Urban Planning Processes*, 4, 15–20; Hamukoma et al., "Lagos," 4, 11; Fourchard, "Between World History and State Formation."

110. Fourchard, "Between World History and State Formation," 263; Xuefei Ren and Roger Keil, "Introduction to Part One," in *The Globalizing Cities Reader*.

111. Jennifer Robinson, "Global and World Cities: A View from off the Map," *International Journal of Urban and Regional Research* 263 (September 2002): 545.

9. HONG KONG: A THREATENED GLOBAL CITY

1.   Clare Baldwin, Yimou Lee, and Clare Jim, "Special Report: The Mainland's Coloniza-tion of the Hong Kong Economy," Reuters, December 30, 2014, https://www.reuters.com /article/us-hongkong-china-economy-specialreport/special-report-the-mainlands -colonization-of-the-hong-kong-economy-idUSKBN0K901320141231.

2.   Mark Abrahamson, *Global Cities* (New York: Oxford University Press, 2004), chap. 4.

3.   Abrahamson, *Global Cities*, tables 4.6 and 4.7.

4.   World Integrated Trade Solution, https://wits.worldbank.org/Default.aspx?lang=en.

5.   John M. Carroll, *A Concise History of Hong Kong* (Lanham, MD: Rowman and Littlefield, 2007), e-book pages, 23.

6.   Carroll, *A Concise History of Hong Kong*, 26.

7.   Carroll, *A Concise History of Hong Kong*, 30.

8.   Steve Tsang, *A Modern History of Hong Kong* (London: Bloomsbury Academic, 2007), 11.

9.   Tsang, *A Modern History of Hong Kong*, 269.

10.   Carroll, *A Concise History of Hong Kong*, 45.

11.   Tsang, *A Modern History of Hong Kong*, 36–38.

12.   Carroll, *A Concise History of Hong Kong*, 116.

13.   Carroll, *A Concise History of Hong Kong*, 37.

14.   Carroll, *A Concise History of Hong Kong*, 53.

15.   Carroll, *A Concise History of Hong Kong*, 55.

16.   Carroll, *A Concise History of Hong Kong*, 61.

17.   Carroll, *A Concise History of Hong Kong*, 62.

18.   Carroll, *A Concise History of Hong Kong*, 63.

19.   Carroll, *A Concise History of Hong Kong*, 65, 69.

20.   Carroll, *A Concise History of Hong Kong*, 71, 73.

21.   Tsang, *A Modern History of Hong Kong*, 198, 65.

22.   Carroll, *A Concise History of Hong Kong*, 76–77.

23.   Carroll, *A Concise History of Hong Kong*, 126.

24.   Carroll, *A Concise History of Hong Kong*, 88.

25.   Carroll, *A Concise History of Hong Kong*, 95–98.

26.   Carroll, *A Concise History of Hong Kong*, 108; Tsang, *A Modern History of Hong Kong*, 71.

27.   Carroll, *A Concise History of Hong Kong*, 121.

28.   Carroll, *A Concise History of Hong Kong*, 149.

29.   Carroll, *A Concise History of Hong Kong*, 155.

30.   Carroll, *A Concise History of Hong Kong*, 166; Tsang, *A Modern History of Hong Kong*, 81.

31.   Carroll, *A Concise History of Hong Kong*, 141.

32.   Carroll, *A Concise History of Hong Kong*, 154.

33.   Carroll, *A Concise History of Hong Kong*, 141, 169.

34.   Henry J. Lethbridge, *Hong Kong, Stability and Change: A Collection of Essays* (Hong Kong: Oxford University Press, 1978), 25.

35.   Tsang, *A Modern History of Hong Kong*, 181–182.

36.   Chi Ming Fung, *Reluctant Heroes: Rickshaw Pullers in Hong Kong and Canton, 1874–1954* (Hong Kong: Hong Kong University Press, 2005), 125.

37.   Kongliao Sha, *Xianggang lunxian riji* (Beijing: Sanlian shudian, 1988), 92.

38. Carroll, *A Concise History of Hong Kong*, 209; Tsang, *A Modern History of Hong Kong*, 142.
39. Carroll, *A Concise History of Hong Kong*, 204.
40. Carroll, *A Concise History of Hong Kong*, 213.
41. Steve Tsang, *Hong Kong: An Appointment with China* (London: I. B. Tauris, 1997), 117.
42. Carroll, *A Concise History of Hong Kong*, 228.
43. Robin Hutcheon, *First Sea Lord: The Life and Work of Sir Y. K. Pao* (Hong Kong: Chinese University Press, 1990), 41–45.
44. David R. Meyer, *Hong Kong as a Global Metropolis* (Cambridge: Cambridge University Press, 2009), 159.
45. Carroll, *A Concise History of Hong Kong*, 264; Hong Kong Heritage Museum Leisure and Cultural Services Department, *Xìtái shàngxià—xiānggǎng xìyuàn yǔ yuèjù*, accessed January 19, 2021, https://www.heritagemuseum.gov.hk/documents/2199315/2199705/The_Majestic_Stage-C.pdf.
46. Richard Meyers, *Great Martial Arts Movies: From Bruce Lee to Jackie Chan—and More* (New York: Citadel, 2001).
47. Carroll, *A Concise History of Hong Kong*, 254.
48. Carroll, *A Concise History of Hong Kong*, 237.
49. Carroll, *A Concise History of Hong Kong*, 248–249.
50. Carroll, *A Concise History of Hong Kong*, 274.
51. Carroll, *A Concise History of Hong Kong*, 256–257; Tsang, *A Modern History of Hong Kong*, 178; Yun-wing Sung, *The China-Hong Kong Connection: The Key to China's Open Door Policy* (Cambridge: Cambridge University Press, 2011), 100–101.
52. Interview with Hong Kong residents (Bernie, Charles, Nathan), July/ August, 2020.
53. Carroll, *A Concise History of Hong Kong*, 267.
54. From HK$8,000 to HK$10,000, and from HK$25,000 to HK$30,200, respectively; see "Labour Force: Table E033: Median Monthly Employment Earnings of Employed Persons by Educational Attainment," Government of Hong Kong, Census and Statistics Department, https://www.censtatd.gov.hk/en/EIndexbySubject.html?scode=200&pcode=D5250037.
55. Tsang, *A Modern History of Hong Kong*, 216; Limin Guo, ed., *Zhonggong du Tai Zhengze Zhiliao Xuanji: 1949–1991* (Taipei: Lifework, 1992), 1:413.
56. Carroll, *A Concise History of Hong Kong*, 284.
57. Carroll, *A Concise History of Hong Kong*, 294.
58. Carroll, *A Concise History of Hong Kong*, 308.
59. Charles Goddard, *City of Darkness: Life in Kowloon Walled City* (Chiddingfold, UK: Watermark, 2011), 208–211; "History/Background," Kowloon Walled City Park, https://www.lcsd.gov.hk/en/parks/kwcp/historical.html.
60. Liang Zhang, *The Tiananmen Papers: The Chinese Leadership's Decision to Use Force, in Their Own Words*, ed. Andrew Nathan and Perry Link (New York: Public Affairs, 2001), 355–362.
61. Carroll, *A Concise History of Hong Kong*, 301; Mark Hampton, *Hong Kong and British Culture, 1945–97* (Oxford: Oxford University Press, 2015), 196.
62. Tsang, *A Modern History of Hong Kong*, 252.
63. Hong Kong Government, *An Introduction to Hong Kong Bill of Rights Ordinance*, 1991, https://www.cmab.gov.hk/doc/en/documents/policy_responsibilities/the_rights_of_the_individuals/human/BORO-InductoryChapterandBooklet-Eng.pdf.

64. Christopher Patten, *Our Next Five Years: The Agenda for Hong Kong* (Hong Kong: Government Printer, 1992), 32–33.

65. Quote in Mark Bray and W. O. Lee, "Education, Democracy and Colonial Transition: The Case of Hong Kong," *International Review of Education / Internationale Zeitschrift Für Erziehungswissenschaft / Revue Internationale De L'Education* 39, no. 6 (1993): 541–560, 548; also see Anna Wu, "Government by Whom?," in *Hong Kong Remembers*, ed. Sally Blyth and Ian Wotherspoon (Hong Kong: Oxford University Press, 1997), 158–166, 165.

66. Tsang, *A Modern History of Hong Kong*, 269.

67. "Zhòngsuǒzhōuzhī, zhímín guójiā duì zhímíndì de tǒngzhì, wú yī bù bāohán cánkù zhěnyā, wénhuà zhímín hé jīngjì lüèduó (bāokuò rénkǒu). Yīngguó zài dì yī cì yāpiàn zhànzhēng hòu qiángzhàn xiānggǎng, yòu xiānhòu tōngguò . . . bù píngděng tiáoyuē bàchí xiānggǎng zhì 1997 nián 6 yuè 30 rì." Sun Haichao, "Did Hong Kong Ever Have Democracy Under British Colonial Rule?," *Beijing Daily*, July 10, 2019, https://theory.gmw.cn/2019-07/10/content_32987595.htm.

68. Tsang, *A Modern History of Hong Kong*, 269.

69. Agnes J. Bundy, "The Reunification of China with Hong Kong and Its Implications for Taiwan: An Analysis of the 'One Country, Two Systems' Model," *California Western International Law Journal* 19, no. 2 (2015): 271–286, 285.

70. Wikipedia, s.v. "1997 Asian Financial Crisis," https://en.wikipedia.org/wiki/1997_Asian_financial_crisis#Hong_Kong.

71. Lee Shiu Hung, "The SARS Epidemic in Hong Kong: What Lessons Have We Learned?," *Journal of the Royal Society of Medicine* 96, no. 8 (2003): 374–378. Hong Kong has also been affected by the Covid-19 pandemic, with nearly 10,000 cases and over 160 deaths by January 2021. Nonetheless, Hong Kong was managing much better than big cities elsewhere, as many Hong Kong residents have been willing to wear masks in public and adhere strictly to quarantine and isolation guidelines. However, in February/ March 2022 there was a flare-up in cases and deaths, in part, due to the high vaccine skepticism among the old age. Alexandra Stevenson and Austin Ramzy, "'I Don't Dare Get the Shot': Virus Ravages Unvaccinated Older Hong Kongers," *New York Times*, February 25, 2022.

72. Ming K. Chan, *The Challenge of Hong Kong's Reintegration with China* (Hong Kong: Hong Kong University Press, 1997).

73. Interview with Hong Kong residents (Nathan and Tim), July/ August 2020.

74. Alice Truong, "How to Make Web 3.0 a Reality," *Wall Street Journal*, December 7, 2010. https://www.wsj.com/articles/BL-HKB-292.

75. Jeffrey Wassermann, *Vigil: Hong Kong on the Brink* (New York: Columbia Global Reports, 2020), 38.

76. The median household income is HK$300,000, and the median home cost is HK$5.4 million. "Global Cities and Affordable Housing: Hong Kong," U.S. Department of Housing and Urban Development, August 14, 2017, https://www.huduser.gov/portal/pdredge/pdr-edge-trending-081417.html.

77. "Global Cities and Affordable Housing: Hong Kong."

78. Jing Li, *"I Am NOT Leaving Home": Post-80s' Housing Attitudes and Aspirations in Hong Kong*, CityU on Cities Working Paper Series, WP No. 2/2014, Urban Research Group, http://www.cityu.edu.hk/cityuoncities/upload/file/original/705520140620145010.pdf.

79. Alvin Y. So, "Hong Kong After 1997: The Rise of the Anti-Mainland Movement," *Taiwan Insight*, March 20, 2018; interview with Hong Kong expert (Nicole), August 2020.

80. Yi-Lee Wong and Anita Koo, "Is Hong Kong No Longer a Land of Opportunities After the 1997 Handover? A Comparison of Patterns of Social Mobility Between 1989 and 2007," *Asian Journal of Social Science* 44, no. 4–5 (2016): 516–545, 524, 530; Duncan A. W. Abate and Hong Tran, "Increased Minimum Wage Rate to Take Effect from 1 May 2017 in Hong Kong," Mayer/Brown LLP, January 24, 2017, https://www.mayerbrown.com/en/perspectives-events/publications/2017/01/increased-minimum-wage-rate-to-take-effect-from-1.

81. "Foreign Domestic Helper Levy in Effect from Oct," *News.gov.hk*, August 29, 2003; "WHAT'S NEW: Minimum Allowable Wage and Food Allowance for Foreign Domestic Helpers to Increase," Labour Department, HKSAR Government, September 27, 2019. https://www.info.gov.hk/gia/general/201909/27/P2019092500606.htm

82. C. George Kleeman, "The Proposal to Implement Article 23 of the Basic Law in Hong Kong: A Missed Opportunity for Reconciliation and Reunification Between China and Taiwan," *Georgia Journal of International and Comparative Law* 23, no. 3 (2005): 705–720.

83. "Full Text of NPC Decision on Universal Suffrage for HKSAR Chief Selection," Xinhua News Agency, August 31, 2014; Wassermann, *Vigil*, 43.

84. "Hong Kong Legislators Reject China-Backed Reform Bill," *CNN*, June 19, 2015.

85. Kris Cheng, "Hong Kong Pro-Democracy Activist Runs for China's Legislature, Claiming Support for Xi Jinping Thought," Hong Kong Free Press, December 4, 2017; "Joshua Wong's Party Named 'Demosisto,'" *RTHK*, April 6, 2016.

86. Emma Graham-Harrison and Verna Yu, "Hong Kong Voters Deliver Landslide Victory for Pro-Democracy Campaigners," *The Guardian*, November 24, 2019.

87. "Beijing Unanimously Passes National Security Law for Hong Kong as Chief Exec. Carrie Lam Evades Questions," Hong Kong Free Press, June 30, 2020; Kelly Ho and Tom Grundy, "Joshua Wong's Pro-Democracy Group Demosisto Disbands Hours After Hong Kong Security Law Passed," Hong Kong Free Press, June 30, 2020.

88. "Hong Kong: Joshua Wong and Fellow Pro-Democracy Activists Jailed," *BBC*, December 2, 2020; Emma Graham-Harrison and Verna Yu, "Leading Democracy Campaigner Nathan Law Leaves Hong Kong," *The Guardian*, July 2, 2020.

89. Opposition lawmakers could not prevent government laws, but they delayed them via filibuster. Vivian Tang and Tiffany May, "As Hong Kong Opposition Quits Council, Pro-Beijing Forces Reign," *New York Times*, November 12, 2020.

90. Naomi Xu Elegant, "Hong Kong Passport Holders Used to Get Special Perks in the U.S. Not Anymore," *Fortune*, July 15, 2020.

91. "Britain Confirms Details of Visa Offer for Some Hong Kong Citizens," Reuters, October 22, 2020.

92. Enoch You, "Hong Kong Protests 2019 vs Occupy Central: After 79 Days, Retailers, Investors, Developers Hit Far Worse by This Year's Demonstrations," *South China Morning Post*, August 27, 2019.

93. Alexandra Stevenson, "Business Embraces Hong Kong's Security Law. The Money Helps," *New York Times*, June 30, 2020.

94. Hong Kong Monetary Authority, "Hong Kong's Financial System: Robust and Advancing," June 2020, https://www2.deloitte.com/content/dam/Deloitte/cn/Documents/ined/deloitte-cn-ined-hk-financial-system-210106.pdf.

95. "Hong Kong Capital Flows," Trading Economics, https://tradingeconomics.com/hong-kong/capital-flows.

96. "Together, We Fight the Virus!," Government of Hong Kong, accessed November 2, 2021. https://www.coronavirus.gov.hk/eng/index.html.

97. Harsh V. Pant and Nandini Sarma, "India Cracks Down on Chinese Investment as Mood Turns Against Beijing," *Foreign Policy*, April 28, 2020.

98. Vivian Wang, "Hong Kong's M+ Museum Is Open. It's Already in Danger," *New York Times*, November 12, 2021.

99. Interview with chief financial officer (CFO) of a large commercial real estate corporation operating in China and India with headquarters in Singapore, February 2, 2021.

100. Jenny Surane and Mary Biekert, "Wall Street's China Dreams Get Jolt from U.S. Hong Kong Warning," *Yahoo Finance*, July 16, 2021.

101. Interview with Singapore board CFO, February 2, 2021.

102. Interview with Singapore board CFO, February 2, 2021.

CONCLUSION: THEORETICAL IMPLICATIONS, CLIMATE CHANGE, AND FUTURE CHALLENGES

1. See chapter 1. Henri Pirenne, *Medieval Cities: Their Origins and the Revival of Trade* (Princeton, NJ: Princeton University Press, 1969).

2. Maurice Dobb, *Studies in the Development of Capitalism* (New York: International Publishers, 1963); Pirenne, *Medieval Cities*.

3. See chapter 1. Giovanni Arrighi, *The Long Twentieth Century: Money, Power and the Origins of Our Times* (London: Verso, 1994); Immanuel Wallerstein, *The Modern World-System I: Capitalist Agriculture and the Origins of the European World-Economy in the Sixteenth Century* (New York: Academic Press, 1974).

4. Georg Simmel, "The Metropolis and Mental Life," in *The Sociology of George Simmel*, ed. K. H. Wolf (New York: Free Press, 1962); Barry Bluestone and Bennett Harrison, *The Deindustrialization of America* (New York: Wiley, 1982).

5. Thorstein Veblen, *The Theory of the Leisure Class* (New York: MacMillan, 1899); Matthew Josephson, *The Robber Barons* (New York: Harcourt Brace, 1934); Gerald Rosenblum, *Immigrant Workers: Their Impact on American Labor Radicalism* (New York: Basic Books, 1973).

6. See chapter 1. Richard Edwards, *Contested Terrain: The Transformation of the Workplace in the Twentieth Century* (New York: Harper Torchbooks, 1979).

7. See chapter 1. Robert Heilbroner, *The Worldly Philosophers*, 7th ed. (London: Penguin, 1999).

8. Douglas S. Massey, *Categorically Unequal: The American Stratification System* (New York: Russell Sage Foundation, 2007), 34–35; Saskia Sassen, *The Global City: New York, London, Tokyo* (Princeton, NJ: Princeton University Press, 1991), chap. 1; Edwards, *Contested Terrain*.

9. Bluestone and Harrison, *The Deindustrialization of America*; Massey, *Categorically Unequal*.

10. Sassen, *The Global City*; Bluestone and Harrison, *The Deindustrialization of America*; David Harvey, *The Condition of Postmodernity* (Cambridge, MA: Basil Blackwell, 1989).

11. See chapter 1. Sassen, *The Global City*; Robert Sampson, *Great American City: Chicago and the Enduring Neighborhood Effect* (Chicago: University of Chicago Press, 2013).

12. Jennifer Robinson, "Global and World Cities: A View from off the Map," *International Journal of Urban and Regional Research* 26, no. 3 (September 2002): 531–554; Neil Brenner, "Theses on Urbanization," *Public Culture* 25, no. 1 (2013): 85–114.

13. Richard Florida, *The Rise of the Creative Class: And How It's Transforming Work, Leisure, Community, and Everyday Life* (New York: Basic Books, 2002); Sharon Zukin, *Naked City: The Death and Life of Authentic Urban Places* (New York: Oxford University Press, 2010); Alejandro Portes and Ariel C. Armony, *The Global Edge: Miami in the Twenty-First Century* (Berkeley: University of California Press, 2018), chaps. 1, 8.

14. See chapter 2. David Dunn, "Dubai's Audacious 'Heart of Europe' Megaproject Nears First Stage of Completion," *CNN Travel*, December 2, 2020, https://edition.cnn.com/travel/article/dubai-heart-of-europe-nears-completion/index.html.

15. See chapter 5 for additional examples. Ephrat Livni, "The Mayor of Miami Is Trying to Rebrand the City as a Crypto Hub," *New York Times*, March 23, 2021, https://www.nytimes.com/2021/03/23/business/the-mayor-of-miami-is-trying-to-rebrand-the-city-as-a-crypto-hub.html; Jemima Kelly, "Maybe 'Bitcoin Bros' Aren't Really a Thing After All," *Financial Times*, June 8, 2021, https://www.ft.com/content/f18a0e38-ffc4-4e11-8b82-a6c22a27ea36.

16. Pirenne, *Medieval Cities*; Dobb, *Studies in the Development of Capitalism*; Max Weber, *The City*, ed. Don Martindale and Gertrud Neuwirth (New York: Free Press, 1958); Steven E. Ozment, *The Reformation of Cities* (New Haven, CT: Yale University Press, 1975); Alejandro Portes, "Migration and Underdevelopment," *Politics and Society* 8 (1978): 1–48.

17. Brinley Thomas, *Migration and Economic Growth*, 2nd ed. (Cambridge: Cambridge University Press, 1973); Rosenblum, *Immigrant Workers*; Dobb, *Studies in the Development of Capitalism*; Alejandro Portes and Ruben R. Rumbaut, *Immigrant America: A Portrait*, 4th ed. (Berkeley: University of California Press, 2014), chap. 1.

18. See chapters 2 and 4. Harvey Molotch and David Ponzini, *The New Arab Urban* (New York: New York University Press, 2019); Lee Kuan Yew, *From Third World to First: The Singapore Story, 1965–2000*, vol. 2 (New York: HarperCollins, 2000).

19. See chapter 3. Portes and Armony, *The Global Edge*, chaps. 1, 4.

20. "2018 Revision of World Urbanization Prospects," United Nations Department of Economic and Social Affairs, May 16, 2018, https://www.un.org/development/desa/en/news/population/2018-revision-of-world-urbanizationprospects.html#:~:text=Today%2C%2055%25%20of%20the%20world's,increase%20to%2068%25%20by%202050; "Urban Population," World Bank, https://data.worldbank.org/indicator/SP.URB.TOTL.IN.ZS; "School of Cities: 2019–2020 Annual Report Release," School of Cities, University of Toronto, October 13, 2020, https://www.schoolofcities.utoronto.ca/news/SofC-2019-2020-Annual-Report-released; Talia Lakritz, "These 11 Sinking Cities Could Disappear by 2100," World Economic Forum, September 10, 2019, https://www.weforum.org/agenda/2019/09/11-sinking-cities-that-could-soon-be-underwater/.

21. "Extreme Weather and Climate Change," Center for Climate and Energy Solutions (C2ES), 2021, https://www.c2es.org/content/extreme-weather-and-climate-change/.

22. *What Climate Change Means for Louisiana*, U.S. Environmental Protection Agency, August 2016, https://19january2017snapshot.epa.gov/sites/production/files/2016-09/documents/climate-change-la.pdf.

23. Rick Jervis, "Fifteen Years and $15 Billion Since Katrina, New Orleans Is More Prepared for a Major Hurricane—for Now," *USA Today*, August 24, 2020, https://www.usatoday.com/story/news/nation/2020/08/24/new-orleans-hurricane-protection-system-marco-laura/5624092002/; Todd Woody, "Will the 'Great Wall' of New Orleans Save It from the Next Killer Hurricane?," TakePart, August 17, 2015, http://www.takepart.com/feature/2015/08/17/katrina-new-orleans-walled-city/.

24. Tim McDonnell, "Louisiana's Population Is Already Moving to Escape Climate Catastrophe," *Quartz*, September 1, 2020, https://qz.com/1895269/louisianas-population-is-moving-to-escape-climate-catastrophe/.

25. Chris Mooney et al., "2020 Rivals Hottest Year on Record, Pushing Earth Closer to a Critical Climate Threshold," *Washington Post*, January 14, 2021, https://www.washingtonpost.com/climate-environment/interactive/2021/2020-tied-for-hottest-year-on-record/.

26. Dawei Li, Jiacan Yuan, and Robert Kopp, "Escalating Global Exposure to Compound Heat-Humidity Extremes with Warming," *Environmental Research Letters* 15, no. 6 (2020).

27. "Louisiana," States at Risk, 2021, https://statesatrisk.org/louisiana.

28. Oleson et al., "Interactions Between Urbanization, Heat Stress, and Climate Change," *Climatic Change* 129, no. 3–4 (2015): 526.

29. Araujo et al., "São Paulo Urban Heat Islands Have a Higher Incidence of Dengue than Other Urban Areas," *Brazilian Journal of Infectious Diseases* 19, no. 2 (2015): 146–155; Helena Ribeiro Sobral, "Heat Island in São Paulo, Brazil: Effects on Health," *Critical Public Health* 15, no. 2 (2005): 147–156; Felicia Keesing et al., "Impacts of Biodiversity on the Emergence and Transmission of Infectious Diseases," *Nature* 468 (2010).

30. Felipe Vemado and Augusto José Pereira Filho, "Severe Weather Caused by Heat Island and Sea Breeze Effects in the Metropolitan Area of São Paulo, Brazil," *Advances in Meteorology* 3 (2016): 1–13.

31. Rebecca Lindsey, "Climate Change: Global Sea Level," NOAA, Climate.gov, January 25, 2021, https://www.climate.gov/news-features/understanding-climate/climate-change-global-sea-level.

32. Kanta Kumari Rigaud et al., *Groundswell: Preparing for Internal Climate Migration* (Washington, DC: World Bank, 2018), http://hdl.handle.net/10986/29461.

33. Jeff Goodell, *The Water Will Come: Rising Seas, Sinking Cities, and the Remaking of the Civilized World* (New York: Little, Brown, 2017), 220.

34. Caleb Robinson, Bistra Dilkina, and Juan Moreno-Cruz, "Modeling Migration Patterns in the USA Under Sea Level Rise," *PLOS ONE* 15, no. 1 (2020). See McDonnell, "Louisiana's Population."

35. "Climate Change," Government of the United Arab Emirates, 2021, https://u.ae/en/information-and-services/environment-and-energy/climate-change/climate-change.

36. "Dubai Population Are 3.3 Million by Q3-19," Dubai Statistics Center (DSC), November 6, 2019, https://www.dsc.gov.ae/en-us/DSC-News/Pages/Dubai-Population-Are-3.3-Million-by-Q3-19.aspx.

37. Gökçe Günel, "The Infinity of Water: Climate Change Adaptation in the Arabian Peninsula," *Public Culture* 28, no. 2 (2016).

38. "Providing Water Security in Arid Regions," World Future Energy Summit, https://www.worldfutureenergysummit.com/en-gb/future-insights-blog/providing-water-security-in-arid-regions.html.

39. Mathew E. Hauer, "Migration Induced by Sea-Level Rise Could Reshape the US Population Landscape," *Nature Climate Change* 7 (2017): 321–325; Robinson et al., "Modeling Migration Patterns."

40. Hauer, "Migration Induced by Sea-Level Rise," 324.

41. Abrahm Lustgarten, "How Climate Migration Will Reshape America," *New York Times Magazine*, September 15, 2020, https://www.nytimes.com/interactive/2020/09/15/magazine /climate-crisis-migration-america.html.

42. Ashlee Cunsolo and Neville Ellis, "Ecological Grief as a Mental Health Response to Climate Change-Related Loss," *Nature Climate Change* 8 (2018): 278; Neville Ellis and Ashlee Cunsolo, "Hope and Mourning in the Anthropocene: Understanding Ecological Grief," The Conversation, April 4, 2018, https://theconversation.com/hope-and-mourning -in-the-anthropocene-understanding-ecological-grief-88630.

43. Portes and Armony, *The Global Edge*, 46.

44. Neil Brenner and Christian Schmid, "Planetary Urbanisation," in *Urban Constellations*, ed. Mathew Gandy (Berlin: Jovis, 2011); Cunsolo and Ellis, "Ecological Grief." See Glenn Albrecht et al., "Solastalgia: The Distress Caused by Environmental Change," *Australasian Psychiatry* 15, no. 1 (2007): S95–S98; Mario Alejandro Ariza, *Disposable City: Miami's Future on the Shores of Climate Catastrophe* (New York: Public Affairs, 2020); Mario Alejandro Ariza, "As Miami Keeps Building, Rising Seas Deepen Its Social Divide," *Yale Environment 360*, September 29, 2020, https://e360.yale.edu/features/as-miami-keeps -building-rising-seas-deepen-its-social-divide.

45. Peter Guest, "The Impossible Fight to Save Jakarta, the Sinking Megacity," *Wired*, October 15, 2019, https://www.wired.co.uk/article/jakarta-sinking.

46. Bill Chappell, "Jakarta Is Crowded and Sinking, So Indonesia Is Moving Its Capital to Borneo," *NPR*, August 26, 2019, https://www.npr.org/2019/08/26/754291131/indonesia -plans-to-move-capital-to-borneo-from-jakarta.

47. Matthew Cappucci, "Sea Level Rise Is Combining with Other Factors to Regularly Flood Miami," *Washington Post*, August 8, 2019, https://www.washingtonpost.com/weather/2019 /08/08/analysis-sea-level-rise-is-combining-with-other-factors-regularly-flood-miami/.

48. Hauer, "Migration Induced by Sea-Level Rise." See Ariza, *Disposable City*; Robinson et al., "Modeling Migration Patterns"; Daniel Hoornweg and Kevin Pope, "Population Predictions for the World's Largest Cities in the 21st Century," *Environment and Urbanization* 29, no. 1 (2016): 195–216.

49. Denise Lu and Christopher Flavelle, "Rising Seas Will Erase More Cities by 2050, New Research Shows," *New York Times*, October 29, 2019, https://www.nytimes.com/interactive /2019/10/29/climate/coastal-cities-underwater.html?smid=nytcore-ios-share.

50. Joshua Partlow et al., "Before Condo Collapse, Rising Seas Long Pressured Miami Coastal Properties," *Washington Post*, June 25, 2021, https://www.washingtonpost.com/climate -environment/2021/06/25/rising-sea-levels-condo-collapse/.

51. Goodell, *The Water Will Come*, 242, 257–260.

52. Ariza, *Disposable City*.

53. Vesa Barileva, "Climate Gentrification, a Crisis That Is Deepening Inequality in Many Cities," Medium, July 22, 2019, https://medium.com/@vesabarileva/climate-gentrification -a-crisis-that-is-deepening-inequality-in-many-cities-4b0518220983; Goodell, *The Water Will Come*, 115.

54.   Barileva, "Climate Gentrification."

55.   Ariza, *Disposable City*; Patricia Mazzei, "A 20-Foot Sea Wall? Miami Faces the Hard Choices of Climate Change," *New York Times*, June 2, 2021, https://www.nytimes.com/2021/06/02 /us/miami-fl-seawall-hurricanes.html?referringSource=articleShare; Goodell, *The Water Will Come*, 103.

56.   Robert Frank, "Real-Estate Brokers Brace for 'Flood' of Wealthy Buyers from Overseas as Travel Restrictions Lift," *CNBC*, November 5, 2021, https://www.cnbc.com/2021/11/05 /real-estate-brokers-brace-for-flood-of-wealthy-buyers-from-overseas-.html.

57.   Portes and Armony, *The Global Edge*, 180–187.

58.   Annalee Newitz, *Four Lost Cities: A Secret History of the Urban Age* (New York: Norton, 2021), 72.

59.   Portes and Armony, *The Global Edge*, 186, 196.

60.   Goodell, *The Water Will Come*, 214–216, quote from 214.

61.   Goodell, *The Water Will Come*, 214–220; Bianca Nogrady, "The Benefits and Downsides of Building into the Sea," *BBC*, November 1, 2016, https://www.bbc.com/future/article /20161101-the-benefits-and-downsides-of-building-into-the-sea#.

62.   Oluwafemi Ayodeji Olajide, Muyiwa Elijah Agunbiade, and Hakeem Babatunde Bishi, "The Realities of Lagos Urban Development Vision on Livelihoods of the Urban Poor," *Journal of Urban Management* 7, no. 1 (2018): 22.

63.   Nchimunya Hamukoma, Nicola Doyle, Sara Calburn, and Dickie Davis, "Lagos: Is It Possible to Fix Africa's Largest City?," The Brenthurst Foundation, Discussion Paper, March 2019, 1–23.

64.   Audra D. S. Burch, "One Historic Black Neighborhood's Stake in the Infrastructure Bill," *New York Times*, November 20, 2021, https://www.nytimes.com/2021/11/20/us/claiborne -expressway-new-orleans-infrastructure.html.

65.   "Inside the Strategy Room on Apple Podcasts," https://podcasts.apple.com/ug/podcast /inside-the-strategy-room/id1422814215?.

66.   Daniel Newman, "The New Future of Work Requires Greater Focus on Employee Engagement," *Forbes*, June 21, 2021, https://www.forbes.com/sites/danielnewman/2021/06/21 /the-new-future-of-work-requires-greater-focus-on-employee-engagement/; John Engler et al., *The Work Ahead: Machines, Skills, and U.S. Leadership in the Twenty-First Century*, Independent Task Force Report No. 76 (New York: Council on Foreign Affairs, 2018).

67.   Sarah Holder, "The 5 Cities Ready to Build with Remote Workers in Mind," *Bloomberg. com*, January 26, 2021, https://www.bloomberg.com/news/articles/2021-01-26/how-small -cities-are-trying-to-lure-remote-workers.

68.   Catherine Shu, "Singapore Is Poised to Become Asia's Silicon Valley," TechCrunch, December 14, 2020, https://techcrunch.com/2020/12/14/singapore-is-poised-to-become -asias-silicon-valley/; J. E. Lee-Partridge, T. S. H. Teo, and V. K. G. Lim, "Information Technology Management: The Case of the Port of Singapore Authority," *Journal of Strategic Information Systems* 9, no. 1 (2000): 91–92.

69.   Shu, "Singapore Is Poised"; Costas Paris, "Singapore Looks to Tech to Bolster Its Role in Shipping," *Wall Street Journal*, April 8, 2021, https://www.wsj.com/articles/singapore -looks-to-tech-to-bolster-its-role-in-shipping-11617909788. See Jonathan Haskel and Stian Westlake, *Capitalism Without Capital: The Rise of the Intangible Economy* (Princeton, NJ: Princeton University Press, 2017).

70.   *C40 Annual Report 2020* (New York: C40 Cities Climate Leadership Group, 2020).

71.   Carlos Moreno et al., "Introducing the '15-Minute City': Sustainability, Resilience and Place Identity in Future Post Pandemic Cities," *Smart Cities* 4, no. 1 (2021): 103–104.

72.   *The Global Fintech Index 2020*, Findexable, December 2019, https://findexable.com/wp-content/uploads/2019/12/Findexable_Global-Fintech-Rankings-2020exSFA.pdf. São Paulo ranks fifth globally compared to Miami's twentieth placement.

73.   "Brave New Worlds: Abu Dhabi's Latest Museum Aims to Rewrite the Story of Modernism," *The Economist*, November 20, 2021, 81.

REFERENCES

Abate, Duncan A. W., and Hong Tran. "Increased Minimum Wage Rate to Take Effect from 1 May 2017 in Hong Kong." Mayer/ Brown LLP, January 24, 2017. https://www.mayerbrown.com/en/perspectives-events/publications/2017/01/increased-minimum-wage-rate-to-take-effect-from-1.

Abdul-Hamid, Husein, Donald Baum, Oni Lusk-Stover, and Huge Wesley. "The Role of the Private Sector in Lagos, Nigeria." World Bank Group Technical Paper, Washington, DC, June 30, 2017.

Abdullah, Asma, and Paul B. Pedersen. *Understanding Multicultural Malaysia: Delights, Puzzles, and Irritations*. Petaling Jaya, Malaysia: Pearson, 2003.

Abrahamson, Mark. *Global Cities*. New York: Oxford University Press, 2004.

Abu-Lughood, Janet. *Third World Urbanization*. New York: Routledge, 1977.

Acayaba, Cintia, and Leo Acroverde. "Batalhões da Grande SP matam 60 percent mais em 2020; na capital, aumento de mortes por policiais militares chega a 44 percent." *O Globo*, June 23, 2020. https://g1.globo.com/sp/sao-paulo/noticia/2020/06/23/batalhoes-da-grande-sp-matam-60percent-mais-em-2020-na-capital-aumento-de-mortes-por-policiais-militares-chega-a-44percent.ghtml.

Addie, Jean-Paul. "Review of New Urban Spaces: Urban Theory and the Scale Question by Neil Brenner." *Regional Studies*, October 18, 2019.

Adebajo, Adekeye. "Nollywood as a Pan-African Cultural Phenomenon." Institute for Pan African Thought and Conversation, May 25, 2017. https://ipatc.joburg/nollywood-as-a-pan-african-cultural-phenomenon/.

Adepetun, Adeyemi. "New Tech Experience Center Debuts in Lagos." *The Guardian NG*, September 23, 2020. https://guardian.ng/technology/tech/new-tech-experience-centre-debuts-in-lagos/.

Adewale Yagboyaju, Dhikru. "Nigeria's Fourth Republic and the Challenge of a Faltering Democratization." *African Studies Quarterly* 12, no. 3 (2011): 93–106.

Aerotime. "Situation in South America's Busiest Airports." Aerotime. Accessed February 25, 2021. https://www.aerotime.aero/26482-situation-in-south-america-s-busiest-airports.

African Press Organization. "The 8th Edition of the NollywoodWeek Film Festival Goes Global." Newswires, April 27, 2021. https://www.einnews.com/pr_news/539540099/the-8th -edition-of-the-nollywoodweek-film-festival-goes-global-selection-includes-films-from -other-african-countries-and-the-african-diaspora/.

Agbiboa, Daniel, ed. Transport, Transgression and Politics in African Cities: The Rhythm of Chaos. New York: Routledge, 2019.

Agbo, Mathias. "The Tragic Human Cost of Africa's New Megacities." ArchDaily, May 24, 2017. https://www.archdaily.com/872025/the-tragic-human-cost-of-africas-new-megacities.

Aglionby, John. "A Tick in the Only Box." The Guardian, October 26, 2001.

Airbus. "Airbus' Assembly Facility Marks 10 Years of Quality Manufacturing for A320 Family Jetliners." Airbus, September 28, 2018. https://www.airbus.com/en/newsroom/news/2018-09 -airbus-china-assembly-facility-marks-10-years-of-quality-manufacturing-for.

AirMundo. "Busiest Airports in South America." Airmundo. Accessed June 30, 2021. https:// airmundo.com/en/blog/busiest-airports-in-south-america/.

Akhavan, Mina. "Gateway: Revisiting Dubai as a Port City." In The New Arab Urban: Gulf Cities of Wealth, Ambition, and Distress, ed. Harvey Molotch and Davide Ponzini, 175–193. New York: New York University Press, 2019.

Akinrinade, Sola, and Olukoya Ogen. "Globalization and De-Industrialization: South-South Neo-Liberalism and the Collapse of the Nigerian Textile Industry." The Global South 2, no. 2 (2008): 159–170.

Akinwotu, Emmanuel. "Waves of Change: Nigeria's Lagos Battles Erosion." Phys.org, July 10, 2019. https://phys.org/news/2019-07-nigeria-lagos-atlantic-erosion.html.

Al-Sayegh, Fatma. "Merchants' Role in a Changing Society: The Case of Dubai, 1900–90." Middle Eastern Studies 34, no.1 (2019): 87–102.

Albrecht, Glenn, Gina-Maree Sartore, Linda Connor, Nick Higginbotham, Sonia Freeman, Brian Kelly, Helen Stain, Anna Tonna, and Georgia Pollard. "Solastalgia: The Distress Caused by Environmental Change." Australasian Psychiatry 15, no. 1 (2007): S95–S98.

Aljunied, Syed Muhd Khairudin. "Beyond the Rhetoric of Communalism: Violence and the Process of Reconciliation in 1950s Singapore." In Reframing Singapore, ed. Derek Heng and Syed Muhd Khairudin Aljunied, 69–87. Amsterdam: Amsterdam University Press, 2009.

Allman, T. D. Miami: City of the Future. Rev. ed. Gainesville: University of Florida Press, 2013.

——. Miami: City of the Future. New York: Atlantic Monthly Press, 1987.

Alozie, Bright. "Space and Colonial Alterity: Interrogating British Residential Segregation in Nigeria, 1899–1919." Ufahamu: A Journal of African Studies 41, no. 2 (2020): 1–26.

AlShehabi, Omar. "Histories of Migration to the Gulf." In Transit States: Labour, Migration and Citizenship in the Gulf, ed. Abdulhadi Khalaf, Omar AlShehabi, and Adam Hanieh, 3–38. London: Pluto, 2014.

Amin, Ash, and Stephen Graham. "The Ordinary City." Transactions of the Institute of British Geographers 22, no. 4 (1997): 411–429.

Andrews, Sally. "'Soft' Repression: The Struggle for Democracy in Singapore." The Diplomat, February 6, 2015.

Ansari, Minaam. "Dubai's Iconic Burj Khalifa Honours Argentine Great Maradona with Dazzling Gesture." Republic World, December 1, 2020. https://www.republicworld.com/sports

-news/football-news/dubais-iconic-burj-khalifa-honours-argentine-great-maradona-with
-dazzling-gesture.html.

Appadurai, Arjun. "Disjuncture and Difference in the Global Cultural Economy." *Theory, Culture, and Society* 7 (1990): 295–310.

Aranda, Elizabeth, Sally Hughes, and Elena Sabogal. *Making a Life in Metropolitan Miami*. Boulder, CO: Lynne Rienner, 2014.

Araujo, Ricardo Vieira, Marcos Roberto Albertini, André Luis Costa-da-Silva, Lincoln Suesdek, Nathália Cristina Soares Franceschi, Nancy Marçal Bastos, Gizelda Katz, Vivian Ailt Cardoso, Bronislawa Ciotek Castro, Margareth Lara Capurro, and Vera Lúcia Anacleto Cardoso Allegro. "São Paulo Urban Heat Islands Have a Higher Incidence of Dengue than Other Urban Areas." *Brazilian Journal of Infectious Diseases* 19, no. 2 (2015): 146–155.

Arcadis Global. "Sustainable Cities Index." Arcadis. Accessed February 18, 2021. https://www.arcadis.com/campaigns/citizencentriccities/index.html.

Ariza, Marina, and Juan Carlos Ramírez. "Urbanización, Mercados de Trabajo y Escenarios Sociales en el México Finisecular." In *Ciudades Latinoamericanas*, ed. Alejandro Portes, Bryan R. Roberts, and A. Grimson, 299–362. Buenos Aires: Prometeo Editores, 2005.

Ariza, Mario Alejandro. "As Miami Keeps Building, Rising Seas Deepen Its Social Divide." *Yale Environment 360*, September 29, 2020. https://e360.yale.edu/features/as-miami-keeps-building-rising-seas-deepen-its-social-divide.

——. *Disposable City: Miami's Future on the Shores of Climate Catastrophe*. New York: Public Affairs, 2020.

Armijo, Leslie Elliott, and Sybil D. Rhodes. "Explaining Infrastructure Underperformance in Brazil: Cash, Political Institutions, Corruption, and Policy Gestalts." *Policy Studies* 38, no. 3 (2017): 231–247.

Armony, Ariel C., Lucilene Cury, and Bruno Massola Moda. "A Discussion on Global Cities and Immigration: The Case of São Paulo and Miami." Conference paper, IPSA World Congress of Political Science, July 10–15, 2021.

——. "As Cidades Globais e Seus Habitantes: Uma Reflexão Transdisciplinar." Unpublished manuscript, 2020.

Arrighi, Giovanni. *The Long Twentieth Century: Money, Power, and the Origins of Our Times*. London: Verso, 1994.

Arrighi, Giovanni, Beverly J. Silver, and Benjamin D. Brewer. "Industrial Convergence and the Persistence of the North-South Divide." *Studies in Comparative International Development* 38, no. 1 (2003): 3–31.

ASDA'A BCW. "A Call for Reform: 11th Annual ASDA'A BCW Arab Youth Survey 2019." 2019. https://www.chathamhouse.org/sites/default/files/2019%20Arab%20Youth%20Survey.pdf.

Ashbolt, Alan. Interview with Lee Kuan Yew. Canberra: ABC Studios. March 24, 1965.

ATTA. "Tourism Holds Positive Growth for Business in Nigeria." February 7, 2020. https://www.atta.travel/news/2020/02/tourism-holds-positive-growth-for-business-in-nigeria/.

Average Salary Survey. "Average Salary Survey." 2021. https://www.averagesalarysurvey.com/.

Baer, Werner. *The Brazilian Economy: Growth and Development*. London: Lynne Rienner, 2008.

Balakrishnan, Sarah. "The Afropolitan Idea: New Perspectives on Cosmopolitanism in African Studies." *History Compass* 15, no. 2 (2017): e12362.

Balassa, Bela, Gerardo Bueno, and Pedro Pablo Kuczynski. *Toward Renewed Economic Growth in Latin America.* Washington, DC: Institute for International Economics, 1986.

Baldwin, Clare, Yimou Lee, and Clare Jim. "Special Report: The Mainland's Colonization of the Hong Kong Economy." Reuters, December 30, 2014. https://www.reuters.com/article/us-hongkong-china-economy-specialreport/special-report-the-mainlands-colonization-of-the-hong-kong-economy-idUSKBN0K901320141231.

Balibrea, Mari Paz. "Urbanism, Culture and the Post-Industrial City: Challenging the 'Barcelona Model.'" *Journal of Spanish Cultural Studies* 2, no. 2 (September 2001): 187–210.

Barileva, Vesa. "Climate Gentrification, a Crisis That Is Deepening Inequality in Many Cities." Medium, July 22, 2019. https://medium.com/@vesabarileva/climate-gentrification-a-crisis-that-is-deepening-inequality-in-many-cities-4b0518220983.

Barr, Michael D. "Lee Kuan Yew: Race, Culture, and Genes." *Journal of Contemporary Asia* 29, no. 2 (1999): 145–166.

——. *Singapore: A Modern History.* London: I. B. Tauris, 2019.

Bassett, R., P. J. Young, G. S. Blair, F. Samreen, and W. Simm. "The Megacity Lagos and Three Decades of Urban Heat Island Growth." *Journal of Applied Meteorology and Climatology* 59, no. 12 (2020): 2041–2055.

BBC. "Hong Kong: Joshua Wong and Fellow Pro-Democracy Activists Jailed." December 2, 2020.

——. "Nigeria Housing: 'I Live in a Floating Slum' in Lagos." March 5, 2020. https://www.bbc.com/news/world-africa-51677371.

Beblawi, Hazem. "The Rentier State in the Arab World." In *The Rentier State*, ed. Hazem Beblawi and Giacomo Luciani, 49–62. London: Routledge, 2016.

Bendix, Reinhard. *Max Weber: An Intellectual Portrait.* Berkeley: University of California Press, 1960.

Berthelsen, John. "A Lee Dynasty in Singapore After All?" *Asia Sentinel*, May 4, 2021.

Berube, Alan, Jesus Leal Trujillo, Tao Ran, and Joseph Parilla. *Global Metro Monitor.* Brookings, January 22, 2015. https://www.brookings.edu/research/global-metro-monitor/.

Bethell, Leslie. "Brazil—the Last 15 Years." *Index on Censorship* 8, no. 4 (1979): 3–7.

Biennial Foundation. "São Paulo Biennial (Brazil)—Biennial Foundation." Accessed February 15, 2021. https://www.biennialfoundation.org/biennials/sao-paolo-biennial/.

Bloomberg News. "Banker Shocked by 45 Percent China Tax Rate Mull Leaving Hong Kong." July 14, 2020.

Bluestone, Barry, and Bennett Harrison. *The Deindustrialization of America.* New York: Wiley, 1982.

Boadle, Anthony, and Gabriel Stargardter. "Far-Right Bolsonaro Rides Anti-Corruption Rage to Brazil Presidency." Reuters, October 28, 2018. https://www.reuters.com/article/us-brazil-election/far-right-bolsonaro-rides-anti-corruption-rage-to-brazil-presidency-idUSKCN1N203K.

Bok, Rachel. "Airports on the Move? The Policy Mobilities of Singapore Changi Airport at Home and Abroad." *Urban Studies* 52 (2014): 2724–2740.

Bonjean, Charles M., Bernic M. Moore, and Adreain A. Ross. *The Junior League of New Orleans: A Profile of Member Attitudes and Orientations.* Report for National Association of Junior Leagues. Austin, TX: The Hogg Foundation for Mental Health, May 1976.

Boodrookas, Alex, and Arang Keshavarzian. "Giving the Transnational a History: Gulf Cities Across Time and Space." In *The New Arab Urban: Gulf Cities of Wealth, Ambition, and Distress*, ed. Harvey Molotch and Davide Ponzini, 35–57. New York: New York University Press, 2019.

Borschberg, Peter. *The Singapore and Melaka Straits: Violence, Security, and Diplomacy in the 17th Century*. Singapore: National University of Singapore Press, 2010.

Botifoll, Luis. "How Miami's New Image Was Created." Occasional Papers Series, Institute of Inter-American Studies, University of Miami, 1985.

Bouchet, Max, Sifan Liu, Joseph Parilla, and Nader Kabbani. "Global Metro Monitor 2018." Brookings Institution, June 2018. https://www.brookings.edu/wp-content/uploads/2018/06/Brookings-Metro_Global-Metro-Monitor-2018.pdf.

Bray, Mark, and W. O. Lee. "Education, Democracy and Colonial Transition: The Case of Hong Kong." *International Review of Education / Internationale Zeitschrift Für Erziehungswissenschaft / Revue Internationale De L'Education* 39, no. 6 (1993): 541–560.

Brenner, Neil. "Global Cities, Glocal States: Global City Formation and State Territorial Restructuring in Contemporary Europe." *Review of International Political Economy* 5, no. 1 (1998): 1–37.

——. "Theses on Planetary Urbanization." *New Society* 243 (2013): 38–66.

——. *Urban Theory and the Scale Question*. New York: Oxford University Press, 2019.

Brenner, Neil, and Christian Schmid. "Planetary Urbanisation." In *Urban Constellations*, ed. Matthew Gandy, 10–13. Berlin: Jovis, 2011.

——. "The Urban Age in Debate." *Latin American Urban and Regional Studies* 127 (2016): 307–339.

Brizotti-Pasquotto, Geise, Leandro Medrano, Geise Brizotti-Pasquotto, and Leandro Medrano. "Iconic Buildings and City Marketing. The Central Area of São Paulo." *Bitácora Urbano Territorial* 24, no. 2 (December 2014): 21–30.

Buckley, Michelle, and Adam Hanieh. "Diversification by Urbanization: Tracing the Property-Finance Nexus in Dubai and the Gulf." *International Journal of Urban and Regional Research* 38, no. 1 (2014): 155–175.

Bundy, Agnes J. "The Reunification of China with Hong Kong and Its Implications for Taiwan: An Analysis of the One Country, Two Systems Model." *California Western International Law Journal* 19 (1988): 271–286.

Burch, Audra D. S. "One Historic Black Neighborhood's Stake in the Infrastructure Bill." *New York Times*, November 20, 2021. https://www.nytimes.com/2021/11/20/us/claiborne-expressway-new-orleans-infrastructure.html.

Butler, Kim D. "Up from Slavery: Afro-Brazilian Activism in São Paulo, 1888–1938." *The Americas* 49, no. 2 (1992): 179–206.

Byrnes, Mark. "Revisiting Pittsburgh's Era of Big Plans." *Bloomberg City Lab*, June 25, 2019. https://www.bloomberg.com/news/articles/2019-06-25/-imagining-the-modern-in-postwar-pittsburgh.

Cadena, Andres, Janna Remes, James Manyika, Richard Dobbs, Charles Roxburgh, Heinz-Peter Elstrodt, Alberto Chaia, and Alejandra Restrepo. "Building Globally Competitive Cities: The Key to Latin American Growth." McKinsey & Company, August 2011. https://www.mckinsey.com/featured-insights/urbanization/building-competitive-cities-key-to-latin-american-growth.

Caldeira, Teresa P. R. *City of Walls*. Berkeley: University of California Press, 2000.

——. "Peripheral Urbanization: Autoconstruction, Transversal Logics, and Politics in Cities of the Global South." *Society and Space* 35, no. 1 (2016): 3–20.

——. "Social Movements, Cultural Production, and Protests: São Paulo's Shifting Political Landscape." *Current Anthropology* 56, no. 11 (2015): S126–S135.

Camayd-Freixas, Yohel. "Crisis in Miami." Special report to the project "Help-Seeking and Services: Use Among Latin American Refugees." Baltimore, MD: Department of Sociology, Johns Hopkins University, 1988.

Cameron, C. R. "Colonization of Immigrants in Brazil." *Monthly Labor Review* 33, no. 4 (1931): 36–46.

Campanella, Richard. "Economic Timeline: Selected Historical Events That Shaped the New Orleans Economy, 1700–2010." Tulane University's Data Center Report, August 2010. https://www.datacenterresearch.org/reports_analysis/economic-timeline/.

——. "New Orleans: A Timeline of Economic History." New Orleans Business Alliance, 2012. https://richcampanella.com/wp-content/uploads/2020/02/article_Campanella_New -Orleans-Timeline-of-Economic-History_NOBA.pdf.

Campos, Nauro, Menelaos Karanasos, Panagiotis Koutroumpis, and Zihui Zhang. "Political Instability, Institutional Change and Economic Growth in Brazil Since 1870." *Journal of Institutional Economics* 16, no. 6 (December 2020): 883–910.

Cantor, Marcelo. *Market Analysis—Airport Sector Brazil.* The Hague: Netherlands Enterprise Agency, 2020. https://www.rvo.nl/sites/default/files/2020/06/Airport-Sector-in-Brazil.pdf.

Cappucci, Matthew. "Sea Level Rise Is Combining with Other Factors to Regularly Flood Miami." *Washington Post,* August 8, 2019. https://www.washingtonpost.com/weather/2019/08/08 /analysis-sea-level-rise-is-combining-with-other-factors-regularly-flood-miami/.

Cardoso, Fernando H., and Enzo Faletto. *Dependency and Development in Latin America.* Berkeley: University of California Press, 1984.

Carroll, John M. *A Concise History of Hong Kong.* Lanham, MD: Rowman and Littlefield, 2007.

Carter, Donald, ed. *Remaking Post-Industrial Cities: Lessons from North America and Europe.* London: Routledge, 2016.

CBRE Research. "Global Living 2020." April 2020. https://www.cbreresidential.com/uk/sites/uk -residential/files/CBRE-Global%20Living_2020_Final.pdf.

Center for Climate and Energy Solutions (C2ES). "Extreme Weather and Climate Change." 2021. https://www.c2es.org/content/extreme-weather-and-climate-change/.

Chan, Ming K. *The Challenge of Hong Kong's Reintegration with China.* Hong Kong: Hong Kong University Press, 1997.

Chappell, Bill. "Jakarta Is Crowded and Sinking, So Indonesia Is Moving Its Capital to Borneo." *NPR,* August 26, 2019. https://www.npr.org/2019/08/26/754291131/indonesia-plans-to-move -capital-to-borneo-from-jakarta.

Chaudhry, Kiren. "The 'Uncanny' Writ Regional: New and Recurring Forms of Poverty and Inequality in the Arab World." In *Rebuilding Devastated Economies in the Middle East,* ed. Leonard Binder. New York: Palgrave MacMillan, 2007.

Chen, Xiangming, and Ahmed Kanna, eds. *Rethinking Global Urbanism: Comparative Insights from Secondary Cities.* New York: Routledge, 2012.

Cheng, Kris. "Hong Kong Pro-Democracy Activist Runs for China's Legislature, Claiming Support for Xi Jinping Thought." *Hong Kong Free Press,* December 4, 2017.

Chete, L. N., J. O. Adeoti, F. M. Adeyinka, and O. Ogundele. *Industrial Development and Growth in Nigeria: Lessons and Challenges.* Africa Growth Initiative of Brookings, 2016. https://www .brookings.edu/wp-content/uploads/2016/07/l2c_wp8_chete-et-al-1.pdf.

Chew, Valerie. "Public Housing in Singapore." National Library Board Singapore, 2009. https:// eresources.nlb.gov.sg/infopedia/articles/SIP_1585_2009-10-26.html.

Chua, Beng Huat. *Liberalism Disavowed: Communitarianism and State Capitalism in Singapore*. Singapore: National University of Singapore Press, 2017.

Clark, Greg. *Global Cities: A Short History*. Washington, DC: Brookings, 2016.

Clark, Greg, Marek Gootman, Max Bouchet, and Tim Moonen. *The Global Identity of Cities: Seven Steps to Build Reputation and Visibility for Competitiveness and Resilience*. Washington, DC: Brookings, July 28, 2020. https://www.brookings.edu/research/seven-steps-build-reputation-visibility-for-competitiveness/.

Clark, Greg, and Tim Moonen. *The 10 Traits of Globally Fluent Metro Areas*. Washington, DC: Brookings, 2013. https://www.brookings.edu/wp-content/uploads/2016/06/TenTraitsIntnl.pdf.

——. *The 10 Traits of Globally Fluent Metro Areas: Barcelona's Compelling Global Identity*. Washington, DC: Brookings, 2013. https://www.brookings.edu/blog/the-avenue/2013/09/03/the-10-traits-of-globally-fluent-metro-areas-barcelonas-compelling-global-identity/.

CNN. "Hong Kong Legislators Reject China-Backed Reform Bill." June 19, 2015.

Cobbinah, Patrick Brandful, Ellis Adjei Adams, and Michael Odei Erdiaw-Kwasie. "Can COVID-19 Inspire a New Way of Planning African Cities?" The Conversation, September 20, 2020. https://theconversation.com/can-covid-19-inspire-a-new-way-of-planning-african-cities-145933.

Cohen, Daniel Aldana. "The Rationed City: The Politics of Water, Housing, and Land Use in Drought-Parched São Paulo." *Public Culture* 28, no. 2 (2016): 261–289.

Cohen, John. "An Intriguing—but Far from Proven—HIV Cure in the 'São Paulo Patient.'" *ScienceMag*, July 7, 2020. https://www.sciencemag.org/news/2020/07/intriguing-far-proven-hiv-cure-s-o-paulo-patient.

Colburn, David R., and Jeffrey S. Adler, eds. *African-American Mayors: Race, Politics, and the American City*. Champaign: University of Illinois Press, 2005.

Connolly, N. D. B. *A World More Concrete: Real Estate and the Remaking of Jim Crow South Florida*. Chicago: University of Chicago Press, 2014.

Contel, Fabio Betioli. *The Financialization of the Brazilian Territory: From Global Forces to Local Dynamisms*. Cham, Switzerland: Springer, 2020.

Contel, Fabio Betioli, and Dariusz Wójcik. "Brazil's Financial Centers in the Twenty-First Century: Hierarchy, Specialization, and Concentration." *The Professional Geographer* 71, no. 4 (2019): 681–691.

Corrupt Practices Investigation Bureau (CPIB). "Singapore's Corruption Control Framework." June 2, 2020. https://www.cpib.gov.sg/about-corruption/prevention-and-corruption/singapores-corruption-control-framework/.

Cowan, Walter. *New Orleans Yesterday and Today: A Guide to the City*. Baton Rouge: Louisiana State University Press, 1983.

Coy, Martin. "Gated Communities and Urban Fragmentation in Latin America: The Brazilian Experience." *GeoJournal* 66 (2006): 121–132.

Coy, Martin, and Tobias Töpfer. "Inner-City Development in Megacities Between Degradation and Renewal: The Case of São Paulo." In *Megacities: Our Urban Global Future*, ed. F. Kraas, S. Aggarwal, M. Coy, and G. Mertins, 101–119. Dordrecht: Springer, 2014.

Croitoru, Lelia, Juan José Miranda, Abdellatif Khattabi, and Jia Jun Lee. "The Cost of Coastal Zone Degradation in Nigeria: Cross River, Delta and Lagos States." World Bank Group, October 2020.

Cunsolo, Ashlee, and Neville Ellis. "Ecological Grief as a Mental Health Response to Climate Change-Related Loss." *Nature Climate Change* 8 (2018): 275–281.

da Gama Torres, Haroldo. "Residential Segregation and Public Policies: São Paulo in the 1990's." *Revista Brasileria de Ciências Sociais* 2 (2006): 41–55.

Dano, Umar Lawal, Abdul-Lateef Balogun, Ismaila Rimi Abubakar, and Yusuf Adedoyin Aina. "Transformative Urban Governance: Confronting Urbanization Challenges with Geospatial Technologies in Lagos, Nigeria." *GeoJournal* 85, no. 4 (August 2020): 1039–1056.

Danseyar, Susan. "Jean Monestime Wants Details." *Miami Today*, May 11, 2017.

Davidson, Christopher. "Dubai: Foreclosure of a Dream." *Middle East Report* 251 (Summer 2009): 8–13.

Davidson, Christopher M. *Dubai: The Vulnerability of Success.* New York: Columbia University Press, 2008.

Davies, Larne. "Gentrification in Lagos: 1929–1990." *Urban History* 45, no. 4 (2018): 712–732.

Dawei Li, Jiacan Yuan, and Robert Kopp. "Escalating Global Exposure to Compound Heat -Humidity Extremes with Warming." *Environmental Research Letters* 15, no. 6 (2020).

Dayo, Bernard. "Netflix Is Launching in Nigeria, but Not Everyone Is Happy." *Vice*, December 28, 2020. https://www.vice.com/en/article/k7agzn/netflix-naija-launch-nigeria.

de Gramont, Diane. "Governing Lagos: Unlocking the Politics of Reform." Carnegie Endowment for International Peace, January 12, 2015, 15–23.

de Melo, José Roberto. "Superintendência Regional do Trabalho e Emprego em São Paulo." SRTE/SP 92, June 10, 2010. http://www.normaslegais.com.br/legislacao/portariasrtesp92 _2010.htm.

de Sousa Damiani, J. H. "The Innovation System of Sao Jose dos Campos: Main Institutions, Architecture, Contributions to Economic and Social Development, Perspectives and Future Challenges." Paper presented at Portland International Conference on Management of Engineering and Technology (PICMET), Portland, OR, 2018.

Dean, Warren. *The Planter as Entrepreneur: The Case of São Paulo.* Austin: Institute of Latin American Studies, University of Texas, 1966.

Deckrow, Andre Kobayashi. "São Paulo as Migrant-Colony: Pre-World War II Japanese State-Sponsored Agricultural Migration to Brazil." PhD diss., Columbia University, 2019.

Delgado-Wise, Raul. "Replanteando la cuestion del Desarrollo y su Relación Dialéctica con la Exportación de la Fuerza de Trabajo." Paper presented at the conference Immigration and Development at a Global Turning Point, University of Miami, October 22, 2020.

Department of Economic Development-Government of Dubai. "Dubai Economic Report 2019." 2019. https://ded.ae/page_report/en/report_2019.

Desmond, Matthew. *Evicted: Poverty and Profit in the American City.* New York: Crown, 2016.

DeWitt, Dennis. *History of the Dutch in Malaysia.* Petaling Jaya, Malaysia: Nutmeg, 2007.

Dews, Fred. "Charts of the Week: Africa's Changing Demographics." Brookings, January 18, 2019. https://www.brookings.edu/blog/brookings-now/2019/01/18/charts-of-the-week-africas -changing-demographics/.

Didion, Joan. *Miami.* New York: Simon and Schuster, 1987.

Dobb, Maurice. *Studies in the Development of Capitalism.* New York: International Publishers, 1963.

Dubai Statistics Center (DSC). "Dubai Population Are 3.3 Million by Q3-19." Dubai Statistics Center (DSC), November 6, 2019. https://www.dsc.gov.ae/en-us/DSC-News/Pages/Dubai -Population-Are-3.3-Million-by-Q3-19.aspx.

Duneier, Mitchell. *Sidewalk.* New York: Farrar, Strauss, and Giroux, 2000.

——. *Slim's Table: Race, Respectability, and Masculinity.* Chicago: University of Chicago Press, 1992.

Dunn, David. "Dubai's Audacious 'Heart of Europe' Megaproject Nears First Stage of Completion." *CNN Travel*, December 2, 2020.

Dupont, Véronique. "The Dream of Delhi as a Global City." *International Journal of Urban and Regional Research* 35, no. 3 (2011): 533–554.

Durán-Almarza, Emilia María, Ananya Jahanara Kabir, and Carla Rodríguez González, eds. *Debating the Afropolitan.* New York: Routledge, 2019.

Durdin, Peggy. "Lee Kuan Yew and Singapore: A Profile." *Asian Affairs* 1, no. 3 (1974): 151–169.

Earle, Lucy. *Transgressive Citizenship and the Struggle for Social Justice.* London: Palgrave Macmillan, 2017.

Economist, The. "Brave New Worlds: Abu Dhabi's Latest Museum Aims to Rewrite the Story of Modernism." *The Economist*, November 20, 2021, 81.

——. "Can Dubai Enter the Premier League of Financial Centers?" *The Economist*, August 22, 2020. https://www.economist.com/finance-and-economics/2020/08/22/can-dubai-enter-the-premier-league-of-financial-centres.

——. "Capital Cities: The Countries Dreaming of Becoming Africa's Singapore." *The Economist*, October 23, 2021, 47.

——. "A Dream Deferred." *The Economist*, June 5, 2021. https://www.economist.com/special-report/2021/06/05/a-dream-deferred.

——. "Housing for All (Singapore Survey)." *The Economist*, December 29, 1979.

——. "A Night at the Cathay." *The Economist*, July 4, 2020.

——. "Quick Study: Ricky Burdett on Changing Cities: Man Versus City." *The Economist*, September 30, 2014. https://www.economist.com/prospero/2014/09/30/man-v-city.

Edwards, Richard. *Contested Terrain: The Transformation of the Workplace in the Twentieth Century.* New York: Harper Torchbooks, 1979.

Ekanade, Olumide Victor. "The Dynamics of Forced Neoliberalism in Nigeria Since the 1980s." *Journal of Retracing Africa* 1, no.1 (2014): 1–24.

Ekundare, R. O. "Nigeria's Second National Development Plan as a Weapon of Social Change." *African Affairs* 70, no. 279 (1971): 146–158.

Elegant, Naomi Xu. "Hong Kong Passport Holders Used to Get Special Perks in the U.S. Not Anymore." *Fortune*, July 15, 2020.

Ellis, Neville, and Ashlee Cunsolo. "Hope and Mourning in the Anthropocene: Understanding Ecological Grief." The Conversation, April 4, 2018. https://theconversation.com/hope-and-mourning-in-the-anthropocene-understanding-ecological-grief-88630.

Elsheshtawy, Yasser. "Real Estate Speculation and Transnational Development in Dubai." In *The New Arab Urban: Gulf Cities of Wealth, Ambition, and Distress*, ed. H. Molotch and D. Ponzini, 235–255. New York: New York University Press, 2019.

——. "Redrawing Boundaries: Dubai, an Emerging Global City." In *Planning Middle Eastern Cities: An Urban Kaleidoscope in a Globalizing World*, ed. Yasser Elsheshtawy, 169–200. London: Routledge, 2011.

——. "Resituating the Dubai Spectacle." In *The Superlative City: Dubai and the Urban Condition in the Early Twenty-First Century*, ed. Ahmed Kanna, 104–121. Cambridge, MA: Harvard University Press, 2013.

Embassy of the UAE, Washington, DC. "How the UAE Became the Center for Art in the Middle East." *Smithsonian.com*, April 3, 2018. https://www.smithsonianmag.com/sponsored/uae-center-for-art-middle-east-180968375/.

Embraer. "About Us." Accessed June 28, 2021. https://embraer.com/global/en/about-us.

——. "Eve Announces Halo as Launch Partner in the Urban Air Mobility Market with an Order for 200 eVTOL Aircraft." June 1, 2021. https://embraer.com/global/en/news?slug=1206878-eve-announces-halo-as-launch-partner-in-the-urban-air-mobility-market-with-an-order-for-200-evtol-aircraft.

Engels, Friedrich. *The Condition of the Working Class in England*. Trans. W. O. Henderson and W. H. Chaloner. Stanford, CA: Stanford University Press, 1968.

Engler, John, Penny Pritzker, Edward Alden, and Laura Taylor-Kale. *The Work Ahead: Machines, Skills, and U.S. Leadership in the Twenty-First Century*. Independent Task Force Report No. 76. New York: Council on Foreign Affairs, 2018.

Environmental Protection Agency. "What Climate Change Means for Louisiana." August 2016. https://19january2017snapshot.epa.gov/sites/production/files/2016-09/documents/climate-change-la.pdf.

Evans, Peter. *Embedded Autonomy: States and Industrial Transformation*. Princeton, NJ: Princeton University Press, 1995.

"Expo 2020 Dubai Will Yield an AED 122 Billion Investment Windfall for the UAE." Expo 2020 Dubai, April 15, 2019. http://elementsglobe.com/expo-2020/expo-2020-dubai-will-yield-an-aed-122-billion-investment-windfall-for-the-uae/.

Ezema, I. C., O. J. Ediae, and E. N. Ekhaese. "Prospects, Barriers and Development Control Implications in the Use of Green Roofs in Lagos State, Nigeria." *Covenant Journal in Research and Built Environment* 4, no. 2 (2016): 54–70.

Faleiros, Gustavo. "How Science Supports São Paulo." *Nature* 563 (November 28, 2018): S179–S181. https://www.nature.com/articles/d41586-018-07536-1.

Falola, Toyin, and Matthew M. Heaton. *A History of Nigeria*. Cambridge: Cambridge University Press, 2008.

Fan, Jason. "PM Lee's 1st Big Speech to Singapore Featured Casinos, 5-Day Work Week & Slayed Other Sacred Cows." *Mothership*, August 12, 2019.

Fernandez-Kelly, Patricia. *The Hero's Fight: African-Americans in West Baltimore*. Princeton, NJ: Princeton University Press, 2017.

Fernandez-Kelly, Patricia, and Sara Curran. "Nicaraguans: Voices Lost, Voices Found." In *Ethnicities: Children of Immigrants in America*, ed. R. G. Rumbaut and Alejandro Portes, 127–155. New York: Russell Sage Foundation, 2001.

Findexable Limited and The Global Fintech Index. "The Global Fintech Index 2020." 2019. https://findexable.com/wp-content/uploads/2019/12/Findexable_Global-Fintech-Rankings-2020exSFA.pdf.

Finn, Kathy. "Oil Boom and Bust." *My New Orleans*, May 1, 2017. https://www.myneworleans.com/oil-boom-and-bust/.

Florida, Richard. *The Flight of the Creative Class*. New York: Collins, 2007.

——. *The Rise of the Creative Class: And How It's Transforming Work, Leisure, Community, and Everyday Life*. New York: Basic Books, 2002.

Fontes, Paulo, and Francisco Barbosa de Macedo. "Strikes and Pickets in Brazil: Working-Class Mobilization in the 'Old' and 'New' Unionism, the Strikes of 1957 and 1980." *International Labor and Working-Class History* 83 (2013): 86–111.

Fontes, Paulo, and Larissa R. Corrêa. "Labor and Dictatorship in Brazil: A Historiographical Review." *International Labor and Working-Class History* 93 (2018): 27–51.

Fossier, Albert A. *New Orleans: The Glamour Period, 1800–1840.* New Orleans, LA: Pelican, 1957.

Fourchard, Laurent. "Between World History and State Formation: New Perspectives on Africa's Cities." *Journal of African History* 52, no. 2 (July 2011): 223–248.

Francis, D., and A. Harris. "Introduction: Looking for Black Miami." *Anthurium: A Caribbean Studies Journal* 16, no. 1 (2020).

Frank, Robert. "Real-Estate Brokers Brace for 'Flood' of Wealthy Buyers from Overseas as Travel Restrictions Lift." *CNBC*, November 5, 2021. https://www.cnbc.com/2021/11/05/real -estate-brokers-brace-for-flood-of-wealthy-buyers-from-overseas-.html.

Frenk, Julio. Opening address to the External Advisory Council of the University of Miami Advanced Institute of the Americas, March 2019.

Fung, Chi Ming. *Reluctant Heroes: Rickshaw Pullers in Hong Kong and Canton, 1874–1954.* Hong Kong: Hong Kong University Press, 2005.

Garmany, Jeff, and Matthew Richmond. "Hygienisation, Gentrification, and Urban Displacement in Brazil." *Antipode* 52, no. 1 (2020): 124–144.

Geromel, Ricardo. "All You Need to Know About Sao Paulo, Brazil's Largest City." *Forbes*, June 12, 2013. https://www.forbes.com/sites/ricardogeromel/2013/07/12/all-you-need-to-know -about-sao-paulo-brazils-largest-city/?sh=7defcd6121ad.

Giuliani, Dario, and Sam Ajadi, "618 Active Tech Hubs: The Backbone of Africa's Tech Ecosystem." *GSMA Blog*, July 10, 2019. https://www.gsma.com/mobilefordevelopment/blog /618-active-tech-hubs-the-backbone-of-africas-tech-ecosystem/.

Global Slavery Index. "Global Slavery Index: Brazil." Global Slavery Index. Accessed February 23, 2021. https://www.globalslaveryindex.org/2018/findings/country-studies/brazil/.

Goddard, Charles. *City of Darkness: Life in Kowloon Walled City.* Chiddingfold, UK: Watermark, 2011.

Godfrey, Brian J. "Modernizing the Brazilian City." *Geographical Review* 81, no. 1 (1991): 18–34.

Goffman, Alice. *On the Run: Fugitive Life in an American City.* Chicago: University of Chicago Press, 2014.

Goldbaum, Christina. "South African Filmmakers Move Beyond Apartheid Stories." *New York Times*, May 10, 2021. https://www.nytimes.com/2021/05/10/world/africa/south-african-filmmakers -move-beyond-apartheid-stories.html.

Gondim de Oliveira, Roberta, Ana Paula da Cunha, Ana Giselle dos Santos Gadelha, Christiane Goulart Carpio, Rachel Barros de Oliveira, and Roseane Maria Corrêa. "Racial Inequalities and Death on the Horizon: COVID-19 and Structural Racism." *Cadernos de Saúde Pública* 36, no. 9 (2020): 1–14.

Goode, Erica. "Miami Police Department Is Accused of Pattern of Excessive Force." *New York Times*, July 9, 2013. https://www.nytimes.com/2013/07/10/us/miami-police-dept-is-accused -of-pattern-of-excessive-force.html.

Goodell, Jeff. *The Water Will Come: Rising Seas, Sinking Cities, and the Remaking of the Civilized World.* New York: Little, Brown, 2017.

Google Search. "New Orleans Economy." Accessed October 5, 2020.

Gough, Paul. "How Pittsburgh Is Finding Its Niche as a Life-Sciences Hub." *Pittsburgh Business Times*, December 16, 2020. https://www.bizjournals.com/pittsburgh/news/2020/12/16/pittsburgh-life-sciences-hub-liftoff-pgh.html.

Government of Hong Kong. "Coronavirus," Accessed November 2, 2021. https://www.coronavirus.gov.hk/eng/index.html.

Government of Hong Kong, Census and Statistics Department. "Labour Force: Table E033: Median Monthly Employment Earnings of Employed Persons by Educational Attainment." Accessed January 19, 2021. https://www.censtatd.gov.hk/hkstat/sub/sp200.jsp?productCode=D5250037.

Government of the United Arab Emirates. "Climate Change." 2021. https:/u.ae/en/information-and-services/environment-and-energy/climate-change/climate-change.

Govers, R. "Brand Dubai and Its Competitors in the Middle East: An Image and Reputation Analysis." *Place Branding and Public Diplomacy* 8 (2012): 48–57.

Graham, Stephen. *Cities Under Siege: The New Military Urbanism*. London: Verso, 2010.

——. *Vertical: The City from Satellites to Bunkers*. London: Verso, 2016.

——. "Vertical Noir: Histories of the Future in Urban Science Fiction." *City* 20, no. 3 (2016): 389–406.

Graham-Harrison, Emma, and Verna Yu. "Hong Kong Voters Deliver Landslide Victory for Pro-Democracy Campaigners." *The Guardian*, November 24, 2019.

Greer, Scott. *The Emerging City: Myth and Reality*. New York: Free Press, 1962.

Griggs, Mary Beth. "You Could Visit Dubai and Never Step Outside: The Proposed Mall of the World Features Temperature-Controlled Walkways." *Smithsonian.com*, July 8, 2014.

Guest, Peter. "The Impossible Fight to Save Jakarta, the Sinking Megacity." *Wired*, October 15, 2019. https://www.wired.co.uk/article/jakarta-sinking.

Günel, Gökçe. "The Infinity of Water: Climate Change Adaptation in the Arabian Peninsula." *Public Culture* 28, no. 2 (2016).

Guo, Limin, ed. *Zhonggong du Tai Zhengze Zhiliao Xuanji: 1949–1991*. Taipei: Lifework, 1992.

Guo, Rongxing. *Intercultural Economic Analysis: Theory and Method*. New York: Springer, 2009.

Habans, Robert, Jenna Losh, Rachel Weinstein, and Amy Tello. "Placing Prosperity: Neighborhoods and Life Expectancy in New Orleans Metro." The Data Center, Tulane University, August 13, 2020.

Hampton, Mark. *Hong Kong and British Culture, 1945–97*. Oxford: Oxford University Press, 2015.

Hamukoma, Nchimunya, Nicola Doyle, Sara Calburn, and Dickie Davis. "Lagos: Is it Possible to Fix Africa's Largest City?" The Brenthurst Foundation, Discussion Paper, March 2019, 1–23.

Hanieh, Adam. *Capitalism and Class in the Gulf Arab States*. New York: Palgrave MacMillan, 2011.

——. *Money, Markets, and Monarchies: The Gulf Cooperation Council and the Political Economy of the Contemporary Middle East*. Cambridge: Cambridge University Press, 2018.

Hanley, Anne. "Is It Who You Know? Entrepreneurs and Bankers in São Paulo, Brazil, at the Turn of the Twentieth Century." *Enterprise and Society* 5, no. 2 (2004): 187–255.

Hardoy, Jorge Enrique. "Two Thousand Years of Latin American Urbanization." In *Urbanization in Latin America: Approaches and Issues*, ed. J. E. Hardoy, 3–55. Garden City, NY: Anchor, 1975.

Harley, Flora. "Where's Best: The Knight Frank Global Cities Index." Knight Frank, March 3, 2020. https://www.knightfrank.com/wealthreport/article/2020-03-03-wheres-best-the-knight-frank-global-cities-index.

Harvey, David. *The Condition of Post-modernity*. Cambridge, MA.: Basil Blackwell, 1989.

Haskel, Jonathan, and Stian Westlake. *Capitalism Without Capital: The Rise of the Intangible Economy*. Princeton, NJ: Princeton University Press, 2018.

Hauer, Mathew E. "Migration Induced by Sea-Level Rise Could Reshape the US Population Landscape." *Nature Climate Change* 7 (2017): 321–325.

Heilbroner, Robert. *The Worldly Philosophers*. 7th ed. London: Penguin, 1999.

Hemingway, Ernest. *A Moveable Feast*. New York: Simon and Schuster, 1961.

Henderson, Joan. "Destination Development: Singapore and Dubai Compared." *Journal of Travel and Tourism* 20, no. 3–4 (2006): 33–45.

Heyman, Stephan. "Hurray for Nollywood." *New York Times*, October 22, 2014. https://www.nytimes.com/2014/10/23/arts/international/hurray-for-nollywood.html.

Hill, Richard Child, and June Woo Kim. "Global Cities and Developmental States: New York, Tokyo and Seoul." *Urban Studies* 37, no. 12 (November 2000): 2167–2195.

History SG. "1877: First Rubber Trees Are Planted in Singapore." Last updated August 1, 2019. http://eresources.nlb.gov.sg/history/events/a8ceea4c-1c8b-4c9a-885c-b85038b39e4c.

Ho, Kelly, and Tom Grundy. "Joshua Wong's Pro-Democracy Group Demosisto Disbands Hours After Hong Kong Security Law Passed." Hong Kong Free Press, June 30, 2020.

Ho, Li-Ching. "Global Multicultural Citizenship Education: A Singapore Experience." *Social Studies* 100, no. 6 (2009): 285–293.

Hoelzel, Fabienne, ed. *Urban Planning Processes in Lagos: Policies, Laws, Planning Instruments, Strategies and Actors of Urban Projects, Urban Development, and Urban Services in Africa's Largest City*. Abuja, Nigeria and Zürich, Switzerland: Heinrich Böll Stiftung Nigeria and Fabulous Urban, 2018. https://ng.boell.org/sites/default/files/160206_urban_planning_processes_digital_new.pdf.

Hong Kong Free Press. "Beijing Unanimously Passes National Security Law for Hong Kong as Chief Exec. Carrie Lam Evades Questions." June 30, 2020.

Hong Kong Government. *An Introduction to Hong Kong Bill of Rights Ordinance*. 1991. https://www.cmab.gov.hk/doc/en/documents/policy_responsibilities/the_rights_of_the_individuals/human/BORO-InductoryChapterandBooklet-Eng.pdf.

Hong Kong Heritage Museum Leisure and Cultural Services Department. *Xìtái shàngxià—xiānggǎng xìyuàn yǔ yuèjù*. Accessed January 19, 2021. https://www.heritagemuseum.gov.hk/documents/2199315/2199705/The_Majestic_Stage-C.pdf.

Hong Kong Monetary Authority. *Hong Kong's Financial System: Robust and Advancing*. June 2020. https://www2.deloitte.com/content/dam/Deloitte/cn/Documents/ined/deloitte-cn-ined-hk-financial-system-210106.pdf.

Hoornweg, Daniel, and Kevin Pope. "Population Predictions for the World's Largest Cities in the 21st Century." *Environment and Urbanization* 29, no. 1 (2016): 195–216.

——. "Socioeconomic Pathways and Regional Distribution of the World's 101 Largest Cities." Global Cities Institute Working Paper No. 4 (2014). https://shared.uoit.ca/shared/faculty-sites/sustainability-today/publications/population-predictions-of-the-101-largest-cities-in-the-21st-century.pdf.

Hopewell, John. "São Paulo Launches Production Incentive to Grab Post-COVID Shoots." *Variety*, May 18, 2020. https://variety.com/2020/film/spotlight/brazil-city-incentives-productions-1234607311/.

HSE University. "HSE Global Cities Innovation Index." HSE University, 2020. https://gcii.hse.ru/en/.

Huber, Leonard. *New Orleans Architecture*. New Orleans, LA: Pelican, 1975.

Huff, W. G. "The Developmental State, Government and Singapore's Economic Development Since 1960." *World Development* 23, no. 8 (1995): 1421–1438.

Hung, Lee Shiu. "The SARS Epidemic in Hong Kong: What Lessons Have We Learned?" *Journal of the Royal Society of Medicine* 96, no. 8 (2003): 374–378.

Hunter, Wendy, and Timothy Power. "Bolsonaro and Brazil's Illiberal Backlash." *Journal of Democracy* 30, no. 1 (2019): 68–82.

Hutcheon, Robin. *First Sea Lord: The Life and Work of Sir Y. K. Pao*. Hong Kong: Chinese University Press, 1990.

Hvidt, Martin. "The Dubai Model: An Outline of Key Development-Process Elements in Dubai." *International Journal of Middle East Studies* 41, no. 3 (August 2009): 397–418.

——. "Economic and Institutional Reforms in the Arab Gulf Countries." *Middle East Journal* 65, no. 1 (2011): 85–102.

IATA. "The Importance of Air Transport to Brazil." Accessed June 30, 2021. https://www.iata .org/contentassets/bc041f5b6b96476a80db109f220f8904/brazil-the-value-of-air-transport .pdf.

IBGE. "Índice de Gini da distribuição do rendimento domiciliar per capita, segundo as Grandes Regiões, as Unidades da Federação e os Municípios das Capitais." 2019. https://ftp.ibge.gov .br/Indicadores_Sociais/Sintese_de_Indicadores_Sociais/Sintese_de_Indicadores_Sociais _2020/indice_das_tabelas_sis2020.pdf.

Ibukun, Yinka, Sophie Mongalvy, and Antony Sguazzin. "Dream of a Lagos Champs-Élysées Banks on Nigerian Recovery." *Bloomberg*, May 29, 2018. https://www.bloomberg.com/news /articles/2018-05-29/eko-atlantic-city-eyes-2023-finish-as-nigeria-economy-rebounds.

IESE Business School. "IESE Cities in Motion Index 2020." IESE Business School, October 27, 2020. https://blog.iese.edu/cities-challenges-and-management/2020/10/27/iese-cities-in-motion -index-2020/.

Illes, Paulo, Gabrielle Louise Soares Timóteo, and Elaine da Silva Fiorucci. "Human Trafficking for Labour Exploitation in the City of São Paulo." *Cadernos Pagu* 31 (2008): 199–217.

IMD World Competitiveness Center. "Smart City Index 2019." October 2019. https://www .imd.org/research-knowledge/reports/imd-smart-city-index-2019/.

Institute for Urban Strategies. *Global Power City Index*. 2018. http://mori-m-foundation.or.jp /pdf/GPCI2018_summary.pdf.

International Finance Corporation. "Public-Private Partnership Stories, Brazil: São Paulo Roads." February 2019. https://www.ifc.org/wps/wcm/connect/6a30d7b8-99e0-4425-809d -6749b843ef56/PPP-Stories-Brazil-SP+Roads.pdf?MOD=AJPERES&CVID=mz3AneC.

InvestSP. "Technology Parks." 2021. https://www.en.investe.sp.gov.br/why-sao-paulo/innovation -science-and-technology/technology-parks//.

Jackson, Nancy Beth. "Miami Real Estate Market Embraces Brazilians." *New York Times*, December 29, 2011. https://www.nytimes.com/2011/12/30/greathomesanddestinations/30iht -remiami30.html.

Jervis, Rick. "Fifteen Years and $15 Billion Since Katrina, New Orleans Is More Prepared for a Major Hurricane—for Now." *USA Today*, August 24, 2020. https://www.usatoday.com /story/news/nation/2020/08/24/new-orleans-hurricane-protection-system-marco-laura /5624092002/.

Jones, Matthew. "Creating Malaysia: Singapore Security, the Borneo Territories, and the Contours of British Policy." *Journal of Imperial and Commonwealth History* 28, no. 2 (2000): 85–109.

Joseph, Damilola Mary. "An Exploration of Trustworthiness in the Nigerian Investment Field: Perspective of Financial Advisors and Investors." PhD diss., University of Portsmouth, UK, 2019. https://researchportal.port.ac.uk/portal/files/20507142/Suggested_Revisions_for _Dr_Sara_2.pdf.

Josephson, Matthew. *The Robber Barons.* New York: Harcourt Brace, 1934.

Juzwiak, Teressa. "Sao Paulo, Brazil, a Case Study from 'Migrant and Refugee Integration in Global Cities—The Role of Cities and Businesses.'" The Hague Process on Refugees and Migration, 2014.

Kanna, Ahmed. *Dubai: The City as Corporation.* Minneapolis: University of Minnesota Press, 2011.

——. "Introduction." In *The Superlative City: Dubai and the Urban Condition in the Early Twenty -First Century*, ed. Ahmed Kanna. Cambridge, MA: Harvard University Press, 2013.

——. "The Trajectories of Two 'Asian Tigers': The Imperial Roots of Capitalism in Dubai and Singapore." In *Rethinking Global Urbanism: Comparative Insights from Secondary Cities*, ed. Xiangming Chen and Ahmed Kanna, 35–52. New York: Routledge, 2012.

Kasinitz, Philip. Remarks on "The Global Edge: Miami in the Twenty-First Century." University of Miami Institute for Advanced Study of the Americas, Miami, FL, April 15, 2019.

Kearney. "Global Cities Report 2020." Accessed February 18, 2021. https://www.kearney.com /global-cities/2020.

Kelly, Jemima. "Maybe 'Bitcoin Bros' Aren't Really a Thing After All." *Financial Times*, June 8, 2021. https://www.ft.com/content/f18a0e38-ffc4-4e11-8b82-a6c22a27ea36.

Kendall, John S. *History of New Orleans.* Chicago: Lewis, 1922.

Kephart, Josiah L., Ione Avila-Palencia, Usama Bilal, Nelson Gouveia, Waleska T. Caiaffa, and Ana V. Diez Roux. "COVID-19, Ambient Air Pollution, and Environmental Health Inequities in Latin American Cities." *Journal of Urban Health* 98, no. 3 (January 20, 2021): 1–5.

Kerbel, Marcos, and Richard Westlund. *Leading the Way: A Comprehensive History of International Banking in South Florida.* Miami: Florida International Bankers' Association, 2004.

Kerr, Simeon, and Andrew England. "Dubai Contemplates a Downsized Future After the Pandemic." *Financial Times*, May 10, 2020. https://www.ft.com/content/5ff1cc05-64eb-4e1a -bf53-62c7e62d5a2c.

——. "Saudi Arabia Tries to Lure Multinationals from Dubai." *Financial Times*, January 10, 2021.

Keshavarzian, Arang. "From Port Cities to Cities with Ports: Toward a Multiscalar History of Persian Gulf Urbanism in the Twentieth Century." In *Gateways to the World: Port Cities in the Persian Gulf*, ed. Mehran Kamrava. Oxford: Oxford University Press, 2016.

——. "Geopolitics and the Genealogy of Free Trade Zones in the Persian Gulf." *Geopolitics* 15, no. 2 (May 2010): 263–289.

Keshavarzian, Arang, and Waleed Hazbun. "Re-Mapping Transnational Connections in the Middle East." *Geopolitics* 15, no. 2 (May 2010): 203–209.

Kester, Adebayo Akesanju. "Emerging 'New Cities' in Africa and Socio-Spatial Inequality: A Case Study of the Eko Atlantic City Project in Lagos, Nigeria." MA thesis, Urban and Regional Planning, University of Amsterdam, 2014.

Khalaf, Abdulhadi. "The Politics of Migration." In *Transit States: Labour, Migration and Citizenship in the Gulf*, ed. Abdulhadi Khalaf, Omar AlShehabi, and Adam Hanieh, 39–56. London: Pluto, 2014.

Kleeman, C. George. "The Proposal to Implement Article 23 of the Basic Law in Hong Kong: A Missed Opportunity for Reconciliation and Reunification Between China and Taiwan." *Georgia Journal of International and Comparative Law* 23, no.3 (2005): 705–720.

Knight Foundation. "Evolving Arts Ecosystem: A Study of Miami." Knight Foundation Arts Division. December 2018. https://knightfoundation.org/reports/evolving-arts-ecosystems -a-study-of-miami/.

Knight Frank. *Branded Residences Report, 2019*. 2019. https://www.knightfrank.com/research /report-library/global-branded-residences-2019-5874.aspx.

——. *Prime Global Cities Index*. 2019. https://www.knightfrank.com/research/report-library /prime-global-cities-index-q1-2021-8017.aspx.

Koh, William, Richard M. Steers, and James R. Terborg. "The Effects of Transformational Leadership on Teacher Attitudes and Student Performance in Singapore." *Journal of Organizational Behavior* 16 (1995): 319–333.

Kola-Oyeneyin, Topsy, Mayowa Kuyoro, and Tunde Olanreqaju. "Harnessing Nigeria's Fintech Potential." McKinsey & Company, September 23, 2020. https://www.mckinsey.com /featured-insights/middle-east-and-africa/harnessing-nigerias-fintech-potential.

Kolawole Ojo, Thomas. "Passenger Movements Development and Structure at Murtala Muhammed International Airport, Lagos." *Public Transport* 7 (2015): 223–234.

Kolkert, Elizabeth. "Louisiana's Disappearing Coast." *New Yorker*, March 25, 2019. https://www .newyorker.com/magazine/2019/04/01/louisianas-disappearing-coast.

Kotkin, Joel. "Size Is Not the Answer: The Changing Face of the Global City." Research Report, Civil Service College, Singapore, 2014.

Kowloon Walled City Park. "History/Background." Accessed January 19, 2021. https://web .archive.org/web/20100207014453/http://www.lcsd.gov.hk/parks/kwcp/en/.

Krane, Jim. *City of Gold: Dubai and the Dream of Capitalism*. New York: St. Martin's, 2009.

Krätke, Stefan. "'Global Media Cities': Major Nodes of Globalising Culture and Media Industries." In *The Globalizing Cities Reader*, 2nd ed., ed. Xuefei Ren and Roger Keil, 348–354. New York: Routledge, 2018.

Kumari Rigaud, Kanta, Alex de Sherbinin, Bryan Jones, Jonas Bergmann, Viviane Clement, Kayly Ober, Jacob Schewe, Susana Adamo, Brent McCusker, Silke Heuser, and Amelia Midgley. *Groundswell: Preparing for Internal Climate Migration*. Washington, DC: World Bank, 2018. http://hdl.handle.net/10986/29461.

Kuznesof, Elizabeth Anne. *Household Economy and Urban Development: São Paulo, 1765 to 1836*. Boulder, CO: Westview, 1986.

Labour Department, HKSAR Government. "WHAT'S NEW Minimum Allowable Wage and Food Allowance for Foreign Domestic Helpers to Increase." September 27, 2019.

Lagos State Government. *Lagos State Development Plan 2012–2015*. Accessed May 10, 2021. https:// dokumen.tips/documents/lagos-state-development-plan-2012-2025.html?page=1.

Lakritz, Talia. "These 11 Sinking Cities Could Disappear by 2100." World Economic Forum, September 10, 2019. https://www.weforum.org/agenda/2019/09/11-sinking-cities-that-could -soon-be-underwater/.

Lawanson, Taibat. "Lagos' Size and Slums Will Make Stopping the Spread of COVID-19 a Tough Task." The Conversation, April 1, 2020. http://theconversation.com/lagos-size-and -slums-will-make-stopping-the-spread-of-covid-19-a-tough-task-134723.

Lawrence, Sidra. "Afropolitan Detroit: Counterpublics, Sound, and the African City." *Africa Today* 65, no. 4 (Summer 2019): 19–37.

Lebergott, Stanley. *Manpower in Economic Growth: The American Record Since 1800.* New York: McGraw-Hill, 1964.

Lee, Tsao Yuan. *Growth Triangle: The Johor-Singapore-Riau Experience.* Singapore: Institute of Southeast Asian Studies and Institute of Policy Studies, 1991.

Lee-Partridge, J. E., T. S. H. Teo, and V. K. G. Lim, "Information Technology Management: The Case of the Port of Singapore Authority." *Journal of Strategic Information* Systems 9, no. 1 (2000): 85–99.

Leke, Acha, and Landry Signé. "Africa's Untapped Business Potential: Countries, Sectors, and Strategies: Spotlighting Opportunities for Business in Africa and Strategies to Succeed in the World's Next Big Growth Market." Washington, DC: Brookings, 2019.

León Contrera, X. I. "Projeto inovador: Comitê Paulista para Imigrantes e Refugiados foi lançado." *Jornal da CMDH—Informativo Bimestral da Comissão Municipal de Direitos Humanos* (January 2008).

Lepoer, Barbara Leitch. *Singapore: A Country Study.* Washington, DC: Government Printing Office, 1989.

Lesser, Jeffrey. "Immigration and Shifting Concepts of National Identity in Brazil During the Vargas Era." *Luso-Brazilian Review* 31, no. 2 (1994): 23–44.

Lethbridge, Henry J. *Hong Kong, Stability, and Change: A Collection of Essays.* Hong Kong: Oxford University Press, 1978.

Leyden, John. *Malay Annals.* London: Longman, Hurst, Rees, Orme and Brown, 1821.

Li, Jing. *"I Am NOT Leaving Home": Post-80s' Housing Attitudes and Aspirations in Hong Kong.* CityU on Cities Working Paper Series, WP No.2/2014. Urban Research Group. http://www.cityu .edu.hk/cityuoncities/upload/file/original/705520140620145010.pdf.

Lim, Jason. "The Dynamics of Trans-Regional Business and National Politics: The Impact of Events in China on Fujian-Singapore Tea Trading Networks, 1920–1960." In *Singapore in Global History*, ed. Derek Heng and Syed Muhd Khairudin Aljunied, 135–150. Amsterdam: Amsterdam University Press, 2009.

Limongi, Fernando, and Laura Mesquita. "Estratégia Partidária e Clivagens Eleitorais: As Eleições Municipais pós redemocratização." In *São Paulo: Novos Percursos e Atores*, ed. Lúcio Kowarick and Eduardo Marques. São Paulo: Editora 34, 2011.

Lindsey, Rebecca. "Climate Change: Global Sea Level." NOAA, Climate.gov., January 25, 2021. https://www.climate.gov/news-features/understanding-climate/climate-change-global -sea-level.

Liu, Amy, and Allison Plyer. *The New Orleans Index at Five: Measuring Greater New Orleans' Progress Toward Prosperity.* New Orleans, LA: Brookings Metropolitan Policy Program and Greater New Orleans Community Data Center, 2010.

Livni, Ephrat. "The Mayor of Miami Is Trying to Rebrand the City as a Crypto Hub." *New York Times*, March 23, 2021. https://www.nytimes.com/2021/03/23/business/the-mayor-of-miami -is-trying-to-rebrand-the-city-as-a-crypto-hub.html.

Logan, John R., and Harvey Molotch. *Urban Fortunes: The Political Economy of Place*. Berkeley: University of California Press, 1987.

Lu, Denise, and Christopher Flavelle. "Rising Seas Will Erase More Cities by 2050, New Research Shows." *New York Times*, October 29, 2019. https://www.nytimes.com/interactive/2019/10/29/climate/coastal-cities-underwater.html?smid=nytcore-ios-share.

Lukacs, Martin. "New, Privatized African City Heralds Climate Apartheid." *The Guardian*, January 21, 2014. https://www.theguardian.com/environment/true-north/2014/jan/21/new-privatized-african-city-heralds-climate-apartheid.

Luna, Francisco Vidal, and Herbert S. Klein. *An Economic and Demographic History of São Paulo, 1850–1950*. Stanford, CA: Stanford University Press, 2018.

——. "Slave Economy and Society in Minas Gerais and São Paulo, Brazil in 1830." *Journal of Latin American Studies* 36, no. 1 (February 2004): 1–28.

Lunden, Ingrid. "Language Learning App Duolingo Confirms It Has Raised $35M on a $2.4B Valuation." TechCrunch, November 18, 2020. https://techcrunch.com/2020/11/18/language-learning-app-duolingo-confirms-it-has-raised-35m-on-a-2-4b-valuation/.

Lustgarten, Abrahm. "How Climate Migration Will Reshape America." *New York Times Magazine*, September 15, 2020. https://www.nytimes.com/interactive/2020/09/15/magazine/climate-crisis-migration-america.html.

Macedo, Carlos G., Marcelo Cintra, Steven Goncalves, and Nelson Catala. *Fintech's Brazil Moment*. Goldman Sachs, May 12, 2017. https://www.gspublishing.com/content/research/en/reports/2017/05/12/f21e671e-dad0-4ef4-ba07-d694211b0c94.pdf.

Macrotrends. "Lagos, Nigeria Metro Area Population 1950–2021." Accessed April 22, 2021. https://www.macrotrends.net/cities/22007/lagos/population.

Maio, Alyssa. "What Is Nollywood and How Did It Become the 2nd Largest Film Industry?" StudioBinder. Accessed April 19, 2021. https://www.studiobinder.com/blog/what-is-nollywood/.

Makinde, Olusola Oladapo. "Typological Analysis of Gated Communities Characteristics in Ibadan, Nigeria." IntechOpen, October 5, 2020. https://www.intechopen.com/online-first/76444.

Mallach, Alan. *The Divided City: Poverty and Prosperity in Urban America*. Washington, DC: Island Press, 2018.

Mann, Kristin. *Slavery and the Birth of an African City: Lagos 1760–1900*. Bloomington: Indiana University Press, 2007.

Mann, Richard. "São Paulo Governor Plans R$18 Billion Infrastructure Investments by 2022." *Rio Times*, February 15, 2021. https://riotimesonline.com/brazil-news/sao-paulo/politics-sao-paulo/brazils-sao-paulo-governor-plans-r18-billion-investments-by-2022/.

Marchal, Roland. "Dubai: Global City and Transnational Hub." In *Transnational Connections and the Arab Gulf*, ed. Madawi Al-Rasheed, 93–110. London: Routledge, 2005.

Marcuse, Peter, and Ronald van Kempen, eds. *Globalizing Cities: A New Spatial Order?* Malden, MA: Blackwell, 2000.

——. *Of States and Cities: The Partitioning of Urban Space*. Oxford: Oxford University Press, 2002.

Markoff, John, and Silvio R. Duncan Baretta. "Economic Crisis and Regime Change in Brazil: The 1960s and the 1980s." *Comparative Politics* 22, no. 4 (1990): 421–444.

Marler, Scott P. *The Merchants' Capital: New Orleans and the Political Economy of the Nineteenth-Century South*. New York: Cambridge University Press, 2013.

Marques, Eduardo. "Governing a Large Metropolis: São Paulo—Urban Policies and Segregation in a Highly Unequal Metropolis." Conference paper, Second ISA Forum of Sociology. Buenos Aires, Argentina, August 1–4, 2012.

Marques Di Giulio, Gabriela, Ana Maria Barbieri Bedran-Martins, Maria da Penha Vasconcellos, Wagner Costa Ribeiro, and Maria Carmen Lemos. "Mainstreaming Climate Adaptation in the Megacity of São Paulo, Brazil." *Cities* 72, Part B (2018): 237–244.

Martinez, Brandon, and Alejandro Portes. "Latin American Cities: Their Evolution Under Neoliberalism and Beyond." *Sociology of Development* 7, no. 1 (2021): 25–51.

Marx, Karl. *Capital.* Moscow: Foreign Languages Publishing House, 1959.

——. *The Eighteenth Brumaire of Louis Bonaparte.* New York: International Publishers, 1963.

Marx, Karl, and Friedrich Engels. *The Communist Manifesto.* New York: Penguin, 1967.

Massey, Douglas S. *Categorically Unequal: The American Stratification System.* New York: Russell Sage Foundation, 2007.

Massey, Douglas S., and Nancy Denton. *American Apartheid: Segregation and the Making of the Underclass.* Cambridge, MA: Harvard University Press, 1993.

Mauzy, Diane K., and R. S. Milne. *Singapore Politics Under the People's Action Party.* London: Routledge, 2002.

Mazzei, Patricia. "A 20-Foot Sea Wall? Miami Faces the Hard Choices of Climate Change." *New York Times,* June 2, 2021. https://www.nytimes.com/2021/06/02/us/miami-fl-seawall -hurricanes.html?referringSource=articleShare.

Mbembe, Achille, and Laurent Chauvet. "Afropolitanism." *Nka: Journal of Contemporary African Art* 46 (2020): 56–61.

McAuley, Anthony. "Amazon Is Expanding in New Orleans with Its 'Last Mile' Delivery Partners." Nola.com, August 10, 2020.

McCann, Eugene, and Kevin Ward. "Relationality/Territoriality: Toward a Conceptualization of Cities in the World." *Geoforum* 41, no. 2 (March 2010): 175–184.

McDonnell, Tim. "Louisiana's Population Is Already Moving to Escape Climate Catastrophe." *Quartz,* September 1, 2020. https://qz.com/1895269/louisianas-population-is-moving-to -escape-climate-catastrophe/.

McKinsey Global Institute. "Building Globally Competitive Cities: The Key to Latin American Growth." August 1, 2011. https://www.mckinsey.com/featured-insights/urbanization /building-competitive-cities-key-to-latin-american-growth.

Metaxas, Theodore, Eleni Bouka, and Maria-Marina Merkouri. "Bollywood, India and Economic Growth: A Hundred Year History." *Journal of Economic and Social Thought* 3, no. 2 (2016): 285–301.

Meyer, David R. *Hong Kong as a Global Metropolis.* Cambridge: Cambridge University Press, 2009.

Meyers, Richard. *Great Martial Arts Movies: From Bruce Lee to Jackie Chan—and More.* New York: Citadel, 2001.

Miami Today. "Flying Goldmine." *Miami Today,* April 20, 2017.

Miami Today. "Port Asian Service Volume Rises, 11 Percent." *Miami Today,* April 20, 2017. Miami-Dade Aviation Department. *Miami International Airport Cargo Hub.* 2014. https:// www.miami-airport.com/home-cargo.asp.

Miami-Dade County. *Comprehensive Financial Annual Report, 2019.* https://www.miamidade.gov /finance/library/CAFR2019-complete.pdf.

Miami-Dade County Department of Planning. *General Statistical Data*. 2020. https://www
.miamidade.gov/finance/library/genstat03.pdf.

Miami-Dade Planning Metropolitan Organization. *Miami-Dade County Compendium of Transportation: Facts and Trends Report*. July 2014. http://miamidadetpo.org/library/studies/compendium
-of-transportation-facts-and-trends-report-2014-07.pdf.

Miksic, John N. *Singapore and the Silk Road of the Sea, 1300–1800*. Singapore: National University
of Singapore Press, 2013.

Mills, L. A. *Southeast Asia: Illusion and Reality in Politics and Economics*. Minneapolis: University
of Minnesota Press, 1964.

Molotch, Harvey, and Davide Ponzini. *The New Arab Urban: Gulf Cities of Wealth, Ambition, and
Distress*. New York: New York University Press, 2019.

Monteiro, John M. *Blacks of the Land: Indian Slavery, Settler Society, and the Portuguese Colonial
Enterprise in South America*. Ed. and trans. James Woodard and Barbara Weinstein. Cambridge:
Cambridge University Press, 2018.

Mooney, Chris, Andrew Freedman, and John Muyskens. "2020 Rivals Hottest Year on Record,
Pushing Earth Closer to a Critical Climate Threshold." *Washington Post*, January 14, 2021.
https://www.washingtonpost.com/climate-environment/interactive/2021/2020-tied-for
-hottest-year-on-record/.

Moreno, Carlos, Zaheer Allam, Didier Chabaud, Catherine Gall, and Florent Pratlong. "Introducing the '15-Minute City': Sustainability, Resilience and Place Identity in Future Post
Pandemic Cities." *Smart Cities* 4, no. 1 (2021): 93–111.

Mori Memorial Foundation. "Global Power City Index 2020." January 15, 2021. http://mori
-m-foundation.or.jp/english/ius2/gpci2/index.shtml.

Morse, Richard. "Trends and Issues in Latin American Urban Research." *Latin American Research
Review* 6 (Spring 1971): 3–52.

Moudio, Rebecca. "Nigeria's Film Industry: A Potential Gold Mine?" *Africa Renewal*, May 2013.
https://www.un.org/africarenewal/magazine/may-2013/nigeria%E2%80%99s-film-industry
-potential-gold-mine.

Mostra. "São Paulo International Film Festival." Accessed February 18, 2021, https://44.mostra.org/.

Muggah, Robert, and Ilona Szabó de Carvalho. "Violent Crime in São Paulo Has Dropped
Dramatically. Is This Why?" World Economic Forum, March 7, 2018. https://www.weforum
.org/agenda/2018/03/violent-crime-in-sao-paulo-has-dropped-dramatically-this-may
-be-why/.

Munshi, Neil. "Nigeria's Port Crisis: The $4,000 Charge to Carry Goods Across Lagos."
Financial Times, December 28, 2020. https://www.ft.com/content/a807f714-7542-4464-b359
-b9bb35bddab10.

National, The. "Dubai Moves to Attract World's Remote Workers with New Residency Programme." October 14, 2020. https://www.thenationalnews.com/uae/government/dubai-moves
-to-attract-world-s-remote-workers-with-new-residency-programme-1.1093699.

National Bureau of Statistics. "Nigerian Ports Statistics 2012–2017." March 2018. https://
nigerianstat.gov.ng/elibrary/read/735.

Nergal, Ory Mazar. *Encyclopedia of American Cities*. New York: Dutton, 1980.

Neumann, Tracy. *Remaking the Rust Belt: The Postindustrial Transformation of North America*. Philadelphia: University of Pennsylvania Press, 2016.

New Orleans Business Alliance. "Doing Business in New Orleans." https://www.neworleans.com/.

New Orleans Public Library. *Records*. 2005. https://louisianadigitallibrary.org/islandora/object/fpoc-p16313coll51%3A35429.

Newitz, Annalee. *Four Lost Cities: A Secret History of the Urban Age*. New York: Norton, 2021.

News.gov.hk. "Foreign Domestic Helper Levy in Effect from Oct." August 29, 2003.

Ng, Jun Sen. "New Ideas to Feed a Growing Island." *Straits Times*, February 4, 2018.

Ng, Pak Tee. "The Evolution and Nature of School Accountability in the Singaporean Educational System." *Educational Assessment, Evaluation, and Accountability* 22 (2010): 275–292.

Nguyen, Sam. "The Modern Image of Global City." Medium, June 23, 2017. https://medium.com/@sannguyen/the-modern-image-of-global-city-13b8eae96a49.

Nigeria Property Centre. "Average Price of Houses for Sale in Lagos." Accessed May 2021, https://nigeriapropertycentre.com/market-trends/average-prices/for-sale/houses/lagos.

Nijman, Jan. *Miami: Mistress of the Americas*. Philadelphia: University of Pennsylvania Press, 2010.

Njoh, Ambe J. "Urban Planning as a Tool of Power and Social Control in Colonial Africa." *Planning Perspectives* 24, no. 3 (June 16, 2009): 301–317.

Nogrady, Bianca. "The Benefits and Downsides of Building into the Sea." *BBC*, November 1, 2016. https://www.bbc.com/future/article/20161101-the-benefits-and-downsides-of-building-into-the-sea#.

NollywoodWeek. "What's Nollywood?" Accessed April 21, 2021. http://www.nollywoodweek.com/en/whats-nollywood/.

Nsehe, Mfonobong. "The Black Billionaires 2018." *Forbes*, March 7, 2018. https://www.forbes.com/sites/mfonobongnsehe/2018/03/07/the-black-billionaires-2018/.

Nyarko, Yaw. "The United Arab Emirates: Some Lessons in Economic Development." Working paper, World Institute for Economic Development, Helsinki, 2010.

Nystrom, Justin A. *New Orleans After the Civil War*. Baltimore, MD: Johns Hopkins University Press, 2010.

——. "The Vanished World of the New Orleans Longshoreman." *Southern Spaces*, March 5, 2014. https://southernspaces.org/2014/vanished-world-new-orleans-longshoreman/.

Obono, Oka. "A Lagos Thing: Rules and Realities in the Nigerian Megacity." *Georgetown Journal of International Affairs* 8, no. 2 (Summer/Fall 2007): 31–37.

Observatory of Economic Complexity. "São Paulo." Last modified March 2021. https://oec.world/en/profile/subnational_bra_state/sao-paulo.

Ojo, Folayan. "Nigeria's Export Performance: Trends, Problems, and Prospects." *Pakistan Economic and Social Review* 15, no. 3–4 (1977): 174–188.

Okoi, Obasesam. "The Paradox of Nigeria's Oil Dependency." Africa Portal. Accessed June 1, 2021. https://www.africaportal.org/features/paradox-nigerias-oil-dependency/.

Okome, Onookome. "Nollywood: Spectatorship, Audience and the Sites of Consumption." *Postcolonial Text* 3, no. 2 (2007): 1–21.

Olajide, Oluwafemi Ayodeji, Muyiwa Elijah Agunbiade, and Hakeem Babatunde Bishi. "The Realities of Lagos Urban Development Vision on Livelihoods of the Urban Poor." *Journal of Urban Management* 7, no. 1 (2018): 21–31.

Oleson, K. W., A. Monaghan, O. Wilhelmi, M. Barlage, N. Brunsell, J. Feddema, L. Hu, and D. F. Steinhoff. "Interactions Between Urbanization, Heat Stress, and Climate Change." *Climatic Change* 129, no. 3–4 (2015): 525–541.

Olson, James S., and Robert Shadle. *Historical Dictionary of the British Empire, K–Z*. Westport, CT: Greenwood, 1996.

Olson, Steve. *Increasing National Resilience to Hazards and Disasters: The Perspective from the Gulf Coast of Louisiana and Mississippi: Summary of a Workshop*. Washington, DC: National Academies Press, 2011.

Olukoju, Ayodeji. "The Port of Lagos, 1850–1929: The Rise of West Africa's Leading Seaport." In *Atlantic Ports and the First Globalisation, c. 1850–1930*, ed. M. S. Bosa, 112–129. London: Palgrave Macmillan, 2014.

Omeje, Kenneth. "The Rentier State: Oil-Related Legislation and Conflict in the Niger Delta, Nigeria." *Conflict, Security, and Development* 6, no. 2 (2006): 211–230.

Ong, Aihwa. "Worlding Cities, or the Art of Being Global." In *Worlding Cities: Asian Experiments and the Art of Being Global*, ed. Ananya Roy and Aihwa Ong, 1–26. West Sussex, UK: Wiley-Blackwell, 2011.

Onishi, Norimitsu. "Nigeria's Booming Film Industry Redefines African Life." *New York Times*, February 18, 2016. https://www.nytimes.com/2016/02/19/world/africa/with-a-boom-before -the-cameras-nigeria-redefines-african-life.html.

Onuoha, Mimi. "A 5-Mile Island Built to Save Lagos's Economy Has a Worrying Design Flaw." *Quartz Africa*, March 18, 2020. https://qz.com/africa/923142/the-flaw-in-the-construction -of-eko-atlantic-island-in-lagos/.

Oolasunkanmi, "Lagos to Establish Anti-Corruption Agency, as Sanwo-Olu Signs Bill Deepening Accountability in Governance." Lagos State Government, April 19, 2021. https:// lagosstate.gov.ng/blog/2021/04/19/lagos-to-establish-anti-corruption-agency-as-sanwo -olu-signs-bill-deepening-accountability-in-governance/.

Open Democracy. "Why Is the Brazilian Right Afraid of Paulo Freire?" Accessed June 3, 2021. https://www.opendemocracy.net/en/democraciaabierta/why-is-the-brazilian-right-afraid -of-paulo-freire/.

Osmond, Iroham Chukquemeka, Durodola Olufemi Daniel, Ayedum Caleb Abiodum, and Ogunbola Mayowa Fadeke. "Comparative Study of Rental Values of Two Gated Estates in Lekki Peninsula Lagos." *Journal of Sustainable Development Studies* 5, no. 2 (2014): 218–235.

Otani, Akane. "Elon Musk Has Become Bitcoin's Biggest Influencer, Like It or Not." *Wall Street Journal*, May 23, 2021. https://www.wsj.com/articles/elon-musk-has-become-bitcoins-biggest -influencer-like-it-or-not-11621762202.

Owen, K. A. "The Sydney 2000 Olympics and Urban Entrepreneurialism: Local Variations in Urban Governance." *Australian Geographical Studies* 40, no. 3 (2002): 323–336.

Oxford Economics. *Global Cities 2030*. December 2016. https://resources.oxfordeconomics.com /global-cities-2030.

Ozment, Steven E. *The Reformation in the Cities*. New Haven, CT: Yale University Press, 1975.

Pande, Pranjal. "Why Asia Is a Big Market for Embraer's E2 Series." *Simple Flying*, May 9, 2021. https://simpleflying.com/asia-embraer-e2-series/.

Pant, Harsh V., and Nandini Sarma. "India Cracks Down on Chinese Investment as Mood Turns Against Beijing." *Foreign Policy*, April 28, 2020.

Paris, Costas. "Singapore Looks to Tech to Bolster Its Role in Shipping." *Wall Street Journal*, April 8, 2021. https://www.wsj.com/articles/singapore-looks-to-tech-to-bolster-its-role-in -shipping-11617909788.

Parque Tecnológico. "Welcome to One of the Largest Innovation and Entrepreneurship Hubs in Brazil." Accessed June 28, 2021. https://pqtec.org.br/en/.

Partlow, Joshua, Darryl Fears, Jim Morrison, Jon Swaine, and Caroline Anders. "Before Condo Collapse, Rising Seas Long Pressured Miami Coastal Properties." *Washington Post*, June 25, 2021. https://www.washingtonpost.com/climate-environment/2021/06/25/rising-sea-levels-condo-collapse/.

Patten, Christopher. *Our Next Five Years: The Agenda for Hong Kong.* Hong Kong: Government Printer, 1992.

Perrotta-Bosch, Francesco. "Electric Avenue: Avenida Paulista as a Microcosm of Urban Brazil." *Architectural Review* (blog), October 21, 2019. https://www.architectural-review.com/essays/electric-avenue-avenida-paulista-as-a-microcosm-of-urban-brazil.

Phang, Sock-Yong. "Strategic Development of Airport and Rail Infrastructure: The Case of Singapore." *Transport Policy* 10 (2003): 27–33.

Piore, Michael. "Notes for a Theory of Labor Market Segmentation." In *Labor Market Segmentation*, ed. R. C. Edwards, M. Reich, and D. Gordon, 125–171. Lexington, MA: D. C. Heath, 1975.

Pirenne, Henri. *Medieval Cities: Their Origins and the Revival of Trade.* Princeton, NJ: Princeton University Press, 1969.

PittMed. "The White House at Our House." Fall 2016. https://www.pittmed.health.pitt.edu/story/white-house-our-house.

Planetizen. "Can a New Master Plan Fix What Ails São Paulo, Brazil?" February 16, 2016. https://www.planetizen.com/node/84067/can-new-master-plan-fix-what-ails-s%C3%A3o-paulo-brazil.

Portada. "Brazil Corner: How São Paulo Intends to Become a Center of Film Production." April 8, 2017. https://www.portada-online.com/latin-america/brazil-corner-how-sao-paulo-intends-to-become-a-center-of-film-production/.

Portero, Ashley. "Cryptocurrency Company Blockchain.com Chooses Brickell for US Headquarters." *South Florida Business Journal*, June 3, 2021. https://www.bizjournals.com/southflorida/news/2021/06/03/crypto-company-blockchaincom-chooses-brickell-for.html.

Portes, Alejandro. *Economic Sociology: A Systematic Inquiry.* Princeton, NJ: Princeton University Press, 2010.

——. "Migration and Underdevelopment." *Politics and Society* 8 (1978): 1–48.

——. "Neoliberalism and the Sociology of Development: Emerging Trends and Unanticipated Facts." *Population and Development Review* 23 (June 1997): 229–259.

Portes, Alejandro, and Ariel C. Armony. *The Global Edge: Miami in the Twenty-First Century.* Berkeley: University of California Press, 2018.

Portes, Alejandro, and William Haller. "The Informal Economy." In *The Handbook of Economic Sociology*, ed. Neil. J. Smelser and Richard Swedberg, 403–426. Princeton, NJ: Princeton University Press, 2010.

Portes, Alejandro, and Brandon Martinez. "Emerging Global Cities: Structural Similarities and Historical Differences." *Spanish Sociological Review* 28, no. 3 (2019): 9–21.

Portes, Alejandro, and Jean C. Nava, "Institutions and National Development: A Comparative Study." *Spanish Sociological Review* 26 (2017): 1–23.

Portes, Alejandro, and Bryan R. Roberts. "The Free-Market City: Latin American Urbanization in the Years of the Neoliberal Experiment." *Studies in Comparative and International Development* 40, no. 1 (Spring 2005): 43–82.

——. "La Urbanización en América Latina durante los Años del Experimento Neoliberal." In *Ciudades Latinoamericanas*, ed. Alejandro Portes, Bryan R. Roberts, and Alan Grimson, 19–74. Buenos Aires: Prometeo Editores, 2005.

Portes, Alejandro, and Ruben G. Rumbaut. *Immigrant America: A Portrait*. 4th ed. Berkeley: University of California Press, 2014.

Portes, Alejandro, and Lori D. Smith. *Institutions Count: Their Role and Significance in Latin American Development*. Berkeley: University of California Press, 2012.

Portes, Alejandro, and Alex Stepick. *City on the Edge: The Transformation of Miami*. Berkeley: University of California Press, 1993.

Portes, Alejandro, and John Walton. *Labor, Class, and the International System*. New York: Academic Press, 1981.

——. *Urban Latin America: The Political Condition from Above and Below*. Austin: University of Texas Press, 1976.

Porto de Santos. "Santos Port Authority Statistics." Accessed February 18, 2021. http://www .portodesantos.com.br/informacoes-operacionais/estatisticas/relatorio-de-analise-do -movimento-fisico/.

Prebisch, Raúl. "A Critique of Peripheral Capitalism." *CEPAL Review* 1 (1976): 9–76.

——. "Notes on Trade from the Standpoint of the Periphery." *CEPAL Review* 28 (1986): 203–216.

Preen, Mark. "China's City Clusters: The Plan to Develop 19 Super-Regions." *China Briefing News*, August 14, 2018. https://www.china-briefing.com/news/chinas-city-clusters-plan-to -transform-into-19-super-regions/.

Puff, Jefferson. "Racismo contra imigrantes no Brasil é constante, diz pesquisador." *BBC*, August 26, 2015. https://www.bbc.com/portuguese/noticias/2015/08/150819_racismo_imigrantes _jp_rm.

Quah, Jon S. T. "Why Singapore Works: Five Secrets of Singapore's Success." *Public Administration and Policy* 21, no. 1 (2018): 5–21.

Quijano, Anibal. "La Colonialidad del Poder y la Experiencia Latinoamericana." In *Pueblo, Época y Desarrollo*, ed. R. Briceño-Leon and H. R. Sonntag, 27–38. Caracas: Nueva Sociedad, 1998.

Rabin, Charles. "Art Acevedo Sworn in as Miami Police Chief." *Miami Herald*, April 29, 2021.

Ramli, David, and Lulu Chen. "The Super Rich Are Choosing Singapore as the World's Safest Haven." *Bloomberg*, May 26, 2021.

Ramos, Stephen J. *The Blueprint: A History of Dubai's Spatial Development Through Oil Discovery*. The Dubai Initiative working paper, Harvard Kennedy School, 2010.

Ramos, Stephen, and Peter G. Rowe. "Planning, Prototyping, and Replication in Dubai." In *The Superlative City: Dubai and the Urban Condition in the Early Twenty-First Century*, ed. Ahmed Kanna, 18–33. Cambridge, MA: Harvard University Press, 2013.

Ray, Talton. *The Politics of the Barrios of Venezuela*. Berkeley: University of California Press, 1969.

Redford, Polly. *Billion Dollar Sandbar: A Biography of Miami Beach*. New York: E. P. Dutton, 1970.

Reinders, Robert, and John Duffy. *End of an Era: New Orleans, 1850–1860*. New Orleans, LA: Pelican, 1964.

Ren, Xuefei. "Global City Building in China and Its Discontents." In *The Globalizing Cities Reader*, 2nd ed., ed. Xuefei Ren and Roger Keil. New York: Routledge, 2018.

——. *Urban China*. Cambridge: Polity, 2013.

Ren, Xuefei, and Roger Keil, eds. *The Globalizing Cities Reader*. 2nd ed. New York: Routledge, 2018.

——. "Introduction to Part One." In *The Globalizing Cities Reader*, 2nd ed., ed. Xuefei Ren and Roger Keil, 3–6. New York: Routledge, 2018.

Rest of World. "Beyond Silicon Valley: The Six Cities Building the Future of the Global Tech Industry." July 16, 2021. https://restofworld.org/2021/beyond-silicon-valley/.

Reuters. "Britain Confirms Details of Visa Offer for Some Hong Kong Citizens." October 22, 2020.

Reynolds, Rory, Nick Webster, and Anam Rizvi. "UAE to Expand 10-Year Golden Visa System to All Doctors, PhD Holders and Highly Skilled Workers." *The National*, November 17, 2020.

Ribeiro Sobral, Helena. "Heat Island in São Paulo, Brazil: Effects on Health." *Critical Public Health* 15, no. 2 (2005): 147–156.

Rieff, David. *Going to Miami: Exiles, Tourists, and Refugees in the New America*. Boston: Little, Brown, 1987.

Roberts, Bryan. *Cities of Peasants: The Political Economy of Urbanization in the Third World*. London: Edward Arnold, 1978.

Roberts, Rebecca Enobong. "Displaced and Isolated: The Realities of Covid19 for Internally Displaced People in Lagos, Nigeria." Internal Displacement Monitoring Centre (IDMC), April 2020. https://www.internal-displacement.org/expert-opinion/displaced-and-isolated -the-realities-of-covid19-for-internally-displaced-people-in.

Robertson, Linda. "The Battle for Wynwood." *Miami Herald*, March 9, 2020.

Robinson, Caleb, Bistra Dilkina, and Juan Moreno-Cruz. "Modeling Migration Patterns in the USA Under Sea Level Rise." *PLoS ONE* 15, no. 1 (2020). https://journals.plos.org/plosone/article ?id=10.1371/journal.pone.0227436.

Robinson, Jennifer. "Global and World Cities: A View from Off the Map." *International Journal of Urban and Regional Research* 26, no. 3 (September 2002): 531–554.

——. "New Geographies of Theorizing the Urban: Putting Comparison to Work for Global Urban Studies." In *The Globalizing Cities Reader*, 2nd ed., ed. Xuefei Ren and Roger Keil, 453–458. New York: Routledge, 2018.

Robinson, William. *Promoting Polyarchy: Globalization, U.S. Intervention, and Hegemony*. Cambridge: Cambridge University Press, 1996.

Rocco, Roberto. "Towards a Polycentric Metropolis: Global Strategies and Unequal Development in São Paulo." *Urbani Izziv* 17, no. 2 (2006): 193–198.

Rodan, Garry. "Singapore Exceptionalism: Authoritarian Rule and State Transformation." In *Political Transitions in Dominant Party Systems: Learning to Lose*, ed. J. Wong and E. Friedman, 231–251. New York: Routledge, 2008.

Rodriguez, Margarita. "Navigating Uneven Development: The Dynamics of Fractured Transnationalism." In *The State and the Grassroots*, ed. Alejandro Portes and Patricia Fernandez-Kelly, 139–159. Oxford: Berghahn, 2015.

Romero, Simon. "Immigrants Stir New Life into São Paulo's Gritty Old Center." *New York Times*, April 14, 2014. https://www.nytimes.com/2014/04/15/world/americas/immigrants-stir -new-life-into-sao-paulos-gritty-old-center.html.

Rosenblum, Gerald. *Immigrant Workers: Their Impact on American Labor Radicalism*. New York: Basic Books, 1973.

Rossetti de Toledo, Carolina. "Population Flows in São Paulo." *Pesquisa FAPESP* 215 (2014).

Rotinwa, Ayodeji. "Lagos: The Taxman Cometh." *The Africa Report*, July 2, 2018. https://www.theafricareport.com/600/lagos-the-taxman-cometh/.

RTHK. "Joshua Wong's Party Named 'Demosisto.'" April 6, 2016.

Ruhling, Nancy. "Banana Island in Lagos Is a Billionaire's Paradise." *Mansion Global*, February 2, 2019. https://www.mansionglobal.com/articles/banana-island-in-lagos-is-a-billionaire-s-paradise-120592.

Sachs, Ignacy, Jorge Wilheim, Paulo Sergio Pinheiro, Robert N. Anderson, and Jerry Davila. *Brazil: A Century of Change.* Chapel Hill: University of North Carolina Press, 2009.

Saldiva, Paulo Hilario Nascimento. "Opening Roundtable: Applying Research to Address Community Health Disparities and Wellness." Paper presented at Place-Based Conference: The Role of Universities in Sustainable, Just and Inclusive Cities, Pittsburgh, PA, January 21–22, 2021.

Sammonds, Charlie. "Lagos: The Heart of Africa's Tech Scene." Medium, March 27, 2019. https://medium.com/primalbase/lagos-a-cluster-of-booming-tech-hubs-3e633058ad4c.

Sampson, Robert. *Great American City: Chicago and the Enduring Neighborhood Effect.* Chicago: University of Chicago Press, 2013.

Santos, Milton. "São Paulo: Metrópole Internacional do Terceiro Mundo." *Revista Do Departamento De Geografia* 7 (2011): 7–24.

Sassen, Saskia. *The Global City: New York, London, Tokyo.* Princeton, NJ: Princeton University Press, 1991.

Schaedel, Richard, Jorge E. Hardoy, and Nora Scott-Kinzer. "Two Thousand Years of Latin American Urbanization." In *Urbanization in the Americas from Its Beginning to the Present,* ed. Richard Schaedel, Jorge E. Hardoy, and Nora Scott-Kinzer, 1–24. Berlin: De Gruyter Mouton, 2011.

Schipani, Andres. "Nubank Shakes Up Brazil's Banking Bureaucracy." *Financial Times*, March 30, 2020. https://www.ft.com/content/c0014ce4-6273-11ea-abcc-910c5b38d9ed.

Schmidt, Benicio Viero. "Modernization and Urban Planning in 19th-Century Brazil." *Current Anthropology* 23, no. 3 (1982): 255–262.

School of Cities. "School of Cities 2019–2020 Annual Report Release." School of Cities, October 13, 2020. https://www.schoolofcities.utoronto.ca/news/SofC-2019-2020-Annual-Report-released.

Schuermans, Nick. "J. Robinson, Ordinary Cities: Between Modernity and Development." Review of *Ordinary Cities: Between Modernity and Development,* by Jennifer Robinson. *Belgeo: Revue Belge de Géographie*, March 31, 2009.

Sesay, Amadu, and Charles Ugochukwu Ukeje. "The Military, the West, and Nigerian Politics in the 1990s." *International Journal of Politics, Culture, and Society* 11, no. 1 (1997): 25–48.

Sha, Kongliao. *Xianggang lunxian riji.* Beijing: Sanlian shudian, 1988.

Sharma, Ruchir. *The Rise and Fall of Nations: Forces of Change in the Post-Crisis World.* New York: Norton, 2016.

Shu, Catherine. "Singapore Is Poised to Become Asia's Silicon Valley." TechCrunch, December 14, 2020. https://techcrunch.com/2020/12/14/singapore-is-poised-to-become-asias-silicon-valley/.

Siegel, Martin. *New Orleans: A Chronological and Documentary History, 1539–1970.* Dobbs Ferry, NY: Oceana, 1975.

Sierra, Gabriella. *The Future Is African* (podcast). Council on Foreign Relations, December 11, 2020, 33:09. https://www.cfr.org/podcasts/future-african#:~:text=Projections%20show%20that%20by%202050,young%20people%20in%20the%20world.

Simmel, Georg. "The Metropolis and Mental Life." In *The Sociology of Georg Simmel*, ed. Kurt H. Wolff, 409–424. New York: Free Press, 1962.

Sims, Shannon. "How One of Brazil's Largest Favelas Confronts Coronavirus." *Bloomberg*, May 3, 2020. https://www.bloomberg.com/news/features/2020-05-03/how-one-of-brazil-s-largest-favelas-confronts-coronavirus.

Singapore Department of Statistics. "Population and Population Structure." Retrieved on November 1, 2021. https://www.singstat.gov.sg/find-data/search-by-theme/population/population-and-population-structure/latest-data.

Singh, Prahalad. "Delhi Master Plan 2021: Introduction, Analysis, Vision, Major Highlights, and Amendments." CommonFloor, April 26, 2020. https://www.commonfloor.com/guide/dda-master-plan-for-delhi-2021-56810.

Skidmore, Thomas E. *Brazil: Five Centuries of Change*. 2nd ed. Oxford: Oxford University Press, 2010.

Skyscraper Center. "São Paulo." Accessed February 15, 2021. https://www.skyscrapercenter.com/city/sao-paulo.

Smith, Richard G. "The Ordinary City Trap." *Environment and Planning* A, no. 45 (2013): 2290–2304.

——. "The Ordinary City Trap Snaps Back." *Environment and Planning* A, no. 45 (2013): 2318–2322.

So, Alvin Y. "Hong Kong After 1997: The Rise of the Anti-Mainland Movement." *Taiwan Insight*, March 20, 2018.

Sobral, Helena Ribeiro. "Heat Island in São Paulo, Brazil: Effects on Health." *Critical Public Health* 15, no. 2 (2005): 147–156.

SPCINE. "São Paulo Film Commission." Accessed February 18, 2021. http://spcine.com.br/spfilmcommission/

Spice, Byron. "CMU's Zoë Rover Shows Robots Can Find Subterranean Organisms." *Carnegie Mellon University News*, February 28, 2019. https://www.cmu.edu/news/stories/archives/2019/february/rover-finds-subterranean-organisms.html.

States at Risk. "Louisiana." 2021. https://statesatrisk.org/louisiana.

Stepick, Alex. "The Refugees Nobody Wants: Haitians in Miami." In *Miami Now! Immigration, Ethnicity, and Social Change*, ed. Alex Stepick and Guillermo Grenier, 58–82. Gainesville: University of Florida Press, 1992.

Stevenson, Alexandra. "Business Embraces Hong Kong's Security Law. The Money Helps," *New York Times*, June 30, 2020.

Straits Times. "PM Lee Talks About Casinos, Population, Family, in Part 2 of Chinese TV Interview." November 30, 2014.

Stuart, John A., and John F. Stack. *The New Deal in South Florida: Design, Policy, and Community Building, 1933–1940*. Gainesville: University of Florida Press, 2008.

Sun, Haichao. "Did Hong Kong Ever Have Democracy Under British Colonial Rule?" *Beijing Daily*, July 10, 2019. https://theory.gmw.cn/2019-07/10/content_32987595.htm.

Sung, Yun-wing. *The China-Hong Kong Connection: The Key to China's Open Door Policy*. Cambridge: Cambridge University Press, 2011.

Sunkel, Osvaldo. "The Unbearable Lightness of Neoliberalism." In *Rethinking Development in Latin America*, ed. C. Wood and Bryan Roberts, 55–78. University Park: Pennsylvania State University Press, 2005.

Surane, Jenny, and Mary Biekert. "Wall Street's China Dreams Get Jolt from U.S. Hong Kong Warning." *Yahoo Finance*, July 16, 2021.

Suttles, Gerald. *The Social Order of the Slum: Ethnicity and Territory in the Inner City*. Chicago: University of Chicago Press, 1968.

Swanston, James. "Is Dubai Facing Another Debt Crisis?" *Capital Economics*, April 20, 2020. https://www.capitaleconomics.com/publications/middle-east-north-africa-economics/middle-east-economics-focus/is-dubai-facing-another-debt-crisis/.

Swee-Hock, Saw. "Population Trends in Singapore, 1819–1967." *Journal of Southeast Asian History* 10, no. 1 (1969): 36–49.

Szmigiera, M. "Ranking of the 20 Countries with Most Patent Grants." Statista. Accessed July 2, 2021. https://www.statista.com/statistics/257152/ranking-of-the-20-countries-with-the-most-patent-grants/.

Tan, Eugene Kheng-Boon. "Law and Values in Governance: The Singapore Way." *Hong Kong Law Journal* 30 (2005): 91–102.

Tang, Vivian, and Tiffany May. "As Hong Kong Opposition Quits Council, Pro-Beijing Forces Reign." *New York Times*, November 12, 2020.

Taylor, Joe Gray. *Louisiana Reconstructed 1863–77*. Baton Rouge: Louisiana State University Press, 1974.

Tham, Yuen-C. "Good Governance Eroding, Says Tan Cheng Bock." *Straits Times*, July 27, 2019.

Thomas, Brinley. *Migration and Economic Growth*. 2nd ed. Cambridge: Cambridge University Press, 1973.

Tilly, Charles. *The Contentious French: Four Centuries of Popular Struggle*. Cambridge, MA: Harvard University Press, 1986.

——. *Durable Inequality*. Berkeley: University of California Press, 1998.

Töpfer, Tobias. "São Paulo: Big, Bigger, Global? The Development of a Megacity in the Global South." In *Globalization and the City: Two Connected Phenomena in Past and Present*, ed. Andreas Exenberger, Philipp Strobl, Günter Bischof, and James Mokhiber, 163–178. Innsbruck, Austria: Innsbruck University Press, 2013.

Torres, Aurora, Jodi Brandt, Kristen Lear, and Jianguo Liu. "A Looming Tragedy of the Sand Commons." *Science* 357, no. 6355 (2017): 970–971.

Torres, Carlos Alberto. "Paulo Freire as Secretary of Education in the Municipality of São Paulo." *Comparative Education Review* 38, no. 2 (1994): 181–214.

Trading Economics. "Hong Kong Capital Flows." Accessed November 2, 2021. https://tradingeconomics.com/hong-kong/capital-flows.

Transparency International. "Corruption Perceptions Index." 2021. https://www.transparency.org/en/cpi/2020/index/nga.

Troyjo, Marcos. "São Paulo Offers Blueprint for What Brazil Could Achieve." *Financial Times*, March 13, 2018. https://www.ft.com/content/5138c8e4-2127-11e8-8d6c-a1920d9e946f.

Truong, Alice. "How to Make Web 3.0 Reality." *Wall Street Journal*, December 7, 2010.

Tsang, Steve. *Hong Kong: An Appointment with China*. London: I. B.Tauris, 1997.

——. *A Modern History of Hong Kong*. London: Bloomsbury Academic, 2007.

Tsang, Susan, and Audrey Perera. *Singapore at Random*. Singapore: Didier Millet, 2011.

Turak, Natasha. "'Dramatic and Risky'—and a Shot at Dubai? Saudi Arabia Issues Bold Business Ultimatum to Pull Regional HQ Offices into the Kingdom." *CNBC*, February 16, 2021.

Ugochukwu, Françoise. "Language and Identity: Nigerian Video-Films and Diasporic Communities." *African Renaissance* 13, no. 3–4 (2016): 57–76.

——. "Nollywood in Diaspora: A Cultural Tool." Paper presented at Reading and Producing Nollywood: An International Symposium, Lagos, Nigeria, March 23–25, 2011.

——. "Why Nigerians Living Abroad Love to Watch Nollywood Movies." The Conversation, March 22, 2020. https://theconversation.com/why-nigerians-living-abroad-love-to-watch -nollywood-movies-132983.

Umpierre, Chris. "International Home Sales Totaled $6.9 Billion in the Miami Mega Region in 2019; According to Latest MIAMI Realtors International Report." Miami Realtors, June 10, 2020. https://www.miamirealtors.com/2020/06/10/international-home-sales-totaled -6-9-billion-in-the-miami-mega-region-in-2019-according-to-latest-miami-realtors -international-report/.

United Nations, Department of Economic and Social Affairs. "68% of the World Population Projected to Live in Urban Areas by 2050, Says UN." May 16, 2018. https://www.un.org /development/desa/en/news/population/2018-revision-of-world-urbanization-prospects .html#:~:text=Today%2C%2055%25%20of%20the%20world's,increase%20to%2068%25 %20by%202050.---check.

United Nations, Department of Economic and Social Information and Policy Analysis. *Population Growth and Policies in Mega-Cities: São Paulo.* New York: UN Headquarters, 1993.

United Nations Human Settlements Programme. *São Paulo: A Tale of Two Cities.* Nairobi: UN Habitat, 2010.

United Nations, International Organization for Migration. *Migration Governance Indicators, City of São Paulo.* Geneva: International Organization for Migration, 2019. https:// migrationdataportal.org/overviews/mgi/Sao-Paulo#0.

United States Census Bureau. *American Community Survey*, 2021.

——. "Opa Locka: Breakdown of Families in Poverty." *American Community Survey*, 2015.

——. "Quick Facts: Miami-Dade County, Florida." https://www.census.gov/quickfacts/fact /table/miamidadecountyflorida/POP060210.

——. "Quick Facts: Miami Gardens City, Florida." *American Community Survey*. 2020.

——. "Quick Facts: New Orleans, Louisiana." Accessed October 28, 2021. https://www.census .gov/quickfacts/fact/table/neworleanscitylouisiana/PST120219.

Upson, Sandra. "Singapore's Water Cycle Wizardry." *IEEE Spectrum*, May 28, 2010.

US Department of Housing and Urban Development, "Global Cities and Affordable Housing: Hong Kong." August 14, 2017. https://www.huduser.gov/portal/pdredge/pdr-edge-trending -081417.html.

US Department of State. "2012 Investment Climate Statement—Singapore." Bureau of Economic and Business Affairs, 2012.

USA Today. "Dismantling Pittsburgh: Death of an Airline Hub." *USA Today*, October 16, 2007. https://abcnews.go.com/Travel/story?id=3724036&page=1.

Uwaegbulam, Chinedum. "How Rising Seas May Wipe Off Lagos, Others by 2050." *The Guardian*, November 6, 2019. https://guardian.ng/news/how-rising-seas-may-wipe-off-lagos-others -by-2050/#:~:text=The%20dividends%20accruing%20to%20Nigeria,world's%20coastal %20cities%20by%202050.

Varrella, Simona. "Direct Tourism Contribution of Lagos to the Gross Domestic Product of Nigeria from 2006 to 2026." Statista, February 22, 2021. https://www.statista.com/statistics/795082/nigeria-lagos-tourism-contribution-to-gdp/.

Veblen, Thorstein. *The Theory of the Leisure Class.* New York: MacMillan, 1899.

Vemado, Felipe, and Augusto José Pereira Filho. "Severe Weather Caused by Heat Island and Sea Breeze Effects in the Metropolitan Area of São Paulo, Brazil." *Advances in Meteorology* 3 (2016): 1–13.

Vertovec, Steven. "Low-Skilled Migrants After COVID-19: Singapore Futures?" Compas, April 21, 2020.

Villaça, Flavio, "São Paulo: Urban Segregation and Inequality." *Estudos Avançados* 25, no. 71 (2011): 37–58.

Visnevskyte, Elzbieta. "Situation in South America's Busiest Airports." Aerotime Hub, November 20, 2020. https://www.aerotime.aero/26482-situation-in-south-america-s-busiest-airports.

Vora, Shivani. "Luxury Living in Miami Moves North." *New York Times*, June 18, 2019. https://www.nytimes.com/2019/06/18/realestate/luxury-living-miami-north-beach-sunny-isles.html.

Wacquant, Loïc. "The Militarization of Urban Marginality: Lessons from the Brazilian Metropolis." *International Political Sociology* 2, no. 1 (2008): 56–74.

Waitt, G. "Playing Games with Sydney: Marketing Sydney for the 2000 Olympics." *Urban Studies* 37, no. 7 (1999): 1055–1077.

Wallace, Paul, and Tope Alake. "Lagos Building Luxury Homes in Face of Affordable Housing Crisis." *Bloomberg*, December 20, 2019. https://www.bloomberg.com/news/articles/2019-12-20/lagos-building-luxury-homes-in-face-of-affordable-housing-crisis.

Wallerstein, Immanuel. *The Modern World-System I: Capitalist Agriculture and the Origins of the European World-Economy in the Sixteenth Century.* New York: Academic Press, 1974.

——. *The Modern World-System III: The Second Era of Great Expansion of the Capitalist World-Economy, 1730s–1840s.* San Diego: Academic Press, 1989.

Wang, Vivian. "Hong Kong's M+ Museum Is Open. It's Already in Danger." *New York Times*, November 12, 2021.

Wassermann, Jeffrey. *Vigil: Hong Kong on the Brink.* New York: Columbia Global Reports, 2020.

Weber, Max. *The City.* Ed. Don Martindale and Gertrud Neuwirth. New York: Free Press, 1958.

——. *The Protestant Ethic and the Spirit of Capitalism.* Trans. T. Parsons. London: Unwin, 1985.

——. "The Sociology of Charismatic Authority." In *From Max Weber: Essays in Sociology*, ed. H. H. Gerth and C. Wright Mills, 245–264. New York: Oxford University Press, [1922] 1946.

——. *The Sociology of Religion.* Trans. E. Fistchoff. Boston: Beacon, [1922] 1964.

Weinstein, Barbara. *The Color of Modernity: São Paulo and the Making of Race and Nation in Brazil.* Durham, NC: Duke University Press, 2015.

Weyland, Kurt. *Democracy Without Equity.* Pittsburgh, PA: University of Pittsburgh Press, 1996.

Whiteman, Kaye. *Lagos.* Oxford: Signal Books, 2012.

Wikipedia. "1997 Asian Financial Crisis# Hong Kong." Accessed January 18, 2021. https://en.wikipedia.org/wiki/1997_Asian_financial_crisis#Hong_Kong.

——. "History of New Orleans." Accessed September 20, 2020. https://en.wikipedia.org/wiki/History_of_New_Orleans.

——. "List of U.S. Metropolitan Areas by GDP." Accessed September 27, 2020. https://en.wikipedia.org/wiki/List_of_U.S._metropolitan_areas_by_GDP.

——. "The Louisiana Purchase." Accessed October 5, 2020. https://en.wikipedia.org/wiki/Louisiana_Purchase.

——. "Miami-Dade County." Accessed June 13, 2021, https://en.wikipedia.org/wiki/Miami-Dade_County,_Florida.

——. "Miami Gardens." Accessed June 21, 2021. https://en.wikipedia.org/wiki/Miami_Gardens,_Florida.

——. "Moon Landrieu." Accessed November 18, 2020. https://en.wikipedia.org/wiki/Moon_Landrieu.

——. "Nicaraguan Adjustment and Central American Relief Act." Accessed June 18, 2021. https://en.wikipedia.org/wiki/Nicaraguan_Adjustment_and_Central_American_Relief_Act.

Wile, Rob. "700 Jobs Are Coming to Downtown, Some with Barry's Bootcamp and Steve Cohen's Hedge Fund." *Miami Herald*, March 5, 2021. https://www.miamidda.com/wp-content/uploads/3.5.21-Miami-Herald-700-Jobs-are-Coming-to-downtown-some-with-Barrys-Bootcamp-and-Steven-Cohens-hedge-fund.pdf.

Williams, N. *All Power to All People.* 2019. Sculpture on display at Adrienne Arsht Center, Miami. https://www.olcdc.org/post/allpower.

Wilson, Ben. *Metropolis: A History of the City, Humankind's Greatest Invention.* New York: Doubleday, 2020.

Wilson, William J. *The Truly Disadvantaged: The Inner City, the Underclass, and Public Policy.* Chicago: University of Chicago Press, 1987.

Winter, Brian. "On Sao Paulo Subway, a Leap for Brazil Infrastructure." Reuters, February 1, 2013. https://www.reuters.com/article/brazil-infrastructure-subway/on-sao-paulo-subway-a-leap-for-brazil-infrastructure-idUKL1N0B11EC20130201?edition-redirect=uk.

Wiseman, Andreas. "Will Smith & Jada Pinkett Smith's Westbrook Teams with Nigeria's EbonyLife on Film & TV Slate." Deadline, February 16, 2021. https://deadline.com/2021/02/jada-pinkett-smith-will-smith-westbrook-nigeria-ebonylife-film-tv-slate-1234694457/.

Wong, Yi-Lee, and Anita Koo. "Is Hong Kong No Longer a Land of Opportunities After the 1997 Handover? A Comparison of Patterns of Social Mobility Between 1989 and 2007." *Asian Journal of Social Science* 44, no. 4–5 (2016): 516–545.

Woodridge, Jane. "Art Basel Parent Committed to Art Fairs." *Miami Herald*, December 8, 2019.

Woody, Todd. "Will the 'Great Wall' of New Orleans Save It from the Next Killer Hurricane?" TakePart, August 17, 2015. http://www.takepart.com/feature/2015/08/17/katrina-new-orleans-walled-city/.

World Bank Database. Accessed November 1, 2021. https://data.worldbank.org/country/singapore.

World Bank Group. "Urban population." Accessed July 20, 2021, https://data.worldbank.org/indicator/SP.URB.TOTL.IN.ZS.

World Bank Integrated Trade. "Trade Summary." Accessed November 10, 2021. https://wits.worldbank.org/Default.aspx?lang=en

World Economic Forum. *The Future of Urban Development Initiative: Dalian and Zhangjiakou Champion City Strategy.* July 2014. www3.weforum.org/docs/WEF_IU_FutureUrbanDevelopment_DalianZhangjiakou_ChampionCityStrategy_2014.pdf.

World Future Energy Summit. "Providing Water Security in Arid Regions." Accessed June 17, 2021. https://www.worldfutureenergysummit.com/en-gb/future-insights-blog/providing-water-security-in-arid-regions.html.

World Population Review. "Lagos Population 2021." Accessed April 14, 2021. https://world populationreview.com/world-cities/lagos-population.

——. "São Paulo Population 2021." Accessed April 4, 2021. https://worldpopulationreview.com /world-cities/sao-paulo-population.

Wright, Frederick D. "The Voting Rights Act and Louisiana: Twenty Years of Enforcement." *Publius* 16, no. 4 (1986): 97–108.

Wu, Anna. "Government by Whom?" In *Hong Kong Remembers*, ed. Sally Blyth and Ian Wotherspoon. Hong Kong: Oxford University Press, 1997.

Wu, Fulong. "From 'State-Owned' to 'City Inc.': The Case of Shanghai." In *The Making of Global City Regions: Johannesburg, Mumbai/Bombay, São Paulo, and Shanghai*, ed. Klaus Segbers, 207–232. Baltimore, MD: Johns Hopkins University Press, 2007.

Wuthnow, Robert. *The Left Behind: Decline and Rage in Small Town America*. Princeton, NJ: Princeton University Press, 2018.

Xiao, Allen Hai. "Interfered Rhythms, Navigating Mobilities: Chinese Migrants on the Roads in Lagos, Nigeria." In *Transport, Transgression and Politics in African Cities*, ed. Daniel E. Agbiboa, 99–118. New York: Routledge, 2019.

Xinhua News Agency. "Full Text of NPC Decision on Universal Suffrage for HKSAR Chief Selection." August 31, 2014.

Yaakoubi, Aziz, Marwa Rashad, and Davide Barbuscia. "Saudi Arabia Amends Import Rules from Gulf in Challenge to UAE." Reuters, July 5, 2021.

Yeoh, Brenda, and Weiqiang Lin. "Rapid Growth in Singapore's Immigrant Population Brings Policy Challenges." Migration Policy Institute, April 3, 2012.

Yew, Lee Kuan. *From Third World to First: The Singapore Story, 1965–2000*. Vol. 2. New York: HarperCollins, 2000.

——. *Hard Truths to Keep Singapore Going*. Singapore: Straits Times, 2011.

——. "Prime Minister's Press Conference." Singapore, August 26, 1965.

——. *The Singapore Story*. Vol. 1. Singapore: Times Editions, 1998.

Yong, Mun Cheong, and V. V. Bhanoji Rao. *Singapore-India Relations: A Primer*. Singapore: National University of Singapore Press, 1995.

You, Enoch. "Hong Kong Protests 2019 vs Occupy Central: After 79 Days, Retailers, Investors, Developers Hit Far Worse by This Year's Demonstrations." *South China Morning Post*, August 27, 2019.

Zabalbeascoa, Anatxu. "Los arquitectos quieren menos Dubái y más Venecia." *El País*, June 16, 2018. https://elpais.com/cultura/2018/06/16/actualidad/1529159142_487847.html?rel=listapoyo.

Zhang, Liang. *The Tiananmen Papers: The Chinese Leadership's Decision to Use Force, in Their Own Words*. Ed. Andrew Nathan and Perry Link, 355–362. New York: Public Affairs, 2001.

Zukin, Sharon. "Competitive Globalization and Urban Change: The Allure of Cultural Strategies." In *Rethinking Global Urbanism: Comparative Insights from Secondary Cities*, ed. Xiangming Chen and Ahmed Kanna, 17–34. New York: Routledge, 2012.

——. *Naked City: The Death and Life of Authentic Urban Places*. New York: Oxford University Press, 2010.

INDEX

U.N. Economic Commission for Latin
America, 26
unemployment, 49, 50, 112, 170, 173, 177, 218,
228
United African Company, 197
United Arab Emirates (UAE), 1, 39, 43, 53, 58;
art festivals in, 51–52; land ownership in,
56; Water Security Strategy, 245. *See also*
Dubai
United Malays National Organization
(UMNO), 108, 109
United States: as capitalist power, 239; Civil
War, 145; education in, 198; as export
market, 165; and the Gulf states, 37, 39;
as import market, 165; industry in, 20–21;
innovation in, 154, 239; Reconstruction,
146; Rust Belt, 21, 133, 242. *See also* Miami;
New Orleans; New York
Universidad de São Paulo (USP), 163
universities: in Abu Dhabi, 1; historically
Black colleges and universities (HBCUs),
198; in Hong Kong, 221; in Miami, 66, 73;
in New Orleans, 154; in São Paulo, 163–164;
in the United States, 2, 66, 73, 198
University of Campinas (UNICAMP), 163
University of Hong Kong, 221
University of Miami, 66, 73
University of Pittsburgh, 2
urban air mobility (UAM), 164
urban branding, 135–136. *See also* branding
urban expansion, 171
urban geography, 30
urbanism, 201; in the Middle Ages, 14–16
urbanization, 10, 13, 53, 237; as global
process, 246; history of, 238; and import
substitution industrialization, 26–27; in
Lagos, 187, 190; and land reclamation, 249;
peripheral, 32; planetary, 31, 127–128; in
São Paulo, 171; and the social sciences, 30;
Third World, 27, 31
urban landscapes, 132
urban planning, 131; in Lagos, 206
urban populations, 4; African American,
73, 75, 77–83; Cuban Americans, 84;

in Dubai, 45–46, 47–50, *48*, 54; ethnic
groups, 13; of global cities, 6; Haitian,
78, 80–83; Hispanic, 75, 79; in irregular
settlements, 5; and the labor market,
29; in Lagos, *189*; in Miami, 73–89, *74t*,
76; middle-class housing, 20–21; in New
Orleans, *149f*, *150*; Nicaraguans, 83–87;
racial and ethnic minorities, 5; in São
Paulo, *161*, 166–167; in Singapore, 102, *103*,
104, *104*, 115–116; Venezuelan, 87
urban poverty, 135, 166, 170, 174, 175, 177, 191,
192–193, 201–202, 250; in global cities, 187;
in Hong Kong, 229; quality of housing
and access to urban services, *192*
urban primacy, 26–27, *27*
urban redevelopment, 179
urban reinvention/restructuring, 127, 133
urban renewal, 134, 175, 179, 180, 200
urban studies, 4–6, 30–33
urban theory, 10, 31, 241, 242
urban transformation, 202–203

Vargas, Getúlio, 168, 169–170
Venezuela, 76, 87, 161
Venice, 15
Venice Biennale, 52
Vietnam, 27
violence: endemic, 174; police, 79–80, 174,
178, 202, 208, 230; in São Paulo, 178, 179,
181
Voting Rights Act, 150
Votorantim, 162

Wahabi movement, 38
Ward, Kevin, 130
Warmouth, Henry Clay, 146
War of 1812, 144
Washington Consensus, 27, 200
Water Security Strategy (UAE), 245
Weber, Max, 15, 23, 116, 118, 241
welfare system benefits, 22, 47, 223–224
Wenski, Thomas, 80–81
Westbrook Studios, 205
white flight, 150

GPSR Authorized Representative: Easy Access System Europe, Mustamäe tee
50, 10621 Tallinn, Estonia, gpsr.requests@easproject.com

www.ingramcontent.com/pod-product-compliance
Lightning Source LLC
Chambersburg PA
CBHW022134020426
42334CB00015B/890